PIETÀ

Divide up the family

Organise your searches by the name of the ancestor you're researching, and keep separate files or folders for each branch of the family. Under each family member, make a list of websites visited and pages searched. If you're using abbreviations, make sure you keep a key. For a list of family history abbreviations, see page 8.

If you're searching for variations on name spellings, write down each version of the name that you come across and whether you've run a search on it. This will save you time in the long run and avoids duplication of searches.

Try wherever possible to link an event in your files (such as the marriage of a great-grandparent) with the source from which you took this information (marriage certificate, parish register entry or banns, for instance) so that you can revisit the site if necessary.

Bookmarking the best sites

Here's how to use your computer to bookmark your favourite family history websites.

● Go to the website you want to bookmark.

● On the toolbar at the top of your computer, click on the option for **Bookmarks** or **Favorites**. Select the option that lets you save the site.

● The next time you want to access the page, you can find it in the drop-down menu under the **Bookmarks** or **Favorites** tab.

● You can then organise these websites into folders or rank them in terms of usefulness.

● If you don't have your own PC, keep a paper trail of your favourite websites so you don't have to go trawling through various search engines every time you want to update your research.

Practical 'housekeeping'

Make sure you back-up the information held on your PC, and save master copies of your notes in case of loss or corruption of files – there's nothing worse than losing months of work. With this in mind, make sure your anti-virus software and firewalls are regularly updated, too. See page 41 for information about the importance of anti-virus software and firewalls.

Storing information from the internet

Most software allows you to copy and save useful documents into your own folders for future use. To save text, use the mouse to highlight the text that you want to copy. On the toolbar, go to **Edit**, and then select **Copy**. Find or create the document that you wish to save the information into. Click on this so that the text cursor is blinking. Return to the toolbar, go to **Edit**, and then select **Paste**. Save the document and label it clearly. To find out how to save images, see below.

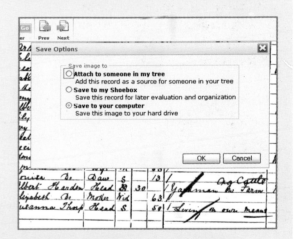

Saving images from the internet

1 Many sites, such as Ancestry, allow you to save images of their original documents to your PC. This means you can view the return as often as you like without having to log back into the website. Select the image that you wish to save – in this case, a page from the 1901 Census. Click on the **Save** icon on the top right-hand side of the image.

Storing saved images on your PC

2 You are then given three options. Select the third option, **Save to your computer**. Click **OK**. You'll then be asked to name the file and select where you'd like it to be stored. It's important to name the file as precisely as possible so that you can recognise it easily for future use. This is how you'd save on the Ancestry site; other webites may offer different methods, but the principle will be the same.

The National Archives – history under one roof

More than 1,000 years of British history is captured within the concrete and glass of The National Archives – if it happened, it's here. Among the collections are documents that have shaped the nation, as well as priceless artefacts, many of which you can see online as well as in person.

Beside the River Thames at Kew in southwest London, a stone's throw from the Royal Botanic Gardens, is the official repository for the records of England, Wales and the UK government. Millions of documents, from wills, census returns and military service records to royal seals and treaties, are kept in 29,000 m² of storage, carefully controlled at a temperature of 16°C and humidity of 50°, and protected from sunlight, pests and water or fire damage.

It all began in 1838, when the Public Record Office (PRO) was established in Chancery Lane, London, pulling together many disparate national records. In 1977 a second site was built at Kew, then extended in 1995, with all records transferred from Chancery Lane two years later. The PRO then merged with the Historic Manuscripts Commission in 2003 to create The National Archives (TNA).

To anyone researching family history in England and Wales, TNA is the most important repository. It contains the story of almost all our families spread across a vast array of official records that minute the stages and events of our ancestors' lives from the cradle to the grave.

People who made history

Perhaps the most fascinating treasures at TNA are the records associated with famous or infamous individuals in our history. These documents bring the past vividly to life, and many can be viewed online at **nationalarchives.gov.uk/museum/.**

Ancient and modern *The National Archives (below) holds the records of a millennium of history. The nation's past is stacked in boxes, in 16 repositories on 100 miles of shelving that grows by a mile annually.*

INSTRUMENT OF ABDICATION

I, Edward the Eighth, of Great
ain, Ireland, and the British Dominions
d the Seas, King, Emperor of India, do
y declare My irrevocable determination
ounce the Throne for Myself and for
cendants, and My desire that effect
d be given to this Instrument of
cation immediately.

   In token whereof I have hereunto set
and this tenth day of December, nineteen
red and thirty six, in the presence of
witnesses whose signatures are subscribed.

Edward RI

Albert

Henry

George

Making history *Edward VIII's 1936 abdication letter can be viewed on The National Archives website.*

Guy Fawkes ranks high in the rogues gallery of British history, and at TNA you can see two versions of his confession to taking part in the Gunpowder Plot of 1605. One he shakily signed 'Guido' straight after torture, the other he marked with a more steady hand eight days later. A miscreant that history has treated more heroically is highwayman Dick Turpin, although the indictment for him held at TNA that led to his final trial and execution was simply for stealing two horses worth four pounds.

Other famed people were the unwitting makers of history. Among the documents at TNA, for instance, is the page from the logbook of HMS *Bounty*, written by Captain William Bligh, that details the dramatic moment of mutiny on Tuesday, April 28, 1789:

'Just before sun rise Mr. Christian, Mate, Charles Churchill, Ships Corporal, John Mills Gunners Mate and Thomas Buskitt, Seaman, came into my cabbin while I was asleep and scizing me tyed my hands, with a cord behind my back and threatened me with instant death if I spoke or made the least noise.'

Nearly 150 years later, on December 10, 1936, another momentous piece of writing secured its place in history. This time it was a typed letter, signed by Edward VIII, declaring his 'irrevocable determination to renounce the Throne for Myself and for My descendants'. This 'Instrument of Abdication', as it's headed, marks the only time an English monarch has voluntarily given up the throne.

The bigger picture

At TNA you'll also find the official documents that have played a key part in the nation's history, many of which you can see online at **nationalarchives.gov.uk/museum/**. Your ancestors are unlikely to appear in these records, but the social or political changes they wrought will have affected them. Understanding these events helps to put your own family history into a wider, national context.

For two of the most ground-breaking documents the story goes back 800 or more years. It begins with the Domesday Book (see page 222) and continues with the Magna Carta or 'great charter', which helped to shape our system of constitutional law. Drawn up in 1215 by the English barons in protest against the arbitrary policies of King John, the Magna Carta's purpose was to restrict the rights of the king and bring them within the law of England. One of the most important clauses – 'no free man shall be seized or imprisoned, or stripped of his rights or possessions … except by the lawful judgement of his peers' – enshrined the principle of a right to a fair trial by your equals, reflected in today's jury system.

A great wrong righted

In 1807, an Act of Parliament formally abolished the slave trade. Until then, slaves were bought and sold throughout the British Empire – and the rest of the world – as chattels.

The Act was the culmination of a widespread campaign led by prominent political figures of the time, such as William Wilberforce, Charles Fox and Lord Grenville. A bronze medal (right) was cast when slavery was finally eradicated from the British Empire in 1834.

TNA has hundreds of documents relating to the abolition campaign, some of which you can see at **nationalarchives.gov.uk/imagelibrary/slavery.** This includes a signed 'Engagement' (right) between Queen Victoria and the King and Chiefs of the Bonny, Nigeria, for the abolition of slavery on November 21, 1848.

Getting started online

You're on the brink of a great adventure: rather than remaining faint ghosts of the past, your ancestors are about to join the family you know. Prepare to be enthralled and absorbed by this fascinating journey.

Making the internet work for you

There's a wealth of original material available online, and the scope increases by the day. It's a goldmine of information, just waiting for you to start digging.

Using the internet to research your family tree is the future for family historians. With so much available, and so easily accessible, there should be no stopping you.

You'll find digitised images of an amazing array of documents – civil registration records dating back 170 years, Victorian census returns, elaborately written medieval wills, maps that are hundreds of years old, ships' passenger lists going back to about 1890, First World War service papers and Prisoner of War interviews. And that's just a small part. The range of surviving material that will enable you to piece together the jigsaw of your family heritage is astounding.

Not so long ago, these documents would have been tucked away in inaccessible archives, only to be seen by determined genealogists prepared to spend hours trawling through paper indexes and rolls of microfilm. Now they're accessible to you simply at the click of a mouse.

Get to know the websites

The number of family history-related websites is growing rapidly. If you're new to online research, start by familiarising yourself with some of the most useful sites mentioned in

Across the generations *Using the internet to trace family relatives is fun for all ages. Children will enjoy showing off their computer skills.*

this book. Many of the more popular websites work in a similar way, so once you've mastered a few, you'll be well on your way to finding the records you want quickly and easily.

Most of them explain how to navigate around the website and search each type of record. There's also usually an FAQ (Frequently Asked Questions) page, which can be helpful if you get stuck.

As well as updating their content, many family history sites regularly change the design of their pages, so you may find you'll have to reacquaint yourself with the look and feel of the site every now and then.

Avoiding confusion

There's so much material online that it's easy to get bogged down trying to work out what's relevant to you. You can avoid this if you have a plan before you start, listing exactly what you want to find for each ancestor or family line. There are many different websites that hold similar documents, so once any initial bewilderment has been overcome, you should find it relatively straightforward to find what you're looking for.

The internet has revolutionised the way we access information. Embrace all these newly available resources and you may find that researching your family history becomes your most rewarding hobby.

The birth of the internet and the World Wide Web

It all began with the US Government in the 1960s. First they compiled a report outlining a way to link up all the computerised data they used, then followed this, in the 1970s, with a research network that they eventually called Internet.

A decade later, across the world in the Swiss Alps, a young British software consultant named Tim Berners-Lee (left), who was on a six-month contract with CERN (the European Organisation for Nuclear Research), had a moment of illumination. He was trying to find a way to organise his notes by creating a program that would work rather like a brain, monitoring random information. In his own words, he devised a piece of software that would keep 'track of all the random associations one comes across in real life, and brains are supposed to be so good at remembering, but sometimes mine wouldn't'.

He went on to create a system that could link a word in one document to other files on his computer – and from there it was only a matter of time before his files could be linked to others at CERN, and then to other organisations. The concept of the World Wide Web was born – where information could be shared freely, at no cost, around the world. Tim then built the first website while still working at CERN and it went live on August 6, 1991.

Using family history software

Once you've started your research and made some progress with your family tree, you'll want to explore different ways of storing all the details on your computer. No matter how complicated your family's story, there'll be a software package that can hold the information.

Family history software becomes increasingly sophisticated as more and more people are gripped by the fun of discovering their ancestry. There's nothing wrong with keeping records on paper, or typing them up, but there are advantages to using specially designed software to store all that vital information.

Putting it all on the computer

Because these software packages are designed specifically for the needs of family historians, you don't need to keep on repeating the basic relationship and other terms used in family history. A program will have tables already set up to receive the data you want to enter, with all the headings you could ever need for each person. This means it's quick and easy to transfer the information from your handwritten notes into a master database.

For example, a database entry will let you add a person's full name and nickname; their dates and places of birth, baptism, marriage, death and burial; their occupation(s) and various addresses; as well as their children's, siblings' and parents' names. Most packages will usually also allow space to add a photo album with a set number of pictures, a timeline showing the major events in a person's life and a full biography.

Advantages of digital records

You might wonder why you should bother keeping an electronic record, especially if you've taken thorough, detailed notes and have copies of all the documents that you've found. Although keeping your paper notes is important, especially copies of official documents, there are a number of advantages to having it all recorded digitally as well.

GOOD SOURCES Most family tree-building packages have the facility to add a list of sources to an individual's notes, which is vital when you're researching your family history. It becomes even more relevant if you choose to send your saved tree to another researcher or family member – they can see at a glance that you've used reliable sources and can also double-check them if they want to.

UNLIMITED STORAGE An electronic database offers almost limitless storage of your findings, from statistics and source references

Pulling it together

With family history software you can store all your information and use it to create family trees. Family Tree Maker, Family Historian and other packages – see pages 38-39 – can usually be bought online or from your local computer retailer.

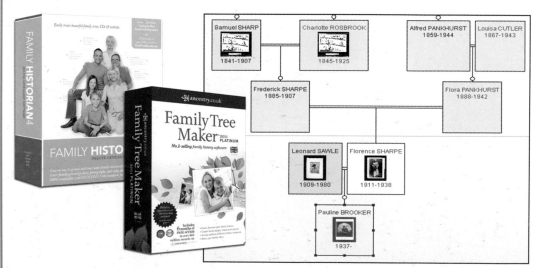

to family photographs and images of documents. Most software packages are designed to let you flick from one type of record to another with just a few mouse clicks. Having all the research together helps you to take in the overall picture, so that you can spot any gaps that need filling.

EASY SHARING If you're keen to show snippets of your research to other family members and share the information, you'll probably find that they'll prefer receiving an electronic file to browse and enjoy, rather than wading through a pile of paperwork. With electronic files you can isolate sections and pass them on, without having to copy and post records.

FASTER RESEARCH Sharing your family tree with other researchers is much easier with electronic files. Recent advances in family history software mean that most packages save your data as a Gedcom file (see page 278), which can be shared with other PCs. Most genealogy websites have a family tree-sharing facility where you can upload your Gedcom file and save it on their database (see pages 270-77 for a description of the best sites for this purpose).

Sharing information in this way can help other researchers to learn from your work and may speed up your own research. Perhaps a distant cousin you've never met, who's exploring a branch of your family tree, will find a common ancestor in your two trees and get in touch with you. This may help you to work back even further, or save you wasting time on an ancestral dead-end.

When your family doesn't fit the format

Many software packages are set up for families that fit into a traditional framework. Explaining to a computer package that your grandmother had a child with an unknown American soldier before she married your grandfather, then divorced him two years after your father was born, could be tricky. Nevertheless, software companies are continually refining their products to reflect changing family dynamics so that several, such as 3D Family Tree and GenoPro, have options to include more than one marriage and explain which children were the product of which marriage. Illegitimacy and adoption are less easy to indicate on computerised family trees, so you may have to resort to making a note on an individual's page about the circumstances of their birth. If you have a high number of unusual relationships in your tree it's worth shopping around to find a package that gives you the flexibility to enter this data.

Much married *Henry VIII married six times and had children by three different wives, which makes his family tree complicated to draw up.*

Choosing the right software

There are many excellent family history software packages on the market, from basic programs for building family trees to more advanced products that also help you to search online records.

Family history software packages make compiling a family tree easier than doing it on paper. They also often offer regular upgrades, which can make them even more effective.

Most packages allow you to upload family photos and scanned images of important documents, as well as video and audio files that will really bring your research and family tree to life. These software packages are specifically designed to simplify the storage of records, with sensible organisation and easy access. The beauty of using a digital package is that you can display as much or as little information as you need to view at any time, and yet have instant access to all the data you've collected.

Gone are the days of rummaging through mountains of paperwork; with modern family history software packages you simply specify what you want and it's presented to you within seconds. Some packages even have direct links to the internet, guiding you to recommended sources and helping you to find vital information.

Check the reviews

There are reviews of software packages on **genealogyreviews.co.uk/genealogysoftware. htm**. The website **www.my-history.co.uk** regularly reviews the latest releases in family history software, and illustrates the main features of each program. Forums hosted by genealogy websites (see pages 280-5) are also good for recommendations. Online stores, such as Amazon (**amazon.co.uk**), also often feature customer reviews of software. Browse before buying.

Family tree software packages to consider

The four software products shown here are among the most popular on the market. Remember that this is an ever-changing area – new packages are introduced regularly and older ones are upgraded – so always check reviews and look out for the latest editions.

Family Historian

Family Historian allows you to create different styles of family tree, to which you can add pictures, audio files and videos. If you have a group photo, people within the shot can be linked to one or several individual ancestors. The software also lets you record details of your sources – vital for verifying your research. All the people in your database can be listed in one window, from where you can go into and edit each person's details. You'll find the Family Historian website at **family-historian.co.uk**.

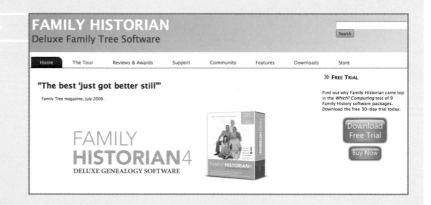

Family Tree Maker

This software allows you to display your data in a diagrammatic form that combines elements of a pedigree chart and a family tree. You'll be able to view your ancestors on a chart that shows up to seven generations at one time. Most versions of Family Tree Maker have an interactive map facility so you can see where your ancestors lived, and you can upload video and audio files as well as digital images. The software can be ordered from **ancestry.co.uk**.

RootsMagic

For a free trial of the RootsMagic Version 4 program, go to **rootsmagic.co.uk**. The software lets you create photo trees, pedigree charts and relationship charts, as well as designing wall charts which you can customise by adding pictures, moving boxes and altering the colour and background. You can publish your family tree in a book format easily with RootsMagic: the software creates an index for you, and lets you choose what information and images you'd like to include.

Legacy Family Tree

You can download a basic edition of Legacy Family Tree free of charge from **legacyfamilytree.com**. It has links to family history sites such as **familysearch.com** and **ancestry.co.uk**. A deluxe version of the software can be bought from the Legacy website and gives you access to useful extra features such as Research Guidance (help with your family research), Publishing Center (where you can publish the results of your research in a book) and Timelines (which provides a chronological review of your ancestors' lives).

Getting the best from the web

When you're searching online, it helps to understand the way your computer interacts with the internet and how to get the most out of your search engine.

There are a number of terms you'll need to know for your searches online.

Browser

A web browser is a software program such as Internet Explorer or Mozilla Firefox that you can use to view web pages and 'browse' websites. All web browsers are the same in principle – they are made up of an address box, into which you type a web address, and an area in which web pages can be viewed. Text and images on a web page often contain links to other web pages on the same or different websites. Web browsers activate these links so you can view the relevant pages.

Cookies

A cookie is a small piece of information that is sent to your computer through your web browser when you've visited particular websites. Cookies store information about you for the next time you go to that site – the pages you visited, any actions you took or links you followed. They're stored on the hard drive of your computer and are dormant until you come back to that site again, at which point they're activated.

When a cookie is placed on your computer, it records the website that will be allowed to open it in the future. For example, if **ancestry.co.uk** places a cookie in its name,

only **ancestry.co.uk** will be able to open it. You can set your browser so that it doesn't accept cookies, but the problem with this is that sites that allow payment for instant access, or those with checkout facilities, won't function correctly and you won't be able to get what is called 'user authorisation' unless the settings are reconfigured to accept cookies. As you're likely to need to pay for searches and certificates, this could be really inconvenient.

Plug-ins

A plug-in is a small piece of computer software that a web browser uses to let you view a document, interact with an image, listen to music or watch a video. If your computer doesn't have the correct plug-in, you can't listen to audio footage or see animations and video on-screen. If you need a plug-in that you don't already have on your

How to search effectively

There are many well-known search engines on the internet, including **google.co.uk** and **yahoo.co.uk**. Although you can do simple searches by just typing in words in the search box, this will often bring up far too many results which aren't relevant to what you want.

To get the best from a search engine, there are a few basic techniques that will make finding what you want easier and quicker. If an initial search doesn't turn up what you're looking for, you should try these.

Looking for phrases If you want to search for a particular phrase, you can improve the search results by enclosing the phrase in inverted

commas, rather than just typing in the individual words. This isn't so important if the words are often used together anyway (such as 'Bodmin Moor'), but it's useful for finding names. Putting 'Mary Ann Brown' in inverted commas will find only the pages where those three names are next to each other in that order, not just any page which may have Mary, Ann and Brown, in any context, on it.

Looking for alternatives If you have a surname that may have different spellings, it's a good idea to look for all variants. Unfortunately search engines don't know anything about surnames, so you'll have to list all the variants, separated by the word OR (which must be in capital letters) – 'Bishop OR Bishopp OR Bisshopp', for example.

Advanced searching All search engines have a wide range of options beyond the basic ones mentioned here. The easiest way to find out about these is to click on the **Advanced Search** link that most search engines have on their homepage. The Advanced Search page should have a link to a help page which will explain what all the options do and how you should use them.

Incorrect spellings Sometimes you don't find what you want because you've spelled it incorrectly yourself. For example, if you type 'English Sivil War' into a search engine such as Google, it will manage to find hundreds of entries despite a misspelling. Fortunately, Google has a spelling checker and asks you: **Did you mean: 'English Civil War'?**

computer you'll be prompted to install it. Most websites offer step-by-step help to install the program, so don't feel alarmed if you're told you need to load one. There are hundreds of different types of plug-in, but only a handful of family history websites are likely to ask you to install one.

Antivirus software

A computer virus is a piece of code that's capable of copying itself. Viruses spread from computer to computer by attaching themselves to email messages or hiding in the code of some programs. As well as replicating themselves so that you'll inadvertently send them to your friends and contacts, many viruses delete files on your computer, or even disrupt pre-loaded software.

Because of the problems that these viruses can cause, it's absolutely vital that you take steps to protect your computer with antivirus software. It consists of computer programs that identify, thwart and eliminate computer viruses and other potentially harmful software. If the antivirus software spots a virus hidden in an email message or web page, it attempts to disable the virus and prevents it from damaging your computer.

You can download basic antivirus software, free of charge, for personal use from websites such as **free.avg.com** from AVG, **avast.com** from Avast or **clamav.net** from ClamAV. If you'd like a higher level of security, you should buy an antivirus software package, such as Norton's Antivirus at **symantec.com**, McAfee's Total Protection at **home.mcafee.com** or the commercial version of AGV's Anti-Virus at **avg.com**.

Firewalls

A firewall is a software program that forms a barrier between your computer and the rest of the internet. It protects your computer from hackers, viruses and any other type of harmful element. Quite simply, a firewall has the ability to stop anything you don't know about from passing between the internet and your computer.

Some internet service providers, such as BT and AOL, actually provide a free copy of a firewall program to their broadband customers. You can also buy firewall software just as you'd buy the antivirus software already described, fromMcAfee at **mcafeestore.com** or from ZoneAlarm at **zonealarm.com**. If a firewall isn't provided automatically, you should invest in one.

Using a credit card safely on the internet

If you want to sign up to family history websites and spend money online, there are a few basic security precautions you should take, to avoid becoming the victim of fraud.

First, you'll need to make sure that you're shopping on a site that you can trust. To help you to follow best practice online, take a look at **getsafeonline.org** and **consumerdirect.gov.uk**.

Some websites let you see their products and decide what you want before you register. Others will insist that you register first. Where you need to pay is usually known as the 'checkout'. You can pay by either credit or debit card, and to complete the transaction you'll need to enter the card number and expiry date.

Some sites also ask you for the security code (the last three numbers printed on the back of your card) as extra security.

Before you hand over your details, make sure that the site you're using has a safe checkout. Regardless of which web browser you're using, a small padlock should appear in the bar at the bottom of the screen. This symbol indicates that other online users can't see any of the data you're sending to the shop.

Play it safe Be very careful when you put any of your banking details online. Never give your PIN number or password to anyone. Keep a record of any transaction you make until you've received an email confirmation of your purchase.

Where to start online

You've decided what you want to research and where you want to end up, but just where do you begin, faced with the treasure trove of information that's available on the internet?

Your search will usually start with finding civil registration certificates. A government website, **direct.gov.uk/gro**, tells you about the information on these certificates, and how it will help you to trace your own family tree. It explains how to order certificates and how to pay for them. You will also find advice on

how to discover relevant certificates in England and Wales, as well as details about Scotland and Ireland, and other registries such as the Isle of Man and the Channel Islands. Other records held by the General Record Office for England and Wales, and for abroad, are also listed.

The other important records you will want to seek out early in your investigations are the national collections of census returns. For advice on the returns for England and Wales, that were held every ten years between 1841 and 1911, go to **nationalarchives.gov.uk/ records/census-records.htm**. This site explains what you need to know before you begin a search and what records are available for you to view online. It also provides basic information about what you might find, and a link to an in-depth research guide.

For Scotland, see **scotlandspeople.gov.uk** and for Ireland, **nationalarchives.ie**.

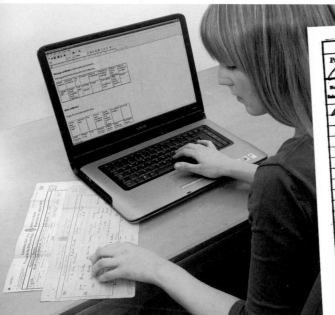

Upload your notes *Transfer information onto your computer as you go along, making sure you record your sources. Details from certificates (above) or a census return (right) will be much easier to access once they are correctly filed on your PC.*

Top tips for keeping online records

● Keep separate notes for each section of the family, so that they don't become confused.

● Record and keep a reference for all the web searches that you do. This will make it easier to remember details at a later date.

● Record and reference any documents you've viewed online, linked to the original archive from which they were taken.

● Make sure you record the time and date each time you update your research.

● Store your favourite websites as bookmarks in your browser.

● Multi-tagging bookmarking websites, such as **delicious.com** or **diigo.com**, provide more sophisticated techniques for cross-referencing your research.

● Consider buying scrapbook software to help you keep all your findings together: MemoryMixer (**memorymixer.com**) and iScrapbook (**iscrapbook.com**) are good examples.

● Remember to back up your information regularly – on a different hard drive or storage medium. A serious computer problem could wipe out months of work.

First Steps

1 On the homepage, click on **Researching family history**, then **First steps in researching your family history**. Look for the link labelled **Download 'Discover your family history'**. This small (364K) PDF document is an ideal introduction to the subject.

The General Register Office (GRO)

2 Return to the **direct.gov.uk/gro** homepage. Now click on **Using the General Register Office to research family history**. This describes everything contained within the GRO, and how you can use it to help trace your ancestry.

Using Official Records

3 Return to the homepage. Now click on the link labelled **Researching family history using official records**. This page tells you where you can order birth, marriage and death certificates, and what they can teach you about your family history.

Finding local knowledge

A number of sites will point you to national information and records, but once you've found out where your ancestors came from, you'll want local information to help you to fill in missing details. This is where Genuki comes in, steering you to the local archives and other resources you may need.

Genuki (at **genuki.org.uk**) is an acronym of Genealogy in the UK and Ireland. It's a free, non-commercial website that provides information and links to online resources for all six regions of the British Isles: England, Scotland, Wales, Ireland (covering both Northern Ireland and the Republic of Ireland), the Isle of Man and the Channel Islands.

The entry for each region holds national information and has links to separate pages for each county. It's these county pages which you'll probably find most useful. They have details of the records offices and libraries where you'll find original records, and many links to online resources for genealogy and history relating to the county.

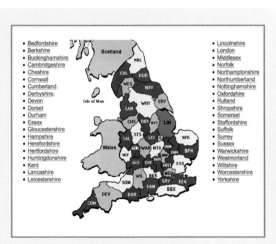

How to search on Genuki

1 Key in **genuki.org.uk** to get to the homepage. To access the site's collections, click **United Kingdom and Ireland** in the top left-hand corner.

Select a region

2 Up comes a map of the British Isles, broken into six regions. There's also a general list offering information on everything from cemeteries to taxation, from which you can choose without selecting a region. Click on a region to see the specific collections held there.

Find your area

3 In this example, by clicking on **England** you're presented with all the English counties. You'll also be offered links to information relating to all of England.

Every county page has a set of headings such as Church Records, Maps and Occupations, so it's easy to find the topic you're looking for. You'll find links to a list of all the towns and parishes in the county. Many individual parishes have a page devoted to them, with more links to local sites.

Because it's designed for family historians, Genuki is organised around the counties as they were in the early 19th century, so you won't find pages for London Boroughs or post-1974 counties such as West Midlands or Avon. But you can use Genuki's Gazetteer at **genuki.org.uk/big/Gazetteer/** to find out in which county a place used to be – the search results give a grid reference and link to the relevant page on Genuki.

In addition, Genuki has many useful tools and lists that you should visit:
☛ There is a list of all family history societies in the British Isles at **genuki.org.uk/Societies/**
☛ All the mailing lists for British and Irish genealogy are listed at **genuki.org.uk/ indexes/MailingLists.html**
☛ The Genuki Church Database (also called the Parish Locator) at **genuki.org.uk/big/ churchdb** lists all the churches within a chosen radius of a particular place – ideal for trying to work out where your ancestor may have been baptised or married.
☛ The Genuki Search at **genuki.org.uk/search/** lets you search all of Genuki, and many other major websites for British and Irish family history research, such as the National Archives, the Society of Genealogists, and most local family history societies.

Find your county

4 Click on the county in which your ancestors lived (**Oxfordshire** is shown here). You'll be taken to a brief description of the county, links to the main archives, and any relevant online resources. There's also a list of parishes and often a separate page devoted to each parish.

Tracing your ancestral home

You may come across an old photograph or painting of an ancestor's home – perhaps one that has since been sold and is no longer owned by a family member. With a house name or address, it may be possible to identify the location on an old map. If the house was large enough, it might be named on the map. This can be invaluable in pinpointing the local archives that may contain records of its ownership and when it was sold.

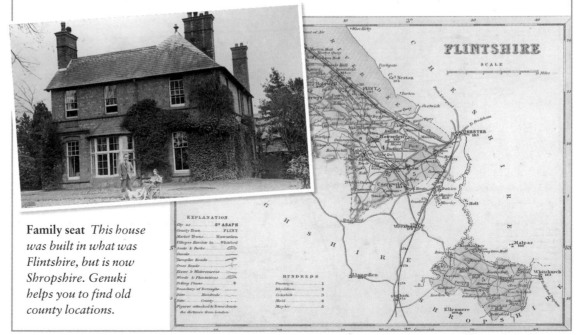

Family seat *This house was built in what was Flintshire, but is now Shropshire. Genuki helps you to find old county locations.*

Cyndi's List – gateway to family history sites

Probably the world's largest family history 'portal' site is run by Cyndi Howells, who has been a genealogist for more than 20 years. Her site provides you with links to a huge range of websites that could help in the search for your ancestors.

There are over 300,000 web links available through Cyndi's List, all updated and checked regularly. Its value to family historians is enormous and there's nothing else on the internet that quite compares.

One of the most appealing aspects of the website, **cyndislist.com**, is its sense of community – you can contribute to it and edit information that appears, as well as email Cyndi with suggestions and comments. There are links to groups and societies, most of which have message boards or chat rooms putting you in touch with the global family history community. You can also subscribe to Cyndi's newsletter to keep up with news.

The site is an excellent resource if you're stuck for information or need a little more guidance about where to look. There are links to thousands of websites, so make a note of every site you search; the sheer size of Cyndi's List makes it tricky to find your way back to a site if you haven't recorded your route carefully.

Navigating the site

Although slightly skewed towards North America, Cyndi's List has plenty of resources that you'll find relevant to your searches. The homepage displays a simple welcome screen aimed at telling newcomers what the site is all about. You can navigate Cyndi's List using the links (shown as purple arrows) on the left-hand side of the home page. These enable you browse, search categories, connect to Cyndi's List via social networking sites such as Facebook or Twitter, join the site's mailing list or suggest new genealogy links that you feel should be added.

The two most significant links as far as your research is concerned will be **Categories** and **Browse New Links**.

CATEGORIES Arranged under a wide array of headings, all of the information held on Cyndi's List is contained somewhere here. The nature of these categories varies enormously. Some, such as **Newsgroups, Books, Newspapers** and **Obituaries**, are quite general; but others are more specific, focussing on particular regions, ethnic groups or religions. If you are researching ancestors from the North of Spain, for instance, the category **Spain and the Basque Country/España y El País Vasco** will be the place you want to look. Also to be found in the list are a number of useful starting points for beginners, such as the category **How To: Tutorials & Guides**.

BROWSE NEW LINKS This is an archive of new links that have been put forward by users and accepted by Cyndi's List. Each archive represents a single day's worth of entries. These are worth browsing from time to time as they often contain interesting new strands of research, some of which may be relevant to your own enquiries.

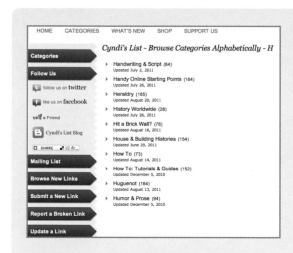

A search for a Huguenot ancestor

1 You can search under a variety of topics using Cyndi's List. For example, if you're looking for an ancestor, Jean du Plessy from Poitiers, who was a Huguenot and who may have escaped persecution by sailing to South Africa, go to the homepage, and click on **H** in the alphabetical list at the foot of the page. This will take you to the link for Huguenot sources. Click on **Huguenot**.

Using the main index

One of the most useful aspects of Cyndi's List is the ease with which you can research almost anything. For example, if you want to find an ancestor who went to New Zealand in the 19th century, and you believe he became a fireman, click on the **Categories** button on the main menu and then scroll down to **New Zealand**. You'll get a long list of topics on the left, and a shorter list of related categories on the right. To find your ancestor, click on **People & Families**. The list that's offered has

a link for the **Palmerston North Firemen in the 1800's**. Click on this, and up comes a list of all the firemen, with their dates of service. When you check the bar at the top of the screen, you'll see you're no longer on the Cyndi's List website, but have been connected directly to **angelfire.com**, the site that offered the information to Cyndi's List. You'll find all the information on the website is contributed by outside sources.

Finding Huguenot ships

2 You're now provided with a list of sources that you can search to trace your Huguenot ancestor. Under **Records: Census, Cemeteries, Land, Obituaries, Personal, Taxes and Vital**, you'll see a link to **Huguenot Ships** with names and dates of vessels that took Huguenots to the Cape. Click on this link.

Huguenot

Category Index	Related Categories
General Resources	Baptist
History & Culture	Catholic
Libraries, Archives & Museums	France
Locality Specific	Germany / Deutschland
Mailing Lists, Newsgroups & Chat	Jewish
People & Families	Mennonite
Publications, Software & Supplies	Methodist
Queries, Message Boards & Surname Lists	Netherlands / Nederland
	Presbyterian
Records: Census, Cemeteries, Land, Obituaries, Personal, Taxes and Vital	Quaker
	Religion & Churches
Societies & Groups	South Africa / Suid-Afrika
	Switzerland / Suisse / Schweiz
	United Kingdom & Ireland
	United States

Find the ship

3 Up comes a list of ships' names. You'll need to know the name of the ship that your ancestor served on, or you may have to undertake a lengthy search. If you know the name of the ship, in this case *Oosterland*, and a rough date, click on the ship's name.

WELCOME

Huguenot ships that arrived in South Africa between 1686 and 1726.

Search this Site

Name of Ship	Port of Departure	Date of Departure	Port of Arrival	Date of Arrival
Vrijheit	?	?	?	1686
Voorschoten	Delft	31 Dec 1687	Saldanha	13 Apr 1688
Borssenburg[1]	Texel	06 Jan 1688	Table Bay	12 May 1688
Oosterland	Middleburg	29 Jan 1688	Table Bay	12 May 1688
Berg China	Rotterdam	20 Mar 1688	Table Bay	04 Aug 1688
Zuid Beverland	Middleburg	22 Apr 1688	Table Bay	19 Aug 1688
Wapen van Alkmaar	Texel	27 Jul 1688	Table Bay	27 Jan 1689
Schelde	?	19 Feb 1688	Table Bay	5 Jun 1688
Zion	Holland	08 Jan 1689	Table Bay	06 May 1689
Spierdijk	-	-	Table Bay	1691
Vosmaar	Holland	April 1696	Table Bay	Oct 1696
Driebergen	Holland	25 May 1698	Table Bay	3 Sept 1698
Westhoven[2]	?	?	Table Bay	16 Jun 1699
Donkervliet	?	?	Table Bay	20 Jul 1699
Reygersdal	?	?	Table Bay	1700

Find your ancestor

4 Now you can search through a list of passengers who sailed on the ship that you have chosen. Jean du Plessy is there, and you can see that he was a surgeon. He travelled with his wife, Madeline Menanteau, and their son Charles, who was born on the voyage. The list also tells you the date and port of departure and the date and port of arrival.

The OOSTERLAND sailed from Middleburg on 29 January 1688 and arrived at Table Bay, South May 1688.

PASSENGERS

Surname	First Name(s)	Origin	Age	Died	Occupation	Spouse	Children
Avicé	Sara	Chateaudun	-	-	-	-	-
Briet	Suzanne	Chateau Thierry, Champagne	-	-	-	Isaac Taillefert	Eliabeth (14), Isaac (7), Pier Susanne (2 1/
Carnoy	Antoinette	Tournai, Flanders	-	-	-	-	-
Clouden	Jean	Condé	-	-	Shoemaker	-	-
Cochet	Sara[2]	-	-	-	-	-	Abraham, Joc Jeanne le Clo
de Buiyse (du Buis, Buis,Buys)	Jan[3]	Picardy	-	-	Agriculturist	-	-
de Savoie or Savoye	Jacques[4]	Ath (Aeth)	52	1717	-	Marie-Madeline le Clerq of Tournay	Marguéite-Th Barbe-Thérès Jacques (9 m
du Plessy (Plessis)	Jean Prieur[5]	Poiters	50	1708	Surgeon	Madeline Menanteau of Poiters	Charles (born voyage)
Menanteau (Menanto)	Madeline	Poiters		Bef. 1700		Jean Prieur du Plessis	Charles (born voyage)

What you'll find online

Family history information on the internet is constantly changing. Not all records are there yet, but an amazing number are, and it's growing all the time.

This is an exciting time to be researching your ancestry. You can access ever-increasing amounts of information about your family from the comfort of your own home.

Most key records are available online, to some degree at least, including those listed below. Each of these categories is dealt with in greater detail later in the book. Website addresses for major collections or indexes are given here, but there are other smaller collections on a wide range of sites. You can find these by entering key words such as 'mineworkers' records' or 'methodist ministers' into a search engine such as Yahoo! or Google.

CIVIL REGISTRATION Indexes for birth, marriage and death certificates in England and Wales are available at **findmypast.co.uk** and **ancestry.co.uk**. For Scotland, you'll find indexes for birth, marriage and death certificates, with access to digitised images of the Old Parish Registers and early census books, at **scotlandspeople.gov.uk**.

CENSUS RETURNS For England, Scotland, Wales and the Channel Islands, from 1841 to 1911, go to **ancestry.co.uk**; for Scotland, from 1841 to 1911, visit **scotlandspeople.gov.uk**.

WILLS You can view English wills from 1384 to 1858 at **nationalarchives.gov.uk**. Testaments and wills for Scotland, from 1513 to 1901, are at **scotlandspeople.gov.uk**.

PARISH REGISTERS Transcripts of parish registers prepared by the Church of Jesus Christ of Latter-day Saints (LDS or Mormons) are freely available at **familysearch.org**.

PASSENGER LISTS You'll find passenger lists for every ship leaving any British port between 1890 and 1919, including the list of the *Titanic*, at **findmypast.co.uk**.

MILITARY RECORDS First World War service records are at **ancestry.co.uk**. You can search the Medal Card Index for the First World War at **nationalarchives.gov.uk**. For lists of war graves, go to the Commonwealth War Graves Commission at **cwgc.org**.

Fateful voyage *The passenger list (far left) for RMS Titanic records all those who embarked on her maiden voyage on April 10, 1912. You can see the details at* **findmypast.co.uk**. *Some 1400 passengers and 800 crew were on board when the ship hit an iceberg on her way to New York. More than 1500 people died, including The Reverend John Harper, a widower and a Baptist minister from Glasgow, (left). His daughter, Nina, survived. Here they are seen before the fateful journey, with Miss Jessie Wills Leitch who also survived.*

What's now online

Enormous quantities of records have been put online in recent years.

Images of civil registration certificates

Digitised images of birth, marriage and death certificates for England and Wales are available on two commercial sites: **ancestry.co.uk** and **findmypast.co.uk**. These are available for Scotland at **scotlandspeople.gov.uk**.

The 1911 census

This is the most recent census that is available for searching. It is now fully available on **findmypast.co.uk** and **ancestry.co.uk**. The next census is that taken in 1921, which will be fully available in 2022, after the mandatory 100 years has elapsed.

Military service records

British Army Service Records, 1760-1915, are available on **findmypast.co.uk**. British Army World War One Service Records, 1914-1920, can now be seen on **ancestry.co.uk**.

Passenger lists

The details of over 24 million passengers who left the United Kingdom on long-haul voyages between 1890 and 1960 are now available on **findmypast.co.uk**.

Using online data services
ancestry.co.uk

A number of key websites, including Ancestry, offer vast amounts of information – your ancestors will be in there somewhere. You may have to pay for the information, but it's well worth it.

Some of the information on Ancestry is free – for example, the birth, marriage and death indexes for England and Wales. You can search these indexes by clicking the **Family Trees** link near the top of the homepage. But to access most of the data collections you'll need either to

Ancestry records include:

- UK censuses (1841-1911)
- Birth, marriage and death indexes for England and Wales (1837-2005)
- Parish and probate records (1538-1980)
- British Army WW1 service records (1914-20)
- London Metropolitan Archives
- Pallot's Marriage Index for England (1780-1837)
- UK Incoming Passenger Lists (1878-1960)

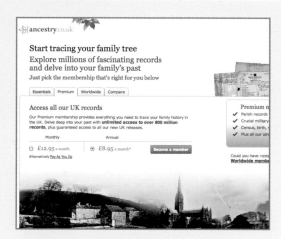

Go to the homepage

1 The design of the **ancestry.co.uk** homepage changes often, but it always gives you details of the records on offer. The tabs at the top provide further information about what you can do on the site. Access is via a registration and subscription service, but you can usually have a free 14 day trial. To register as a member, click on **Subscribe** on the top right-hand side of the page.

Register and subscribe

2 On the registration page you'll be asked to select an annual or monthly membership package. There are three different packages available: The basic subscription (**Essentials**) is sufficient for most uses; you'll want the **Premium** subscription if want to view military records; and **Worldwide** if you think your ancestry stretches beyond the UK. There are also pay-per-view options available. Select your preferred plan and click on **Become a member**.

Give your details

3 Enter your name and email address and click on **Continue**. This takes you to another page where you enter your contact details. Then enter your credit card details. Make sure you read and accept the terms and conditions of the site. Once you're registered, you have access to the records via a series of search screens.

take out a subscription (which gives you access to all the records without further payment) or use the pay-per-view system, where you pay for a fixed number of record searches. Whichever you choose, you'll pay by credit card and your subscription will be renewed automatically unless you cancel it.

There are separate UK and World subscriptions, but unless you know that Ancestry has records for a country your ancestors came from or went to, the UK membership should cover all your needs.

What's in the indexes

Take a look at the yellow box opposite, to see what information is held on the Ancestry site. Like most other data services, it has relatively little material for Scotland – most of which is available only on ScotlandsPeople (see page 56).

Ancestry has an enormous number of different datasets, and in many cases they provide not only an index or transcription of the records but also images of the original records. This means you can see all the details for yourself, to check against the information given in the index.

Seeing the images

To display these images, Ancestry has a special image viewer with facilities for saving, printing and zooming. Once you've saved an image on your own computer, you can view or print it as you need.

In addition to the basic image viewer, Ancestry also has an Enhanced Image Viewer, which provides a wider range of options, including a facility for magnifying individual

sections of a page. There are also options to download higher-quality images – these take longer to download, but you may be able to read the writing in the image more easily.

The Enhanced Image Viewer is designed to be used with the browser Internet Explorer, version 5.5 or later. It doesn't work with some other browsers, so you may need to switch to Internet Explorer to get the best out of the Ancestry site. To use the Enhanced Image Viewer, you'll need to install a special piece of browser software, or plug-in, on your computer (see page 40). Usually your computer will prompt you to install the plug-ins you need. If your browser settings or anti-virus software try to prevent installation, you'll find Ancestry's help pages have the information to solve the problem.

Lawful union

There's a double chance that you'll be able to trace your ancestors' wedding because most Anglican marriages generate two records: of the banns and of the marriage itself. In the 19th and early 20th centuries, weddings usually took place in the bride's parish church. Then, as now, the banns would be read by the vicar on three Sundays before the wedding. The banns publicly proclaim the couple's intention so help to avoid a bigamous or unlawful marriage. Records of banns and marriages can be found at **ancestry.co.uk**.

DNA testing service

Ancestry offers a range of DNA tests which allow you to find out if others with the same surname are related to you. You can buy a testing kit through the website and send off a simple mouth swab to get the results.

Using online data services
findmypast.co.uk

This website was originally called 1837online, named after the year in which civil registration of births, deaths and marriages began in England and Wales – you may still see it referred to by that name on websites and message boards. Using **findmypast.co.uk** you can access all the indexes held in the General Register Office (GRO), apart from those of the past 18 months, which aren't yet accessible (see pages 78-81). You can also view images of the original indexes. To get all the information you need, you'll have to order the certificates using a GRO reference number, which you can find on the website.

Many hands *Men of the Royal Marine Artillery unload howitzer shells at Ypres in 1917. First World War records on* **findmypast.co.uk** *will tell you about your fighting ancestors.*

Sign in to the site

1 To sign in, go to the **findmypast.co.uk** homepage. Click on the **Register** link, at the top right-hand corner of the page. This will take you to the registration screen.

Register your own details

2 You'll be asked to confirm your registration details, which include your email address and a password of your own choosing, as well as your name, country of origin and phone number. As with most sites, you'll also be asked to agree to its terms and conditions.

Main screen

3 After you've completed your registration, you'll be directed to the main Findmypast screen, which gives you a variety of options. From here, if you wish, you can make your first record search. You can also manage your account details or assess the benefits of paid subscription.

The findmypast information includes:

- Civil registration indexes to birth, marriage and death certificates for England and Wales 1837-2005
- Census returns for England and Wales 1841-1911
- Parish records for England and Wales (from 1538, updates ongoing)
- Passenger lists leaving the UK 1890-1960 and other migration records showing passport applications 1851-1903, as well as several sets of Indian records such as the Bengal Civil Service Graduation List 1869
- Indexes of living people, where you can look for a relative, address or business

- Military records, including British Army service records 1760-1915, soldiers who died in the First World War 1914-18, Army births 1761-2005), marriages 1796-2005, deaths 1796-2005, National Roll of the Great War 1914-18, Army Roll of Honour 1939-45, Boer War records 1899-1902, World War II Prisoners of War, and other Army lists roll calls 1656-1888
- Occupational sources, including Apprentices of Great Britain 1710-1774, Teachers' Registration Council Registers 1914-1948, the Clergy List 1896, Dental Surgeons' Directory 1925, Medical Register 1913 and Medical Directory for Ireland 1858

Get to know the site

4 It's a good idea to familiarise yourself with the site. Click on **Getting started** at the top of the list of useful links, and you'll be directed to a screen showing a variety of help options. These are worth exploring before you begin your work in earnest.

Start your search

5 Once you've familiarised yourself with the site, you can begin your search. Click on the **Search records** tab at the top of the page. Enter the name and dates for the person you are tracing, and then choose the category in which you wish to search. Military records, for example, are listed in the category **Armed forces and conflict**.

Wedding paperwork *A Victorian bride and groom sign the register – the original record of the event, which was forwarded to the GRO. Findmypast lets you view a transcription of the details.*

Using online data services
familysearch.org

The Church of Jesus Christ of Latter-day Saints (LDS), also known as the Mormons, maintains an online resources called **familysearch.org**. You can use its indexes free of charge. Its 'Discover Your Family History' facility is useful if you're looking for ancestors born before civil registration was introduced in the UK in 1837, because LDS has transcribed information, mostly from parish registers, known as 'British Isles Vital Records' from 1530 to 1906. These records appear in their International Genealogical Index (IGI).

FamilySearch records include:

● Census records, including a full transcript of the 1881 English and Welsh census, as well as US and Canadian records

● The International Genealogical Index (IGI) – a list of births, marriages, deaths and burials, transcribed from parish registers around the world

● Family trees, ancestral information and family pedigrees from other users of the website

● Links to Family History Centres worldwide

Start your search

1 On the **familysearch.org** home page you are immediately presented with a page entitled Discover Your Family History, where you can enter the first and last name of the ancestor you are seeking. Restrict the date ranges and the geographical area as much as possible. On clicking **Search**, a list of matches appears. If there is a problem displaying the matches, try repeating the process using a different browser.

Select by country

2 An alternative way to search is to browse by location on the Discover Your Family History page (see step 1). Under **Browse by Location**, click on **Europe**. Then on the page that appears click on **United Kingdom** in the left column. This takes you to the Historical Record Collections for the United Kingdom. You can now choose between parish registers, census returns and so on.

Narrow your search

3 If you click on **England Births and Christenings 1538-1975**, for instance, you are taken to a page (see above) where you can enter a name, place and dates for the person you are researching. Enter the details and click on **Search** and you are taken to a page showing matches for your search data.

Using online data services
origins.net

As well as census records, the **origins.net** site provides access to less commonly found records, such as Irish wills, livery company apprenticeships and court disputes going back at least 400 years. It's able to do this through partnerships with rich archive sources, such as the National Library of Ireland, York University's Borthwick Institute and the Society of Genealogists.

The King's shilling
Recruiting sergeants in Westminster try to encourage young men to sign up. The Origins website holds useful data of the young men who enlisted.

The Origins collections include:

British Origins britishorigins.com
- British Record Society Probate Collection 1320-1858, and other indexes of wills.
- Marriage Licence Allegations Index 1694-1850
- Militia Attestations Index 1886-1910
- Bank of England Will Extracts Index 1717-1845
- Apprentices of Great Britain 1710-74
- Passenger lists for 1890
- Teachers' Registrations 1870-1948
- Boyd's Inhabitants of London index

Irish Origins irishorigins.com
- Dublin City Census for 1851
- Irish Wills Index 1484-1858
- Passenger lists: Irish ports to USA for 1890
- Militia Attestations Index 1872-1915
- Griffith's Valuation of Ireland 1847-64

Scots Origins scotsorigins.com
- Access to experts' research of Old Parish Registers, detailing births, baptisms, marriages and death records in Scotland
- The 1861 and 1871 census records
- Free search for Scottish places
- Articles and discussions on Scottish history

Sign up

1 From the home page you can make a free search by name. To access this information, you need to sign up as a subscriber. Click on the **Find out more** link at the centre left-hand side of the homepage. Click on the **Login** link on the top right-hand side of the home page to see a range of subscription options.

Select a subscription package

2 You can choose to subscribe to all or parts of the Origins collections. Prices vary from package to package and on the length of your subscription. Click on your chosen package and follow the registration and payment details.

Using online data services
scotlandspeople.gov.uk

If you have Scottish ancestors, visit the 'one-stop shop' for Scottish family history, **scotlandspeople.gov.uk**. It's the government-sponsored online resource for Scottish records, and holds most of the birth, marriage and death indexes, known as statutory registers, as well as images of the original documents online.

The website will give you access to what is known as Old Parish Registers, which are the records kept by individual parishes of the Church of Scotland before the introduction of civil registration in 1855. Some date back as far as 1552. Many parish boundaries were changed over time, often more than once, and on this site you can find information about these changes to ensure you're looking in the right place.

The website also offers research guides, background information about the records, discussion groups and a comprehensive Frequently Asked Questions (FAQ) section. Browsing the contents list is free, but you'll have to pay to access the data (the fee is a contribution to the cost of indexing and digitising the records).

Getting more information

As well as searching for facts about your ancestors, you can read about the significance of the data you're looking at. This is important since it gives you an overall picture of how your ancestors lived, not just where and when.

The indexes on the site are listed in the box below. To access more recent statutory registers for births, marriages and deaths, as well as burial records from the parish registers, you need to go to the National Records of Scotland, in Edinburgh – a merger

Original images *Each hand-written two-line entry in the Old Parish Register of births and baptisms records whether the child was 'lawful' or 'natural' – a euphemism for illegitimate.*

The ScotlandsPeople indexes include:

● Indexes and images of Statutory Registers: births 1855-1906, marriages 1855-1931 and deaths 1855-1956

● Indexes and images of census records for Scotland 1841-1911

● Indexes and images of Old Parish Registers for births, baptisms, banns and marriages 1553-1854

● Indexes to wills and testaments 1513-1901. This area is free to search.

Go to the homepage

1 This provides information about the ScotlandsPeople Centre and the major classes of records. Click on **Register now** at the top right of the page.

in 2011 of the National Archives for Scotland and the General Register Office for Scotland (*see* **nrscotland.gov.uk**). Read more about using ScotlandsPeople on pages 96-99, and about searching Scottish parish records on page 144.

For the record *A class of children pose with their teacher at Eddleston School in Peeblesshire in 1899. Their names and family details would have been entered in the Scottish records when they were born, and again when they were baptised.*

Register and get a password

2 Enter your name, postal and email addresses as well as your chosen username. (A password will be emailed to you.) Once you've filled in the details, click on **Register your account now** at the bottom of the page. If you check your email you should find that you have received your password. Login at the top right of the screen.

Buy credits

3 Many of the most useful areas of scotlandspeople.gov.uk require payment. To go to the payment screen, click on the **Buy more credits** button.

Making your payment

4 The minimum payment you can make is £7.00, which buys you seven credits. These are valid for one year. Select **Number of credits** from the drop-down menu. Click on the **Proceed to payment** button and follow the instructions. The number of credits you own and their expiry date is shown at the top right of the screen.

Surnames and family history

If you have an uncommon surname you will usually be able to trace your family tree more quickly than if your name is Smith or Jones. Knowing where your surname was likely to be found in early times will help to direct your research in the right direction.

What's in a name?

Looking for the origins of the surname Loy shows how family historians can combine online sources with those available in print and in original documents. A good place to start online is **surnamedb.com**, which reveals that the name Loy became popular in France and that it was a shortened form of Eligius. The page on Loy on this site is full of interesting information.

Broadening the research to printed sources, *A Dictionary of Surnames*, by Patrick Hanks and Flavia Hodges, says that the name was of French origin and that it was made popular by St. Eligius, a goldsmith who became a priest and eventually a bishop. Furthermore, French dictionaries of surnames report that the surname is found principally in Lorraine, near the German border. In medieval England St Eloy, or St Loy as he was commonly called, was the patron saint of smiths, including the Worshipful Company of Blacksmiths in London. In *The Canterbury Tales*, the favourite oath of Chaucer's Prioress was 'By St Eloi!'

Where a name occurs

A number of sources can be used to provide data showing where specific family names are principally located. One such source – this time on a CD-ROM – is Stephen Archer's, *The British 19th Century Surname Atlas* (see page 62), which provides distribution maps of all the 400,000 plus surnames recorded in the 1881 census. This reveals that in 1881 there were only 263 Loys in the United Kingdom. Of these, 94 were living in Sheffield and neighbouring parts of South Yorkshire. Other small concentrations of the name were located in Scotland and north-east England. London had only 18 Loys.

So it seems that the surname came from France, perhaps Lorraine, and by mid-Victorian times it was particularly strong in and around the Yorkshire city of Sheffield. This is all extremely useful background.

Homing in on Thomas Loy

This information should make it easier to delve into the antecedents of someone named Loy. One such is Thomas Loy, who died in Romford in 1897, and whose birth certificate shows that he was born on November 2, 1861 in St Pancras, just a few months too late to be included in the 1861 census. The information on the birth certificate is confirmed by the baptismal record (see left) at St Pancras Church on November 28, 1861, which is available on the **ancestry.co.uk** site. This names his parents as Thomas and Sarah Loy and gives the father's occupation as 'Cutler'. This immediately suggests a possible connection with Sheffield – once the great centre of cutlery manufacture.

The Sheffield connection

A search for Thomas and Sarah Loy in the 1861 census for St Pancras was frustrated for a time because the surname was wrongly transcribed on the website as 'Log'. This is a common experience. Another member of the family in the 1851 census was transcribed as 'William Lay'. It is often necessary to try different spellings of names before the correct identity appears. When the Loys were eventually found, Thomas senior's birthplace was given as Sheffield.

To go back in time before the census returns and the birth, marriage and death certificates, the first place to turn to is **familysearch.org** to look for names in the parish baptism, marriage and burial registers in the International Genealogical Index. There it can be discovered that Thomas Loy (the father) was baptised at St Peter's Church, Sheffield (now the Cathedral) on September 7, 1817, the son of William and Harriet Loy, who were married on September 12, 1814 (see left).

This William Loy was baptised at the same church on December 31, 1740, but a direct line cannot be traced further back than his father. However, the name was a rare one that was confined to a single family or two, so it is reasonably certain that earlier people

A Sheffield family *The 1881 census reveals that of the 263 Loys living in the United Kingdom, more than a third lived in the industrial city of Sheffield and surrounding villages.*

with the surname Loy in Sheffield parish were William's ancestors. In fact, after a gap in the records, five more generations can be traced back through the parish register to Richard Loy, a cutler of Wincobank in the parish of Sheffield, who married in 1618.

Now the broader picture provided by the local history of Sheffield can be extremely useful. In the 1570s the Earl of Shrewsbury, lord of the manor, brought a group of ironworkers from the Weald of Kent and Sussex to build and work the first charcoal blast furnaces in the Sheffield district. These ironworkers had come to England from Lorraine. Their surnames included Gelley, Hussey, Perioge, Vintin and Loy. A John Loye was recorded among a group of Lorraine ironworkers in Kent in 1543.

Where did your surname come from?

The starting point for your family research will probably be your surname. Whether it's rare or common, it will tell you something about your family background and help you to trace other ancestors.

The Normans brought surnames to Britain after the Conquest in 1066. Before then, most people simply had Anglo-Saxon or Viking personal names, such as Edgar or Eric. Some Normans took their names from the towns they had left in France, such as the Laceys from Lassy. Others used their fathers' names, adding 'fitz', meaning 'son of', to form new names such as Fitzwilliam. Biblical names, such as John and Peter, were also used. As the population grew, so did the need for surnames, in order to distinguish people.

LOCATION Linking a name to a location started in the 13th century. More than a quarter of English surnames came from the position of a person's home, such as Underwood or Bywater, or from geographical features, such as Banks, Ford, Hill or Wood. Surnames that developed from place names often took the form used in local dialect, so someone from Braithwell in Yorkshire may have been called Brewell. People who moved to a new area were often named after the place they had come from, such as Welshman.

FAMILY NAMES Many surnames came from a father's name – so the son of James may have become known as Jameson. These are called patronymic names. Less frequently, names came from the mother's line – matronymic. This was likely if the woman were a widow or a wealthy landowner. Matronymic last names were also given to children of unwed mothers. Their descendants would adopt a matronym based on her name, such as Marriott from Mary, and Beaton from Beatrice.

FEATURES People were often named after their physical appearance, character or nickname – Sweet, Strong, Short or Ball (a nickname for a bald man), for instance.

OCCUPATION This is the most common derivation of English names. Clerk, Cook, Hunter, Butcher, Baker and Smith are all self-explanatory. Some occupational names are no longer quite so obvious. Cooper, for example, is derived from the maker of casks; Fletcher

The Luttrell Psalter *In the first half of the 14th century, Geoffrey Luttrell, a wealthy Lincolnshire landowner, commissioned a richly illustrated copy of the Psalms. The illustrations give an insight into rural and domestic medieval life and show some of the occupations that later gave rise to surnames used today. This portion shows a butcher, two cooks and two dispensers or butlers.*

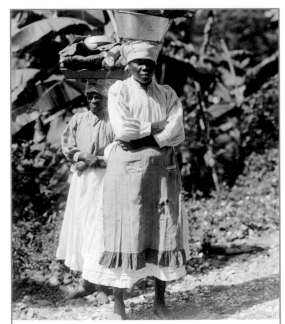

New names imposed
Many people taken as slaves from Africa to the West Indies in the 17th and 18th centuries were deprived of their own family names and given the surnames of the plantation owners or the estate on which they worked.

made arrows; Coward herded cows; Webster was a weaver and Butler, Spence or Spencer were dispensers of food and drink.

NO STANDARD SPELLINGS Until the late 19th century, few people were literate, so names weren't often written down, and when they were, similar-sounding names may have been spelled differently, such as Smith and Smythe. People also changed their names to avoid prejudice. During and after the two World Wars, many German or Jewish names were anglicised – Braun to Brown, for example.

Learning more about your surname

Someone who shares your surname may have already made a start on researching it. Try the Internet Surname Database at **surnamedb.com**, which is free to use (see page 58). Enter your name in the search box on the homepage. The site offers explanations of the origins of the name, its meaning, its likely geographical source and the changes in its location over time, as well as some of the holders of the name who've appeared in various parish and county records. Treat this information as a useful starting point. Your researches into your family history may well come up with a different explanation.

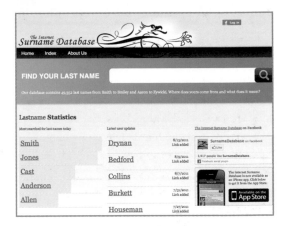

Links to other sites
On the **surnamedb.com** homepage there are several links taking you to other sites that will help with family research. One of them is **onegreatfamily.com**. It has a bank of 190 million already researched names, and displays them in the form of a simple family tree.

Origins and meanings
Back on the **surnamedb** homepage, click on **Surname origins** and you'll get a link to **ask.com**. Click on this and a list of family history sites is offered, including **dnaancestryproject.com** and **last-names.net**, both of which are helpful for surname searches.

For an insight into the meaning of surnames, go to **ramsdale.org/surname.htm**. It has a section on modern names and their long-forgotten origins.

It is important to remember that information on websites is largely compiled by amateurs. The advice given in the following pages may well lead you to different conclusions from those on offer.

The spread of a name
The Guild of One-Name Studies researches all appearances of a name (its distribution and frequency of appearance, for example). There are about 8000 names on the Guild's site, **one-name.org**, and you can check what's held there by clicking on **Online records** on the homepage. An A to Z index comes up. Choose the first letter of the name you want, and if it's shown, click on it and you'll see who's researching it and how to contact them.

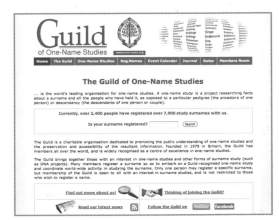

Tracking family names

Your surname provides important clues to your roots, especially if it's derived from a particular geographical region, place or feature.

All but the commonest surnames have a geographical distribution that can help you to trace the origins of your family. Thanks to the large data collections now available, studies in surnames and their worldwide geographical spread can be accessed on a new website, **gbnames.publicprofiler.org**. Just click on **Search for a surname** on this site to get information on 25,000 of the most widespread names.

Family business *Mr Davies stands outside his Cardiff boot shop in 1903. Then, you'd have been hard-pressed to find a Davies beyond Wales.*

Find your relatives

Key in your name and you can call up maps of how people with your name were spread across Britain at the time of the 1881 census and in 1998. This will give you clues about how your family has moved over the past century. You'll also be able to pinpoint where most people with your name are concentrated, not only in Britain, Northern Ireland and the Republic of Ireland, but also in the USA and Commonwealth countries, too.

The 1881 census returns are also mapped on *The British 19th Century Surname Atlas*, a CD-ROM available from **archersoftware. co.uk** (see also page 58). The surnames and forenames in the census are mapped in more localised detail than on the publicprofiler site.

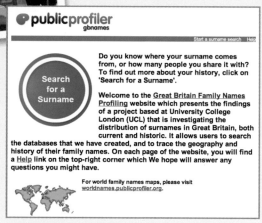

Do you know where your surname comes from, or how many people you share it with? To find out more about your history, click on 'Search for a Surname'.

Welcome to the Great Britain Family Names Profiling website which presents the findings of a project based at University College London (UCL) that is investigating the distribution of surnames in Great Britain, both current and historic. It allows users to search the databases that we have created, and to trace the geography and history of their family names. On each page of the website, you will find a Help link on the top-right corner which We hope will answer any questions you might have.

For world family names maps, please visit worldnames.publicprofiler.org.

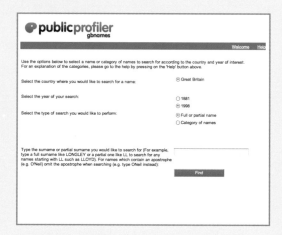

Use the options below to select a name or category of names to search for according to the country and year of interest. For an explanation of the categories, please go to the help by pressing on the 'Help' button above.

Select the country where you would like to search for a name: ⦿ Great Britain

Select the year of your search: ○ 1881 ⦿ 1998

Select the type of search you would like to perform: ⦿ Full or partial name ○ Category of names

Type the surname or partial surname you would like to search for (For example, type a full surname like LONGLEY or a partial one like LL to search for any names starting with LL such as LLOYD). For names which contain an apostrophe (e.g. ONeil) omit the apostrophe when searching (e.g. type ONeil instead):

[Find]

Start your search

1 To search for the spread in Great Britain of the surname Newberry, for example, go to the **gbnames.publicprofiler.org** homepage and click on **Search for a Surname** on the left-hand side of the page. The data is taken from the 1881 census and the 1998 electoral roll, so when you start to search, you can choose to see how the distribution of your surname has changed over time.

Fill in your details

2 Great Britain is already selected as the country to check. You then need to select either **1881** or **1998**. Once you have your results it's easy to change your selection to see how the distribution of your surname has changed. If you're looking for a specific surname search, select **Full or partial name**. Type the name you're searching for in the box provided – in this case, Newberry. For a wider search, use **Category of names**. Click on **Find** to view the results.

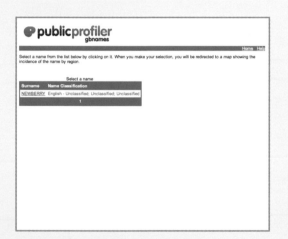

The 1881 Dafts

The 1998 Dafts

Least

Most

They weren't daft!

What could the names Cock, Hickinbottom and Smellie have in common? The research behind the creation of **gbnames.publicprofiler.org** reveals that these are among the six least popular surnames in Britain and have disappeared from the records over the past century or so. Another in this category is 'Daft'. Call it up on the distribution map of 1881 (left) and you'll see that the name is concentrated in the east Midlands, in Nottinghamshire, Lincolnshire and Leicestershire. Click on the map of 1998 (right) and the picture has changed little, apart from a small exodus to Dorset. The surname of Daft probably began with a single family – and just to set the record straight, in the Middle Ages it meant 'meek', not 'stupid'.

View the spread of a name

3 If you selected **Full or partial name**, you'll be presented with either a single match (as above) or a list of surnames, showing you the basic ethnic and geographical background for each one. If your name doesn't appear in the 1881 search, try again, this time selecting 1998 to see if it appears there. Then select the name and click on the link.

British concentrations

4 This page will show you a map of England, Scotland and Wales, showing the distribution of your surname, colour-coded to indicate the areas of the most and least coverage. Now you can begin to build up a picture of where the heartland of your family surname was located in 1881. In this case, you can see Newberry is mostly of southwest origin. At the top of the map, there's an option to view the map of 1998. Click on this link to see the corresponding distribution a century later.

Find out more

5 From the map screen, click on **Geographical Location** to see how common your surname is in other parts of the world and for more information on its spread within Britain. This may lead you to broaden your search for family members (see pages 254-61). From this screen you can also click on **Frequency and Ethnicity**, to see your surname distribution data in terms of numbers for 1881 and 1998, followed by a listing that shows the ethnic origins of your name.

When a name doesn't match

If you have difficulty finding a match for the surname of an ancestor, it may well be because it has been presented differently in the records or indexes you've been searching. This situation is usually easy to resolve.

One reason your ancestor's surname appears differently in the records could be because the spelling has changed over time. A Shepherd could become a Sheppard, for example, or a Rumball a Rumbold. Or perhaps a census enumerator, encountering someone with an unfamiliar accent, didn't take down the name the way you'd expect. It could also be that a modern data processor has made a mistake reading Victorian handwriting – when you look at the originals yourself, you'll see how hard they are to read. (For more about how to read old handwriting, see page 174.)

Most of the material available online has been created by large groups of people working from digital records or microfilm, rather than the original documents. The reproduction of some of the original images is often less than perfect, making them difficult to read. Add the possibility of simple human error and the 100 per cent accuracy of surname transcription can't be guaranteed.

All of this means you have to be open-minded about surname spellings and be prepared to search for that elusive person. But looking through huge lists of possible variants is a tedious process, so most data services offer a range of options for finding variants in a single search.

Search tips for finding names

Many websites automatically offer variations on the spelling of a name and you have to select the **Exact match** option if you want to find only the spelling you've entered. The disadvantage in doing a wider search is that you may have too many results to check.

There are ways to widen your search, though, without being overwhelmed by results. If you're having no luck trying to match a name exactly, a Wildcard, Soundex or Namex search can be helpful.

WILDCARD SEARCH One way to improve on an **Exact match** search is to use a Wildcard to stand for any letter or group of letters. Most

sites use an asterisk for this purpose. For example, W*lsh will find Walsh, Welsh, Wailsh and so on. Will* finds Will, Wills, Willis, Williams and Willoughby. You can use more than one wildcard: W*l*h will find both Walsh and Welch. Wildcards are particularly useful at coping with transcription errors, as they allow you to ignore letters that have been entered wrongly.

SEARCHING WITH SOUNDEX This technique for name-matching was invented in pre-computer days for the US census to try to get round spelling variations. Many records sites, such as ScotlandsPeople (left), make it available as a search option.

Soundex gives each surname a code based on the first letter and the remaining consonants, with similar codes for similar-variants have different codes and won't turn up as matches, so Hill has a code H400, while Hills is H420.

SEARCHING WITH NAMEX The surname-matching technique NameX is a more recent option to Soundex. It averages out the results of several name-matching systems to give a score of how closely another name matches what you've searched for. So if you search for Walsh, you'll find Wallsh scores 99 per cent, Welsh 95 per cent, Walshaw 82 per cent and so on. In Soundex, two spellings either match or they don't. But NameX tells you how closely they match. The Origins site, for example, uses NameX to give you a choice between **Close variants** and **All variants.**

Searching for a surname, offline

If you can't match a name online, there are a number of dictionaries and books in print that might help.

☛ George Redmonds, *Surnames and Genealogy: A New Approach* is the best introduction to modern studies of surnames.

☛ John Titford, *Penguin Dictionary of British Surnames* is the most up-to-date dictionary.

☛ George Redmonds, Turi King and David Hey, *Surnames, DNA and Family History* uses a multi-disciplinary approach, combining linguistics, distribution maps, genetics and genealogy to show how surnames were formed and how they spread and sometimes changed over time.

Saints' names *Many saints, such as John and Matthew (above), inspired both forenames and surnames. With time, their spelling may have changed, giving variations such as Johns, Johnson and Jonson, or Matthews, Matheson and Mathieson. A wildcard, Soundex or NameX search will help to find a name as it once was.*

sounding names. The code for Walsh, for example, is W420 and a Soundex search for Walsh will look for all names that are coded W420. These will include names like Welsh, Welch, Walch, Walshe as well as many that are less likely to be misspellings or genuine variants of Walsh, such as Wallace, Wells, Wills, Wheelock, Wolsey and Wyles. So a Soundex search will always give you a lot of names to search through. Another limitation of Soundex is that some obvious surname

The Bard fails the spelling test

William Shakespeare's will is remembered not only for the leaving of his second-best bed to his wife, Anne Hathaway, but also because his name is spelled differently twice in the same document. In one place it's given as 'Shackspeare', but the

signature at the end of the will appears as 'Shakspeare'. His name is spelled differently on other documents, too, and illustrates the relaxed attitude towards spelling in many official and private records of the time.

Signature at the top of the will

Signature at the bottom of the will

Building your family tree

Once you've gathered all your preliminary data, you'll want to find and collect the information that links one generation to the next – birth, marriage and death certificates, census forms, church records and other original documents. This is where you turn family history detective, following the clues and making great discoveries.

Setting out your family tree

When you've gathered a certain amount of information about your family going back a few generations, you'll want to start putting it into some sort of order. A family tree is the most obvious and most manageable format for this.

The simplest family tree is known as a pedigree chart or birth brief (see page 70). It starts with one person (usually yourself) and works backwards in time, generation by generation. At its most basic level, a pedigree chart names direct ancestors only – parents and grandparents on both the maternal and paternal line – and to keep things simple, it doesn't include aunts, uncles, cousins or siblings. As your research widens, you may find that you expand your pedigree chart which can encompass these relatives and any new ones that appear as you make progress. You can then work forward in time to record any children or grandchildren you may have.

Putting it down on paper

When you start drawing up your family tree, you'll use the information you've acquired from your family interviews as well as from your initial research. These are your building blocks and should include facts about:
- your children
- your brothers and sisters and their children
- your parents
- your grandparents
- any further generations about whom you have concrete evidence.

Working backwards, write your parents' names above your own, and link them with a double line to indicate their marriage (see

the tree-drawing tips, right). Then add the names of your siblings, again linking them to you. As you add each person, list their dates and places of birth under their names for easy reference. Where marriages have taken place, write the date and place of marriage under each entry. And if anyone has died, write the date and place of death, if known.

List your grandparents, using the same principles, and go back as far as you can. Leave spaces for any information you don't know, or insert question marks if you're not certain of the date of an event or the full name of the person. These flagged areas will need follow-up research later on.

Starting your family tree on paper is the obvious way to go, but as you begin to add more and more information, using your computer becomes more practical. You'll find plenty of help in this book to help you to get your family tree into an electronic form, but it's worth waiting until you've amassed quite a bit of detail.

Check and double-check

Make sure that any information you add to your tree is verified and accurate. Remember to double-check everything you've been told against documented sources such as certificates and census records. You'll discover in this chapter how to find all this

information and get copies of details. Once you've drawn up your immediate family tree based on interviews, it's a good idea to make it a rule that you add further information only after you've verified it.

Making duplicates

As your family tree expands, it's a good idea to take copies of smaller sections of it with you if you have to go to libraries or record offices in the course of your research. They'll help you to maintain your focus on a specific area of research without becoming bogged down in the larger tree and stop you being tempted to fly off in a dozen different directions on possible wild goose chases.

If you do find new information, add it to the master copy as soon as possible and be sure to date any additions as you write them onto the tree. From time to time, print out or draw up a new tree, so that you always have a clean, up-to-date version to refer to.

Facing hurdles

Be realistic about what you can expect to find. Although the ideal tree traces all lines back as far as possible, you're bound to encounter obstacles – especially as your search widens beyond your immediate family. Sometimes these problems can seem almost insurmountable – and every family historian dreads coming up against a 'brick wall'. But as you gain experience and amass more information, you'll discover that there are ways around apparent dead ends. The key is to be prepared to use the family history community, experiment with new sources and not to give up.

GRANDMA

THE PANKHURST GIRLS!

MUM → WEDDING PICS?

MY FAMILY TREE

Try to find birth/death certificates

Check photographs

Need to build on tree here

| WILLIAM SAWLE ? ? | CAROLINE PARSONS 1851-1921 | | J. PERRIN b. 1843 d. ? | ALICE HALL ? -1921 | | SAMUEL SHARPE 1841-1907 | CHARLOTTE ROSBROOK 1845-1925 | | ALFRED PANKHURST 1859-? | LOUISA CUTLER 1867-1943 |
| ggf | ggm | | ggf | ggm | | ggf | ggm | | ggf | ggm |

Marriage certificate - might have missing dates?

| CHARLES SAWLE 1874-1945 | | SARAH PERRIN 1880-1945 |
| gf | | gm |

| FREDERICK SHARPE 1885-1911 | | FLORA PANKHURST 1888-1942 |
| gf | | gm |

Find birth certificate

- Fought in WW1?
- Check regiment.
- Find old medal

| LEONARD SAWLE 1909-1980 |

| FLORENCE SHARPE 1911-1938 |

Things to do:
- Order certificates
- Search photos
- Fill in gaps!
- Build on tree

| PAULINE BROOKER 1937- |

| LAWRENCE BROOKER | | TIFFANY BROOKER |

DAD
* SCAN PHOTO FOR TREE

First attempts *Start by putting your family tree together on paper, using all the documents you've collected. At first you may find it easier to write the names of your ancestors on pieces of card, or on sticky notes, so that you can move them around easily on your tree without having to re-draw it.*

Family tree-drawing tips

To make your tree easier to read and understand, it's a good idea to stick to the accepted conventions for showing relationships.

● Women on the tree are given their maiden name, and are linked to their spouse by = or **m**.

● A vertical line links children to their parents, beneath the marriage symbol.

● A horizontal line links siblings.

● Children are usually listed in chronological (date) order from left to right.

● Members of the same generation are written on the same horizontal line.

Types of family tree

Family trees come in different shapes and sizes. Once you've compiled enough information to start putting your tree onto your computer (see pages 312-5), you can decide which is best for you.

The most commonly used format is the pedigree chart (see right) that starts with yourself at the bottom of the page and works upwards, and backwards in time. Or, you can display the same information in a horizontal format, called a birth brief (below), which starts with you on the left and has each successive generation moving one step to the right. You can even develop a circular chart, with yourself in the centre. These charts are suitable if you are concentrating on just one branch of the family, excluding any siblings.

If you want to expand your tree to include other branches of your family, a drop line chart – where you start with your earliest-known ancestors at the top and work down through the generations – will be the most suitable. This type of tree can become complicated because there's so much information to include, but it has the benefit of showing a complete family history.

There are a number of accepted symbols and conventions to use when drawing up your tree – see pages 8 and 69.

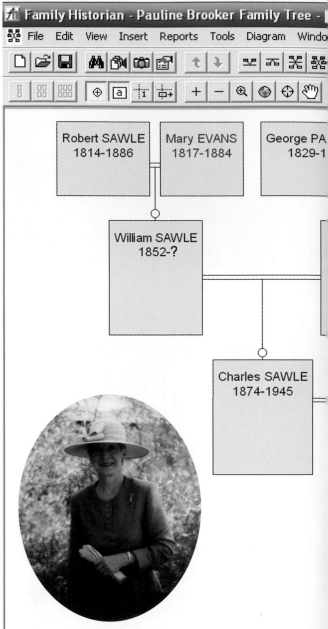

Know your pedigree The style of tree that concentrates on o branch of the family is called a pedigree. Here, the pedigree chart of Pauline Brooker starts at the bottom and works up. No siblings are shown, just direct ancestors. On Pauline's maternal line, the surname Sharp changed over time to Shar

Birth brief – an alternative view

This horizontal format for a family tree is simple and easy to read. On your computer, you can keep on adding generations as you discover more ancestors.

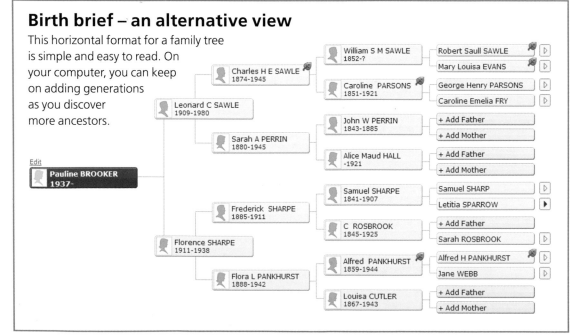

Caroline FRY
?

Samuel SHARP
1804-1883

Letitia SPARROW
1808-1871

Sarah ROSBROOK
?

Alfred PANKHURST
1828-1867

Jane WEBB
1883-?

ARSONS
1921

John PERRIN
1843-1885

Alice HALL
?-1921

Samuel SHARP
1841-1907

Charlotte ROSBROOK
1845-1925

Alfred PANKHURST
1859-1944

Louisa CUTLER
1867-1943

Sarah PERRIN
1880-1945

Frederick SHARPE
1885-1911

Flora PANKHURST
1888-1942

hard SAWLE
909-1980

Florence SHARPE
1911-1938

Pauline BROOKER
1937-

Births, marriages and deaths

Now that you know how to enter material into your family tree, you can start researching the civil registration documents that hold vital information about your ancestors.

Understanding civil registration

The wealth of information collected by the Victorians sheds light on many aspects of our ancestors' lives, including their professions, their property, the size of their families, their age at death and even what they died of.

The established Church in England and Wales has had to record all of its ceremonies since 1538. Until 1837, baptisms, weddings and burials were registered at the church where the ceremony took place and the recorded information stayed there. But with the spread of nonconformist religious groups there were many births, burials and marriages not recorded in this way.

Registration after 1837

On July 1, 1837, soon after Queen Victoria ascended the throne, a national, centralised system of registering the births, marriages and deaths of everybody in England and Wales was set up for the first time. Scotland and Ireland had later starting dates.

THE FIRST NATIONAL INDEXES The new system introduced the concept of a civil marriage and required all religious establishments to forward records of marriages, and all relatives to register births and deaths at local register offices, where local indexes

Wedding days *English artist, Sir Samuel Luke Fildes, painted this picture (left) of a village wedding taking place in high summer in 1883. By contrast, a marriage certificate from 1882 (right) shows that two domestic servants from Walworth in London were married on Christmas Day – their only free day.*

were created. These were sent each quarter (January-March, April-June, July-September and October-December) to the General Register Office (see page 80) with copies of each certificate issued. National indexes were compiled covering these respective quarters.

MISSING CERTIFICATES If you can't find an early certificate, it may be because your ancestor just didn't register the event. It wasn't until 1875 that the rules were tightened, making it more difficult to avoid registration. A large number of births, marriages and deaths were registered before 1875, nonetheless, and the certificates yield more details than the early parish records.

How civil registration worked

In 1837 a Registrar General was created in London with responsibility for the rest of England and Wales. Registration districts were set up with central register offices manned by superintendent registrars. Each registration district was split into sub-districts with a registrar to record local births, marriages and deaths. The new registration districts reflected the existing boundaries of the Poor Law Unions (see page 210).

REGISTRATION DISTRICT BOUNDARIES This system has not changed greatly since it was first established, but some boundaries have moved. You'll find the English and Welsh registration district boundaries for 1837 to 1851, 1852 to 1946 and 1946 to 1965 on maps published by the Institute of Heraldic and Genealogical Studies (see Directory). If you can't find an ancestor in the registration district that seems logical, look in adjacent districts, in case boundaries have changed.

What registration certificates will tell you

First prize in the treasure hunt for your family's records must be the discovery of birth, marriage and death certificates. Not only do they confirm names, dates and places, they may often yield a wealth of other information, too.

Sometimes a certificate may uncover a long-hidden family secret. If, for example, you come across a birth certificate where the father's name has been left blank, this suggests that the child was illegitimate and the father was not present at the registration (the mother couldn't give his name in his absence). When this happened the child usually took the mother's surname.

You can double-check this information by searching for that child's marriage certificate and seeing if the father's name is blank on that, too. Thanks to the Victorians'

scrupulous record-keeping, you can find details of the births, marriages and deaths of many of your ancestors in the records of the General Register Office (GRO).

The National Archives in Kew have microfiche copies of the indexes from 1837 until 1992, and many local record offices and public libraries also have copies. If you'd rather do your research from home, several websites provide online access to the indexes (see pages 82-93). You'll need to use data from the indexes when you order copies of certificates from the GRO (see page 94).

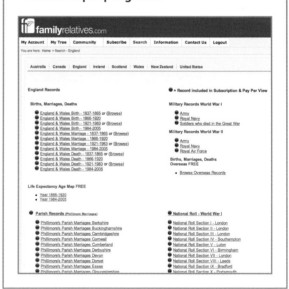

(see pages 82-93)

Improved access to indexes

The following sites provide extensive access to the General Register Office indexes:

- **freebmd.org.uk**
- **findmypast.co.uk**
- **bmdindex.co.uk**
- **familyrelatives.com**
- **ancestry.co.uk**
- **ukbmd.org.uk**
- **scotlandspeople.gov.uk**

The importance of baptismal records

Before civil registration was introduced in 1837, births would not have been recorded officially. But as most babies were baptised within weeks in their local church (left), baptism records act as a guide to the birth date. If your ancestor was born after 1837, you can expect to find a record of both birth and baptism. After 1874, by law, births had to be registered within six weeks of the event.

CERTIFIED COPY OF AN ENTRY OF BIRTH

GIVEN AT THE **GENERAL REGISTER OFFICE**

Application Number.........G209162

REGISTRATION DISTRICT	Amesbury
1858 BIRTH in the Sub-district of Orcheston	in the County of Wilts

Columns:-	1	2	3	4	5	6	7	8	9	10
No.	When and where born	Name, if any	Sex	Name and surname of father	Name, surname and maiden surname of mother	Occupation of father	Signature, description and residence of informant	When registered	Signature of registrar	Name entered after registration
418	Fourth March 1858 Tilshead	Edward	Boy	Thomas Mead	Ellen Mead formerly Payne	Shoemaker	Ellen Mead Mother Tilshead	Tenth March 1858	Edw. Wilson Turner Registrar	

CERTIFIED to be a true copy of an entry in the certified copy of a Register of Births in the District above mentioned.

Given at the GENERAL REGISTER OFFICE, under the Seal of the said Office, the.............13th.............day of.............March.............2007

BXCC 352896

CAUTION: THERE ARE OFFENCES RELATING TO FALSIFYING OR ALTERING A CERTIFICATE
AND USING OR POSSESSING A FALSE CERTIFICATE ©CROWN COPYRIGHT
WARNING: A CERTIFICATE IS NOT EVIDENCE OF IDENTITY.

PDP

039887 10107 08/05 SPSL 012033

What you'll find on a birth certificate

First, you'll see where the birth was registered – the registration district, the sub-district and the county. Then ① the GRO reference number ② where and when the child was born (this can be revealing, as most children were born at home until the National Health Service was set up in 1948, when hospital births became more common) ③ the child's first names ④ the child's sex ⑤ the father's full name ⑥ the mother's full name and maiden name ⑦ the father's occupation ⑧ who registered the birth, their relationship to the child and their address ⑨ when the birth was registered and ⑩ the registrar's signature. The last column is for any later notes. It may show that a child was adopted or that they changed their surname.

CERTIFIED COPY OF AN ENTRY OF MARRIAGE   GIVEN AT THE GENERAL REGISTER OFFICE

Application Number _____ Y006395 _____

1910. Marriage solemnized at *the East Ham Baptist Church, Plashet Grove, East Ham* in the District of *West Ham* in the County of *Essex West Ham C.B*

No.	When Married.	Name and Surname.	Age.	Condition.	Rank or Profession.	Residence at the time of Marriage.	Father's Name and Surname.	Rank or Profession of Father.
84	ninth September 1910	Archie Edgar Hibbert	28 years	Bachelor	Secretary Public Company	130 Clements Road East Ham	John Rison Hibbert	of no Occupation
		Lowie Alice Beatrice Mead	26 years	Spinster	/	76 Bristol Road East Ham	Edward Mead	Commercial Clerk

Married in the *Baptist Church* according to the Rites and Ceremonies of the *Baptists* by *certificate* by me,

This Marriage was solemnized between us. *A. E. Hibbert* *L. A. B. Mead* in the Presence of us. *Jno. R. Hibbert* *E. Mead Y. Mead* *Frank Williams* *S. Mawer Registrar*

CERTIFIED to be a true copy of an entry in the certified copy of a register of Marriages in the Registration District of _____ *West Ham* _____

Given at the GENERAL REGISTER OFFICE, under the Seal of the said Office, the _____ *6th* day of _____ *September* 2001

MXA 895057

This certificate is issued in pursuance of section 65 of the Marriage Act 1949. Sub-section 3 of that section provides that any certified copy of an entry purporting to be sealed or stamped with the seal of the General Register Office shall be received as evidence of the marriage to which it relates without any further or other proof of the entry, and no certified copy purporting to have been given in the said Office shall be of any force or effect unless it is sealed or stamped as aforesaid.

CAUTION: THERE ARE OFFENCES RELATING TO FALSIFYING OR ALTERING A CERTIFICATE AND USING OR POSSESSING A FALSE CERTIFICATE. ©CROWN COPYRIGHT

WARNING: A CERTIFICATE IS NOT EVIDENCE OF IDENTITY.

Form MXA Series   Dd 0730   90M   04/01   SPSL(000153)

What you'll find on a marriage certificate

First, the name of the town and county where the marriage took place. Then ① the GRO reference number ② the date of the marriage ③ the full names of the groom and bride ④ the ages of the groom and bride ('full age' means they were over 21, 'minor' means they were under 21) ⑤ the marital status of the groom and bride ⑥ the groom's occupation or social status ⑦ where the groom and bride were living before they married ⑧ the groom's and bride's fathers' names (if the father has died, the word 'deceased' will normally be written underneath the name) ⑨ the groom's and bride's fathers' occupations or social status ⑩ where the marriage took place, whether it was in a church, synagogue or registry office, and under which religious denomination the ceremony was performed and ⑪ the signatures of the groom, bride and two witnesses.

CERTIFIED COPY OF AN ENTRY OF DEATH

GIVEN AT THE GENERAL REGISTER OFFICE

Application Number Y 006395

REGISTRATION DISTRICT	Ilford	
1946 DEATH in the Sub-district of Ilford North	in the County of Essex	

Columns:–	1	2	3	4	5	6	7	8	9
No.	When and where died	Name and surname	Sex	Age	Occupation	Cause of death	Signature, description and residence of informant	When registered	Signature of registrar
459	Seventeenth April 1946 King George Hospital	William Loving	male	73 years	of 26 St Margarets Road Barking a Council Laration Attendant	Broncho pneumonia due to fractured right femur. Knocked down by motor cycle on highway when crossing on foot PM Accidental cause	Certificate received from P Bernard P Reels Coroner for Metropolitan district of Essex. Inquest held 20 April 1946 25th April 1946	Twenty seventh April 1946	G A Norkett Registrar

CERTIFIED to be a true copy of an entry in the certified copy of a Register of Deaths in the District above mentioned.

Given at the GENERAL REGISTER OFFICE, under the Seal of the said Office, the .... 6th .... day of .... September 2001

DXZ 894350

See note overleaf

What you'll find on a death certificate

It will start with the registration district, the sub-district and the county. Then ① the GRO reference number ② when and where the person died ③ the deceased person's full name ④ the deceased person's sex ⑤ the deceased person's age (death certificates issued after 1984 show the person's date and place of birth instead) ⑥ the deceased person's occupation (women's death certificates prior to 1984 usually state the husband's name and occupation instead of the woman's occupation) ⑦ the cause of death ⑧ who registered the death, their relationship to the deceased person and their own address ⑨ the date the death was registered and, finally, ⑩ the registrar's signature. If the cause of death is a condition or illness that's unfamiliar to you, see how to get help with understanding the terminology on page 74.

How to use General Register Office indexes

Your search for family records is about to get really exciting. The records of the vast majority of births, marriages and deaths in England and Wales since 1837 are listed in the indexes of the General Register Office (GRO), and the information gets easier to access every day.

You can already view many of the indexes online through the pay-per-view websites that appear on the following pages. The ultimate aim is for everyone to be able to search online for images of real certificates.

What the indexes are

The GRO indexes are lists rather like the index in a book. Entries for all certificates are arranged in chronological order, and then alphabetically, by surname. In the past, they were held in book form at the Family Records Centre in Islington, London, but now you can see them on microfiche at The National Archives (TNA) at Kew or through the websites that are making them available online.

Before you begin looking for your family's certificates, you'll need to understand exactly how the indexes are arranged and what information they contain. The page opposite tells you how to find birth certificates; see page 80 for marriage and death certificates.

Don't be misled by the date

Even if you know the exact date of an event such as a birth, the index entry will not necessarily appear in the quarter in which it happened: it will be in the quarter in which it was registered. Births may be registered several weeks after the event.

BETWEEN 1837 AND 1983 In this period, the indexes are arranged in year order, with each year divided into quarters: January-February-March; April-May-June; July-August-September; and October-November-December. Each quarter is known by the name of its last month – so the first quarter is referred to as 'March quarter'. Within each quarter you'll find an alphabetical index of surnames. So if, for example, you know that your ancestor, Grace Abbots, was born on August 4, 1920, find the section of books

How to order a certificate by phone

Having found an entry in the indexes, you may want to order a certificate. You can do this online on the Directgov website, **direct.gov.uk/en**

(see page 94 for how to find the part of the site you need) or, if you're unsure about the information you have and would feel happier speaking to someone about it, you can order by phone (0845 603 7788). If you have the index entry number, which will be a volume and page number, that will be very helpful, but if you haven't found a reference in the indexes, staff at the GRO will look it up for you. There's a cost of £3 for this service.

You can pay by credit or debit card over the phone. Certificates are posted to you after five working days at a cost of £9.25 a certificate. Or you can use a priority service, which despatches the next working day at a cost of £23.40 for each certificate if you order.

covering 1920 and then the quarter covering July, August and September (but see 'Don't be misled by the date', opposite). Now look under 'A' for Abbots and then find 'Grace' in the sub-heading under 'Abbots'.

AFTER 1984 In this period, the books are arranged chronologically by year, then alphabetically by surname and forename, with no quarterly breakdown. To find Mary Abbots born August 4, 1991, find the books covering 1991 and then look under 'A' for Abbots; there's no need to know the quarter in which she was born.

Searching the birth indexes

The birth indexes from September quarter 1837 until June quarter 1911 give only the child's first names, surname, father's name and the registration district of the birth, along with the GRO reference code that you'll need if you intend to order a copy of the certificate.

From September quarter 1911, the indexes will also show the mother's maiden name, making it easier to identify the correct entry. It will also make it possible for you to trace relatives from her side of the family.

WHAT TO WRITE DOWN If you think you've found the entry you want in the birth indexes, and want to order a certificate, make a careful note of:
- the first name and surname of the child
- the year (and quarter, if before 1984) in which the birth was registered
- the registration district in which the birth was registered
- the page number of the entry and the

volume in which it appears – all of which will be shown on-screen. These details are essential if you're going to order a copy of the birth certificate from the GRO and you want to be sure that they'll send you the right one. (For information on ordering, see box, left.)

Given a name *Birth certificates and baptismal records are the earliest official appearances of a person's name. You should be able to find details of your ancestors in the GRO indexes at* **direct.gov.uk/en** *(see page 94).*

Searching for marriage and death details

These two key life events will form an important part of your family history research. The General Register Office's indexes for marriages and deaths are a rich source of the information you need.

Using the GRO's marriage indexes for England and Wales since 1837 will enable you to find the date of a family marriage. It will also allow you to verify other dates, places and names that you may have found from less reliable sources, such as a letter.

Searching the marriage indexes

These are organised in year order, under the 'quarter' system described on page 78. Marriage indexes covering ceremonies that took place before the end of December quarter 1911 will show the name of the person you are searching for (but not the surname of their spouse), the registration district in which the marriage took place and the GRO reference number. The spouse's surname was included from the beginning of the March quarter 1912, making these indexes much more helpful.

BOTH NAMES KNOWN If you're hunting for a marriage that took place before the end of December 1911, and you know the full names of both the bride and groom, you can do two separate marriage searches using each of the names. Then cross-reference the list of possibilities that comes up until you find a pair with matching registration districts and reference numbers for the same year and quarter. This saves you wasting time as well as money.

Love at the double *Although it's traditional for brides to take the surname of their husband, some couples combine their surnames and create a new, shared name that will go into the records. If you're looking for a double-barrelled name, try searching the GRO indexes for both names, separately.*

ONLY ONE NAME KNOWN If you know only one of the surnames, you'll need to order certificates for all possible marriages for the person whose name you do know, and then use the certificates to find a match for the correct forename – a more expensive route. Before buying certificates, it's a good idea to cross-check your information on a free-to-use website, such as **freebmd.org.uk** (see page 82), with a database of transcribed index entries.

Once you've found the details

When you're sure that you've found the right marriage record, but before you attempt to order a copy of the certificate from the GRO, make a careful note of the information that you get from the index – or you could end up paying for a certificate that isn't what you really wanted.

WHAT TO WRITE DOWN These are the details you'll need to note:
- the full name of at least one of the people on the marriage certificate – the bride's first name and surname or the groom's full name are sufficient. Having both is even better
- the year and quarter in which the marriage was registered
- the registration district in which it was registered
- the volume and page number of the entry.

Searching the death indexes

If it's a death certificate you're after, the GRO's indexes from 1837 until the end of December quarter 1865 give the name of the person who died, the registration district in which the death was registered and the GRO reference number you'll need when ordering.

From March quarter 1866 until the end of March quarter 1969, the indexes also give the age of the person who died, making it much

End of the thriller *Agatha Christie's death in 1976 would, like all deaths, have been recorded where she died, and not necessarily where she lived or was buried (below). Her death certificate is held at the GRO and can be accessed online.*

easier to identify the correct entry, especially if you have either of the relevant birth or marriage certificates. From June quarter 1969 the death indexes are even more detailed, giving the date of birth of the deceased person rather than just their age. So if a relative died after April 1969 and you know the date of death, you can quite quickly and easily discover their date of birth.

WHAT TO WRITE DOWN To order a copy of a death certificate from the GRO, you need the following information from the index:
- the first name (or names) and surname
- the age at death or date of birth if given, although this isn't essential

- the year and quarter in which the death was registered
- the registration district
- the volume and page number of the entry.

Suspicious deaths

Sometimes a death certificate may indicate that the death wasn't due to natural causes and therefore a coroner's order was made. It's definitely worth following up on this lead by looking for details of an inquest or inquiry in the local newspaper of the time (see page 216). Some coroners' records are held in the county record offices, but aren't accessible for at least 75 years after the death.

Using the national indexes
freebmd.org.uk

If you're after the birth, marriage or death certificate of an ancestor, the best place to start searching is this free-to-use website. It holds transcriptions of the GRO indexes.

FreeBMD is transcribing the indexes of all registered births, marriages and deaths in England and Wales from 1837 up to 1983, with more being added daily. Transcriptions are held in a database that's searchable by name, which saves you having to trawl through scanned pages of original indexes, searching for the name you want.

To search the registers, click on the **Search** button on the homepage. The website also offers links to FreeCEN (census data) and FreeREG (parish registers).

Using the searchable database

The transcriptions on FreeBMD are held in a database that you can search by first name and surname, or surname only if you're not sure of the person's first name. Narrow down the list of search results by including the county and registration district, if you can, and restricting the range of years.

For searches in the birth index after September quarter 1911 – when the mother's maiden name began to be included – restrict your results by asking the database to find only those entries that include the mother's correct maiden name. Similarly, if you are looking for a marriage from March quarter 1912 – when the spouse's surname was first included in the index – narrow down the results by searching only for entries that include the spouse's correct surname.

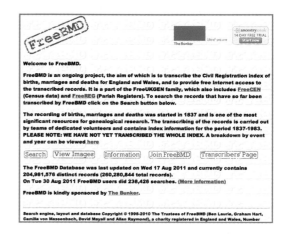

All entries should have a link to a scanned image of the original index. Click on the spectacles symbol next to the entry if you'd like to see the scanned page. Download the image to your computer (see page 31), free of charge, and then you can enlarge it to read the entry more easily.

Facts to bear in mind

This website is a great short cut for getting started with a 19th-century birth, marriage or death search, but you won't get all the details until you can see the certificate itself. If you find a promising lead, make sure you note the district, volume and page numbers, as you'll need these to order original certificates (see pages 78-81 and 94).

Five generations *An elderly woman with her son, grandson, great grandson and great great grandchild. A photograph that captures several generations is a wonderful find, matching faces to the names you'll see on sites such as FreeBMD.*

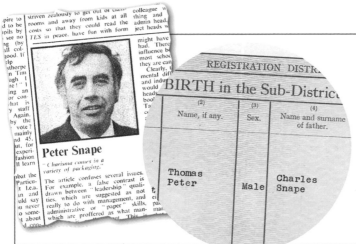

Thomas or Peter?

Confusion over the name by which a person is known can make your search trickier. Headmaster Thomas Peter Snape was always known to both his family and his colleagues as Peter, but looking for a 'Peter Snape' in various records and indexes would have drawn a blank. Always try to search using both forenames.

Search guidelines to help you

- Enter what you know into the search engine.
- If you're looking for the birth of someone with a common name, restrict the search by entering a county or registration district of birth.
- If you're doing a general search for the deaths of everyone with an unusual family name, just enter that surname and a date range.
- If you can't find an ancestor, it may be that the transcriptions are incomplete or contain mistakes. Instead, return to **direct.gov.uk/en** (see page 94).

Search for the name of a spouse

1 In this case history, you know that Cornelius Waite married a woman called Mary Ann some time between the 1861 and 1871 censuses, but you don't know her maiden name. To find their marriage in the indexes, go to the **freebmd.org.uk** homepage and click **Search**. This takes you to a page where you enter all the details you already know. Choose **Marriages** from the **Type** list. Select the registration district and county if you know them. Click on **Find**.

Possible matches

2 You entered 'Waite' in the **Surname** box and 'Cornelius' in the **First name(s)** box, narrowed down the search by entering the years 1860 and 1871 in the **Date range** boxes and put 'Mary' in the **Spouse first name(s)** box. The search engine produces a list of possible results under the name 'Waite'. Click on the highlighted page number. Here, it's page 270.

Spouse's name found

3 You'll see any other names whose reference matches Cornelius Waite's, and find that Mary Ann's maiden name was Johnson. Click on the spectacles icon for a scanned image of the entry. If you were researching a more common name, you could get several results. In that case, you'd need to order all the marriage certificates to discover which was the right one.

Using the national indexes
findmypast.co.uk

On **findmypast.co.uk** you'll find all the digital images of the General Register Office (GRO) indexes from 1837 until 1983, as well as the indexes from 1984 to 2005 in a searchable database. But what makes it particularly useful is that it also has details of births, marriages and deaths of British

subjects that occurred overseas between 1761 and 1994. It wasn't compulsory for a British subject living abroad to register these events, so the indexes aren't necessarily complete. The website also has indexes of births, marriages and deaths that happened at sea in the second half of the 19th century, as well as

divorce proceedings that took place between 1858 and 1903. There's a section that deals with military records – you can search all records from 1656 to 1994, for example, as well as armed forces records for births, marriages and deaths going back as far as the late 18th century. All these indexes are free to search, but there's a small charge to view the image or database transcription. You need to do this, to make sure you've found the correct entry, and to get the references you require for ordering certificates from the GRO.

Go to the homepage

1 Here's how to do a search for details of the departure from the UK of a relative, John Jones, some time between 1890 and 1920. Go to **findmypast.co.uk** and register, as shown on page 52.

Buy units

2 Having registered you can search all the indexes on the site for free, but to see relevant entries in more detail you'll have to buy credits. Choose from subscription or pay-as-you-go options and then click on the relevant button. Give your credit card details. Pay-as-you-go options are valid for a limited time. (See opposite for how to set up an account.)

Enter search details

3 Enter the first and last names of your ancestor. Tick the **Include variants** box, to widen the search in case his name was entered wrongly. Click on **Male**. Set the date range between 1890 and 1920. Click on **Search**.

THE 1837-1983 DATABASE The births, marriages and deaths search engine for 1837 to 1983 looks only for the index pages that cover the surname you're looking for, and doesn't locate an individual entry. Type in the name and the date range you wish to search. The Search Results page shows you a list of all the quarters and years that cover the period for the name. Click on **View** to have a closer look at the scanned image of each quarter to see if you can find your ancestor's name and details.

THE 1984-2005 DATABASE If you're looking for a birth, marriage or death between 1984 and 2005, narrow the search by including the person's middle name, the district in which the event was registered, the mother's maiden name for a birth, the spouse's surname for a marriage and the date of birth for a death search. The Search Results page will give you a list of possible entries but will provide only name, registration district and year of registration. Click **View** to see the full entry, for 1 unit.

Setting up an account

To view images on the Findmypast website you have to register, open an account and buy £5 worth of units – which gives you 50 units at 10p each. There's step-by-step advice for this below, left, and on page 52. You can pay online, using your credit or debit card, or by using BT's Click & Buy service that adds the charge to your phone bill. You can also buy monthly or annual price plans from the site. One unit is deducted from your account each time you view an image.

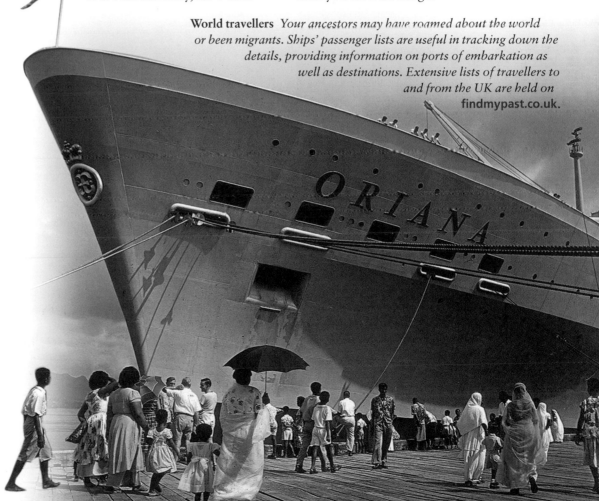

World travellers *Your ancestors may have roamed about the world or been migrants. Ships' passenger lists are useful in tracking down the details, providing information on ports of embarkation as well as destinations. Extensive lists of travellers to and from the UK are held on* **findmypast.co.uk.**

| Home | My family tree | Search records | News | Help & advice | My account |

Passenger list search results

Search criteria used:

Last name: Jones
First name: John(including variants)
Year of departure: 1890 to 1920

Results:
- 2094 records shown include exact matches.
- 5602 records include initial J and exact matches.
- 11095 records include unstated first name, initial J and exact matches.

Cost:
You will be charged 5 credits to view a transcript and 30 credits for an image unless you have purchased a subscription for this set of records.

redefine current search

Viewing Page 1 of 42 [1]2 3 4 5 6 7 8 9 10 >>

Last name ▼	First name	Year of birth	Sex	Departure year	Departure port	Destination country	Destination port	Transcript	Image
JONES	A L Ct John	Unknown		1918	Liverpool	Canada	Saint John NB	VIEW	VIEW
JONES	Alfred John	1908	M	1920	Liverpool	Canada	Quebec	VIEW	VIEW
JONES	Cecil Henry John C	1896	M	1910	Bristol	Canada	Quebec	VIEW	VIEW
JONES	David John	1855	M	1895	London	Australia	Sydney	VIEW	VIEW
JONES	David John	1888	M	1919	Liverpool	India	Calcutta	VIEW	VIEW
JONES	E John	1883	M	1907	Liverpool	Canada	Halifax	VIEW	VIEW
JONES	Ed John	1878	M	1901	Liverpool	USA	Philadelphia	VIEW	VIEW
JONES	Edwin John	1877	M	1896	Plymouth	Australia	Sydney	VIEW	VIEW
JONES	Edwin John	1877	M	1896	Plymouth	Australia	Sydney	VIEW	VIEW
JONES	Evan	1844	M	1890	Liverpool	Argentina	Puerto Madryn	VIEW	VIEW
JONES	Evan	1868	M	1890	London	Australia	Sydney	VIEW	VIEW
JONES	Evan	1886	M	1890	Liverpool	USA	New York	VIEW	VIEW
JONES	Evan	Adult	M	1890	Liverpool	USA	New York	VIEW	VIEW
JONES	Evan	Adult	M	1890	Liverpool	USA	New York	VIEW	VIEW
JONES	Evan	1852	M	1891	Dartmouth	Madeira	Madeira	VIEW	VIEW
JONES	Evan	Adult	M	1891	Liverpool	USA	New York	VIEW	VIEW
JONES	Evan	1821	M	1891	Liverpool	USA	New York	VIEW	VIEW

Choose from the results

4 Your results will be presented as a list that shows you the name, age, sex, year of departure, port, destination country and destination port. Select the entry that seems most likely. Decide whether you want to see a transcript or the image of the entry and click on **View** in the appropriate column on the right. You'll need to use your credits, or register for a voucher. It costs 5 units to see a transcript and 30 to see the image.

Using the national indexes
BMDIndex.co.uk

The BMD site specialises in births, marriages and deaths, holding scanned images of the General Register Office (GRO) indexes from 1837 to 1983 and a database of transcriptions from the GRO indexes for 1984 until 2005. You'll have to pay to use **bmdindex.co.uk**, but it's not expensive.

Searching the records

There are four ways to search the records. You can choose from the basic search engine, an advanced search engine or two 'SmartSearch' options – one for births and one for deaths. There's also a facility that displays your results as a printable map.

BASIC SEARCH ENGINE This searches the indexes for all records between 1837 and 1983 by surname, forename and year range. You'll get a list of results with links to scanned images of the pages on which your entry might be found. The search engine looks for initials only, even if you've supplied full details of the first names, so there may be two or more pages to check for one quarter, particularly if the surname is a reasonably common one. It's best to use this type of search when the surname is uncommon.

Log in and set date parameters

1 In this case history, the search is for the children of a John Pickering and a Janet Holmes, whom you know were born after 1984, probably in Sheffield. On the homepage enter your email and password and click on **Sign in**. If you have not already registered, click on **Sign Up.** and follow the intructions. Press the **Search** link that takes you back to BMD Indexes 1837-2005. Under **Search Options** click on the **Search Now** button for records between 1984 and 2005.

Choose your search method

2 The BMDIndex Basic Search page shows how you can search the records. Choose from birth, marriage and death registrations, SmartSearch for birth dates from 1865 within the deaths list, or SmartSearch to find birth records from family and maiden names. Click on the second **SmartSearch** option, and the search engine will be displayed. Set the dates to cover 1984-2005 in the **Select a period** panel.

Find the children

3 Under **Search parameters** enter 'Pickering' in the **Father or mother's surname** box. Type 'Holmes' in the **Mother's maiden surname** box and scroll down the **Optional registration district** list to find Sheffield. Click on **Find children from parent's names** under **Search options**. Five children come up with the surname Pickering and mother's maiden surname Holmes born in Sheffield between 1984 and 1992.

ADVANCED SEARCH ENGINE Records from 1984 to 2005 can be accessed by an advanced search engine. To narrow down the list of results – useful if you are searching for a common name – enter a middle name and mother's maiden name for birth searches, or partner's surname for marriage searches, or a date of birth for death searches. If you click on the link to the spouse's surname in a marriage search, for example, you'll see the page showing the groom's or bride's entry – and discover his or her first name.

View the records

4 Click on the **View** icon to find the GRO references needed to order each birth certificate, which is the only way you can be sure that all the children have the same parents. You can print the on screen record, or cut and paste it into a document on your computer (see page 31).

USING SMARTSEARCH FOR DEATHS To find death records between 1984 and 2005, use the first SmartSearch option. Its death records contain the dates of birth, so a search for one will yield the other. You'll be given a list of surnames, first names and the month, year and district of registration for anyone matching your criteria who died between 1984 and 2005. Click **View** to see the fully transcribed record, which confirms the date of birth and the GRO reference. On the **Full record** page, you'll find an option to view the page in the birth indexes where your ancestor's birth entry should be found. For the death registration for a married woman, you need to enter her maiden name in the **Surname at birth** box to find her birth date.

USING SMARTSEARCH FOR SIBLING BIRTHS Trace the births of siblings born between 1984 and 2005 by using a second SmartSearch option. This finds children whose surnames and mother's maiden names match. You can narrow down the results by restricting the year range.

Bear in mind that people shown as sharing surnames and mother's maiden name are not necessarily siblings. To cut out confusion, restrict the district search to the area in which the parents married if you think they might have stayed in the same region.

A final farewell *Parish burial records are important in tracing the dates of deaths occurring before the start of civil registration in 1837.*

How to pay
It's free to search the site's indexes and view results pages, but you'll have to register and buy a subscription before you can access the search engines. Credits are deducted from your account every time you view a new image of the indexes or a full transcription.

There's a range of price plans for viewing the information held by **bmdindex.co.uk**. A low-cost, pay-as-you-go subscription lets you view the birth, marriage and death indexes. You get 50 credits, valid for 90 days – it costs one credit to view an image. If you want to view the same image more than once in a 30-day period, you won't be charged a second time. There's also an option to have a year's subscription, which works out cheaper if you have a lot of searching to do.

Bear in mind that your account can be activated only on one computer – so you can't access the search engines unless you're using the computer on which you signed up to the account. But you can change your registered computer as many as three times, if you find you have to.

Using the national indexes
familyrelatives.com

The wide range of information available at **familyrelatives.com** includes some of the more unusual records, such as overseas births, marriages and deaths, and Army, Navy and RAF deaths from the two world wars. In addition, records from hundreds of parishes have been transcribed.

The civil registration indexes for England and Wales from 1837 to 2005 are being transcribed, and the site has divided the period into four sections: 1837 to 1865, 1866 to 1920, 1921 to 1983 and 1984 to 2005. You can access the site's 400 million records by subscription or by a pay-per-view system.

BEFORE YOU BEGIN Before you can search the site's databases you'll need to register – which won't cost you anything. Just as with most other sites, the registration form will ask for your email address, a password, your name and contact details. Once you've filled in the form, click on **Continue** to be taken to the **Search** page, where you can choose which database you're interested in.

It makes sense to buy units or set up a subscription before you begin searching. You'll need credits to be able to view any

Life in the colonies *In the late 19th century, the three Hewitt sisters went out as nurses to what was then Rhodesia. Annie Hewitt (centre) married Joseph Nesbitt on October 10, 1900. Many colonial marriages can be found in the overseas records.*

Search for a birth

1 Once you've registered (see above), go to the search page and choose the type of event and year range you wish to search. For example, if you want to search the website's transcriptions for the birth of a Mary King born between 1911 and 1915, click on the **Birth – 1866-1920** link.

of the results you find that could help your research, and it's frustrating to have to stop and set up your credits when you've actually found what you want to see. Click on the **Subscribe** link along the top panel and you'll be offered a choice of an annual unlimited subscription for £30, or pay-per-view units in blocks of 60 for £6, or 150 for £12.

INCOMPLETE TRANSCRIPTIONS The periods 1837 to 1865 and 1921 to 1983 aren't yet fully transcribed, but you can browse the scanned index pages. You can use the search engine for these years free of charge, but you'll have to pay one unit (about 10p) to download each scanned page. You can search the two databases by surname, first name, year and quarter. You'll get a list of all the pages you need to download and browse for the entry you're looking for. It costs two units to view a page of up to 20 transcribed results showing the name, year, quarter, district and reference number, plus one additional unit to view an image of the index page.

FULLY TRANSCRIBED INDEXES The indexes for 1866 to 1920 and 1984 to 2005 have been fully transcribed and can be searched by name, district, year and quarter range (see page 73). You can also opt to match a person's name with the spouse's surname in the indexes that cover information after 1912, and a child's name with the mother's maiden name if you're searching after 1911. As the number of fully transcribed indexes increases, so do your chances of finding your relatives.

Enter the details you know

2 Enter 'Mary' in the **Forename(s)** box, 'King' in the **Last Name** box, restrict the **From Year** to 1911 and set the **To Year** to 1915. You know her mother's maiden name was Payling, so enter that, too. You can further restrict the search by **District** and **Quarter** if you know these details. Click on **Search Records**.

Read the results

3 The next page shows the results that match your search criteria in a table format. Only one match was found for the birth of Mary King, with the mother's maiden name Payling. If your search gives more results, you can choose to arrange them chronologically or alphabetically by clicking on the up and down arrows next to the **Name** or **Year** fields.

View the transcription

4 The transcribed result gives you all the information you need to order Mary King's birth certificate from the General Register Office (see page 83). But if you want to make sure the transcription is accurate, click on **View image** and, for the price of one unit, you'll see a scanned image of the original index page showing Mary's birth. To see the image, you'll be prompted to download the free DjVu viewer, available from the 'Information' page.

Using the national indexes
ancestry.co.uk

Access to online birth, marriage and death (BMD) indexes is completely free on **ancestry.co.uk**. Scan the indexes to see if the information you want is there, then just register your name and email address on the site, when you're prompted, if you want to view the actual images of the documents you've found.

The website has three types of search engine for the indexes of the General Register Office (GRO).

● A complete set of scanned images of the GRO indexes from 1837 to 1983.
● Access to the partially transcribed FreeBMD indexes (see page 82) for 1837 to 1983 with links to scanned images.
● A database of indexes from 1984 to 2005.

Complete BMDs for 1837-1983

This set of scanned index images is searched in the same way as the original GRO indexes (see page 94). Choose whether you want to research births, marriages or deaths. The search engine will ask you for the name you are looking for, as well as the appropriate years and the quarters to search.

You'll then see a list of pages that you can search. Click on **View** to see the scanned image of each page from the indexes and search the page to see if your ancestor is there. Many family history websites charge you to look at these pages; here it's free, so this is a good site to start with.

A MISSING QUARTER Check that the search engine has found all four quarters for each year. Sometimes one or two quarters may be left out, because the search engine has been confused by something such as an entry being added to the page by hand, so the names are no longer in alphabetical order. If this

happens, you can find the missing quarter by going back to the search engine and keying in a surname that's close in spelling to the one you're looking for in the missing year and quarter. If you're looking for the surname Berry, for example, a useful trick is to ask the search engine to find Barry instead, which is

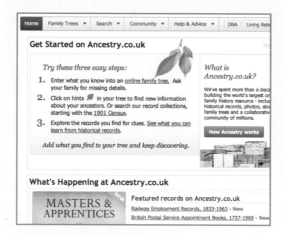

Search for a death

1 To trace the death of Sinah Price between 1928 and 1930, go to the homepage and click **Search**. Enter her first and last name. Under Any Event click **Death**. Under Year enter 1929 and under Location enter **Manchester, Lancashire**. Click **Search**.

Scan the results

2 The Results page show that her death was registered in March 1929 in South Manchester. Click the **View Image** icon for each quarter, and check the index entries. Sinah Price's death appears on the fifth image, and gives the information needed for ordering her death certificate. Note the date of death (March quarter 1929), the district (Manchester S), the volume (8d) and the page (515). See pages 78-81 and 94 to order a copy of the certificate from the GRO.

earlier in the list than Berry. On the page that comes up, keep clicking on the **Next** button until you find the page with Berry on it.

Partial BMDs for 1837-1983
When you use this search engine, there's no trawling through pages of surnames until you find the right first name. Here, your search takes you directly to the name and gives you a list of transcribed names and references from the indexes and links to scanned images of the pages. The drawback is that it's not as comprehensive as the Complete BMD as it uses transcriptions from FreeBMD that aren't yet complete.

The search engine will also find transcriptions of names that look or sound similar to the one you're looking for, unless you restrict your search instructions to include exact matches only.

Complete indexes for 1984-2005
Unlike the other two, this database contains no scanned images, because all the data was entered electronically to start with. The death indexes, for example, show the person's name, the year and quarter of registration of the death, the registration district and the deceased person's date of birth. These pieces of information will help you to widen your search for further details.

Common ground *The population of Britain grew significantly in the 19th and early 20th centuries, and an increase in leisure time, affordable public transport and a delight in new and exciting events drew people of all classes together. Your Victorian ancestors could have been among the crowd flocking to see the spectacle of a balloon ascent at Crystal Palace Park in Sydenham, in London.*

Discovering local indexes
ukbmd.org.uk

For fewer transcription errors, try this website, linked to local authority and family history society sites, which takes you direct to local register copies.

The acronym UK BMD stands for United Kingdom births, marriages and deaths. The site is valuable if you're tracing your family, because it transcribes from original sources of information, significantly reducing the chances of errors that arise when material is re-transcribed by the General Register Office (GRO). Use of the UK BMD website is free.

What's on the website

The site provides links to 465 other websites that have transcriptions from local civil registration birth, marriage and death indexes. The website suggests that, whenever possible, you search these local indexes first, before consulting the GRO indexes, to cut down the chances of coming across transcription errors.

The best links on the website for tracing your ancestors fall into three general categories: Local, GRO and County.

❯ Start your search

1 To search for the birth of an Alan Victor Jones in Bath or Berkshire between 1935 and 1937, click **Local BMD** in the left-hand margin of the homepage. The next page has links to each county's database. Click on **Select a county** and choose one from the list. Alternatively, to search more than one county's records at once, click on the **UKBMDSearch** link in the **UK BMD's Multi-region search** panel to the right.

❯ Give the event and date

2 Click on **Births** in the **Search type** section. Scroll down the **Date ranges** box, to find the year you want. Click on the year **1935** to select it.

❯ Add name and place

3 If you decide to spread the search, in terms of years, select all three years, **1935**, **1936** and **1937** by holding down the **Shift** key while you click on the years. In **Regions** highlight **Bath** and **Berkshire** in the same way. Type 'Jones' in the **Surname** box, 'A' in the **Forename** box and click on **Search** at the bottom of the screen.

Local BMD

Here you can access websites that provide free indexes for whole counties. Search these individually by county or as a whole via the UK BMD multi-region search engine (see the case history, below). Local BMD also provides links to records transcribed by smaller areas, but you'll have to consult these individually – they aren't associated with a centralised search engine.

Various local authorities and family history societies are creating new indexes based on the local register offices, rather than taking information from the GRO's national indexes. There are millions of entries, with more added each day. Each local area website shows how complete its online records are.

GRO

This service provides links to sites whose records are based on the GRO national indexes. Most are commercial 'pay-per-view' sites, though some – such as FreeBMD – are run by volunteers and are free of charge.

County BMD

Find out which websites from both the Local and GRO categories have online records for your county by selecting the name of the county from the drop-down list on the left-hand side of the homepage and clicking on **County**. This displays links to all the websites that hold records relevant to the county you've chosen, with brief descriptions.

Bonny baby *Christina McColl with her son Hugh in 1893. At this time, baby boys wore dresses, so it's hard to tell from a photo whether you should be searching online for the birth of a boy or a girl.*

UK BMD Search

In the results below, the reference number will be a link to a printable application which can be used to order the certificate for the index entry. Full details of the charges and the Register Office address can be found on the form. **Please note** that due to the manner in which some of the Cheshire indexes were compiled into groups of years, you may see results from years outside of the range that you requested in the results from Cheshire.

Surname	First Name(s)	Mother's Maiden Name	Year	District	Region	Registers At	Reference
JONES	Alan Rex		1936	Bucklebury, Reading	Berkshire Reading		BUC/33/67
JONES	Alan Stanley	ROBERTS	1935	Keynsham	Bath	Bath	KEY/30/295
JONES	Alan Victor	BLACKER	1936	Norton Radstock - First Series	Bath	Bath	NR1/1/163
JONES	Alison Mary Bradley	TAGGART	1936	Twerton - Second Series	Bath	Bath	TW2/14A/267
JONES	Ann Marguerite	WILTON	1937	Norton Radstock - First Series	Bath	Bath	NR1/1/466
JONES	Francis Arthur		1937	St Giles, Reading	Berkshire Reading		STG/134/54
JONES	Gordon Arthur	WICKHAM	1936	Bath - First Series	Bath	Bath	BT1/1/284
JONES	Josephine Anne Therese	HOBBS	1937	Norton Radstock - First Series	Bath	Bath	NR1/1/329
JONES	Keith Arthur	HILLIER	1936	Bath - First Series	Bath	Bath	BT1/1/139
JONES	Kenneth Albert	GARDINER	1935	Walcot - Second Series	Bath	Bath	WL2/18A/350
JONES	Rosemary Ann	BRAY	1936	Norton Radstock - First Series	Bath	Bath	NR1/1/031
JONES	Shirley Ann		1936	St Giles, Reading	Berkshire Reading		STG/132/7
JONES	Tania Ann	GARDNER	1936	Bath - First Series	Bath	Bath	BT1/1/252

A total of 13 Births were found that matched your search criteria.
If you do not find the registration indexes that you are seeking it could be that they have not yet been transcribed. Few of these indexes are complete.
Full details of the coverage of these sites can be found on the individual sites. Also, the individual sites offer extra features such as the ability to download to a file.

Ordering of Copy Certificates.
To order a copy certificate you can either:
- Click on the reference number to display a printable application form
or
- Where available you can order **on-line** by clicking on the check-boxes for the entries you wish to purchase, then click on the **Start On-line Order Process** at the bottom of the page to proceed to the next stage of the on-line ordering process.

To return to your previous search screen, please use the **Return to Searches** links below.

				Birth Indexes				
Surname	Forename(s)	Mother's Maiden Name	Year	Sub-District	Registers At	Region	Reference	Order On-line
JONES	Alan Victor	BLACKER	1936	Norton Radstock - First Series	Bath	Bath	NR1/1/163 (Remove)	N/A

Return to Searches.
No Marriages Selected.
Return to Searches.
No Deaths Selected.
Return to Searches.

To Remove all the results from above click: (Remove All)

On-line ordering is available from the following regions:

Scan the first results

4 You'll see the births of all Joneses with first names starting with 'A', in alphabetical order. Alan Victor Jones' transcription shows that his mother's maiden name was Blacker, and his birth was registered in 1936 in Norton Radstock district, which is in the Bath region. Not all counties' transcriptions include the mother's maiden name. Bath does; Berkshire doesn't.

Order your certificate

5 Click on the underlined **Reference** next to the entry. Up comes a printable form containing all the details of the birth. Print it off and send it, with the £9 fee enclosed, or with details filled on of your credit or debit card, to the register office whose address appears on the form, and they'll send you a copy of the birth certificate.

Ordering certificates from Directgov

If you're researching family history at home, it's quick and easy to go online and order birth, marriage and death certificates from the General Register Office (GRO) website.

The General Register Office (GRO) website, available via **direct.gov.uk/en**, provides information on all aspects of civil registration and is a great help to the family historian. When you're ready to order a certificate for a birth, marriage or death, go to the GRO website.

How to use the service

You can order certificates online, by post or by phone or fax. Before you can use the online service you need to register; your email address and chosen password will be your login details for all future transactions.

Buying certificates isn't free of charge. The standard service charge for a certificate is £9.25 and the certificate is posted to you four working days after receipt of your order; the priority service costs £23.40 and the certificate is dispatched the next working day.

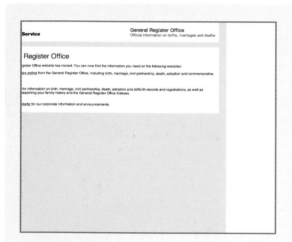

Ordering a certificate online

1 Suppose you wish to order a birth certificate for an ancestor named Peggy King. You know that she was born in Ipswich in 1930. Go to direct.gov.uk/en. On the homepage, click on the link for **Government, citizens and rights**. This takes you to the new page. In the section headed **Registering life events**, click on **Birth, marriage and death certificates**. This opens another new page. Click on **Order birth, marriage and death certificates**, then **Order certificates online**. This takes you to the GRO's ordering service (see above).

Putting in the detail

2 Click on **Order a certificate online now**. Give your login details (or register if you don't have any), and when the 'Certificate choice' page opens click on **Birth certificate (England & Wales)**. Near the foot of the page, where the form requests 'Year in which the event was registered', enter **1930**. Now click on **Submit**.

Giving delivery instructions

3 You'll then be asked to fill in the address you'd like the certificate sent to. You'll also be asked for your phone number in case there are any problems processing your order. When you've completed this page, click on **Submit**.

Add extra detail where possible

To make sure you get the right certificate, add as much detail as you can. Click on the **Reference checking** option at the end of the order form and add at least one of the following details – more, if possible:

- date of death
- place of death
- date of birth of deceased
- occupation of deceased
- marital status (if female)
- other checking point of your choice (for example, the father's name on a birth certificate).

If the office can't find matching details, you won't be sent the certificate but you'll get a partial refund of the certificate fee. After you've completed the form, click on **Resume Application**.

Preparing to order
Certificates are quite expensive, so make sure that you have all the details ready to hand, as well as your credit card, before you go online. Keep a record of what you've ordered – it's easy to lose track when making multiple orders.

Filling in the application

4 This takes you to the 'Application' page, where you have to complete the boxes marked with a red asterisk * – and any further information you have. In this example, enter the name, date and place of birth. Since you also know the names of both parents you can add those as well. At the bottom of the form, choose whether you want **Standard** or **Priority** delivery service, and the number of certificates you require. Now click on the **Submit** button.

Finalising your order

5 The 'Basket summary' page shows your order. Check that the details are correct. Click on **Edit** if you need to go back to change anything. To order further certificates, click on **Add to order**. You'll be taken back to the 'Certificate choice' page, where you can fill in another set of forms. When you've finished, click **Checkout**.

Making a payment

6 If you're happy with your order, click on **Proceed with payment**. If you need to adjust your order, click on **Return to basket**. On the 'Secure payment' page choose the appropriate credit or debit card to reach the next page, where you can enter your card details. Finally, select **Make payment**. Your payment will be processed and you'll receive an email to confirm this.

Civil registration in Scotland

The civil registering of births, marriages and deaths began in Scotland in 1855. If you've Scottish ancestors, you're in luck, as the records offer you more family history information than those for anywhere else in the UK.

Office for Scotland (GROS) at New Register House, Edinburgh (see Directory). But thanks to ScotlandsPeople, **scotlandspeople.gov.uk**, the official government website, you can now search online. The website contains indexes and images of the Statutory Registers for births, marriages and deaths 1855-2005. Its other records include census returns, wills and parish records – and some digital images of paper records from New Register House. ScotlandsPeople is the only website which holds this material.

On January 1, 1855, the recording of baptisms, marriages and burials by Church of Scotland parishes was replaced by civil registration for all denominations. In the first year people had to provide extensive detail – a real boon to family historians. This proved impossible to sustain, so from 1856 the level of information reduced, although the post-1856 records are still more detailed than English and Welsh certificates.

The extra information means that when you find someone in the Scottish registers you can be confident it's the right person. This then saves time when you start looking for the birth, marriage and death certificates for the rest of that branch of your family.

The paper records, known as Statutory Registers, are held in the General Register

STATUTORY BIRTH REGISTERS The registers include all the information you'd normally find on English and Welsh birth certificates, plus the family's home address.

If your relative was born in 1855, you may discover much more – any other siblings, the parents' ages and birthplaces, and where and when they married. Although much of this information was dropped from 1856 for practical reasons, the date and place of the parents' marriage was re-introduced on the registers from 1861.

All Scotland's people *Your Scottish ancestors may have lived in dilapidated buildings like these, which were to be found in the West Bow area of Edinburgh in the 1900s. Wherever they lived, you should be able to find records relating to the significant events in their lives at the GROS.*

STATUTORY MARRIAGE REGISTERS On the registers you'll find details of the bride's and groom's names, ages, marital status, occupations, addresses, date and place of marriage, both their fathers' names and occupations, the witnesses' names and the name of the officiating clergyman.

If your relatives were married in 1855 (see right), you'll again discover a great deal more. You may find out if the bride and groom were related to each other (cousins, for example), what their mothers' names and maiden names were, where they were born, and whether either was married before and had any children by that marriage. All of which information is a huge boost to your research.

After 1855, the GROS stopped including the couple's birthplaces and previous marriages. Then from 1972 the number of former marriages was shown in the registers again, adding further valuable details to help you in your search.

STATUTORY DEATH REGISTERS In all these registers, you'll find the date, time and place of death, the person's name, sex, marital status, age, occupation, cause of death, duration of last illness, doctor's name and informant's details. Again, if your relative's death was registered in 1855 itself, you'll find a wealth of extra detail: their address, place of birth, spouse's name, the names and occupations of their parents and whether they, too, had died, the names and ages of any children (including the age and year of death of any children that had died before the parent), when the doctor last saw the person alive, the burial place and undertaker's name.

From 1856, the deceased's birthplace, names of children and spouse's name were no longer recorded. Then, from 1860 the burial place, name of the undertaker and when the doctor last saw the deceased alive was also omitted. But after 1861, the registers once again showed the spouse's name.

The detail of marriage *Two entries in the 1864 marriage register for the parish of Stornoway provide far more information than would be found in registers in either England or Wales – although by then it was no longer necessary to show the couple's birthplaces and any previous marriages.*

Scottish registers scotlandspeople.gov.uk

If you have Scottish ancestors, you'll find the ScotlandsPeople website a big help in your researches. It's a vast online source of original genealogical information, well organised and remarkably user friendly. Before you start searching, you'll need to register (see pages 56 and 57) and choose a password. Then you can search for a name in the birth, marriage or death records, free of charge. You're told whether any matches have been found. But if you want to look at the results, you'll need to buy credits. You'll see more about how you do this on page 57.

Viewing the register

Before charging you to view a page, the site will always tell you how many credits it will cost and asks if you're sure you want to go ahead. If you want to proceed, click **Yes**, and the 'Search Returns' page will list the transcriptions for every match.

● Births – you're told the year of the entry, the child's full name, the sex of the child and the district name, county and General Register Office for Scotland (GROS) data.

● Marriages – you get the year of the entry, the man's and woman's full name, as well as the district name, county and GROS data.

● Deaths – you're given year of the entry, the deceased's full name, the mother's maiden name, other surnames the deceased may have had (in the case of a woman who has married more than once), the sex of the deceased, the age at death, as well as the district, county and GROS data.

From here you can choose to view an image of the Statutory Register for each match (see page 96). It costs five credits but what you see is marvellous – a scan of the original register page containing the handwritten entry you're interested in, along with any other entries on that page (see opposite). It's exciting when you realise that you've found the right record, and that there's much more information about that person than you had before. You can save the image to your desktop or just print it out.

Find the death registration first

1 Say you want to trace the birth, marriage and death of an ancestor, Alexander Fyfe, who died in 1921, when he was about 60. You also know that the Fyfes had strong links with St Andrews, in Fife, and that Alexander's oldest son, Arnet, was born in 1893. Start by finding Alexander's death certificate. Go to **scotlandspeople.gov.uk** log in and click on **Deaths** on the left of the screen. Then type 'Fyfe' in the **Surname** box, 'Alexander' in the **Forename** box and '1921' in both of the **Year Range** boxes. Then click on **Do the search** near the top of the screen. There's just one match, which can be viewed for the price of one credit. The first entry on the list is located in St Andrews, Fife, which seems appropriate. Now for five credits you can look at the page. You can discover Alexander's profession, his wife's name (Jessie Mason), when and where he died, his parents' names, his father's profession and his mother's maiden name. You're also told how he died, how long he'd been ill and that his death was reported by his son, Arnet. You now have enough information to search for Alexander's marriage and his birth records.

Find the marriage record

2 Click on **Marriages** on the left of the screen and then enter the known facts into the relevant boxes – Fyfe/Alexander/Mason/Jessie. Alexander and Jessie's first-born, Arnet, arrived in 1893, so key in a year range of ten years preceding this date – '1883-1893' – to cover the probable years of marriage. Click on **Do the search**. Interestingly, this registration that appears (see above) isn't in St Andrews but in Dennistoun, Glasgow. Following Scottish tradition, it's likely that Alexander's father was also called Arnet. As it's the only match, it's probably worth investing five credits to look at the page. All the information correlates to the information you found earlier on the death registration, confirming it to be the entry you want. What it adds is Alexander's home address in Glasgow, the date and place of the marriage, Jessie's home address, her profession and her parents' details.

Search for the birth record

3 Click on **Births** on the left of the screen and then key your known facts into the relevant boxes. You know from the death registration that Alexander was 59 when he died in 1921, so he must have been born around 1862. Put '1861' and '1863' into the **Year range** boxes and St Andrews, Fife in **District**. Click on **Do the search**. There is one entry so click on **View** to see the handwritten entry in the register – this will cost you five credits. This shows Alexander's name, address and date of birth, both his parents' names, including mother's maiden name, and the date of his parents' marriage – four months before his birth. His father's name is, as suspected, Arnet – the final confirmation, if any were needed, that you've found the correct entry.

Civil registration in Ireland

When researching your Irish ancestors it's important to be sure of your dates, so that you can go straight to the correct source of the records. Ireland was divided in 1922, and so were its records.

Deciphering the past
Many Catholic parish registers which were originally written in Latin, have been copied into the indexes.

Civil registration for all births, marriages and deaths, whatever the denomination, began in Ireland on January 1, 1864. However, a fire at Dublin's Four Courts in 1922 destroyed many Irish records. This doesn't mean that tracking down births, marriages and deaths before 1922 is trouble-free, as not all of these events were registered. Until April 1, 1845, only Catholic baptisms, marriages and deaths were registered, by the church itself. Then, in 1845, registration was extended to include non-Catholic marriages. It was not until January 1, 1864, that the registration of all events – births, marriages and deaths – whatever the denomination, was made compulsory.

Until the partition of Ireland in 1922 into the Irish Free State (later the Republic of Ireland) and Northern Ireland, records were held in Dublin. After 1922, they were split between Dublin and Belfast.

How to find the records
Records for 1864 to 1921 for the whole of Ireland, and from 1922 onwards for the Republic of Ireland, are held at the General Register Office (GRO) in Dublin; the website is **groireland.ie**. Northern Irish records, since 1922, are held at the GRO in Belfast; the website is at **nidirect.gov.uk/gro** Both sites give you contact details – or see the Directory. Few Irish records have been digitised, so

if you're researching your Irish roots you'll need to visit the archives. Alternatively, you can hire a researcher to trace your family history from the Irish archives.

What the records contain
The records from 1864 to 1877 are indexed chronologically by year; those from 1878 onwards are indexed quarterly. The registers contain all the information you'd expect: names, ages, dates, addresses, witnesses or informants and details about fathers' professions. In birth records you sometimes get a baptismal name if one was added after registration of the birth.

Understanding the registration
To research your Irish ancestry, it helps to understand how the registration districts worked. Under the Irish Poor Law Act of 1838, the country was divided into 159 areas called Poor Law Unions. Each area centered on a market town and covered a radius of about 10 miles – often crossing county boundaries. Every union was responsible for providing relief to the poor and destitute within its boundaries. In the 1850s, the Poor Law Unions were subdivided into smaller 'Dispensary Districts' as part of a nationwide public health system and, in 1864, each

Dispensary District also became a local registration district. A registrar sent the records to a superintendent registrar who was in charge of assembling all the records within his Poor Law Union boundary. These were then sent on to Dublin, copied into a central index at the Office of the Registrar General and then returned to the local offices. It's this central index that you'll need to use to find birth, marriage and death records.

As well as the master indexes for the entire country, the Dublin GRO also holds microfilm copies of all the local registers.

Searching the indexes

In Dublin, you can search for a particular name over a five-year period for a fee of €2, or you can have access to all the indexes for up to seven hours for €20, but it'll be only the indexes that you can view. To see a full entry, you'll have to pay €6 per entry for a microfilm print. Or you can buy the certificate of any entry for €10, but this tells you no more than the microfilm copies.

HERITAGE CENTRES Each county also has a local Heritage Centre that will provide search services for a fee. You'll find them by going to **groireland.ie**.

FAMILY HISTORY CENTRES The Church of Jesus Christ of Latter-day Saints (the Mormons) has made copies of most of the Irish indexes and registers, which can be viewed at its local Family History Centres. Details of how to find a Family History Centre are found on the Mormon website **familysearch.org** (see page 137). You'll probably have more success with these records than searching the indexes at the GRO in Dublin, because you can search both the indexes and the registers simultaneously.

The Mormons have also transcribed birth and marriage registrations, from as early as the year 1530, into their family history database.

Heritage in flames *Thousands of records were destroyed when Dublin's Four Courts building went up in flames in 1922. The loss was catastrophic, but you can still access much of the information through Family History Centres.*

What to do when data is missing

Sometimes, an ancestor may prove elusive. You know the person lived – you have several pieces of information to confirm it – but they're lost in the records. Don't worry – help is at hand.

There's an art to searching indexes for birth, marriage and death records, especially when looking for early 19th-century events. English and Welsh civil registration may have begun in 1837, but it wasn't until 1875 that the system began to be really efficient. In the early days, it was possible simply to avoid registration, which explains why some names are missing from the indexes of that period.

Why you might not find a name

There are also some other obstacles to finding information. These guidelines will help you to track down your ancestor.

EXTEND THE NAME SEARCH Variations in spellings, of both forenames and surnames, may explain why you can't find your ancestor in the indexes, or that person may have been known by their middle name. Try looking in the indexes under a variety of spellings. If you can't find Mary Ann Price, try looking for her under Mary Ann Pryce. Search for shortened versions of forenames – for example, Sarah Ann was sometimes shortened to Saran, Elizabeth might be recorded as Betsy, and many a Margaret was known as Peggy. Also, try looking for a person under a middle name.

Gypsy wedding *Romany or gypsy weddings like this one in Holsworthy, Devon, in about 1910, were traditionally held in the open air. Despite the elaborate ritual, it was unlikely that anyone would offer the details for registration.*

Britons abroad

If your ancestor doesn't appear in any UK records, he may have spent time overseas, perhaps with the British Army, such as these soldiers (right). They were stationed in Egypt during the First World War, to protect the Suez Canal and keep it open for the transport of troops from the Colonies to the Western Front.

Many sites, including The National Archives have indexes of regimental births, marriages and deaths online (see also findmypast on page 84).

CHECK REGISTRATION DETAILS When looking for a specific date, remember that the record will be found in the quarter in which the event was registered – which isn't necessarily the quarter in which it occurred. Search the quarter that includes the month in which the event took place and also the following quarter: it's perfectly legal to register a birth or a death up to six weeks after the event. When checking dates given to you by elderly relatives, remember that it's possible they've got their 'facts' wrong.

WIDEN THE DATE RANGE Even if you're fairly sure of the date, widen the year range you're searching by a decade or more. Some people in the 19th century simply did not know when they were born, so ages on census returns may not be accurate. Others lied about their age on marriage certificates, claiming to be older. And for a death, the person reporting it may not have known the deceased's true age and just guessed at it.

WIDEN THE AREA Try using local indexes (see page 92) rather than national ones, as the national indexes are more likely to contain errors, having been retranscribed. Alternatively, if you've been looking in a specific region because a census return told you the person was born there, it could be that they grew up in that place but were actually born elsewhere. For example, Manchester and other large cities have many registration districts very close together, so search a range of districts in the general area in which your family lived.

LOOK EVEN FURTHER AFIELD Migration around the country was fairly common during the Victorian period, as people moved from villages and farms to industrialised towns looking for work. When searching for records of someone's marriage and death, bear in mind that these events may have occurred some distance from the village or town where they were born.

CONSULT ORIGINAL SOURCES Sometimes the transcriptions are wrong, often simply due to human error. If you're having no luck in finding a person, you may have to consult the original paper indexes at the relevant archive. With more and more people transcribing information onto the internet, the margin of error becomes greater, so always double check your findings.

Living rough *It's hard to trace relatives who fell on hard times. This homeless woman, sitting outside a workhouse in the late 19th century, may not have appeared in the census and could have had an unrecorded death.*

The census

Details about Britain's inhabitants have been recorded in a census every ten years since the early 19th century. After 100 years, each census is released to the public and provides vital information about our ancestors and fascinating insights into the way they lived.

Understanding the census

When the first census was taken in 1801 its main aim was military. Napoleon was regarded as such a serious threat that the British Government needed to know how many men could be mobilised if French forces invaded.

Since that first head-count, a census has been taken every decade (apart from 1941, when the Second World War prevented it). Census records include personal and, sometimes, sensitive information – such as names of couples who weren't married – which is why the data remains confidential for a century. The 1911 census is the most recent that we can access, so you have to trace your family back to the early 20th century, using civil registration certificates, before the census comes into play.

What the census contains

Before 1841, the census was simply a head-count that – with a few regional exceptions in 1821 and 1831 – contained nothing about individuals. After 1841, the census included details about individuals, such as name, age, sex, occupation, place of birth and any relationship to others in the house, which you can now use to trace family history.

On rare occasions the census takers, known as enumerators, compiled their own lists of the heads of each household; these usually survive only in local record offices.

Mass information *19th-century censuses give a wonderful insight into the social and economic changes experienced by the growing British population.*

When you start to delve into census records, you'll find they're like a snapshot taken on a given night of the year. They capture information about the people residing at a specific address, along with any visitors, servants and lodgers present on the night in question. It also records information about people who were away from home, in institutions such as prisons, schools and workhouses, or on naval vessels.

Inconsistencies in the returns

Levels of detail in census returns can vary according to the whim of each enumerator. Also, it was usually the responsibility of the householder to provide accurate information – and this wasn't verified in any way. Householders were simply asked to fill in forms that were then collected and transcribed by the enumerators. This accounts for some of the oddities in the returns – such as people's names spelled wrongly and discrepancies in the way people's ages progressed, from one census to another.

Britain was divided into census enumeration districts, which were further broken up into sub-districts. From 1841, these were the same as civil registration districts, which makes it easier to move between the two sources in your search.

Census dates

The census returns were recorded on a particular night of each year:

1841 – June 6	1851 – March 30
1861 – April 7	1871 – April 2
1881 – April 3	1891 – April 5
1901 – March 31	1911 – April 2

It may be useful to keep these dates to hand for enabling you to work out and check the ages of your ancestors.

A right puzzler *The early census forms often came as an unwelcome piece of officialdom. In this* Illustrated London News *cartoon, from the 1840s, a bemused householder is visited by the enumerator.*

" WHAT'S THIS ? "

Census records online – a priceless resource

All the major censuses are now available on the internet, so you can search this vast store of records from home on your computer. Here are some of the best websites on which to start your investigations.

You can get to original census images online through databases that are searchable by the name of a person. Access to the census collections is rarely free – companies such as Ancestry and findmypast (see below), which have digitised the censuses, will charge you a subscription to view their images. If you don't want to pay, you'll have to visit local archives to view microfilm versions, or look at the digitised records at The National Archives (TNA) in Kew, in London.

What's in the census records?

All census returns tell you who was staying in a specific property on the night of the census – wherever they normally lived. In addition to the basic information listed by all censuses, the census returns from 1851 to 1911 include marital status, relationship to the head of household and place of birth (county and parish). They declare whether an individual is 'deaf-and-dumb' or 'blind', and by 1891, whether they're 'lunatic, imbecile or idiot'.

By 1901, the records also show a person's employer or employee status. The 1841 census is different; the ages of children under 15 were recorded accurately, but ages over 15 were rounded down to the nearest five-year band – so someone aged 34 in 1841 would be recorded as being 30. Place of birth isn't given, other than whether or not they were born in the county of residence. If someone was born elsewhere, this was indicated with **I** for Ireland, **S** for Scotland or **F** for Foreign.

The National Archives

Lists of census returns and links to relevant websites are provided at the TNA website, **nationalarchives.gov.uk/census**. The links take you to census data at either **ancestry.co.uk** (see below) or **1901censusonline.com**. If you're accessing the records from home, you'll need to pay to view the images; if you're researching at TNA at Kew, you can access all the census records free.

Ancestry

The Ancestry website, **ancestry.co.uk** (see page 112), holds all the census returns for Britain as well as records for Canada and much of the USA. Each census has been individually transcribed. The 1881 England and Wales census index can be searched free of charge; otherwise you'll need to buy a monthly or annual subscription, or pay-per-view if you only want to use the facilities for a limited period.

Origins

At **origins.net** (see page 114) you can look at census collections for different parts of the British Isles. British Origins holds the 1841, 1861 and most of 1871 census for England and Wales. Scots Origins holds censuses transcriptions for 1861 and 1871, but not online. Irish Origins has partial censuses and 'census substitutes' (see page 126). You can subscribe to the entire website, or to one geographical area only, on a 72 hour, monthly or annual basis.

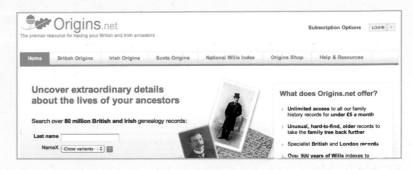

findmypast

The website **findmypast.co.uk** (see page 120) allows you to search the 1841-1911 censuses for England and Wales, and offers the useful function of searching by address as well as by name. You can search the indexes without registering or paying, but if you want to view a transcript or an original image, you'll need to subscribe – which you can do on a monthly or yearly basis.

ScotlandsPeople

Scottish censuses from 1841 to 1901 are at **scotlandspeople.gov.uk**. You can search the collection indexes free of charge once you've registered your details, but you'll need to buy credits to view your search results and the original images (see page 124).

1901censusonline

The usefulness of this website lies in its excellent index, which you can search not only by name, but also by address, institution and navy or merchant vessel (see page 116). You can search **1901censusonline.com** free of charge and without registering. You'll need to buy credits only if you want to view an original image. The website is run by GenesReunited and can be accessed via their site, too (see page 270).

The men behind the census

It was Napoleon who pushed Parliament into the first census. The concept had been around since Roman times but it took the fear of French invasion during the Napoleonic Wars to make it happen. But the unsung heroes of the censuses were the army of men who gathered the mountain of information.

In 1800 Parliament decided it needed to know how many men could be called on to defend the country against the French camped just across the Channel – and also how many aliens were living here. So the first official census was taken on March 10, 1801.

As we scour the records now for information about our ancestors, though, we give little thought to the people who gathered all this detail. The census takers, known as enumerators, had the onerous task of visiting every home in their district on a particular night and recording the occupants' details – and they did it every ten years.

How the enumerators' task grew

At first, from 1801 to 1831, all the enumerator did was record the size of the population of his local parish, based on the number of people living in each house, the numerical breakdown of their occupations, how many houses were occupied and the total number of baptisms, marriages and burials in the parish.

He was usually chosen because he had some standing in the community, perhaps having served on the parish council or undertaken the role of an assessor of local rates. Because the enumerator was part of the community, he'd have known much about the neighbours he was counting and they, in turn, would have trusted him to come into their homes – and perhaps share a little light refreshment with them.

Some enumerators took their jobs so seriously that they made personal notes as they went around. Richard Stopher, for example, the enumerator for Saxmundham, Suffolk, in 1831, and a keen local historian, added biographical notes to the names of householders as he travelled throughout the parish. It was such men, gathering personal data as well as the basic statistical

No one left out *Even Queen Victoria was included in the 1851 census (left), with Prince Albert and her large family at Buckingham Palace. On the other end of the social scale, a gypsy family are counted by an enumerator in 1901 (right).*

information, who helped to change the way the census was perceived and brought about new categories of information, such as the names, ages, occupations and birth places of each occupant, introduced in the 1841 census. This census was also the first to use forms that were filled in by the head of the household, with the help of the enumerator, if necessary. On the night of June 6 that year, 35,000 enumerators recorded the names and biographical data of almost 16 million people.

More trouble than it's worth

Unlike Richard Stopher, not all census takers knew their community. Some enumerators in the large towns and cities encountered suspicion from householders who resented the intrusion, or they were simply not taken seriously. One householder listed 'Dick the Canary' as a member of his household. Sometimes enumerators described the difficulties and

Famous names at home

Despite the difficulties of the job, enumerators could always claim to have met renowned people, even if they were little-known at the time. In 1901, for instance, Charlie Chaplin (right) was recorded as a 12-year-old 'music hall artiste' in south London, at 94 Ferndale Road, Lambeth.

As they carried out their jobs, enumerators also encountered every walk of life – one day, quite possibly, a slum, recording prostitutes and beggars, the next royalty in their palaces. Despite being the ruler of the British Empire, Queen Victoria is recorded on the 1851 census (far left) simply as 'The Queen', with her husband Prince Albert listed as 'Head of Household'. Other enumerators would have had the pleasure of meeting such notables as Florence Nightingale (left, 1861), H.G. Wells (1891), and W.G. Grace and Claude Monet (1901).

frustrations they'd encountered at the end of their written returns. In one such record for Isleworth, Middlesex, the enumerator, Mr Abott, wrote 'This is the first and last of W. Abott's taking the census of England and Wales, unless the price goes up'. It seems the job wasn't worth the 2s 6d for every 100 persons counted, and it was this discouragingly low rate of pay that led to the recruitment of women enumerators from 1891.

There's no accounting for people

Census gathering may have been streamlined over the years, but the task of the enumerator becomes no less problematic. During the foot-and-mouth crisis in 2001, enumerators in Scotland weren't allowed past security cordons for fear of spreading the disease through their door-to-door visits. And despite improvements in technology, and changing ways in which the data is collected, the census still causes controversy. Also in 2001, an online campaign ensured that 390,000 people stated their religion as 'Jedi Knight'. As a result, official reports into the state of the UK were forced to include Jedi on the list of practising religions.

Using the census

All you need to search the census are your ancestor's name and a few basic details. Then get off to a flying start with a choice of websites.

Once you've established information about your family going as far back as the early 20th century, you can access the 1901 census to find out more. To make the most of census returns, you'll need to use the information you've gathered from civil registration certificates (see pages 74-77). For example, by establishing someone's date and place of birth from a birth certificate, you can then work out how old he or she would have been in a particular set of census records and narrow down the likely area in which they might have been living. Bear in mind that people did move around from town to town. The reverse is also true: you can use what you find out from the census to track down further civil registration certificates. For example, by looking at the ages of children born to a couple, you can usually predict a marriage date. A combination of census and certificate information allows you to work backwards through the returns to widen your family tree. You can also use the information to fill out the branches by including siblings listed on the returns.

Online census indexes

In addition to the websites described on pages 106-7, you could try visiting Family Search at **familysearch.org** (see page 54). It has an excellent index to the 1881 census.

Many family history societies have created census indexes for their local area – go to the FFHS website **familyhistoryonline.net** or visit their online shop at **genfair.com** for more information.

Estate life *Photographs and census records make it possible to reconstruct vanished communities. In Sulham, Berkshire, the family (left) were tenants of the Reverend Wilder; the 1901 census entry (above) reveals his cowman, Aaron Spackman.*

Online search facilities are extremely useful tools, but some of them may have a few transcription errors, which can make it hard to find what you're looking for. If this happens, try another website.

Online census images

You can view the images and transcripts in various ways. Some sites allow you to download the images direct to your PC so that you can view them electronically as often as you like. You can also print most of the images straight from the website. You'll find detailed instructions about the main sites on pages 112-29.

Some of these sites allow you to store your family tree information on their software, and sites such as **ancestry.co.uk** also allow you to upload census images to your family tree to back-up your findings.

A picture of life in the past

The information you discover from census returns can be a great help if you want to put your research into a wider social context. Look at the occupations of your relatives. For example, were trades or professions handed down from generation to generation within your family? Whether they were miners or solicitors – or anything in between – you often find several generations following in the previous one's footsteps.

You'll also notice unfolding social trends brought about by economic change. The rapid industrial growth of the 19th century may have drawn ancestors to towns and cities. Some may appear as railway workers – benefactors of the Victorian 'railway mania'.

The bigger picture
Census data can reveal information of all kinds. The map, left, created from 1851 census detail, shows how occupations were distributed across Britain in the year of the Great Exhibition. Britain was undergoing an industrial transformation and the censuses show vividly how the lives of even the most ordinary families were affected by the big changes of the day.

Using the census
ancestry.co.uk

Ancestry's census indexes cover England, Wales, the Channel Islands, the Isle of Man and Scotland. You can search the whole census collection or choose a specific year and region. All the indexes are free to view, once you've registered your details (see page 50). If you're lucky enough to be searching for an unusual name, you can conduct a simple name search on Ancestry's census search page. But if the name is fairly common, you could end up with a lot of matching results, so it's better to fill in any other details you have – the more you enter, the narrower and more accurate your results will be.

As well as your ancestor's name, add anything else you know – such as his mother's name, where and when he was born and his relationship to the head of the household. If you tick the 'exact match' box, then that's what you'll get – which could be a blank, if the entry was mistranscribed.

When you draw a blank

If you don't get any matching results, don't worry – just delete some of the information in the boxes and try again. It's also a good idea

Fill in the known facts

1 To find a John Peacock, born around 1821 in Cambridgeshire, in the 1861 census, go to the homepage and click on **1861** under **UK Census Records**. On the page that appears click on **1861 England Census** under **Included data collections**. On the page you are taken to (see above), enter 'John' in the **First & Middle Name(s)** box and 'Peacock' in the **Last Name** box. In the **Birth** row, enter '1821' under **Year** and 'Cambridgeshire, England' under **Location**.

Refine your search

2 Click on **Search**. You will now see quite a long list of possible candidates. The John Peacock most closely matching your search criteria is at the top of the list. Click on **View record** to learn more about this particular John Peacock.

Look at the details

3 On this page you can see more details about this John Peacock and you can also opt to view the original image.

to remove the tick from 'exact matches', so the search engine will look for close variations of names and other data you've keyed in – which may find you hundreds of possibilities. You'll need to experiment with your search, but that's what makes it so thrilling when you get a positive result.

Counting heads *Every person in every household would be counted on the night of the census, including servants who 'lived in', such as the driver of this wealthy family's 1910 Humber.*

Who else lived there?

4 Scroll to the bottom of John Peacock's record to see who else was staying at that address on census night 1861. You can see that there was 40-year-old John, his wife Rebecca, two sons, a daughter and three servant girls. You can also see who your ancestor's neighbours were by clicking **View others on page**.

View the original

5 Back at the top of the screen, if you select **View original record** you can look at the original handwritten census page, including other houses in the same street. The zoom tools at the top-left of the page will allow you to change the size at which the image is displayed.

Locate your ancestor

6 John Peacock is near the bottom of the page. The double diagonal lines drawn at the top-left of John Peacock's name indicate the start of a new household. When a household begins near the bottom of the page, it often continues on the next page. If you wish to check, use the navigation buttons at the top-right of the screen. You can also print the image or save it to your computer.

Using the census
origins.net

Origins.net has a wide range of UK and Ireland data collections (see page 55 for more details). They're arranged geographically, with links to British Origins (meaning English and Welsh), Irish Origins and Scots Origins at the top of the homepage. The Irish Origins section is particularly valuable as an online resource if you're researching your Irish ancestry.

IRELAND Because of the destruction of virtually all Ireland's 19th-century census returns in a fire at the Public Record Office in Dublin in 1922, a whole range of different sources (known as 'census substitutes') have become vital to the family historian with Irish roots. The Irish Origins holdings include many of these records – which are searchable online – and they include:

• **Elphin 1749 census** Records for nearly 20,000 people living in the Diocese of Elphin in 1749 tell you the occupation and religion of the head of household, size of the family, who had servants and how many they had.
• **Irish 'strays' in England and Wales** Lists of people identified as Irish in both the 1841 and 1871 England and Wales censuses.
• **Griffith's Valuation 1847-64** An all-Ireland property survey, county by county, published between 1848 and 1864, that holds detailed information about land and buildings – who owned, let or occupied them.
• **William Smith O'Brien Petition 1848-9** A petition listing more than 80,000 names and places from the time of the Great Famine.
• **Dublin City 1851 census** An index of the heads of households in Dublin, which was compiled by a local doctor in order to help old age pension applicants prove their age and make claims.
• **Dublin City Rotunda Ward 1901 census** Details of 13,556 individuals living in more than 1,334 properties in the Rotunda Ward.
• **Irish Wills Index (1484-1858)** Online access to wills and related documents.
• **Transatlantic migration (1858-70)** Lists of passengers returning to Ireland from the USA.
• **Irish Origins library** Collection of rare vintage photos, books, maps and other publications of interest to family researchers.

Heavy work *Many Irish migrants came to the UK to work on large construction projects such as the Manchester Ship Canal. Here, 'navvies', or labourers, are shown at the start of the excavations in 1887.*

Search the Elphin census

1 To search the census for a Sarah Kiernan, go to **origins.net**, log in or register (see above, opposite), and then choose the Irish Origins site. Click on **Census of Elphin 1749**. Follow the instructions to get to the search page. Enter the name in the two relevant boxes. You can search by county, but the Elphin census covers only Galway, Roscommon and Sligo. You can also search by parish. Once you've entered any details that you know, click on **Search**.

ENGLAND AND WALES Origins holds transcriptions and scanned images of the English and Welsh censuses for 1841 and 1861, and part of the 1871 census.

SCOTLAND Access to the Scottish records is free of charge but what you can find there is limited. The site gives free access to an index of place names in the 1881 census, but not to any other census transcriptions. You can request a search of the 1861 and 1871 Scottish censuses and order transcriptions by sending in an order form with details of your search criteria, which must include at least your ancestor's name and where you think they lived.

Researching with Origins

To search the network's indexes for British or Irish ancestors you need to register your email address and a chosen password on the site. The minimum subscription to all the records is £8, which gives unlimited access for 72 hours. You can look at all the census records for one country at the same time. Whether you're searching the censuses or a census substitute, the principle is the same. Enter your ancestor's name and select a specific year range. If you get too many results to sort through, you can narrow down the results by clicking on **Refine search** next to the dataset (census return) you wish to search. You can then expand your search criteria by entering parish and county of residence, birthplace and age range. The website will lead you through other options.

First findings

2 At the top of the page you'll see that three results have been found for your search. You can then choose to refine your search, or view all the results. If you want to view all of them, click on the **View Records** button at the top of the page.

Find your ancestor

3 You'll see a screen, displaying the names, counties, and parishes of the people with the surname you've asked for, as well as the page number for the census return. Scan the list to find the person with details that most closely match your ancestor's. If there's more than one likely name, you may need to check all of them. In this case, the match is the first Sarah Kiernan, the eighth name on the list. Click on the **Image** button next to her name.

See the scanned image

4 If you haven't used the site before, you'll be asked to view a test census image. This is so the site can check that you have the appropriate software. Once you've viewed the test image successfully, the census image will be displayed. It will show you the county, place of abode, name and religion, profession, number of children over and under 14, and number of male and female servants in the house on the night of the census.

Using the census
1901censusonline.com

Some websites only let you search by name, but with this pay-per-view site you have the bonus of getting at information in the 1901 census for England and Wales through an address, institution or ship's name – and even by place, so you can see the census return for a whole area.

The 1901 census was the first census to be digitised and made available to the public online. It was launched on January 2, 2002, by The National Archives (then known as the Public Record Office) and its project partner QinetiQ. They underestimated the popularity of the subject matter, and the site crashed within seconds – it was unable to cope with the millions of family historians who logged on, not only from the UK but from right around the world. Since it was restored, it has proved to be extremely popular and totally reliable.

Types of search

The 1901 census search engine offers several different types of search, each of which has links to scanned images of the census return. If you start with the site's **Search Census** link at the top of the homepage it will take you straight to **Person search** – but using the tabs along the top of this page you can change the basis of your search, and choose other criteria, such as a vessel or institution.

The **Address** search allows you to look for a house name, house number, street name and place. So if you're having trouble finding your ancestors when you search for them by name – and this will often be because the name has

been mistranscribed – you may be able to find them by searching an address found on a marriage or birth certificate dated 1900 or earlier. You can also use the address search to discover the names and other details of people who were living in your own home at the time of the 1901 census. Both types of search are shown overleaf, on page 118.

Using advanced searches

If you're not sure of the spelling of an ancestor's name, the **Advanced search** option allows you to tick an **Include Synonyms?** box next to the person's name. The results will include variants on the name you have entered, which will greatly widen your search.

You may find you get too many results. If this happens, you can narrow the results list by specifying the occupation of the person you're looking for, their relationship to the head of the household, and their marital status.

If you're looking for an address, the **Advanced search** lets you narrow the search right down to the ecclesiastical parish and parliamentary borough the address should come under. But it's important to remember that restricting your results may in fact make

Street life *A crowded London tenement would house hundreds of people, many of them extended families. Pinning down who lived there would have been a full-time job for an enumerator and mistakes were often made.*

it harder to find the correct entry. If, having entered all the known criteria into an advanced search, you still have no luck, try reducing the number of details you fill in. This will widen the search.

The cost of searching

It costs nothing to make a simple search of the indexes. This will let you see, for free, lists with transcriptions of names, ages, places of birth, county and town of the census return and occupations. But if you find a possible ancestor or place you'd like to investigate more fully, you'll be prompted to register and buy credits to see more detail or to view the digital image of the actual census page. You can buy credits using your credit card, or there's the option of buying vouchers, which is explained onscreen. For most people, using a credit card is the quickest and easiest option.

The minimum amount you can spend is £5, which buys you 500 credits that are valid for seven days. It costs 50 credits to view the transcription of a page and 75 credits to view the scanned image of the page. Once you've paid, your search continues.

Other censuses on the site

The website also has online indexes and scanned images of the 1841 to 1891 England and Wales censuses. The search engines for these census returns are less sophisticated than those of the 1901 census and allow you to search only by first name, last name and year of birth.

Start your 1901 census search

1 To search for an Adelaide Archdale in Guy's Hospital, London, in the 1901 census, first sign in and check that you have enough credits to order original material (see above). On the homepage, click on **Search Census** button. Next, click on the **Institution** button and enter 'Guys'. Add any other details you have. Click on **Search**. If you have a lot of detail for your search, use the **Advanced search** option by clicking the link at the bottom of the page.

See the first results

2 The results will come up and you'll be offered a number of viewing options: you can view a description of the institution, the total number of people in the institution or the first page of person details. But if you're searching for a person, it's best to click on the name of the institution – in this case, **Guys**.

Find your relative

3 A list of names of all those present in the hospital on that night will come up. Click on the name you're looking for – in this case, Adelaide Archdale. You'll see that she was a single nurse, aged 26 and born in Colhshaw, Norfolk. To see an image of the original census page, go back to the previous screen and click on the census icon next to her name.

Using the census
1901censusonline.com

The address search feature of **1901censusonline.com**, mentioned on the previous pages, can help you if you're battling to find an ancestor using a name search. When you do an address search you're asked for the house or street name and the place. It's a good idea to omit the words Road, Avenue, Hill, Street or Lane because the spellings of these can vary. 'Avenue', for example, may have been transcribed as 'Ave', 'Av' or 'Avn'. So if you're looking for East Street, for example, just key in East.

Once you've found the name of the people who were at the address on census night in 1901, why not try entering that name into the indexes for the 1891 census, to see if they were living there then. If the house had been passed down through the generations, you could be lucky enough to find a string of census entries in the name of the same family, as you work backwards through the censuses for previous years. You can then build up a vivid picture of the family who lived there.

Finding people using an address

1 Say you're having difficulty locating a Priscilla and Joseph Toulson in the 1901 census, but you know their daughter Vera was born in 1900 at 3 Dillington Road, Barnsley. On the homepage, click the **Address** search link at the top. This takes you to the address search engine. Enter '3 Dillington' in the **House and/or Street** box and 'Barnsley' in the **Place Keywords** box and click **Search**.

View the results as a list

2 The results page shows that there's only one match for '3 Dillington' in Barnsley, and it's 3 Dillington Road. Click the address to see a full transcription of all the occupants there on the night of the 1901 census. This will cost 50 credits.

View the results as an image

3 Alternatively, click on the census icon to see a digital image of the whole census page. You'll find Priscilla and Joseph Toulson living at 3 Dillington Road with their daughter Vera and the rest of their children. This will cost 75 credits. You'll have access to this page for seven days, so it's worth making a copy of it to save to your computer (see page 31).

Who was living in The Hermitage in 1901?

On census night, 1901, The Hermitage in Tonbridge was a full house. The occupants were George and Kate Dain, their five school-age children, George Dain's younger brother, Harry – employed by his brother and presumably a permanent resident – and two servants. The house had four bedrooms, used by the family members, as well as two attic rooms for the servants. Until the 1980s, there were still bell-pushes in the main rooms that rang bells on a labelled board in the kitchen. The 1901 census is the only one that lets you find occupants when you know only the address and not their names.

Searching for previous occupants

1 If you're researching the history of the house where you grew up – for example, The Hermitage, 22 East Street, Tonbridge. Assuming that it was built and occupied by the time of the census in 1901, you can use the address search. From the homepage click the **Search Census** tab, then click on **Address** at the top of search page. Enter '22 The Hermitage' in the **House and/or Street** box and 'Kent' in the **Place Keywords** box. Click **Search**.

Select from the possible matches

2 There are three matches from this search. The transcribed index gives the addresses, whether the buildings are occupied (Y or N), and administrative details of the county and town of the census return.

View the entry

3 Select **22 The Hermitage**, the entry that most closely matches your criteria. You can then read full transcription details of the ten occupants on census night 1901. If you want to see the original census image, click the census icon at the top of the page.

Using the census
findmypast.co.uk

Searching the indexes of **findmypast.co.uk** is free, but you have to pay a small amount to see detailed information (see page 84). You can search for evidence of your family's past, either by person or by address, in the indexes and images of the 1841-1911 census records for England and Wales. If you know the TNA document reference number, click on **Search records** and select **Census, land & surveys** from the drop-down menu. On the page that appears click on **census reference search**.

Searching for a person

You can perform a quick search from the homepage by entering the first name, last name, and – if you have it – the year of birth

and the year of death, and then clicking on the **Search** button. This will provide you with a list of results for each collection of records held by **findmypast.co.uk**. For example, all matches within the 1841 census collection. You can perform a more advanced search by focussing on specific collections. As shown in

the example below, if you go to the **Search records** tab in the main menu you can use a name or address as search criteria within a specific census collection. By including data you may already have at hand – relating perhaps to occupation, place of birth or place of residence – the likelihood of a successful search is increased.

The results list is free and displays the address type (household, institution or vessel), the person's name, age (but this would be rounded up or down to the nearest

Search tips

It's better to fill in fewer fields and read all the results rather than ask the search engine to restrict the results. Only fill in more fields if a list of results is really long or you're searching for common names.

Some names have been transcribed with the surname first, particularly census returns for institutions. If you can't find someone, try entering their surname in the first name field and their first name in the surname field.

In cases where the **findmypast** transcribers have been unable to decipher certain words, they've typed **'999'** or **'…'** instead – which explains why you may sometimes not be able to find an ancestor in the census return.

Start your search

1 You want to find a Joseph Lilly on the 1841 census, but all you know is that he was 28 years old in 1841 and that his wife's name was Elizabeth. You're also unsure where he may have been living in 1841. Click on **Search records** along the top panel and select **Census, land & surveys** from the drop-down menu. Scroll down to the row labelled **1841 Census** and click on **Search by person's name**.

Enter your search criteria

2 The 1841 person search window appears. Enter 'Joseph' in the **First name** field, 'Lilly' in the **Last name** field, tick the **Include variants** box under **First name**, enter '1813' in the **Birth year** field and set the **+/-** age range to '5' (because the 1841 census enumerators rounded adults' ages down). Now press **SEARCH**.

five years in the 1841 census), sex and the registration district. You must subscribe if you want to see a household transcription or view an image of the page. There are several ways of doing this, from annual or monthly subscriptions to pay-as-you-go schemes.

Searching for an address

If you click on **Search records** and then select **Census, land & survey records** from the drop-down menu you have the option of searching either by name or address for each collection (see step 1, left). If you click on **Search by address** this opens a window offering very basic criteria. You can choose **Advanced search** for a more focussed selection of records, which narrows your results by asking you for more information; use this when a basic search yields too many results. If you simply can't find an address, it could have been mistranscribed. Try doing a 'wildcard' search (in which you type an asterisk to replace one or more letters) in either the basic or the advanced address search engine.

Do an advanced search

3 Four Joseph Lillys are found with the correct name and roughly the right age, although none are exactly 28 years old. Click on the **redefine current search** link, then on the **advanced search** tab. Add Joseph's wife's name: under **Other persons living in same household** put 'Elizabeth' in the **First name** box and 'Lilly' in the **Last name** box. Press **SEARCH** to be taken to the results page.

Your ancestor is found

4 Only one of the Joseph Lillys listed previously is now displayed, which means he was the only one living with an Elizabeth Lilly. To view the original census page press the **VIEW** link in the **Original census image** column.

Life on the river *If your ancestors worked the rivers on a barge, you'd expect them to be hard to find on a census. But as the census entry above shows, some bargemen were recorded.*

Using the census
scotlandspeople.gov.uk

The entire collection of Scottish census returns – from 1841 to 1901 – has been indexed and made available online. They can be accessed, along with other Scottish data, at **scotlandspeople.gov.uk**.

Before you can view the census index, you need to register as a new user, choose a password and log in (see page 56). Making a search is free, but you have to pay to view the results pages and each page of the census return, which involves buying credits.

So far, the 1881 census is the only one that has been transcribed on this website. The others have to be viewed as original records, which means there's no option to search for and view a whole household. If the household is spread over two pages, you may not realise that it's incomplete – and to view the following page, just to be sure, will cost you a further 5 credits.

Reading the handwriting

Just about everything you see, apart from the 1881 census, will be in the handwriting of the time. For more information about reading handwriting click the **Help & resources** tab on the homepage and select **Research tools** from the drop-down menu. This offers you a menu of useful links, including one to **Handwriting Help**, which contains a further link to **ScottishHandwriting.com**. This website offers 'Online Tuition in the Palaeography of Scottish Documents'. It

covers the 16th, 17th and 18th centuries, but the information within the site, especially the 'letter finder' section, is invaluable for deciphering the handwriting in some of the 19th-century census returns. See also pages 174-5 for help with reading old handwriting.

Spelling the name correctly

When you begin searching for an ancestor, the search facility page gives you the option to search by name, sex, age range, year, county and district. Scotlandspeople also allows you to use the Soundex system or 'wild card' characters to widen the scope of your searches.

Soundex works by enabling your search to bring up records of similar-sounding names. Suppose, for example, that you believe your ancestor was called James Fyffe, the database will return all entries containing that forename at any position in the forename record. So the results will include James Fife, Alexander James Fyffe, James Robert Fyfe and so forth. This can help you to locate family members whose names were wrongly recorded in the census – but the only disadvantage is that it can give you an excessively long list.

For more information about Soundex codes and wild-card characters, click on the **Help & resources** tab on the homepage and select **Help with searching** from the drop-down menu.

Why you may not find a match

Sometimes a search may yield no records, despite the fact that you know that the person you're looking for definitely existed. This may be because the name wasn't recorded in the way you might have expected – either due to a different spelling or because of illegitimacy. The person may not have been staying where you expected to find them – or even living in Scotland. Sometimes it can help to broaden your search, again by using Soundex or wild card characters.

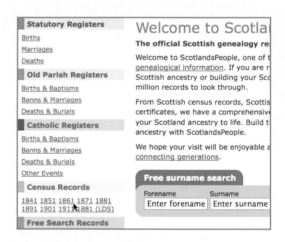

Searching in the 1861 census

1 If you want to search for a Donald John MacDonald in the 1861 census, go to scotlandspeople.gov.uk and log in or register. From the menu of the left of the screen, under **Census records** choose the year that you wish to search – in this case, click on **1861**.

A jumping-off point

It's a good idea to use the information you find in the 1881 census to do some detective work that will take your family research considerably further.

● The birthplaces and ages recorded in the census can be used to look for the registered births or baptisms of these people.

● Because you know the age of the householder you can work out roughly when he married, and find the names of his parents in the marriage indexes.

● The disappearance of an elderly relative or a young child between census years might indicate a death to be pursued.

● A woman might have returned to her family home for her first confinement, therefore the given birthplace of the eldest child might be an indication of where her parents lived.

Son of Perth *John Buchan, author of novels such as* Greenmantle *and* Mr Standfast, *was born in 1875. You can find his name and details in the Perth 1881 census returns.*

Fill in the details

2 On the search page enter 'MacDonald' in **Surname**, 'Donald John' in **Forename** and '1861' in **Year**. Then click the **Do the search** button at the top left of the search page.

First results are shown

3 The index has returned four results for this search. It will cost you 1 credit to view them. To do this, click on **View (1 credit)**. If you haven't already done so, you'll then need to buy credits (see page 56). Having clicked the **View** link, the next page will ask if you want to go ahead. Click the **Yes** button.

Viewing the results

4 If you see a match, you can view the original for 5 credits. If you click the **View (5 credits)** link, you'll be asked again if you want to proceed. Click **Yes**. You'll find the infant Donald John at home with his parents, two sisters and two servants. Clicking on the appropriate icons at the top of the screen will allow you to save the image to your computer for future reference or to print out the page.

Using the census
irishorigins.com

Census records for Ireland are sparse, but this site gives you access to the best alternative there is – Griffith's Valuation.

Although censuses were taken in Ireland from 1821 to 1911, many returns haven't survived. Those for 1861 to 1891 were deliberately destroyed and pulped for paper during the First World War, and most of the census returns for the preceding years – 1821 to 1851 – were lost in the catastrophic fire in Dublin's Public Record Office in 1922.

Fortunately, the returns for 1901 and 1911 are in the public domain, and although they may not be available yet online on this site, you can view them if you visit the National Archives in Dublin or go to the Public Record Office of Northern Ireland (PRONI) in Belfast.

Irish property records

Luckily, the gap left by the destruction of the census returns has been partly filled by another important source of information – 19th-century Irish property records, which can be accessed through **irishorigins.com**. They're known as Griffith's Valuation, and are the most comprehensive survey of

Search Griffith's Valuation Index

1 Once you've subscribed to **irishorigins.com** (see **origins.net**, page 55), you can search Griffith's Valuation. To search for a Patrick Kiernan, go to the homepage and enter the names in the two relevant boxes. You can choose to search by exact match or, if you're not sure of the spelling, by close variants. Once you've entered the name, click on **Search**. You'll be offered the screen shown above. Select **View Records** from the row labelled **Griffith's Valuation Index**.

Choose an image to view

2 The search generates a list of all the Patrick Kiernans held within Griffith's Valuation Index. To view the original handwritten record for the entry that best fits your search criteria, click on the **Image** button, to the right of the name.

Find the address you want

3 You'll then be given an image of the valuation return. The image may look a little fuzzy, but Patrick Kiernan is about a third of the way down the page, and it includes a description of his dwelling. You can print this out for your records. Return to the search page to find out if a map is available. If it is, click on the button to help you to locate the property.

Dispossessed

Many tenant farmers and their families were evicted from their homes when agricultural depression hit Ireland in the late 19th century. Sometimes force was used and the house was destroyed. The cottage (right) of Mathias Magrath in County Clare was demolished by battering ram (a great log slung from a wooden frame) in the late 1880s. Facing homelessness and destitution in Ireland, thousands of people emigrated and made new lives elsewhere. You'll be able to track down stories such as this in the Griffith's Valuation Index.

households for the period covering the years between the Great Famine and the start of civil registration (1848-64). The records cover the entire country: every property in Ireland was included in the valuation, along with the occupier's name and, if the property was rented, the house owner's name.

What's more, the valuation covers not only houses, but every building, as well as land – it lists everyone who paid rates. This linking of land, landowners, property and family members is what makes it such a valuable 'census substitute' for family historians. But before you can make the best use of these property records, you need some idea of where your ancestor lived. Unless he had a very unusual surname, you'll need at least a county of origin.

Accessing the records

To access the Griffith's Valuation records, go to **irishorigins.com** and click on **Irish origins**. You'll also be able to access other Irish census substitutes such as the Dublin City censuses for 1851 and 1901. You can search the index for free, but to view any detailed information, you'll need to register your name and email address, and pay a subscription (see page 100). The site operates on a pay-per-view voucher system.

Finding out more about Irish records

These websites have a lot of useful information about using Irish family history records:

☞ The Public Record Office of Northern Ireland (PRONI) at **proni.gov.uk** has information about freeholders' records.

☞ Genuki's site for Ireland at **genuki.org.uk** gives county-by-county detail.

☞ The family history website **movinghere.org.uk** provides a free online catalogue of material related to migration from local, regional and national archives, libraries and museums. Click on **tracing your roots**, then on the **Irish** button.

Can't find an ancestor?

Don't despair if you have trouble finding a relative on census returns. There are many ways of getting round this brick wall.

When you're hunting for a particular census return, be prepared for two common stumbling blocks: errors made when the original returns were transcribed into a database, and mistakes in the original census returns. Both are most often simply a result of human error. A good way to lessen the effect of any of these mistakes, and get the best results, is to use the census returns along with the civil registration certificates that you'll probably have acquired already.

Tackling transcription errors

Always remember that the online census index you search may not be accurate. The original information has gone through many steps before you see it – from householder to enumerator, then stages of transcription and digitising. Look out for these three areas.

- Bad handwriting – in some cases the original returns may have been illegible, in others careless mistakes were made.
- Abbreviations – in some cases names were abbreviated, with William recorded as Wm and Thomas as Thos, for example.
- Dittos – the form 'do', rather than today's ditto marks, was used by the enumerator when the information in consecutive entries on the same page was the same.

The 'less is more' approach often yields the best results. If you use the **Advanced** search facility on the Ancestry website, for example,

rather than entering the full range of information, including dates of birth, counties and other people that you expect to be in the household, you can widen your search by omitting some of your 'facts'.

DIFFERENT CENSUS, DIFFERENT INFORMATION

Some census indexes can be searched in ways other than by name. For example, the 1881 census on the Ancestry site lets you search by occupation, and the 1901 census on The National Archives site allows you to search by address and street. This will help you to learn more about the local area and your ancestors' neighbours.

NAME SPELLINGS: VARIANTS AND SOUNDEX

If you aren't sure of a spelling, some sites offer Soundex (see page 64), and others list all the variations of a name if you click the appropriate option from a drop-down list. For example, the Origins search engines use NameX, where you can choose **exact matches only**, **close variants** or **all variants** when you're searching.

NAME SPELLINGS: WILDCARDS

When using wildcards (see page 64) you usually have to enter a specific number of characters to make the search work. For example, The National Archive search for the 1901 census specifies a minimum of two characters before a wildcard

entry. So if you're hunting for Louisa, say – which is often mistranscribed Lousia – try entering **Lou*** for a better result.

Errors in the original returns

If you've tried all these search tips and still can't find who you are looking for, it could be a problem that dates back to the night on which the original census was taken.

STAYING AWAY The most common reason that people don't appear where they should is that they weren't at home on that particular night. Your ancestor could have been staying with friends or relations so won't be listed in his own home. Another reason for a non-appearance in the census is that many people travelled about to look for work.

IN AN INSTITUTION An ancestor may have been in an institution. Remember to search the returns for barracks, if you know someone was in the military. A child might have been at boarding school, some distance away from home. Or perhaps your ancestor was in a workhouse or in prison.

DIFFERENT NAMES Although the enumerator may have abbreviated names, it was more common for householders to provide the information themselves, and they may well have used pet names or shortenings. So James is often recorded as Jim, and Elizabeth as Lizzy or Betsy. People were often known by their middle names, too, so the 'John William' you are searching for could well be listed in the census return as 'Bill'. Use lateral thinking in your search.

RELATIONSHIP DISCREPANCIES A householder may have listed someone as a 'brother' or 'cousin', but this doesn't tally with your research. Bear in mind that these terms were sometimes used to describe relations acquired though marriage, or even distant relatives.

ENUMERATOR PROBLEMS Enumerators might have recorded names phonetically; a variant name search or a wildcard can help to overcome this. Examples of phonetic names recorded in the census include Sarah as Sahra or Sara, and Kathrine as Catherine.

MISSING RETURNS Occasionally the page has been lost – between 5 and 10 per cent of the 1861 census is missing. It's most likely that the final page dropped off the enumerator's book – and as there was only one set of returns recorded, your best bet is to search the censuses before or after the one you're in.

There are also a variety of reasons, ranging from being deliberately omitted by the householder, to being homeless and on the streets at the time, that mean at least 5 per cent of the population doesn't appear in census returns.

> ## Top 5 causes for a 'missing' ancestor
> **1** The person was away from home that night
> **2** Your relative travelled a lot, so is hard to trace
> **3** The person was listed under a different name
> **4** The householder lied on the census return, perhaps to hide evidence of an illicit relationship or a fugitive
> **5** The person was away from home on a vessel or in an institution (a boarding school, perhaps, or even a prison).

Multiple identities

Tracking an ancestor can be hard if details have been wrongly recorded or transcribed. Edward Mead, wearing his hat on the beach (right), was a particular challenge. His birth in 1858 in the small village of Tilshead in Wiltshire was registered (below, left) by his mother, Ellen. As a three year old he was recorded as Edwin (instead of Edward) Mead in the 1861 census. At the age of 13, he appears in the 1871 census as E. Mead, scholar, born in Tilshead, living in the household of a baptist minister in Worcestershire (below, middle). But the digital version of the census document (far right) describes him not as a male scholar, but as the granddaughter of the minister. Having his place and date of birth firmly fixed helped his great-granddaughter to solve the puzzle.

DNA and family history

Thanks to the fact that males pass a small amount of genetic information unchanged from generation to generation, evidence from DNA analysis can show, for instance, how family names originate in specific areas.

Family historians have a new technique to enable them to pursue their origins. Geneticists can prove a connection down a male line over the generations, for just as surnames are passed down from father to son, so is that part of the male DNA structure that is known as the 'Y' chromosome.

DNA evidence *People with unusual surnames are likely to share the same Y chromosome.*

This is particularly important in the study of surnames. The DNA evidence can either support or disprove the case for single or multiple origins for a name. But it is most effective when combining the evidence from genetics with traditional genealogical methods. The rarer the surname, the more likely it is that all the bearers will share the same Y chromosome.

Non-paternity events

The picture is often blurred by what scientists call 'non-paternity events'. The chief one of these is illegitimacy, whose rates have varied considerably at different periods of time. They reached a peak of seven per cent in the second quarter of the 19th century, but were usually much lower than this. Other non-paternity events include change of name upon adoption or when a father has died and a child becomes known by the name of his mother's new husband. DNA tests can often confirm a non-paternity event that has long been suspected!

A particularly fruitful use for DNA testing is that it can prove or disprove a connection between variant forms of a surname. Genetics can fill the gaps in the documentary record by establishing a DNA pattern for each family tree. Genetic genealogy also offers the possibility of finding branches of a family tree

in other parts of the world. It is especially popular in Australia, Canada, New Zealand and the USA as it allows families who can trace their ancestors back to Britain to link up with older family branches and perhaps to locate their surname's original home.

Difficulties with genetic evidence

Even when most male bearers of a surname share the same genetic markers, it's not certain that they are the descendants of the man who first had the name. It's possible that an early illegitimate line produced a large number of male offspring. It might even be that the original line died out. Another difficulty is that a surname may have had more than one origin, but that only one of these survives or that only one line has been sampled. DNA testing is not a magic wand. It should be combined with the older techniques of genealogy and surname distribution mapping.

About the Meates One-Name Study

My One-Name Study has been a tremendous adventure of discovery. When I started, very little was known about the surnames, and although people suspected that various family trees were related, no one knew. Most assumed that all Meates were related, since it is a very rare surname, and wondered how the surname ended up in Ireland, Wales, and London. Many people also suspected that those with the surname Meats were related, but could never find any proof.

As with many One-Name Studies, mine evolved from research on my family tree, when I started collecting for Ireland all occurrences of the surname, in the hope to determine who was related. Years later, having a large database of events for multiple countries, and many different family trees, DNA was added as a research tool.

If any of the surnames in my research or in the DNA Project are in your family tree, be sure to contact me. Most likely, I have information that can help with your research.

Variants

For my One-Name Study, the following variants are included:

Mate, Mates, Mayott, Meat, Meats

For my DNA Project, the above variants are included, as well as:

Matt, Matta, Mayot, Miot, Myatt, Myott

And any possible variant, such as Matis as a variant for Mates of Romania.

DNA online databases

There are now a large number of one-name studies online, starting with the Guild of One-Name Studies (**one-name.org**), which has nearly 8,000 surname studies. Enter 'DNA' in the box: **Search the Guild's website** (see opposite) to see them. One of the most interesting is Susan Meates's One-Name Study (**one-name.org/profiles/meates.html**) (see image above), which includes the similar names of Mate, Mates, Mayott, Meat, Meats,

Matt, Matts, Mayot, Miot, Myatt and Myott. Her documentary research came to an end, so she turned to the commercial company, Family Tree DNA. She found that many of these surnames across the world are related and that they descend from the surname Mayott, which originated in Rushton James, north Staffordshire by 1281. The name was also recorded as Mayot and Mayote in early records.

All the following names are related and descend from this origin:

- All Meates whose family tree goes back from America and Canada to Ireland.
- All Mates whose family tree goes back to Ireland, except the Mates family tree of County Kildare.
- All Meats family trees.
- Several Mate and Mates family trees who

What about the female side?

Mitochondrial DNA (mtDNA) is inherited by both males and females, although it is passed on only by females. Both males and females can test for this. These tests inform you about the direct female line through your mother, her mother, and so on back in time. But since a woman's surname usually changes with marriage, mtDNA testing is not of use for one-name studies.

are traced to England and Wales.

- All Myatt family trees, except one tree whose progenitor is found in Longton, Staffordshire in 1820. Discovering the variant Myatt was totally unexpected. The DNA tests have also shown that the distant origin for this group is Nordic.

Commercial DNA testing

Taking a DNA test is simple. A test kit is sent by post to the person taking the test. He swabs the inside of his mouth with the cotton-wool sticks provided in the kit, and sends it back. After a few weeks, the results are sent to the person who supplied the test and to the project administrator – the person conducting a surname study, for instance. Cyndi's List (**cyndislist.com/dna.htm**) names the numerous providers of DNA tests. Tests can be costly, with an average of around £150 a person.

familytreedna.com The largest commercial DNA testing company in the USA.

oxfordancestors.com Britain's biggest DNA testing resource is headed by Bryan Sykes, who made the first single surname study (see left).

ancestry.co.uk A similar service is now offered by this major genealogy site.

smgf.org The Sorenson Molecular Genealogy Foundation (see right) is a non-profit organisation

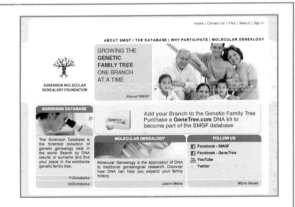

founded in 1999, which connects both DNA and family trees by collecting the pedigrees of all those who takes the DNA tests. Its database is freely accessible. You can make a search by using either genetic or genealogical evidence and you can connect to other family trees.

The Red Cross – in peace and war

For almost 150 years, the Red Cross has helped people suffering through military conflict, many of whom appear in its archives. Just as important is its peacetime role, bringing relief to those caught up in flood, famine, earthquakes and other disasters around the world.

In 1859, a Swiss businessman, Henry Dunant, witnessed horrific scenes on the battlefield of Solferino in northern Italy. He was so appalled by the misery of the thousands left to die that he founded the Red Cross in 1863 to protect the victims of armed conflicts, including the wounded, prisoners of war, refugees and civilians. The British Red Cross was established in 1870, following the start of the Franco-Prussian War.

Wartime roles

When war broke out in 1914, the British Red Cross joined forces with the Order of St John (founder of the St John Ambulance first-aid service) as the Joint War Committee, to work in hospitals, medical supply depots and convalescent homes. They also replaced the old, slow horse-drawn ambulances with motorised ambulances in battlefields. One volunteer driver was the writer Ernest Hemingway who drew on his experiences to write *A Farewell to Arms* after the war. The volunteers helped to keep prisoners of war in touch with their families and, at the end of the war, organised the safe return home of more than 420,000.

The Red Cross fulfilled the same role during the Second World War but was prevented at first

For exceptional service *The Florence Nightingale Medal is awarded to nurses who've shown remarkable bravery. It was instituted in 1912 by the International Committee of the Red Cross in Geneva to commemorate the work of Florence Nightingale.*

from applying pressure on the Nazis about their treatment of Jews in the concentration camps for fear that reprisals would affect its freedom to help other prisoners of war. Some 20 million of the famous Red Cross food parcels were dispatched to prisoners from the UK alone and, in November 1943, it received permission to send parcels to inmates of some concentration camps. As the parcels were often signed for by other internees, the Red Cross managed to compile a list of more than 100,000 camp prisoners.

Aid in peacetime

After the First World War, the Red Cross turned its focus from the battlefield to 'the improvement of health, the prevention of disease and the mitigation of suffering throughout the

Helping hand *A Red Cross nurse (right) lends her support to an injured soldier, a sailor and a pilot wounded during the Battle of Britain in 1940.*

world'. It began fulfilling this ambitious role at home by setting up Britain's first blood transfusion service in 1921. Overseas, the Red Cross provided help and relief to millions of people displaced during the Second World War, and continued to support refugees from conflicts such as the Hungarian Revolution in 1956 and the Vietnam War.

Natural disasters have also spurred the Red Cross into action. Many thousands affected by cataclysms such as the Indian Ocean tsunami of 2004 and Hurricane Katrina in 2005 are grateful for the relief provided by the volunteers wearing the red cross.

Records held by the Red Cross

If someone in your family trained or served in the Red Cross, or was caught up in warfare somewhere around the world, you may find you can discover more from the Red Cross Museum and Archives, which holds records dating from its foundation in 1870. Among these are personnel records for the Voluntary Aid Detachments (VADs) – including those who trained in military hospitals and as nurses. Records since the Second World War are scant and there are none for the inter-war years. The archive also has medals and emblems, posters, postcards and photographs – many of which can be viewed via the website at **redcross.org.uk**.

Researching with the Red Cross

The page at **redcross.org.uk/About-us/Who-we-are/History-and-origin/Museum-and-archives** enables you to see what resources are available. You'll find a link to **Our historical collections**. Click on this to discover what archives are held. There's no online catalogue, but you can make an appointment to visit the museum and archives in London (see Directory). Research hours are from 10am to 1pm and from 2pm to 4pm, Monday to Friday.

Tracing a volunteer or a POW

To find out about an ancestor who worked for the Red Cross, email **enquiry@redcross.org.uk**, giving as much information about the person as possible, or write to the address in the Directory. The records of prisoners of war and civilian internees are held by the International Committee of the Red Cross (ICRC) in Geneva (see Directory). You can write to them and ask for a search, but this can take a long time. You'll need to give the person's name and nationality as well as date and place of birth, father's name, date of capture, regiment and army number, if you have them. Searches are carried out free of charge, but the Red Cross suggests that you make a voluntary donation, if you can, to contribute to the cost of the service.

Church records

To go beyond the early 19th-century limits of civil registration and census records, you'll need to look at parish registers of baptisms, marriages and burials. These could carry you back to the mid 16th century.

Keeping a record *Church registers became more detailed as record-keeping was standardised. The 18th-century burial register (right) gives the bare minimum – and sometimes not even a name – whereas the 1863 marriage certificate (far right) provides a wealth of information.*

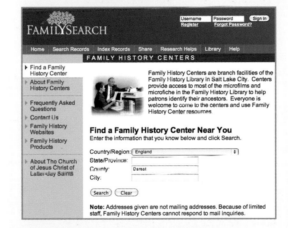

Using Access to Archives

The National Archives Access to Archives site at **nationalarchives.gov.uk/a2a** gives details of more than 400 repositories throughout England and Wales, as well as the scope of their contents. For example, on the home page type 'Nottinghamshire archives' in the search box and over 100,000 results are shown, dating from the eighth century to the present day.

Alternatively, you can type in the name of a place, such as the town or village where an ancestor came from, to see if any early records are available. You can even type in the name of a person and a place, although you would be lucky to find a direct hit.

For tips on how to make further searches, go to the box headed **Need help?** and click **Help with Searching**.

Contact details for record offices and libraries throughout the United Kingdom are given on **nationalarchives.gov.uk/archon**.

Finding a Family History Centre

1 Go to **familysearch.org/eng/library/ fhc/frameset_fhc.asp** (see above). Fill in the information in the boxes provided. For example, to search for centres in Dorset, England, select the **Country** by scrolling down to find 'England'. In the **County** box enter 'Dorset' and click the **Search** button.

Search results

2 All the Family History Centres in the county are listed with their contact details and hours of opening. Dorset has two centres, in Poole and Weymouth, from which you can choose.

Using parish register indexes
familysearch.org

Several websites help you to search parish register indexes online, and most of them have similar information. The trick is to find one that suits you and seems to hold the type of information you want. The free website **familysearch.org/Eng,** run by the Church of Jesus Christ of Latter-day Saints (LDS – the

Mormons), is a good place to start. For more details about what the site contains, see page 54. To use this site to find an LDS Family History Centre near you, see page 137.

The information in this website comes from three main sources. Two, the Ancestral file and Pedigree Resource file, consist of

information submitted by users on a voluntary basis, which means that you'll need to verify it. The third, the International Genealogical Index (IGI) is the most useful: a vast collection of parish record transcriptions for the UK and other countries throughout the world. Some other websites will automatically link you to it.

Below are two examples of the types of parish register search you can do on **familysearch.org/Eng.** One is a simple search to trace a baptism, and the other is an

Start a simple search

1 To find the baptism of a John Sowerbutts in Lancashire in 1753, go to the homepage and start a simple search. Enter 'John' for the **First name** and 'Sowerbutts' for the **Last name**. Choose **Birth/christening** for **Life event**. Enter '1753' in the **Year** box. From the **Country** list choose **England**. Click on the **Search** button.

Success with the first result

2 One possible entry comes up in the International Genealogical Index (IGI). This John Sowerbutts was christened on March 11, 1753, at Ormskirk parish in Lancashire. Click on his name for more details.

Father and mother revealed

3 This screen gives us the names of John Sowerbutts' parents: Thomas Sowerbutts and Elizabeth. You can find out if any more information on them is held in the records by clicking on their names.

ancestors, it's when they came up against the law that their names and details would have entered the records. Also, as Catholics were subject to extra taxes and fines, consider searching the tax records held in The National Archives (TNA) and at local record offices. Because Catholicism was stronger in northern England, the local archives there will be of particular value in your search.

Catholics cradle to grave

From the beginning of the 19th century, Catholic churches began to keep registers of baptisms, marriages and burials. When civil registration began in 1837 only a small number of them were deposited in central archives, along with other non-parochial records. You'll find those that were deposited are mainly from northern England and are in TNA, among the other sets of registers found in a record series called RG4 (see page 148).

The rest of the registers are either still with the individual churches or in local record offices. It's also worth remembering that, in the middle of the 19th century, about three-quarters of Catholics were of Irish origin, so your Catholic ancestors from that era are likely to have come from Ireland.

Risky mass *For many years Roman Catholics were forced to worship in secret, knowing that not only their priest, but they, as well, would be severely punished for participating in unlawful rituals. Often the priest lived with a sympathetic Catholic family and his presence was kept hidden. Restrictions introduced in the 16th century were only lifted in the 18th and 19th centuries.*

Tracing your Catholic ancestors

Apart from TNA indexes, a number of websites offer help in tracing Catholic records.

Two specialist sites are the Catholic Record Society at **www.catholic-history.org.uk/crs** and the Catholic Family History Society at **www.catholic-history.org.uk/cfhs**.

There are also some established sites such as **ancestry.co.uk** and **movinghere.org.uk** that will help. The Society of Genealogists at **sog.org.uk** has good information about Catholic records.

You may well find, though, that most of your searching will have to be done offline. For books about Catholic records, try the Institute of Heraldic and Genealogical Studies (IHGS) online Family History Bookshop at **ihgs.ac.uk**. It holds a number of books that you'll find helpful in tracing Catholic ancestors. Also, you might try the Westminster Library. On the City of Westminster homepage (**westminster.gov.uk**), click on **Libraries & archives** under **Services by category** at the bottom of the page. On the page that appears click on **Archives & local history** at the left. On the page you are taken to click on **Search the Collection**, then on the next page click on **Family History: A Guide to Sources** for more information.

Tracing your Nonconformist ancestors

If your ancestors belonged to one of the Nonconformist religions, it's unlikely you'll find them in the records of the established Church. But there's plenty of information available elsewhere to help you to track them down, whatever their beliefs.

The term 'Nonconformist' was used from the 16th century onwards to describe people who refused to conform to the rites and disciplines of the Anglican church. They included many religious groups – Presbyterians, Unitarians, Congregationalists, Baptists, Methodists, Puritans and other smaller groups – who were fined and penalised for not attending Anglican services. Although Charles II had promised an amnesty to all dissenters when he was restored to the throne in 1660, he

increased persecution and discrimination by introducing the Act of Uniformity two years later. At this point many Nonconformists sailed to North America for refuge; the Quakers, for example, founded Pennsylvania as a haven of religious freedom.

Indexes of Nonconformists and Dissenters (as they were also called) may be found on the website of the Church of Jesus Christ of Latter-day Saints, **familysearch.org**, which has transcribed the registers of a number of

independent churches among the records held in its International Genealogical Index or IGI (see page 138). Another informative website is **nationalarchives.gov.uk/records/research-guides/nonconformists.htm**, which has information about various religions.

The Toleration Act of 1689 made life a little easier for Nonconformists, but until 1828 they were debarred from holding political office. And in 1837, when civil registration began, most Nonconformist registers were collected and deposited with the General Register Office (GRO).

Finding a relative in TNA indexes

The majority of Nonconformist birth, marriage and death records are held in The National Archives (TNA) under the department code RG (see right). Even if you don't know the name of the church or chapel that your ancestor attended, it's possible to find relevant records. The records are listed by county, so try doing a search by county or town.

A different way of baptising *The Baptist movement began in 1612 and was based on the concept of adult baptism and universal access to salvation. One of its greatest supporters was John Bunyan, whose 1678 allegory* Pilgrim's Progress *enhanced the credibility of the movement. Baptist records can be found in series RG4 and RG5 at The National Archives.*

This is how the RG records are grouped:
- RG4 holds registers of births, marriages and deaths surrendered to the Non-parochial Registers Commissions of 1837 and 1857, 1568-1857. Also the Protestant Dissenters' Registry or 'Dr William's Library' of Baptists, Congregationalists and Presbyterians in the London area from 1742
- RG5 has birth certificates from the Presbyterian, Independent and Baptist Registry and from the Wesleyan Methodist Metropolitan Registry, 1742-1840

- RG6 contains Society of Friends' Registers, Notes and Certificates of Births, Marriages and Burials, 1578-1841
- RG7 has the registers of Clandestine Marriages and of Baptisms in the Fleet Prison, King's Bench Prison, the Mint and the May Fair Chapel, 1667-c.1777
- RG8 holds registers of births, marriages and deaths surrendered to the Non-parochial Registers Commission of 1857, and other registers and church records, 1646-1970.

A quiet new faith

The Society of Friends, or the Quakers, was established by the dissenter George Fox in the 17th century. Early Quakers worshipped without preachers or any liturgy, as they believed God would speak to them through members of the congregation. As well as rejecting the established Church, Quakers refused to bear arms or take oaths, and believed in the equality of the sexes.

Violent persecution forced many Quakers to emigrate to North America. Many others stayed, with some, such as the chocolate magnates and industrial reformers, Joseph Fry and George Cadbury, making their mark on British life. The Society of Friends was the first Nonconformist organisation to start using registers and began recording births, marriages and deaths from the mid 17th century. In addition to series RG6 at TNA, Quaker records can also be found at **rootsweb.com/~engqfhs**. Not every register has survived, and you may find gaps in the records when you search for your Quaker ancestors.

Searching for a chapel

1 To find the location and details of the Friar Gate Chapel in Derbyshire, for example, go to **nationalarchives.gov.uk**, click on **The Catalogue**, and then **Search the Catalogue**. In the **Word or phrase** box enter 'Friar Gate'. To narrow the search, enter 'RG4' into the **Department or Series code** box. Click on **Search**.

Accessing the chapel's records

2 You will then be given a list of all the records in this series that relate to Friar Gate Chapel. They're arranged in chronological order, by record number. Make a note of the number on the left of the entry you're interested in. These records are available only on microfilm at TNA, and you'll need this unique reference number in order to locate and view the records you've chosen.

Quaker wedding *Surrounded by 'Friends' in a meeting house, two Quakers make a commitment to a lifelong, equal partnership, without any need for clergy.*

Memorial inscriptions

Finding the words from a tomb or gravestone for an ancestor is poignant, as well as informative. Inscriptions can be traced online, as many local family history societies have transcribed them from graveyards and cemeteries.

Inscriptions on your ancestors' gravestones often contain far more detail than you'll find in official records or parish documents. For example, you may find out their date of birth and age at death, as well as where they lived and what job they did. Many of them give information about the parents and children of the person, helping you to extend your family tree.

A memorial inscription may tell you about the travels of the person, because not all burials take place where the person died. Sometimes a body is brought back to a parish from many miles away, to be interred with other family members. This can help where you have a 'missing' relative, or answer the question 'Where did he get to for all those years?'

Inscriptions online

The online indexes of transcribed memorial inscriptions should tell you the graveyard where the inscription was found. This in turn helps you to find further information in the parish burial register of the church associated with the graveyard.

Since 1978 the Federation of Family History Societies (FFHS) has encouraged its members to transcribe memorial inscriptions from the 17th to the 20th century in many parts of England, Scotland and Wales. The

records of this ongoing project are now available as part of the parish records collection at **findmypast.co.uk**. The largest county collection is that for Cornwall with 319,771 inscriptions.

Inscriptions offline

Although there's plenty of help available for online searches, not all inscriptions have been transcribed yet, so sometimes you simply have to visit a graveyard, church or crematorium to track them down. It could prove a fruitful journey, because graves and monuments offer up hidden treasure to the persistent explorer. Many churches have detailed memorial inscriptions about past parishioners and dignitaries on their walls and set into their floors. You may also be

Finding an inscription

1 GenFair is one of the best sources of genealogy data. It holds many CDs of memorial inscriptions provided by local family history societies. Go to **genfair.co.uk**. From the menu on the left-hand side of the screen select **Monumental Ins**.

Searching the database

2 You can either work through the availability list, scrolling down each page, or you can do a search. In this example we'll see what's available for the Yorkshire village of Monk Bretton.

able to find out about an ancestor at a crematorium, where ashes are interred in urns in a garden of rest.

Closed or redundant graveyards

You may find that the graveyard in which you expected to find your ancestor's gravestone and inscription has been built on or paved over. Before any old or redundant graveyards can be re-used in this way, the information on the gravestones has to be recorded in great detail and deposited with the local council or records office. Sometimes the stones will have been preserved and may still be accessible.

Some closed graveyards are maintained by the council in the area or by a group of local volunteers, and through them you may be able to find a list of the inscriptions of gravestones and monuments that are still there. Many local libraries have lists of memorial inscriptions of gravestones that have long since vanished or have become illegible with the erosion of time.

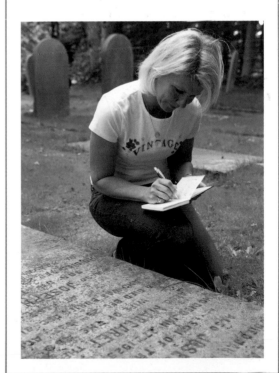

How to prepare for a graveyard visit

• Take a camera, notebook and pencil with you, so that you can record the information accurately. Note the position of the grave you are interested in within the graveyard, too.

• Some old inscriptions are difficult to read, especially if the stone has weathered. Go either early or late in the day, when the sun's slanting rays will light the inscription to best advantage.

• You may be tempted to brush off moss and lichen if they're obscuring the inscription, but be aware that old headstones are fragile, and you must take care not to damage them at all.

• Some graveyards are overgrown, so wear sturdy shoes and have a pair of secateurs in your pocket in case you need to cut back weeds or brambles to expose your ancestor's memorial inscription.

See the results

3 Type the name in the text box and click on **Search**. The search reveals that there is CD-ROM available containing photographs of inscriptions from St Paul's church in Monk Bretton. To buy the CD-ROM, click on **Add to basket**.

Check the source

4 Beneath the description of the CD-ROM the supplier is named. If you want to find out more about them, or other items they may produce, click on the name.

Searching for inscriptions

As more and more local record offices digitise information, the search for memorial inscriptions gets easier and more exciting. The material available online could include the words on your ancestor's gravestone.

Compiling databases of the inscriptions on memorials is a slow business, often carried out by volunteers and students. Tapping into a database that covers memorials in the area you're searching is the family historian's

equivalent of finding a seam of pure gold. The discovery of a detailed memorial inscription can open up new directions for you to explore, and can help you to fill in details of other relatives.

As online databases of memorial inscriptions have been put together by individual societies, they follow no particular pattern or design and each will require searching in a different way. Some ask for a small payment before they will supply the inscription(s) you need; in other cases the inscriptions are available with no charge directly from the website. As much of the transcription work is ongoing and digitising of larger databases takes time, many more sites will come online as teams or individuals finish their work.

Searching local sites

Most areas in Britain have a local record office and many have websites that provide the family historian with detail of memorial inscriptions. If you can't find what you are looking for, don't despair – you may be able to get help direct from your local records office. Below are three examples of good local sites.

Bath Record Office

If your ancestors lived in or near the city of Bath it's worth visiting the website for the local record office, batharchives.co.uk. Clicking on **Family history** at the top of the page will take you to a section of the website where there's a separate page covering memorial inscriptions. Click on **Monumental inscriptions** on the left-hand side of the page and you'll find details of which memorial inscriptions have been transcribed for which parishes around the area. As most of these records are still being compiled, it's worth checking regularly.

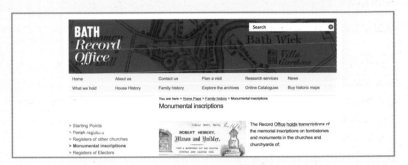

Kent Archaeological Society

For gravestones and monuments in and around Kent, try the Kent Archaeological Society archive of transcriptions at kentarchaeology.org.uk. Go to **Research** from the homepage then click on the **M.I.** (Memorial Inscriptions) link. There are parish maps of West and East Kent and an alphabetical list of locations. Clicking on a link to a place in Kent – Bexley, for example – will take you to a list of all the graveyard inscriptions at St Mary's church, Bexley. Some links also show sketch maps of graveyards, so you can identify the exact plot.

Hertfordshire Family History Society

Memorials from many of the parish churches within its county borders have been transcribed by the Hertfordshire Family History Society, at hertsfhs.org.uk. It lists the parish churches it has covered, and the cost of transcriptions, under the **Publications** section of the website. Click on **Monumental inscriptions** for a list of parish churches. The list is updated regularly, so check from time to time to keep updated on what information has become available recently.

Callington Area Heritage

The Heritage Centre at Callington in Cornwall, **callingtonheritage.org.uk** provides a resource for local history, including monumental inscriptions. The homepage has a **Search our Data** button. Click on this, then click on **Monumental Inscriptions**. You can submit queries by entering a surname into a box. Click on **Submit Query** and any inscriptions under that name will appear.

CEMSEARCH-uk

For ancestors in Lancashire, **Cemsearch.co.uk** hold databases of monumental or headstone inscriptions from cemeteries and graveyards. More than 46,071 gravestones are featured, with 201,130 individuals. You can click on a full alphabetical listing of names from each cemetery. Inscriptions for each name can be ordered from the website at a cost of £2 or £6.

Wills

A will is a uniquely personal document, and can reveal a
wealth of information about your ancestor and the family.
Finding one could be a huge boost to your research.

Understanding wills

Reading ancestors' wills reveals not only their financial state, but an enormous amount about what was important to them in their lifetime.

A will is often used to thank people, or to show appreciation of a spouse or children. Sometimes a nominal gift suggests that the deceased was angry with the recipient, so that they were almost cut out of the will. In some wills, the eldest son inherits just a token shilling because he has already taken over a family business or lives in the family home.

A husband's prerogative

Until 1883 a married woman could not make a will without her husband's permission. Once she married, all her property became part of her husband's estate, which meant that, by law, she had no property to leave. So before 1883, you're unlikely to find a will for a married woman – though you might find one for a widow or a spinster.

Wills made before 1858

You'll need to be quite tenacious to find a will made before 1858, because until that date, there was no central system of 'proving' a will – a term that came into use when a Church court validated the will, allowing the executor or administrator to carry out its instructions. Where this process (which

You can't take it with you *Wine is tasted and valued (left) to assess the amount of tax due on an estate in a 1947 painting entitled* Inventory and valuation for probate *by Frederick W. Elwell.*

A writer's bequests *Jane Austen's will of 1817, with explanations of the terms used, can be viewed on The National Archive's website.*

the person making the Will, (testator for men, testatrix for Women) It also stated the Parish where she lived.

Description of First beneficiary which is usually the Husband /Wife or next of Kin.

Final Beneficiaries This would cover servants and friends and the will would often specify their relationship to the testator or testatrix

is called 'probate') took place, depended on the value of the assets left by the deceased person and where the person had lived. You're not likely to find wills from among the poorer sections of the community – if you had no valuables, you'd have had little or no reason to draw up a will. But anyone with £5 or more to their name would have made a will.

Almost 300 Church courts were responsible for disposing of the possessions of people who had drawn up wills, and most of these wills are still held in local record offices.

There were several kinds of court, ranging from local archdeacon's courts to the Prerogative Courts of Canterbury and York, which dealt only with the wills of the very wealthy. The official records that survive are usually registered copies of 'proved' wills – not the orginals, which may no longer exist.

Wills made after 1858

It's not too difficult to track down wills made since January 1858, as this was when today's centralised system for dealing with legacies began. Unlike census records that stay closed

for 100 years, the contents of a will are in the public domain. Copies of all English and Welsh wills from 1858 to the present day are held at the Principal Registry in London (see Directory). In Scotland, most records are held by the individual courts that granted probate; in Ireland, the records are at the National Archives in Dublin or the Public Record Office in Belfast (see Directory).

When there's no will

Any ancestor who failed to make a will is said to have 'died intestate'. What should be done about the assets – or liabilities – was usually settled by a legal process known as administration. An administrator, often the deceased's brother, eldest son or widow, was appointed to pay the debts and distribute the assets, according to the law.

Despite the fact that there may be no will for you to track down, there'll be legal records of what happened to the estate after death – probably held in the local record office.

What wills can tell you

An ancestor's will is a really exciting find. The document is likely to contain a wealth of detail that you wouldn't get from census returns or registration certificates – and you can reveal the real person behind the name.

Wills or legacies left by your ancestors add layers of colour and texture to simple names and dates, and often tell you so much about their lives and families. You'll find out how well off they were, or discover relationships and even children you never knew existed. In addition, you'll find out where they lived, what they owned, whom they loved, what they cared about. Beneficiaries in the will may include institutions such as schools and

hospitals or charities, and even a mistress or previously unacknowledged illegitimate child. Then there are the wills that reveal a vindictiveness which can be breathtaking – a husband, for example, leaving his money to his wife on the condition that she does not marry again or co-habit with another man.

Whatever it reveals of the writer's nature, finding a will is a great windfall when you're tracking down long-lost ancestors.

Where probate took place

Probate is the official process of validating a will (see page 155), which takes place in the area in which they lived or died.

If your ancestors lived in southern England or Wales and died between 1384 and 1858 (when the centralised probate system was established) and owned assets that were worth more than £5, or stretched over more than one diocese, any will they made would have been proved at the Prerogative Court of Canterbury, in Kent.

Start your search for a will

1 Here's how you would search for the will of a Richard White, an ancestor from Farnham in Surrey, who died between 1700 and 1720. Enter **nationalarchives.gov.uk/documentsonline/ wills.asp** in your browser's address line. The page named 'Prerogative Court of Canterbury WIlls (1384-1858)' will appear. Under **Introduction**, click on **search**.

In the solicitor's office *The secrets of a will are revealed in this Victorian illustration. Wills can yield a surprising amount of information about your ancestors.*

The wills of people who lived in northern England were proved at York. Bequests below £5 were handled in other courts by bishops, and you should be able to find those wills in a local archive.

Most wills were proved within a year or two of the person's death, but it could take several years for probate to be granted, particularly if the terms of the will were disputed. If you don't find the probate records you're looking for, try looking in the records for a year or so later.

The earliest wills are likely to be in Latin; English became more widely used by the 17th century. The records that survive are usually registered copies of 'proved' wills – not the originals. The copied wills vary in length: most are one or two pages long, but if your ancestor was a wealthy aristocrat with vast estates and investments, his will might have run to as much as 15 or 20 pages.

The National Archives has a fascinating collection of more than a million wills online. You can search them using various criteria:

name, place, occupation and date of probate. Search these fields together or individually. The index is free to search, but if you find the will you're looking for, it will cost £3.50 to download. Remember that there may be transcription errors. Also, names may not be spelled as you'd expect them, so it's wise to search all variants of a name.

To have a look at some old wills, go to **nationalarchives.gov.uk**, and enter 'sample wills' in the **Search** box. You'll be offered a huge amount of information about them.

Fill in the details

2 Enter the ancestor's first name and last name. As White is a fairly common name, you should include a **Date range**. Put in the earliest and latest possible dates – in this case '1700' and '1725' – bearing in mind that probate may have not been granted for a few years. If you enter a place it may make the search too limited, so leave it blank and click on **Search**.

Assess the first results

3 From what you know about your ancestor, you can dismiss most of the Richard Whites on the results page. The most promising entry is the will for one from Farnham, Surrey, proved on October 3, 1715. Look at the most likely record first, by clicking **See details**.

Buying the record

4 The result looks right, so buy the record by clicking **Add to shopping**. You'll be taken through a series of screens that guide you to making an online payment of £3.50. Once your payment is accepted, you can download the will.

Looking for wills

You may think your family was too poor to have left any property, but it's always worth searching for a will. Even if your more recent forebears were humble, you could discover more distant ancestors who were wealthy.

The earliest wills were generally left by the rich, but farmers and craftsmen often left wills, too. A blacksmith or a master carpenter might have wanted the tools of his trade to go to a particular son, for example. By the 18th and 19th centuries, you'll find wills made by soldiers and sailors, and in the 20th century, people from all walks of life, whatever their income or assets, were making wills.

The law makes searching easier
On January 12, 1858, responsibility for the granting of probate was shifted from the Church Courts to the State (see page 155).

Since then, probate has been granted in district offices across the UK. Wherever probate is granted, a copy goes to the Principal Registry in London. Calendars giving details of all grants of probates and letters of administration have been published every year since 1858, and these can be searched at the Principal Registry (see Directory) or at major city libraries nationwide.

Looking for older wills
Before the law changed, wills were proved in numerous Church Courts, so pre-1858 you should begin your search at a local or county record office. But before you do, check the online index of The National Archives (TNA) at **nationalarchives.gov.uk** for wills for the Prerogative Court of Canterbury, where many English and Welsh wills were proved between 1384 and 1858. This quick search could save you time and effort.

Using local record offices
Record offices throughout the British Isles hold collections of wills proved in local courts. Few wills are available online, but county record offices are gradually transcribing and uploading indexes of the will collections in their possession. As the work is ongoing in many counties, you'll need help

> **A possible shortcut**
> Until 1906, taxes known as death duties were payable on estates over a certain value. Death Duty Registers containing details of these taxes have been kept since 1796. Before 1805, death duties were charged on about 25 per cent of all estates; by 1815 almost 75 per cent of beneficiaries had to pay some death duties on their inheritance. The Death Duty Registers are now held at TNA, and there's an online index covering 1796 to 1811 at **nationalarchives.gov.uk/documentsonline**. You can search the index free of charge and if you find your ancestor, you can download the details – including which court granted probate – for £3.50.

Reading the will *An 18th-century family wait expectantly to hear who has benefited from the will of a relative. Details of wills from this period are often held at local record offices.*

to find the records you need, so try the ARCHON directory (see below). It's accessed through TNA's website. If you find what you're looking for in an online index, the record office will send you a photocopy of the document for a small fee. The following counties have made this information available online through their record offices.

CHESHIRE The archives and local studies offices for the region covered by what is now the ceremonial county of Cheshire

archives.cheshire.gov.uk/ hold on their database more than 130,000 wills that were proved at Chester from 1492 to 1940. Only the index is available to see online, so if you find your ancestor's will listed and want to see a copy, you'll need to order it. You'll receive onscreen prompts to help you.

WILTSHIRE AND SWINDON The record office at history.wiltshire.gov.uk/heritage contains 105,000 wills proved in Salisbury between 1540 and 1858. At that time, the diocese

covered the whole of Wiltshire and parts of Dorset, as well as the parish of Uffculme in Devon. You can search the index online and order photocopies of the wills you want.

HAMPSHIRE To find wills on this site, go to www3.hants.gov.uk/archives/catalog.htm. The database includes the records for all probate granted at Winchester (excluding the Archdeaconry of Surrey). You can search the index but you can't view the wills online; these can be ordered and posted to you.

Which record office do you need?

1 If you're not sure where the local record office that holds your ancestor's documents might be, then use the ARCHON directory within TNA's website, nationalarchives.gov.uk/archon/. On the homepage, click on the **Search ARCHON Directory** button.

Search the ARCHON directory

2 If you're searching for archives in the Lichfield area, for example, key in 'Lichfield' in the **Repository name** field and click on **Search**. Two results appear, but only one (the lower of the two) looks suitable. Click on it to get its contact details.

Choose a repository

3 If you selected the 'Lichfield Record Office' (which is part of the Staffordshire and Stoke-on-Trent Archive Service), you'll see full contact details and access information. There's also a website link through which you can discover more about the library's holdings.

Other sites to search for wills

If you've had no luck searching for ancestors' wills on The National Archives website, there are other sites to try. Wills were proved in a number of different places, and the trick is to track down the one you want.

You'll find the search for a will enthralling and the results, when you get hold of them, worth all the effort. Knowing where to look is half the battle, and so it helps if you can understand the types of will that were made in the past, and can define what type of will you're after.

Looking for English wills

A number of collections of data relating to wills in England is currently held by several different commercial sites. Along with an index for the Prerogative Court of Canterbury (see pages 155-7), there's also an index for wills proved in London and at the Prerogative Court of York.

Knowing some details about your ancestor will help you to assess which of the indexes is most likely to hold the details of his will and make it easier and quicker to choose from the options that are offered to you.

BANK OF ENGLAND WILLS EXTRACT INDEX

The years 1717 to 1845 are covered in this index, available on **findmypast.co.uk**. Entries include individual stockholders who were declared bankrupt, as well as people who had invested money in public funds – this includes people from all over England, not just London.

PREROGATIVE COURT OF CANTERBURY INDEX

You'll find this index covers the years 1750 to 1800. Wills were proved in the Canterbury court – that is, probate was granted (see page 155) – until responsibility was taken over by the State in 1858. It's possible for you to buy hard copies of these original wills. This data can be found at **nationalarchives.gov.uk**.

ARCHDEACONRY COURT OF LONDON WILLS INDEX

This court in London was responsible for proving wills in the city. The index covers the first half of the 18th century and contains the wills of many sailors. It can be searched at **origins.net**.

YORK MEDIEVAL PROBATE INDEX

Wills proved in the province of York from 1267 to 1500 are held here. Most of the index's coverage is of individuals with estates in Yorkshire, but there are also entries for people who lived in other parts of England. Hard copies are held at the Borthwick Institute in York (see Directory). This and the following York indexes are held online at **origins.net**.

YORK PECULIARS PROBATE INDEX

'Peculiar' is a term used to describe a church or parish that was under the control of a diocese other than the one in which it lies. This index is rare and not widely available. Wills proved in the peculiar courts within the province of York are included in this index. It covers the years 1383 to 1883. Hard copies of these original wills can be bought.

PREROGATIVE AND EXCHEQUER COURTS OF YORK PROBATE INDEX

The Prerogative Court of York was the northern counterpart of the one in Canterbury. If property was in one or more diocese but all these dioceses were in York, the will would be proved in York.

Search for a will

1 The National Wills Index on **origins.net** contains an number of useful collections – some of which are mentioned above. Here we'll look for the probate details of a man named John Preston, who we know died in Suffolk in 1803. Go to origins.net and log in. Click on the **National Wills Index** tab. On the resulting screen, enter the man's name and click on the **Search** button.

The Exchequer Court of York dealt with probate matters for certain laymen and members of the clergy with property in the province only. Indexes are available from 1688 to 1858.

How to find a Scottish will

If you're researching a Scottish ancestor it's possible to find the will through an index on **scotlandspeople.gov.uk**. As a large number of Scottish family history records have been placed on this website, searching for Scottish wills is quite easy. The site holds an index for more than 600,000 wills, proved between the years 1513 to 1901.

The index itself is free to search, but you have to log in first (see page 56 for details). Then click on **Wills & Testaments** under **Free Search Records** to begin the search. Enter everything you know about your ancestor in the appropriate boxes and begin the search to see if any records are held. If you find the will you're looking for, you'll have to pay to get a copy of it.

Finding an Irish will

The loss of so many Irish records in 1922 makes this tricky. But go to **ancestry.co.uk** and click on **Search** at the top of the page. On the page that appears scroll down to the interactive map and click on **Ireland**. On the list of links that appears click on **View all Ireland Tax, Criminal, Land & Wills** under **Ireland Tax, Criminal, Land & Wills**. You'll now see a collection of links. Click on one to be taken to a search page where you can begin.

First search

2 The following screen tells you how many records have been found in each collection. Click on **View Records** for **Probate Record Collection**.

Study the results

3 The list of results show that there have been some matches in Suffolk. If you click on that row, it expands into a drop-down list. There are three sets of records. The first two end at the year 1700, and so are of no interest. The third, however, covers the known date of death. Click on that row and then on **View Results**.

Your ancestor's record is found

4 There are two listings in the Probate Records of the Court of the Archdeacon of Sudbury 1800-1858. Since the second entry is dated as 1803, this could well be your ancestor. To view the record, click on **Image**.

Consulting original records

Once you've made initial discoveries about your ancestors, you may want to see, and even touch, original documents that relate to them. It can be exciting and inspiring to view the proof of their existence.

Record offices and repositories

National archives and libraries hold an extraordinary amount of detail about your family in official government records. Once you've explored your local archives, the next step is to visit national institutions.

It's always worth phoning before you visit to confirm opening hours and to make sure the archive holds the records you require. You will usually need to give proof of identity before being allowed access to files. Charges will be made for photocopying.

The National Archives

Based at Kew in southwest London, The National Archives (TNA) – formerly known as the Public Record Office – is the central archive for England, Wales and the UK Government (see page 32).

Its records exist in different formats. There are original paper and parchment documents, microfilm and microfiche copies, and digital scanned images. Viewing any of these can give you detailed insights into your family's past.

If, for example, your ancestor was a railway worker, or applied for naturalisation as a British subject, or was transported to Australia as a convict, or spent time in one of London's debtors' prisons, you should be able to find out more from the archives. There's also a wealth of material on the

Information is power *The National Archives at Kew holds the more than 900-year-old story of the nation and its people, from the Domesday Book to the present day.*

Metropolitan Police, Army, Royal Air Force, Royal Navy and Merchant Navy, Coastguard and railway company records – most of whose records include service histories.

Catalogue reference codes

Each document held at TNA has a unique reference code which you'll need if you want to order it. The first part of the reference always refers to the government department responsible for the record. So 'HO' stands for Home Office and 'WO' for War Office.

Finding a document

The National Archives Catalogue provides online descriptions of more than 10 million documents that you can search for by keyword, such as a surname or place name. You can narrow the search by year range and

What's available online?

Among the records now available online are First World War British Prisoner of War interviews, Victorian Prisoners' photographs, Death Duty registers, First World War Campaign Medals, Second World War Seamen's Medals and Alien Registration Cards – and the scope is increasing.

To see what else has been digitised, go to the National Archives homepage at **nationalarchives.gov.uk**. Click on **Records** at the top of the page and on the page that appears choose **DocumentsOnline** under **Quick links**. If you find what you're looking for, you can download it for a small fee, or view it free of charge if you choose to visit TNA.

by departmental code – such as HO for Home Office records. The results list will give you a brief description of the document's content, the covering dates for each record and the catalogue reference code.

Making a visit to TNA

If you can't find a document online, you'll need to go through the paper catalogues at TNA. But if you've found a document that you'd like to view, you can place an order for it, in advance of your visit, by clicking on the **About us** tab on the homepage, then **Visit us**, then **Before you visit** and then on **Ordering documents in advance**. Once you're at TNA, you register for a reader's ticket, which allows you to use the reading rooms and order more documents.

You can order up to six documents – for which you'll need to have found reference numbers – online or over the phone.

Searching for records in Scotland

Scotland has its own national archives, which holds government records stretching back 800 years, quite separate from birth, marriage and death registers of the General Register Office for Scotland.

Strange though it may seem, it's always much easier to find ancestors who fell foul of the law. So if you know that one of your Scottish ancestors was a thief or a bigamist, you're likely to find him recorded in the National Archives of Scotland (NAS). You'll also find lighthouse keepers, coal miners, Catholics and canal workers among the esoteric collections on its website at **nas.gov.uk**.

Like England, Ireland and Wales, Scotland has a local record office for each county or shire, with the main repository – the National Archives of Scotland – based in Edinburgh (see Directory). It holds Scottish government records going back as far as the 12th century, along with a variety of records deposited by businesses, landed estates, families, courts, churches and other institutions. At present the NAS doesn't duplicate any of the information held at the General Register Office for Scotland (GROS) – so you won't find any civil registers of births, marriages and deaths, Old Parish Registers of the Church of Scotland or census returns (see right) among its archives. The two merged in April 2011 to become the National Records of Scotland (NRS), and in due course an NRS website will be created.

Most of the NAS records have been indexed and can be searched using its online public catalogue – see right. This database searches by keyword, surname, place name, date and reference number (if you happen to know it). So if you suspect that one of your Scottish forebears may have come into contact with the Scottish government at some time, you may find them with a search here. Getting to the point where you can begin to find relevant information is quite a long-winded process, but it's worth persevering.

There's a knack to searching this collection, as the records aren't catalogued under the most obvious headings. If you enter 'Highland Clearances' into the search engine, for example, you'd get few results. But if you put in names, dates or places that were relevant to the event, you'll get what you're looking for.

Pride of Scotland *The declaration of Scotland's independent status was drawn up at Arbroath Abbey (left) in 1320 – a copy is held in the NAS.*

Other archives that hold Scottish records

- The most important resource for researching Scottish ancestry is the General Register Office for Scotland, **scotlandspeople.gov.uk**, which holds birth, death and marriage registers, and census returns (see pages 96-99).

- Many of Scotland's local authorities, universities, health boards and other corporate bodies have historical records and maintain archive services. The Scottish Archive Network

(SCAN), at **scan.org.uk**, is compiling a unified online catalogue to many of these records – including those held by the National Archives of Scotland.

- The National Library of Scotland (NLS), **nls.uk**, in Edinburgh, holds UK legal deposits (a copy of every British and Irish publication), as well as collections of manuscripts, maps and Scottish newspapers.

- Some historical documents for Scotland are held at The National Archives (TNA) in Kew (see page 163), at **nationalarchives.gov.uk**. They include military service records after the union of Scotland and England in 1707, ships' passenger lists from 1890 and records of immigration to the UK. Using the keyword **Scotland** will reveal hundreds of documents that may be relevant; knowing a date will narrow down your search.

The NAS online public catalogue

1 To reach the online collection's homepage, go to **nas.gov.uk/onlineCatalogue**. Click on the **Search** tab at the top of the screen.

Enter your details

2 To do a search for a MacPherson ancestor who was a petty criminal in the 19th century, enter the name in the **Search for** box. You can also search a specific date range – in this example, enter '1840' in the **Dates from** box, and '1854' in the **Dates to** box. Then click on **Search**. (You can introduce additional criteria by clicking on the **Advanced search** tab in the menu bar at the top of the screen.)

Narrow down the results

3 On the page that appears you will see that a search for your relative has yielded well over a hundred matching records. To narrow these down, you can use add further selection data by clicking on **Refine search**. To see the individual records, click on the **Display Catalogue results** button. From the list that appears (see above) you will see that a number of MacPhersons fell foul of the law between your selected dates.

Record offices and repositories
Ireland, Northern Ireland and Wales

If your ancestors were transported from Ireland to Australia, or signed the Ulster Covenant opposing home rule for Ireland in September 1912, or were buried in a Welsh churchyard, you're likely to find the event recorded in the relevant country's national archive. They'll probably be there even if their lives were quietly unremarkable.

Keeping the records *A country's national library is the guardian of its history – accessible and invaluable to the lay person and specialist alike.*

Searching the record offices in these three areas can be very rewarding once you know how to go about it. Here's an overview of what you can expect to find.

Republic of Ireland archives

The National Archives of the Republic of Ireland, in Dublin, holds official records for the whole of Ireland as well as records relevant to Irish genealogy and local history. The archive is in the process of digitising the 1901 and 1911 Irish censuses, and has an informative website, **nationalarchives.ie**. Online indexes to the archive's collections are held in 24 searchable databases, so you can visit the archive armed with a list of references you'd like to look up. The Ireland-Australia Transportation database – which lists Irish convicts transported to Australia between 1780 and 1868 – is an especially valuable resource. You'll find more about emigration to Australia on page 254.

Northern Ireland explored

Documents relating to Northern Ireland's history are held at the Public Record Office of Northern Ireland (PRONI) in Belfast. The PRONI site, **proni.gov.uk**, is well worth persevering with as it does contain much

valuable information. You can explore what the site has to offer by clicking on the links on the home page. The **Search the archives** link takes you to a page that explains what can be accessed online.

Click on **Research and records held** and the links revealed on the expanded list provide useful insights into what can be discovered. Click on **Introductions to significant privately deposited archives** to see an A-Z list of people and organisations that have deposited papers in the archives, for instance. Another useful link on the home page is **Family History**. Clicking on this reveals many useful links and at the bottom of the page is the link **Some of PRONI's guides and indexes are also available online**, which takes you to a page detailing online guides and indexes.

A record of Wales

The National Library of Wales (NLW), also known as Llyfrgell Genedlaethol Cymru, based in Aberystwyth, is the main Welsh archive. You can browse its website, **llgc.org.uk**, in Welsh or English – choose a language when you start using the site. Its electronic records are free to view online. From the website you can search the NLW collections by clicking on the **Catalogues** link under **Quicklinks** at the left of the home page. The Quick Links that appear on this page are well worth exploring, especially the **Crime and Punishment database** and **Wills Online**. Meanwhile, clicking on **Library Catalogues** takes you to a page with a link to **The Full Catalogue**. When this is clicked you are taken to a search page where you can search for books, periodicals, newspapers, electronic publications, maps, graphics and digitised records. Eventually, all of the library's

collections will be searched for from this catalogue, but until then there is a link on the Full Catalogue search page that takes you to ISYS:web, where material not on the main catalogue can be searched for.

Under **Catalogues** and below **Library Catalogues** is a link to **Electronic Resources**. If you click on the link you'll be taken to a list of links. For family research, you'll find the one of the most useful of these is **Digital Mirror**, which gives quick acccess to a range of useful collections. Another is

the **Marriage bonds** search engine, where you may find an ancestor's marriage, if he applied for a marriage licence between 1616 and 1837.

Look also for the **National Screen and Sound Archive of Wales** (under **Quick Links** on the Catalogues and Electronic Resources page), which holds information about the television and radio programmes recorded by the Archive over the past 20 years. It also holds a cross-section of the Archive's extensive film collection.

Starting a search in Northern Ireland

1 The **proni.gov.uk** site lists the records that are available online. On the home page, click **Search the archives** in the left column, followed by **Will calendars** from the expanded list. Now click on **Search the Will Calendars**. To search for the will of Martin Adams of Drumaroan, County Antrim, farmer, who died in 1910, enter his name and year of death and click on **Search**.

Read the results

2 The results page shows only one entry, listing the probate of the will of Martin Adams of Drumaroan, who died on May 14, 1910. To see further information about the will click on the **Details** button.

Find the will

3 You can see from the full abstract that Martin Adams left effects to the value of £2,006, 6 shillings and 1 penny, and they were granted to John Adams, farmer – most likely his son.

Using online catalogues to explore the archives

Being able to search an archive's catalogue online not only helps you to decide whether a visit to that archive will be worthwhile, but speeds up your search when you get there. This type of preparation pays dividends.

There's a vast array of archives in the UK, many of which may contain useful information about your family and the areas of research that interest you. In the past, as cataloguing techniques varied from one archive to another, you'd have needed an experienced archivist to decipher the index and find material on your behalf. Now, many archives have begun to upload their catalogues into online databases, with searchable indexes, making the catalogues easy for the first-time family researcher to use. The development of integrated online catalogues, where archives across the UK have compiled their indexes onto one database, means that you can locate documents in archives that you may not have considered visiting. Links from one catalogue to other search engines broadens your scope.

Search by corporate name

1 If you had a relative who worked for Boots Pharmaceuticals in the past, you can try to track down their work record. You need to start by finding out if Boots has a company archive and what kind of records it might hold. Go to **nationalarchives.gov.uk/nra**. From the homepage, select **Corporate name** from the list of possible search options.

Find the company

2 Because Boots is a well-known name, start off with a Simple search by entering 'Boots' in the **Name** field and clicking on **Search**.

Read the results

3 There are two results for the Boots company, one for 'Boots Co. Ltd. pharmaceuticals, manufacturers and retailers', and one for 'Boots The Chemist, chemists'. The number in brackets next to the company name indicates how many records have been found for each business, but neither tells you where the archives are held. Click on each company name to see a description of the records and their location.

Archives across the nation

In 1869 the Royal Commission on Historical Manuscripts was formed to produce surveys of British historical records held in private collections, known as the Reports and Calendars. So much material was collected that it was necessary to create the National Register of Archives (NRA) as a means of maintaining catalogues and indexes. Since 1995, the NRA has been available online, at **nationalarchives.gov.uk/nra**, and it updates its collections and provides links to electronic catalogues. The NRA now holds indexes to more than 44,000 unpublished lists and catalogues for archives, both in the UK and overseas, and contains information about the historical records kept by around 46,000 individuals, 9,000 families, 29,000 businesses and 75,000 organisations. There is a printed copy of the NRA catalogue available for consultation in the reading rooms at The National Archives (TNA) in Kew, which has been indexed under five headings: Business, Organisations, Personal, Diaries and Papers, and Family and Estates. The online database has put them into four types of search engine:

Life at work A big company such as Boots will often have archives where an ancestor might appear. Jesse Boot, who founded the business in 1849, was a generous donor to his home town of Nottingham, giving a large area of land (above) to its University College.

Company archives are found

4 If you clicked the link to **Boots Co. Ltd. pharmaceuticals, manufacturers and retailers**, the first of the 17 records reveals that this repository holds corporate records, staff records and photographs. Click on the link to that repository, and you'll be supplied with an address, phone number and map showing the location of the company archive. You can now contact the archive and arrange a visit to see if you can find out more about your ancestor.

CORPORATE NAME You can search the Business and Organisations indexes (see left) using a 'Simple search', which only requires a name or keyword from the organisation's title. Alternatively, you can conduct an 'Advanced search' of either index. The advanced search for businesses allows you to specify a sector, town, county and date. The advanced search for organisations can restrict the results by category, town, county and date. You can also browse an A to Z of both the Business and Organisations indexes.

PERSONAL NAME Here, the search engine combines the Personal index and the Diaries and Papers index. Only a name or description of the papers you're looking for is needed for a 'Simple search'. You can also search the Personal index using an 'Advanced search', which restricts the search by name and description, gender and date. There's also a link to an alphabetical list of the combined Personal index and Diaries and Papers index.

FAMILY NAME To search the Family and Estates index, you can do a 'Simple search' with just a surname. An 'Advanced search' lets you enter a name, the family's seat, a county, country and date. There's also an alphabetical list of the Family and Estates index that you can browse.

PLACE NAME All five indexes are combined in this search engine, which you can search by town and county to see what archives are held for a business, organisation, individual or family from a specific area, and what diaries or papers are relevant to that place.

Finding the archives a2a.org.uk

For a good guide to where records are held, use Access to Archives (a2a), which provides online catalogues of many local archives in England and Wales, some dating right back to the 8th century. Not every archive is catalogued, but new ones are added all the time.

Like the National Register of Archives (see page 168), a2a is a database only. That means it provides catalogued descriptions of documents held in local record offices, archives, museums, universities and libraries around England and Wales – and tells you how to access them. It doesn't contain full transcriptions of documents or digital copies of manuscripts or historical records, but at least you'll know where to start looking.

The database includes descriptions of about 10 million records from more than 400 repositories. You'll be able to search them by keyword, repository, area and date range.

Using the search engine

The **Keyword** search on the main search page (see below) is usually the best way to find documents relevant to your research. But if you'd rather search for a specific archive's catalogues, you can select that archive from the **Location of archives** list on the same page and leave all other fields blank. To ensure the widest range of results, set the **Dates of archives** to look for records added since June 2001. As with most search engines, the more detail you enter, the more specific the results.

Working underground *A 'putter' puts his weight behind a steel tub. He's watched by an overseer at Fourstones Colliery near Hersham in the 1920s. A putter's job was to push the coal to where it could be hauled to the surface by machine or horse.*

Access to Archives
Part of the UK archives network

Quick search	Advanced search	Search result

Find results (enter keyword(s) in **one** or **more** of the search boxes)

all these words
`mining elsecar`

Date range
from
[ ] (dd/mm/yyyy **or** yyyy)

one or more of these words
[ ]

to
[ ] (dd/mm/yyyy **or** yyyy)

this exact wording or phrase
[ ]

Place
[ ]

Repository
[Select Repository]

Region
[Yorkshire Region]

[Search]

Start a new search

Enter your keywords

1 To find the mining records of Elsecar in Yorkshire, click on **Advanced search** on the homepage. Enter 'mining' and 'elsecar' in the box headed **all these words**. Choose **Yorkshire Region** from the **Region** drop-down list. Leave the date range blank. Then click on **Search**.

ARCHON – the local archives directory

You'll find links on some websites to the ARCHON Directory, at **nationalarchives.gov.uk/archon/**, part of The National Archives website. It holds contact details of vast numbers of local archives in the UK, the Republic of Ireland, the Channel Islands and the Isle of Man. It also offers an index of foreign record repositories. You can search the ARCHON Directory in a number of ways, including by county, by A to Z index and by keyword through the **Search ARCHON Directory** facility.

The site offers an extensive list of FAQs that detail:

- what is on the website
- what records The National Archives holds
- what can be viewed online, how to do it and what it costs
- ordering copies of records
- who can help with research (you can pay for TNA researchers or independent researchers)
- what to do if you want to visit in person (including ordering documents online)
- making use of online services such as RSS news feeds (web pages that update you with what's new on their site)

There is a vast collection of online documents available including records listing British International Brigade volunteers who fought in the Spanish Civil War, service record cards for officers' serving in the Royal Navy, RNR, RNVR and WRNS, wills and air combat reports. See pages 158 and 225 for more information on the ARCHON Directory.

Examine the matches

2 The search produces ten matches. Each entry on the list indicates where the archive is stored, its name, the date range covered by that catalogue, and a link to the 'hits' found. On the right of the screen, in the grey box, you can see the archives in which the records are kept. Click on the title of the top heading in the main list: **John Goodchild Collection: Coal Mines Inspection Manuscripts.**

What's held in the archives

3 You can now view the manuscript. If you click on the name of the collection (in the row headed **Held by**) you can view the ARCHON Directory details for that archive.

Getting the archive details

4 On the ARCHON Directory page you will be able to find its postal address and phone number, website, access information and a link to an online street map.

Finding and using libraries

When you're trying to flesh out the picture you have of your ancestors, a local library's records can prove invaluable. You'll be able to read about their trades or professions, as well as discover what local issues affected their lives.

Many libraries hold local archive material, including newspapers, deposited research notes and electoral lists. If your library has a local study centre, it may also hold rare books, trade directories or maps. Library services are usually free of charge.

Most libraries with source material on microfilm or microfiche will supply you with copies, for a fee. Remember that most family history material can't be borrowed – it's for reference use on library premises only. But there's likely to be a photocopier, so you should be able to buy copies of anything that you find useful for your research.

● When visiting a library for the first time, contact it in advance to confirm what it holds and when it's open.

● Check whether you'll need proof of identity.

● If a library offers a booking service, book a microfilm or microfiche reader, or a computer terminal, before your visit.

● Plan your research beforehand by reading the guide you'll find under **Visit us** at **nationalarchives.gov.uk**.

Valuable resource Local libraries provide a wealth of information for researchers. If you want to look further afield, Cyndi's List provides a comprehensive alphabetical list of libraries in Britain and worldwide at cyndislist.com/libraries

Using the Mormon researches

You may live within reach of one of the more than 100 or so Family History Centres of the Church of Jesus Christ of Latter-day Saints (LDS – the Mormons) spread across the UK and Ireland. If so, it would be worthwhile visiting the centre to see what research resources it has. There's information about the organisation and its holdings on page 54, and on page 138 you'll see how to use its website. To search for the Family History Centre nearest to you, see page 137.

Getting help with your research from major libraries

The contact addresses for these libraries are given in the Directory and on their websites.

☛ **The British Library** Known as 'the world's library', this extraordinary facility holds more than 13 million books, manuscripts, journals and newspapers. It's based in London and its website is **bl.uk**.

☛ **The National Library of Scotland** Preserving the history and culture of Scotland is the main aim of the library, which holds a large collection of rare books and manuscripts. The library is in Edinburgh and its web address is **nls.uk**.

☛ **The National Library of Wales** Material specific to Welsh history is held here, including photographs, manuscripts and films. Based in Aberystwyth, its website is **llgc.org.uk**.

☛ **National Library of Ireland** Based in Dublin, the library holds microfilm collections of Roman Catholic parish registers up to 1880, as well as Gaelic manuscripts and estate records. There's a good online catalogue at **nli.ie**.

☛ **Manx National Heritage Library** The library archives contain manorial records, maps and plans. The library is in Douglas and its web address is **gov.im/mnh**.

☛ **Catholic National Library** Mission registers with details of baptisms, confirmations, marriages and deaths dating back to 1694 are held in London. The website is **catholic-library.org.uk**.

A haven for family historians

The Society of Genealogists (SOG) is a charitable organisation that encourages the study of genealogy. Its library holds family trees, pedigrees and research notes deposited by other researchers, and a wealth of records from county sources, including indexes and transcripts of parish registers. It also has poll books, directories, local histories, the International Genealogical Index (IGI) on CD, Scottish civil registration indexes, Boyd's Marriage Index for 2,600 parish registers, and some overseas records   particularly for the British empire.

The Society's library in London (see Directory) charges visitors £4 for an hour's use of its facilities, or £18 for a full day. Alternatively, annual membership costs £43 plus an initial £10 joining fee.

You can search the collections through the SOG's online catalogue. Go to **sog.org.uk** and click on **Use the Library Catalogue** in the bar at the top of the homepage. Then follow the website's instructions. It's wise to consult 'Sogcat' to make sure the library has what you're looking for, before making the trip to London. The library's collections are arranged by title in alphabetical order, so just enter the beginning of a phrase when you search. It will then take you to the point in the list nearest to the first few letters of the phrase you've entered.

Click on **Find out about the library** at the top of the homepage, and then **Library index** in the left-hand panel, to see an index of the collections held, including wills, overseas records or surname studies.

Montagu links with Scotland

Edward Douglas Scott Montagu – whose home is Palace House at Beaulieu – inherited the title of Lord Montagu from his father, John. His coat of arms (right) includes the three parts of his surname (below), each representing the family's history. The Scott connection links the family to a distant kinsman, Sir Walter Scott. You can trace your own family's history through reference books available in local or national libraries.

Douglas

Scott

Montagu

SPECTEMUR AGENDO

Family affair *The present Lord Montagu inherited his father's passion for motoring, founding the National Motor Museum at Beaulieu in 1952. He is seen below with his family.*

How to read old handwriting

Don't be put off by old-fashioned writing on original records and old letters. You can decode it, and doing so will be immensely satisfying.

At first glance, the handwriting you'll find in early documents – from parish records to personal letters – can look illegible. But the websites shown below can help you to decipher them. If you're looking at documents dating from before the mid 18th century, they may be written in Latin. Photocopy difficult documents so that you can take them home to work on them, bearing these points in mind:

● Start building up an alphabet of letters from words you can read and use these to decipher more difficult words.

● Some letters were written differently, such as 's', which was written as 'f' or 'ss' which appeared as 'fs'. The letters 'I' and 'J' were regarded as different forms of the same letter. 'U' and 'V' were treated similarly.

● Capitals and punctuation were arbitrary, and apostrophes were used to show where a letter had been missed out.

● Numbers were often written in Roman numerals, in capitals or lower case – I, i or j = 1; V or v = 5; X or x =10; L or l = 50; C or c = 100; D or d = 500; and M or m = 1000.

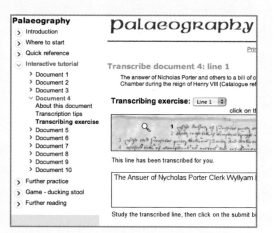

Take an online handwriting tutorial

1 Go to nationalarchives.gov.uk/palaeography/. There is a choice of links. **Where to start** tells how letters were once used and common words abbreviated. **Quick reference** explains the Julian and Gregorian calendars (see opposite), tells you how to read Roman numerals, explains the old monetary system and gives a list of historic counties with abbreviations. Once you've read these sections, click **Interactive tutorial** at the top left of the page.

Learn and practise

2 The interactive tutorial provides ten exercises to work through. To access the text illustrated, click **Document 4**, which takes you to information about the document and some vital transcription tips. When you're ready to have a go, click **Interactive transcribing exercise**. This manuscript has 13 lines. A magnifying glass tool allows you to zoom in and move left or right, and you can fill in your transcription in the box beneath.

Learn more about early documents

The University of Leicester has developed a handwriting website at **paleo.anglo-norman.org**. From the homepage click on the Edward I silver penny for medieval palaeography, the Henry VIII half groat for early modern palaeography. If you select the latter you can view the text shown here by clicking on **Sample text 1** from the options in the left-hand column.

Dating documents using the Julian calendar

We now use the Gregorian calendar, but when you're reading dates in early documents, remember that until 1752 Britain used what was known as the Julian calendar. With this calendar, each new year began on March 25 – Lady Day.

So instead of being the tenth month of the year, October was regarded as the eighth month – and was often written in a combination of Roman numerals and letters to give 'VIIIber'; likewise, December was written 'Xber'.

Adjusting the dates you find

If you're looking at a document from 1728, for example, you'll need to bear in mind that with the Julian calendar, December 31, 1728 was followed by January 1, 1728. The last day of the year fell on March 24, and the new year, 1729, began on March 25. To make things even more complicated, the Scots changed to the Gregorian calendar as early as 1600. And in some indexes, transcribers have already adjusted the dates.

Double dating

If you're studying transcripts of documents and events drawn up before 1752, you may find that dates between January 1 and March 24 have been written covering two years – 'February 15, 1728-9', for example. This means that the date was originally February 15, 1728, according to the old Julian calendar, but would be February 15, 1729, by the Gregorian calendar, which was adopted in 1752.

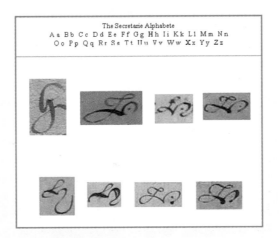

Focus on 1500 to 1700

1 If you fancy an academic challenge, try the online tutorial of 28 lessons that Cambridge University has put together. It concentrates on handwriting from 1500 to 1700. Go to **www.english.cam.ac.uk/ceres/ehoc**. From there, click **historical introduction** to learn about inks, pens and dating manuscripts, or **course lessons** to begin the tutorial. The interactive lessons have difficulty ratings of 1 to 5 and can be 'marked' at the end.

Recognise historic alphabets

2 From the Cambridge University site's homepage click **alphabets**. The modern alphabet is displayed here, and by clicking on any letter, a window will appear showing how the letters used to be written centuries ago. Click the capital **H** to see the images shown here.

Deciphering Scottish handwriting

Scottish documents dating from 1500 to 1750 are interpreted in an online tutorial at **scottishhandwriting.com**, a website created by the Scottish Archives Network (SCAN). From the homepage click **Tutorials** and then work your way through the excellent **1 Hour Basic Tutorial**. When you feel more confident, you can test your knowledge on some 17th-century Scottish court records by clicking on **Glasgow Burgh Court**. Click on **Case 4** to see the manuscript shown here.

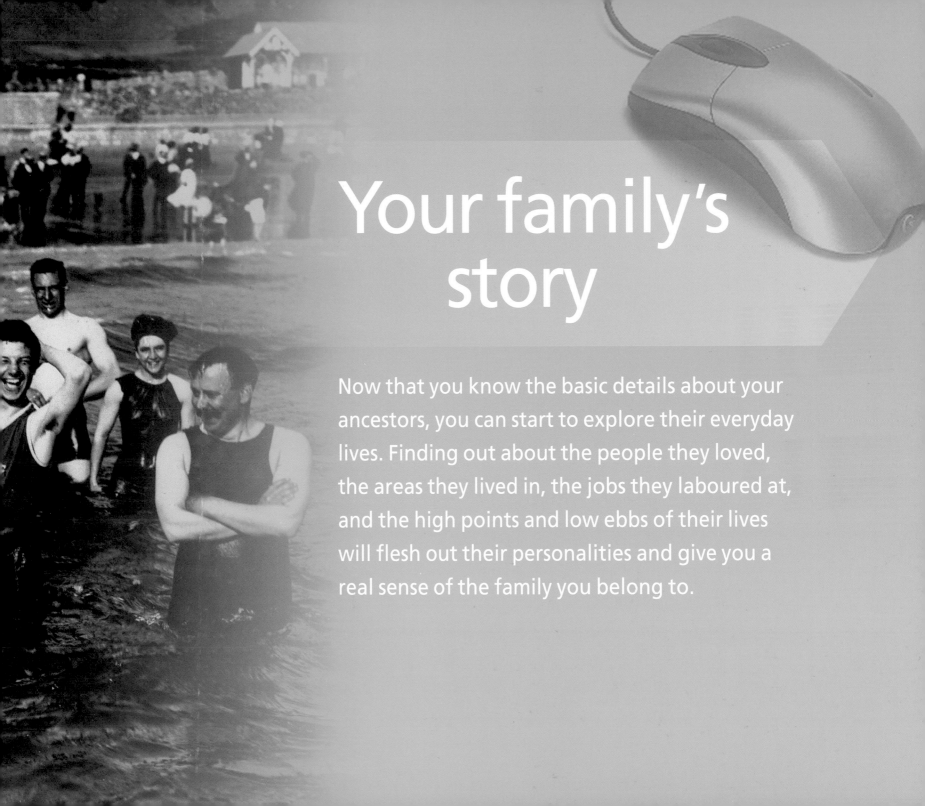

Your family's story

Now that you know the basic details about your ancestors, you can start to explore their everyday lives. Finding out about the people they loved, the areas they lived in, the jobs they laboured at, and the high points and low ebbs of their lives will flesh out their personalities and give you a real sense of the family you belong to.

Real people, not just names

Once you begin to discover more about the lives of your ancestors, they become real people who worked, played and loved, lost and grieved. Only then do the names in your family tree become flesh-and-blood characters.

Finding out more about the daily lives of your ancestors isn't difficult, and you'll find a great deal of help online and in local libraries and archives. You can discover what sort of homes those ancestors lived in, what jobs they did and what was going on in their wider communities. Who was on the throne in their lifetime, and which party was in government? Were they affected by national issues, such as strikes, depressions and even wars?

Where they lived

There are different ways to find out where your ancestors lived, depending on when they were alive. Online censuses from 1841 to 1901 can help, and for 20th-century relatives, you can use civil registration documents (see pages 72-77) and electoral rolls (see page 294).

Until the 20th century, few people owned their homes, most renting in some way or another. In rural areas, people rented houses from wealthy landowners or lords of the

manor. Estate and manorial court records were often deposited in a local library or archive. They can tell you about the transfer of property, the names of occupiers and how much rent they paid. You might also find title deeds, estate maps and surveys.

People also rented from landlords in towns and cities – many wealthy families would leave their country homes to rent in London 'for the season'. You may be able to track down tenancy agreements in local archives. Street and trade directories (see page 230)

were widely published from the 19th century onwards. Similar to modern phone books, the early directories listed people by trade, and later ones covered neighbourhoods on a street-by-street basis. Some of these are available online; others can be viewed at national and local libraries and archives.

The National Archives (TNA) holds a collection of nationwide street and trade directories in its library at Kew. You could also visit libraries and archives in the areas where your ancestors lived. Or go online to **historicaldirectories.org** for details of English and Welsh directories from 1750 to 1919.

What they did for a living

Where you begin your search for an ancestor's work history depends on what he did. Was he in the Navy or the Army,

On the march *Playing their harmonicas, 200 unemployed shipbuilders marched from Jarrow, near Newcastle-upon-Tyne, to London, in 1936. Their protest was sparked off by the closing of Palmer's shipyard, after years of worsening industrial conditions. You can find out more about the whole story when you enter 'Jarrow March' in* **bbc.co.uk**'s *search engine.*

Ancestors in uniform *Men of the Merchant Navy pose formally for a group photo. You can search records at The National Archives for details of your ancestor's service career, the ships he sailed in, as well as when and under what circumstances he left the service.*

Rich discoveries in local libraries

Most local libraries have local studies collections, where you'll find written histories of towns and many villages, with maps of the area, past and present. These give useful clues about the homes of your ancestors, and you may be able to look at historic local postcards and photographs, and copies of old local newspapers.

For example, the Local Studies collection at Leicester library includes:

● information about Leicestershire and Rutland towns and villages

● individual village and town histories arranged in alphabetical order by place name

● a selection of street directories, giving the names of householders and tradesmen in Leicester and Leicestershire in the 19th and 20th centuries.

a tradesman or a master craftsman with apprentices, an agricultural labourer or a doctor? Most military service records are stored at TNA (see page 196). If your ancestor served in the forces, try to find out what his rank was. Army and naval officers were, by and large, educated and wealthy. 'Other ranks' generally came from poorer backgrounds. If they're not in the digitised records at **nationalarchives.gov.uk**, you can view them at TNA, in person.

If your ancestor was in the Metropolitan Police or the Merchant Navy, an employee of HM Customs and Excise or worked for one of the railway companies, his records are probably stored at TNA.

From the 14th century, apprenticeship schemes (see page 186) were common. The Origins site has the largest online collection of apprentice records, and TNA has 18th-century records, though not as yet online.

Other professions are recorded in more specialised places. For example, the Wellcome Library (see page 182) holds records for doctors and surgeons; and records for the Anglican clergy are held at the Lambeth Palace Library at **lambethpalacelibrary.org**.

Did they emigrate?

You may find a branch of your family moved abroad – often, but not always, through choice. The reasons for their departure tell you something about their circumstances. People tended to emigrate voluntarily because they were poor and felt they stood a better chance of success in North America, South Africa, Australia or New Zealand. Or they might have followed their adventurous spirit and indulged a desire to see the world.

Transportation, the other extreme, was the 'humane' alternative to the death penalty for many convicted criminals (see page 254).

Wherever your ancestors ended up, you'll find records to help your research. There are online indexes to a range of Australian archives covering both voluntary immigrants and people who arrived on prison ships.

If you want to find out what 'crime' your ancestor committed, local record offices and TNA hold criminal records and details of transportation. It's believed that 3 per cent of Britons have ancestors who were transported, many for such misdemeanours as fishing in a private river, or setting fire to undergrowth.

Anyone leaving the UK was recorded on ships' passenger lists (see page 255) – now stored in archives in the UK, Canada and Australia. Some are available online and searchable by name at **findmypast.co.uk**; others can be viewed at TNA.

How they lived

Through talent and hard work, our ancestors turned Britain into a world power. Fortunately, many of them left copious records of their lives and achievements.

SINGER'S FACTORY

What did your ancestors do for a living?

Over the centuries people have earned their livings in many ways, some of which might seem strange today. By discovering your ancestors' occupations, you'll get a clear idea of their social class and probable standard of living.

Before the Industrial Revolution, beginning in the late 18th century, most people worked on the land, whether as land-owning farmers, tenant farmers or agricultural labourers. Their occupations might be recorded in tenancy agreements, census returns and sometimes on their gravestones. If you come across a job you've never heard of, you may find it explained online – try **genuki.org.uk** or go to **rmhh.co.uk/occup/a.html**.

Palisters, todmen and telynors

Some job titles are more obvious than others. Most people know what a smith or a collier did for a living, but fewer will recognise a palister as a park keeper, or a wainwright as a wagon-maker. Your Scottish ancestors might have even odder sounding occupations – a chowder sold fish, a fethelar was a fiddle player, a hetheleder gathered and sold heather for fuel, and the todman was responsible for keeping down the tod (Scottish for fox) population on the laird's estate. In Wales, your ancestor might have been described as a bugail (shepherd), crydd (shoemaker), telynor (harpist) or ysgolfeistr (schoolmaster).

Factory life *Vast numbers of people worked in factories such as the Singer sewing machine works in Glasgow (left), where their employment history would have been scrupulously recorded.*

Companies and industry

From the mid 19th century, factories sprang up all over Britain. The irresistible lure of employment triggered a mass migration from the countryside to the towns. Factories offered work for both the skilled and unskilled.

The Singer Manufacturing Company, for example, began making sewing machines in Glasgow in 1867. It soon grew out of its premises and, by 1883, had built the biggest sewing machine factory in the world – with a distinctive clock tower – at Kilbowie on Clydebank, which provided work for 12,000 men and women by the early 1900s. Then, during both the First and Second World Wars the factory produced munitions for the armed forces alongside the sewing machines.

Industries such as this generated a wealth of employment records and many of the documents survive. The National Register of Archives (see page 168) lists the location of records for around 25,000 companies. Access the index at **nationalarchives.gov.uk**.

Working for the government

If your ancestors were government employees – whether in the civil service or the armed forces – it's likely that their employment records are held at The National Archives (TNA), the UK government's official archive. They may even be available online, among TNA's centuries of records from parchment scrolls to digital files and websites. If your ancestors worked in one of the British colonies or for one of the many railway companies that sprang up across Britain in the 19th and 20th centuries, TNA could hold their employment records, too.

Work in town, live in the country

From the mid 19th century the burgeoning railway network enabled people to commute to work in the cities, while continuing to live in the country. In particular, from 1863 the construction of the London Underground network saw the city's suburbs spread rapidly outwards from the commercial centres. So people's work and home life became more separated, making it harder to work out your ancestors' social standing from their homes and the type and place of their employment.

Early commuter chaos *Workers bound for the City crowd Baker Street station, which opened in 1863 on London's first underground line.*

Occupational directories

Over the centuries, many jobs, trades and professions have kept records of the people who worked in them. If you know the occupations of your ancestors, these records can give you an intriguing insight into their lives.

In this section, you'll find out more about where to search for the records of working people, including the clergy, the medical profession, apprentices, industrial workers and rural labour. They'll give you valuable information about what your ancestors did.

Many professional and occupational bodies have excellent records. You can search websites such as **findmypast.co.uk** for some of them (see opposite), but many are available only in local libraries or archives (see below).

Clerical records

Members of the clergy are ordained and allocated to a parish by a bishop, and these appointments are recorded in the bishops' registers. If the ancestor you're looking for was a member of the Anglican clergy, it's likely he was listed in *Crockford's Clerical Directory*. Crockford's was first published in 1858, and is an annual publication that gives biographical details of all members of the clergy, as well as a list of the Anglican parishes throughout the British Isles. For a fee, you can search the website, **www.crockford.org.uk**, although online records go back only to 1968. To find someone registered before 1968, you'll have to view the original directories, which are available in most local libraries.

Another useful clerical website is **theclergydatabase.org.uk**. Although it's not yet complete, this site intends to list all members of the Anglican clergy from 1540

JOHN McCOLL (Small: II, 528), born 1920 30th Sept. 1863 at Glasgow, son of Hugh M. and Janet Roberton; educ. at Glasgow Pollokshields P.S., High School, Univ. of Glasgow, M.A. (1882), U.P. College, Edinburgh; student missionary, Edinburgh John Ker Memorial 1884-5; licen. by U.P. Presb. of Glasgow South 1885; ord. and ind. Paisley Lyles-land U.P. 20th Dec. 1886; trans. to Queenstown Presb. Church, South Africa,

Man of the cloth *Scotland has its own directories, or 'fastis', of clergy and congregations. John McColl (top) appears in* The Fasti of the United Free Church of Scotland: 1900-29. *His entry (above) charts his progress from a childhood in Glasgow to a posting to South Africa in 1910.*

Offline directories

Many occupational directories aren't available online but are accessible in institutions throughout the UK. The addresses for many of them are in the Directory.

Local record offices and archives Local trade directories listing individuals by profession are held, probably in paper form.

Ham's Yearbooks If your ancestor was in either HM Customs or Excise in the late 19th and early 20th centuries, try consulting the yearbooks for these professions. It's possible to trace the career of your ancestor using these sources at The National Archives (TNA).

The Business Archives Council This organisation aims 'to promote the preservation of business records of historical importance',

including records for shipbuilding and brewing. Its library can be used by the public, but an appointment is necessary.

Medical profession Records and directories for medical practitioners may be held at local libraries. Alternatively, the Wellcome Library holds an extensive collection of sources. The library is open to the public and has compiled a detailed guide to its sources that you can download from its website **library.wellcome.ac.uk** to study before you decide to make a visit.

The Law List There are various directories for people who were members of the legal profession. The Law List has been published annually since 1798, and gives details of lawyers in England and Wales. It's usually available in larger reference libraries.

to 1835. Its free-to-use website allows you to search for individuals, locations and bishops, using well-designed drop-down menus, in addition to an A to Z list.

Medical records

The medical profession was divided into three specialist areas until the 19th century: apothecaries, physicians and surgeons. Right up to the late 18th century, they were all regulated by the Church and licensed by its bishops. The issue of each licence was recorded in bishops' registers and held in county record offices. From 1550 to 1875, the details were also held by the Archbishop of Canterbury. Strangely, apothecaries belonged to the Grocers' Company in the Middle Ages, but formed their own society in 1617. Their records are held in the Guildhall Library in London (see Directory).

Midwives also had to be licensed by their bishops and, from 1825 to 1965, their names were published annually by the Royal College of Surgeons.

The *Medical Register*, which lists qualified medical practitioners, was first published in 1859 by the General Medical Council, and *The Roll of the Royal College of Physicians of London, 1518-1825*, was compiled in 1878. The *Medical Directory for Ireland* was first published in 1852. Registration of dentists didn't begin until 1878 – from which time they're listed in the *Dentists' Register*. The British Medical Association Library and the Wellcome Library hold many of the archived records (see Directory).

Select a directory

1 The findmypast.co.co.uk website has a number of searchable occupational directories. In this example we are looking for David Browne, who was a British dentist in the 1920s. Click on the **Search records** tab at the top of the homepage, then choose **Education & work** from the drop-down menu. Scroll down the list to the section headed **Occupations**, and click on **Dental Surgeons Directory 1925**.

Enter the details you know

2 The **Event and year range** will be entered automatically for you, from the previous step. Now enter 'Browne' in the **Last name** box. As Browne can be spelled in more than one way, click on **Include variants**. Now click on the blue **SEARCH** button.

See the entry in the directory

3 In this case, there are two David Brownes. Click on **VIEW** and you'll be offered the chance to see the actual entry in the directory. You'll find that by 1925 the David Browne you want was living and working in Athlone, county Meath, having qualified in 1918. His address is given as Shannon House, which will help you to find him in a local directory. (Note: to view original records you need to buy credits, although searching the index is free of charge.)

The Guildhall – a home to masters of their trades

In the 1420s, London's most famous Lord Mayor, Dick Whittington, set out in his will the foundations of the city's Guildhall. Rooted in the Anglo-Saxon word 'geld', meaning payment, the Guildhall was the place where citizens would come to register their trades when they formed trade associations or 'guilds'. Look in its library for your London ancestors.

The members of merchant guilds, together with the Lord Mayor, effectively ran the City of London and controlled commerce. Each guild had its own hall and coat of arms, but in overall control was the Guildhall, in the heart of the City, where representatives of the guilds met.

The present Guildhall, dating from 1411, now plays a more ceremonial role, used for state and civic banquets, as well as for meetings of the City of London's elected assembly. Its library has many archives that are a great source of information for the family historian. So if you have a craftsman, merchant or trader in your family tree, the Guildhall may have relevant records, and at the least should be able to offer an insight into how they lived and worked.

The importance of guild membership

The earliest guilds were established in the 12th century, in London and other cities such as Bristol and York. Young men entering the trades were given apprenticeships, regulated by local town guilds of merchants and artisans. Once an apprentice became a master of his trade and so a guildsman, he gained certain privileges, such as the right to vote. He could also leave his master and was free to work wherever he wanted, all over the country. Much like the trade unions of today, the guilds looked after the welfare of their members and families. But the great power of the guilds meant that if a tradesman was expelled from his guild, it was almost impossible for him to earn a living elsewhere.

All trades *The earliest reference to a guildhall in London dates from 1128. The hall has long been the centre of trade life for many London livery companies such as the Gardeners (see inset).*

London's ancient guilds

The earliest London guilds, such as the Weavers and the Drapers, are, unsurprisingly, related to ancient crafts or trades. The number of guilds grew as trades such as butchers and goldsmiths became more organised. The Ancient Guild of Apothecaries, for instance, was founded in 1617 but dates back to 1180, when it was linked with the Guild of Pepperers and, from 1316, with the Guild of Spicers, who joined in 1316. The word 'apothecary' comes from the Latin *apotheca* – meaning a storehouse, often for wines, spices and herbs. By the 16th century, the guild was more concerned with medical supplies, rather like the pharmacy of today, and also offered general medical advice and services such as minor surgery.

The Guildhall Library has extensive records relating to the Apothecaries and many other London guilds. It holds, for example, the library and all historic records of the Clockmakers' Company, founded in 1631, including details of 18th and 19th-century apprenticeships.

The special identity of the companies

Each London guild adopted a distinctive style of dress – or livery – to set them apart from each other, and so became known as livery companies. By the early 19th century there were more than 70 companies, each with its own patron saint. St Dunstan, for instance, was adopted by jewellers, locksmiths and armourers, St Boniface protected brewers and tailors, and St Matthew took care of tax-collectors and bankers.

Many of the old livery halls were either destroyed or badly damaged in the Blitz, although some survive, such as the Apothecaries Hall and the Coopers Hall, both

Finest livery *Each year, at the Lord Mayor's Show, guild members parade through the City of London streets dressed in their livery costumes.*

dating from the 17th century. Street names in the City echo the early guilds – Milk Street, Bread Street, Ironmonger Lane, Cloth Fair and Mason's Avenue among them.

Today the City of London has more than 100 livery companies, which include more modern professions such as Environmental Cleaners and Management Consultants; their titles are usually prefaced by the phrase 'The Worshipful Company of...'. Changes in the scale of industry and commercial activity mean that they no longer wield the same political or financial power as they once did, but the companies still work to support and champion their trades, as well as raising money for worthy causes.

Using the Guildhall Library

You'll find many original documents relating to London in the Guildhall Library, ranging from parish registers to records of breweries and football clubs. But its collections aren't just restricted to the capital: it holds many journals from local history societies, as well as county, town and village histories, making it valuable for any family historian. The library's collections are free to use, but you need to register as a reader. The details are all on the website at **cityoflondon.gov.uk**. Although you can't view documents on the site, you can discover what they hold, and the reference numbers you'll need to locate documents when you visit. Go to the homepage, click on **A-Z** in the top bar, select **G** from the drop-down menu and then scroll down to click on **Guildhall.** On Guildhall's main page scroll down and click on **Guildhall library**.

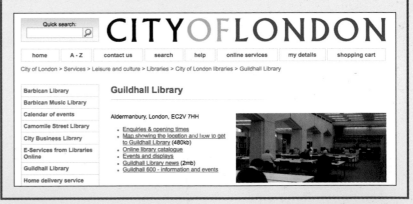

Records of apprenticeships

From the 14th century onwards, apprenticeship was an essential stage in a number of trades and crafts, and copious records were kept. So if your ancestor was apprenticed in his youth, you'll be able to find out what he did.

Apprenticeship was valuable for any young person and had to be paid for, usually by the parents. The young people would be legally bound, for a period of about seven years, to a master from whom they would learn a trade. In 1563, this system was made official by the Statute of Artificers and Apprentices, which stipulated that no one could practise a trade without having first served as an apprentice.

Where to find apprentice records

The National Archives (TNA) has a central register of apprentices, going back as far as 1710. Many apprenticeship records are held in local and county record offices and aren't online yet, so it's a good idea to check what's held in your local archive.

LONDON APPRENTICESHIP ABSTRACTS These records, held by **origins.net**, cover 1442 to 1850 and include apprenticeship records of London's Livery Companies. They name the youth's father and the parish of his residence.

APPRENTICES OF GREAT BRITAIN This database, found at **findmypast.co.uk**, covers the years 1710 to 1774. It has been compiled from the Inland Revenue tax records now held at TNA. It provides similar information to that of the London Apprenticeship Abstracts database, but covers the whole of

Great Britain. You can see digitised images of the originals. On the homepage click on **Search records**, select **Education & work**, then under **Apprentices** click on **Apprentices of Great Britain 1710-1774**.

Unusual professions

Many old professions and occupations have disappeared or changed almost beyond recognition. Coopers (makers of barrels), frobishers (restorers of armour) and mercers (cloth merchants) are just some of the less familiar. If you come across an obscure occupation, a book you'll find helpful is *A Dictionary of Old Trades, Titles and Occupations* by C. Waters, Countryside Books,1999. Or visit **olivetreegenealogy.com/misc/occupations.shtml** and search their list of Obsolete Occupations.

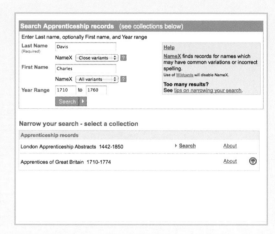

Search apprenticeship records

1 Here's how you'd search for Charles Davis, who was apprenticed between 1700 and 1760. Go to **origins.net**, sign in (see page 55) and click on the **British Origins** tab in the menu bar. Then scroll down the page and click on **London Apprenticeship Abstracts 1442-1850**.

Enter the details you know

2 On the main search page, enter 'Davis' in the **Last Name** box and 'Charles' in the **First Name** box. As it's a fairly common name, it's best to add the date range, 1710 to 1760. Click on the **Search** button.

Irish and Scottish apprenticeships

The completion of an apprenticeship in Ireland qualified you as a freeman. Many such craftsmen and tradesmen are named in the list of free citizens of Dublin from 1225 to 1918, which is held in the Dublin City Archives (see Directory).

Serving out an apprenticeship in Scotland qualified a man to become a burgess in certain chartered cities, giving him voting rights. Records are kept in the National Archives of Scotland (in Burgh records, ref B).

Trainee cobbler *An apprenticeship was a chance to learn a trade with a master. The records show that young people would travel quite a distance to take up an apprenticeship.*

Search results

3 Your search reveals three matches. To look at them click on the **View Records** button. (If the search had yielded a large number of hits, then you could have amended your search parameters by clicking on the **Refine search** button.

View the records

4 The records for the London Apprenticeship Abstracts are shown and the top one on the list looks most likely. Charles Davis was apprenticed to a feltmaker on August 15, 1715.

Widening your search

5 If you were unsure of the exact spelling of ancestor's name or perhaps you thought the surname was something that sounded like 'Davis' and also wanted to widen the date range, then go back to the original search and change the box beneath each name to **All variants** and widen the year range. This produces a much longer list.

Industrial trades and skills

The Industrial Revolution at the beginning of the 19th century completely changed British people's lives and aspirations. Your ancestors may have left their rural homes to work in the new trades that sprang up in towns and cities.

The rise of factory labour meant that more people than ever entered the work force. Records of their employment give rise to information that will prove invaluable to you now. There are some excellent websites with mailing lists that you can visit for information about specific occupations. If you know what your ancestor's job was, one of these occupational websites can give you an insight into how they lived.

The textile industry

If you think your ancestor was a textile worker, **spinningtheweb.org.uk** is a good place to look. Dedicated to the large textile industry of northern England, Spinning the Web gives a thorough history of the cotton manufacture in Lancashire and is divided into different sections, each with a tab at the top of the homepage.

- **Overview** outlines the rise and decline of the industry, divided into chronological periods, from 1760 to the present day.
- **People** analyses the living and working conditions of the many thousands of people employed by the industry, including the use of child labour.
- **Places** describes the environmental and cultural impact of the textile industry.
- **Industry** explains the technical innovation that powered the industry.

- **Clothing & products** shows the industry's products, including clothes and furnishings.
- **Interactives** tells stories related to the cotton industry.

Coalmining

The website of the National Coalmining Museum for England, **ncm.org.uk**, is dedicated to an industry that was one of the country's largest employers in the 19th and 20th centuries. It offers a virtual tour of its museum and provides access to its library catalogue. This fascinating collection includes documents that relate to the history of coalmining, but not the employment records for the miners. Where these survive, they've been deposited with local archives.

Other trades

When researching the kind of work your ancestor may have done, it's useful to visit the following collections. See the Directory for their addresses, or visit their websites.

The People's History Museum

The origins of this museum lie in the Trade Union, Labour and Co-operative Society. It focuses on preserving the history of ordinary working people of Britain and is located in Manchester on two sites. To see its website go to **phm.org.uk**.

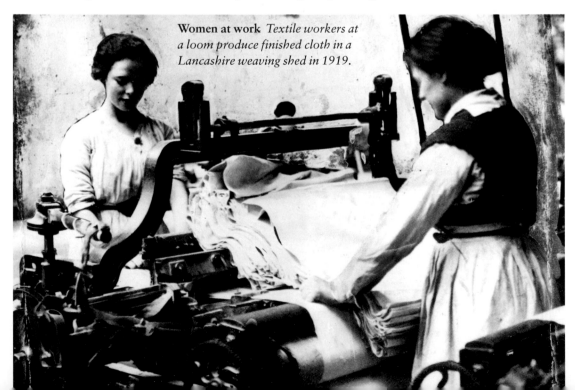

Women at work *Textile workers at a loom produce finished cloth in a Lancashire weaving shed in 1919.*

The Modern Records Centre

The University Library of Warwick hosts **www2.warwick.ac.uk/services/library/mrc**, a free-to-use collection of social, economic and political history archives, mainly from the mid 19th century onwards. For the family historian keen to get into the detail of their ancestor's working lives, these records should prove a rich hunting ground. They include:

• Records of trade unions, which include the archives for the Trade Union Congress (TUC) and similar institutions.

• Records of trade associations, which include archives of the Confederation of British Industry (CBI), employer organisations and related bodies.

THE JOHN RYLAND'S LIBRARY Located in the University of Manchester, the collection holds more than four million printed books and manuscripts. The library has a comprehensive selection of material covering economic and industrial history. This includes archives of the coal industry, the pharmaceutical industry, large mill producers and trade unions, as well as a wide range of other industries.

The website is at **library.manchester.ac.uk**. On the homepage enter 'Economic and industrial history' in the search box at the top right and click on **Go**. On the page of results that appears, look for and click on the link to **Economic and industrial history**. The page that shows up explains what they have. Click on **Resources** in the column on the left for a list of manuscripts and printed matter.

Search the People's History Museum

1 Here's how to do a free online search of the collections. Go to the homepage and click on **Our Collection** in the menu bar, and then **Search our collection**, on the left-hand panel. Say you had an ancestor involved with the radical 19th-century Chartism movement, and you want to know more about it. Enter 'Chartism' into the **Search by keyword** box, and then click on **Search**.

Choose a subject record

2 The results are displayed as a table of 'thumbnail' images, catalogue numbers and object names, looking something like that shown above. The entry you want is a digitised copy of The People's Charter, 1838. Click on the image in the left column to display details of the charter.

See the image and description

3 Information about The People's Charter and its purpose are displayed, as well as a thumbnail image of the charter. Click on the image to view a copy of the original charter.

Life on the land

Not everyone left the country to flock to the new factory jobs on offer in towns. Your farming ancestors may have stayed where their families had always lived and worked the soil. In times of war, this proved invaluable to the nation.

The rich history of Britain's rural life is well documented in museums, art and literature, as well as through cherished collections of old farming tools and well-preserved barns. Ancient building, farming and animal husbandry skills are valued and preserved. These were the stuff of life and survival to your ancestors; the tools and skills they used shaped their lives and attitudes. By visiting the museums, websites and resources listed below, online or in person, you'll gain valuable insights into their daily existence.

The levels of farm worker

Not all rural workers were the same, so it helps to be able to distinguish between them. There was a difference in status between farm servants and farm labourers. A farm servant was employed by the year from about the age of 14, and lived and worked on the farm. A farm labourer was usually a married man, employed on either a regular or casual basis, who lived off the farm, sometimes in a tied cottage that belonged to the landowner.

There were also regional differences in earnings. People working on the land in the north of England had the highest pay because of the competition from industries. The worst-paid farm labourers were found in the southwest counties, such as Somerset.

Rural England captured

The Museum of English Rural Life, at the University of Reading (see Directory), charts the history and importance of England's agricultural life. Entrance is free to the public.

The collections are built from various archives, books, artefacts, photographs and sound and film recordings that have been collected over the years. It's a wonderful resource if you want to research the history of food and farming, and understand how your rural ancestors may have lived. The museum's library contains more than 40,000

Explore the museum *Changing exhibitions mean that there's always something new to discover on the Museum of English Rural Life website, as well as details of the permanent collections.*

different books, pamphlets and journals relating to country life and work. To help you to find what you want, the collection has specific sections on agricultural surveys, the history of British farming, the technology and engineering involved in farming, and conservation.

SEARCHING THE DATABASE You can search the online database of the museum at **reading.ac.uk/merl/**. On the homepage there are links that enable you to explore what the museum has to offer. There is also information for visitors and pages detailing current and future exhibitions, special events and events for the family.

A moment in farming history

Early in the Second World War, Winston Churchill commissioned a survey to find out whether the farms of England and Wales were providing enough food to feed a war-torn nation. The resulting National Farm Survey, completed in 1943, is both an important snapshot of the state of farming during the war and a source of revealing information about your farming ancestors.

The survey tells you about the type and scale of food production on each individual farm (nearly 300,000 of them in total), and includes forms filled out by the farmer and detailed field maps. The records are held in The National Archives (TNA). If you know the name of a farm owned by members of your family at the time, you can learn much about how those ancestors lived and worked the land while the world was at war.

The 'land girls' take over

The Women's Land Army was founded in the First World War to make up the shortfall of male agricultural labour. When war was declared again in 1939, the Land Army was re-established. The women – commonly known as 'land girls' – were recruited from all spheres of life including shops, offices and factories. Many of them had lived all their lives in a city, but by 1943 more than 80,000 women were working on the land. They did a vital job in keeping the country fed during and after the war, often facing prejudice and hostility from farmers and male farm workers.

Although the conditions were often dismal and the pay low, the women had a cheeky 'grin and bear it' attitude that kept their spirits high and earned respect. So many women enjoyed their work on the land that some of them stayed on after the war.

The Land Army was finally disbanded in 1950, and although the service registers don't survive, index cards for the service records do, and are retained by the Imperial War Museum (see Directory, and page 194). You can also view microfiche copies of the cards in person at TNA, although only for the years 1939-45.

Salt of the earth *If you come across a photo of a female relative wearing a headscarf, a jersey and overalls – and looking muddy and cheerful – she was probably a 'land girl'. You might find her records at the Imperial War Museum.*

Did your ancestors fight for their country?

It's likely you'll have ancestors who served in the British Army at some point in history. Searching for their records is much easier when you understand the structure of the army and its regiments.

Before the English Civil Wars (1642-51), an army was raised only when the country faced a specific danger, and it was usually made up of local militia units. Oliver Cromwell created his professional New Model Army in 1644, but the first full-time Army dates from the restoration of Charles II in 1660.

The naming of regiments

Initially, each regiment was named after the colonel that commanded it. Numbering and ranking was introduced in 1694, when the named regiment also acquired a number – for example, the 'Fifth Regiment of Foot'.

By 1751, regiments were no longer known by the name of their colonel, but instead were given a descriptive name. By 1782, this often related to a place or county, but could just as likely reflect a ceremonial link to the sovereign or Royal Family. These descriptions gradually replaced the old regimental numbers so that by 1881 numbering was abolished. Many regiments were merged, and often took the names of the county where they were raised. This means that one regiment might have been known by a number of names over time, so you'll need to investigate fully when looking for a service history of an ancestor.

In addition, there were different types of regiment within the British Army, such as Cavalry, Infantry, Foot Guards and Artillery. Special corps included the Royal Engineers, as well as nursing personnel.

Showcase for the British Army

The National Army Museum in London is dedicated to the army, its regiments and history, and has an online collection of

Joining the regimental ranks *The Royal Fusiliers, painted in 1876 (below), was formed from two companies of the Tower of London Guard.*

records and images that can be accessed via its website at **national-army-museum.ac.uk**. These will help you to identify the correct regiment and understand in more detail the Army's organisation.

The museum itself has a large collection of private, regimental and business papers that tell the story of more than 500 years of regimental history of the British and Commonwealth armies. It also holds information relating to uniforms and medals. The curators of the museum are happy to

answer individual questions, which you'll find helpful if you've come across an old medal or a picture of an ancestor in the course of your research.

Finding regimental museums

Many regimental museums have their own websites. To check if the regiment you're interested in has one, take a look at the Army Museums Ogilby Trust website at **armymuseums.org.uk**. It's a great resource for regimental history, approved by the

Ministry of Defence, which describes itself as the 'definitive guide to the regimental and corps museums of the British Army'. The website's search engine lets you find museums across the UK, either by regiment or location, so you can see if there's a dedicated museum for your ancestor's regiment. It will spell out the location and contact details of any existing regimental museum and provide a brief description of what it holds, along with links to other useful websites that may be pertinent.

Search for a regiment

1 To search for the details of the Duke of Cornwall's Light Infantry, for example, go to armymuseums.org.uk. On the homepage, click on the link for **Museum search** from the tabs along the top.

Choose a regiment

2 You'll be offered a search page that gives you the options of searching the collection or the region, both from drop-down menus. To search for a regiment by name, select one from the list. In this case, select **Duke of Cornwall's Light Infantry museum**. Then click on **Go**.

See the details

3 You're taken to a page which gives you a brief description of the Duke of Cornwall's Light Infantry Museum, what it holds (including, among other treasures, George Washington's Bible, captured in 1777), its opening hours, location and contact details. The page will also point you to the museum's website or email address, if it has them.

Imperial War Museum – serving and surviving

The exhibits and archives at the Imperial War Museum give remarkably vivid insights into what life was like for those who fought for Britain – and the people they left back home. The museum can also help you to identify military memorabilia, such as medals and badges.

War has affected most families in some way over the past 100 years, so a visit to the Imperial War Museum (IWM) in London is enthralling for people interested in their ancestors. As well as the collections of military hardware and memorabilia, there's an ever-changing programme of exhibitions that can cover subjects as diverse as propaganda, the Falklands War and the work of war artists.

The imposing building, fronted by two huge 15 inch naval guns from the First World War, was once the central portion of the old Bethlam Royal Hospital – better known as Bedlam. IWM was founded in 1917 as a tribute to those who fought in the First World War, and today the size and importance of the collections are such that they're spread over several other sites: HMS *Belfast*, moored on the River Thames near Tower Bridge; the Churchill Museum and Cabinet War Rooms, in Whitehall; Duxford in Cambridgeshire, which has a superb aviation collection; and the Daniel Libeskind-designed Imperial War Museum North, in Salford, which opened in 2002.

People caught up in war

The museum's permanent displays cover both World Wars and conflicts since 1945, and include permanent exhibitions on key areas such as the Holocaust and the role of espionage. The many testimonies from people who experienced war at first hand on the battlefield or on the home front make it an important resource if you want to understand more fully what your family went through in wartime.

One example describes a soldier's unforgettable Christmas dinner. Peter Roylance Noakes, who served in 1st Battalion Northamptonshire Regiment in India, Ceylon and Burma, remembers December 25, 1943. He was in the Indian jungle at Dimapur when he received a surprising gift from the Gurkhas. They'd shot a deer and cooked it over an open fire. The soldier had 'never tasted anything like it. Smoked venison if you'd like to call it … a change from bully beef and biscuits'.

To find this and more than 13,000 other records on IWM's documents database, you can use the website (see box, right). The document archive (in the section under IWM Collections) holds letters and diaries, as well as photo albums – with pictures of people or the camps where they were stationed – and identity cards.

It also holds prisoner of war listings, including the Singapore Changi Civilian Internment Camp register, kept until the end of 1942. Here you'll find an internee's full name, age, marital status, occupation, date of internment, and name and address of next of kin.

Identifying medals

If you've unearthed medals that you can't identify, the IWM's display of awards and decorations will help you to identify yours. Shown here is the Victoria Cross awarded posthumously to Boy (1st Class) Jack Cornwell (right) for staying at his post on the cruiser HMS *Chester* during the Battle of Jutland on May 31, 1916. The ship was shelled by four German cruisers and all Cornwell's crewmates were killed.

Keeping the home fires burning

The shortage of men back home, in both World Wars, meant that women took on many jobs that had traditionally been done by men – from running the public transport network to farming and even mining. They also operated machines in factories, including the often dangerous manufacture of munitions. The Women's Work Collection at IWM focuses on the involvement of women in the First World War and includes photographs and letters. It can also be seen online (see below).

Women also had to carry on the role of looking after children unwittingly caught up in the dangers and privations of living on the home front. At IWM a long-term exhibition called The Children's War looks at how war affected children – the excitement and disorientation of evacuation, the terror of blackouts and the joyless experience of rationing. This period is made vividly realistic in the 1940s house – a life-size recreation of a suburban house at the time of the Blitz.

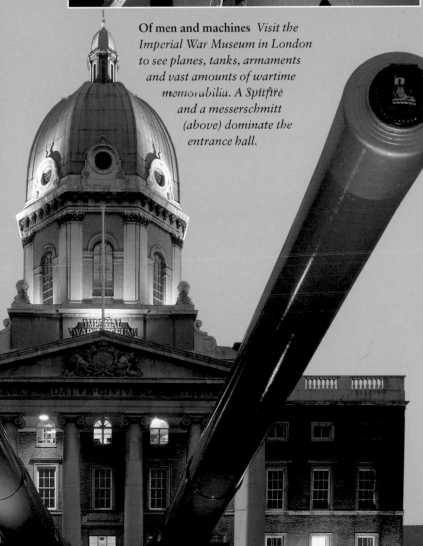

Of men and machines *Visit the Imperial War Museum in London to see planes, tanks, armaments and vast amounts of wartime memorabilia. A Spitfire and a messerschmitt (above) dominate the entrance hall.*

Wartime online

The IWM's website, at **iwm.org.uk**, has a **Family history** page with links to numerous collections, including war graves, rolls of honour, gallantry awards, journals, photos and a section called Women's Work. You can also find advice on how to research your ancestors who may have served in the air force, army, navy or merchant navy, or who were held as prisoners of war. There's a link on the website that takes you to the UK National Inventory of War Memorials, which has the details of the 55,000 war memorials that have been recorded so far. You can also access the site direct at **www.ukniwm.org.uk**.

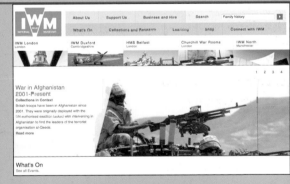

Access to all the other IWM sites, in Whitehall, Duxford and Salford, is through the IWM homepage. The website is both easy to use and free to search and could add immensely to your research into your family history in wartime.

Tracing military records

If you have ancestors who took an active part in either of the World Wars, there should be records that provide details about their service.

The First World War saw the largest ever mobilisation of soldiers in Britain: more than seven million people served in the conflict. Almost everyone who saw service abroad was awarded a campaign medal at the end of the conflict. The National Archives (TNA) has a large set of service records for the Army, some of which are available online. Most online material is from the First World War or earlier. The TNA research guides on army records are worth looking at.

Medal index cards

The index cards for First World War medals have been digitised. You can view and download them at **nationalarchives.gov.uk** under the **DocumentsOnline** section. The cards give the rank, unit and area of operation of each soldier, as well as details about which medal he was entitled to. Because a large number of other service

records were destroyed by enemy bombing in 1940, these cards serve as an effective back-up roll call of all those serving in the First World War. Overall, they consist of more than 5.5 million records.

Searching the index

You can search the medal index free of charge. If you find a document you want to download, there will be a small fee.

To search for a medal index card, go to **nationalarchives.gov.uk/documentsonline/** and click on **Advanced search,** untick **All** categories then tick **WW1 campaign medals.** Enter the name of the soldier, and any other relevant information you might have, before clicking on **Search.**

First World War officers' records

Army personnel records are organised under commissioned officers and non-commissioned officers/other ranks, so TNA has divided its records on this basis, too. The main officer service files were among those destroyed in 1940, but supplementary 'correspondence files' were also created and they survived. These files are catalogued by surname and the

---

First World War pension records online
The National Archives, working in partnership with **ancestry.co.uk**, has begun to put online all the First World War pension records that are found in TNA series WO364.

Ancestry is a subscription-based website but once you've registered, the index for the records can be searched free of charge. If you want to view the actual record, you'll have to subscribe first (see page 50).

On parade *Lord Kitchener reviews troops lined up for inspection at the beginning of the First World War. By January 1915, more than a million men had enlisted in the British Army.*

first initial of each officer, and you can search them by name. They're held in TNA series WO339 (the majority of files for the regular Army and emergency reserve) and WO374 (most of the files for the Territorial Force).

To search for an officer's file, click on **The Catalogue** under **Quick link**s on the **nationalarchives.gov.uk** homepage. Now click on **Search the Catalogue** and enter the name of the officer in the **Word or phrase** box. Also enter the series you wish to search, in this case WO339 or WO374. Click on the **Search** button. Each result will have a catalogue number, starting with WO, which stands for War Office.

Other ranks before 1914

TNA also retains the surviving service records for other ranks that joined the army, prior to the First World War. They're found in the series WO97, and cover the years from 1760 to 1913. Records kept before 1883 have survived, but only for soldiers who were discharged to pension (commonly known as 'Chelsea pensioners').

It was only after 1883 that service records for almost every serving soldier were kept in a systematic fashion. The surviving records contain attestation and discharge papers and often give the soldier's place of birth, age and next of kin – which is very useful extra information if you're not sure of his connection to your family.

The earliest sets of records in WO97, covering the years 1760 to 1854, have been individually catalogued. It's possible to carry out a name search for a soldier discharged to pension between those years, on TNA's

Catalogue. Just navigate to **the Catalogue**, click on **Search the Catalogue** and enter the name of the soldier you're researching. Then put WO97 in the box for **Department or Series code**. Enter a **Year range** of 1760 to 1854 to limit the search. Each result gives the parish of birth and the regiment of the soldier which, along with his full name and age, should be enough information to confirm that you have found the correct record. If you'd not already found your ancestor's parish of birth, this is doubly useful.

Army personnel after 1922

Service records for army personnel who remained with the army after 1922, or who joined after that date, are still held by the Ministry of Defence in Glasgow and aren't available online.

For a fee, the Ministry of Defence will search for the service record of your ancestor, and provide you with the information you want. You'll need to contact the Army Personnel Centre; the address is shown in the Directory.

Search for a campaign medal

1 To search for the medals awarded to an ancestor, Matthew Jackson, go to **nationalarchives.gov.uk/documentsonline** and click on **Advanced search**. Fill in his first and last names. If you know his service number, enter it in **Other keywords**. The **All categories** box is automatically ticked; "untick" it, and then tick only the box labelled **WW1 Campaign Medals**. Click on **Search**. The more details you enter, the more successful your search will be.

View the details

2 Without the service number, 37 results would have appeared. But with the service number entered, the correct card appears. Click on the **+Add to shopping** button and follow the appropriate steps to download and view an image of the card.

Finding sailors and airmen

Britain has a long seafaring history, and many of your ancestors may have served their country in the Royal Navy. The Royal Air Force is much younger, but it has its records, too, and serving ancestors are traceable.

Few centralised records of seamen were kept before 1853, and if you're trying to track down an ancestor from this period you'll need to know the name of at least one ship on which he served and some details of his life.

For example, did he go to sea as a cabin boy or did he join as an adult? Did he have officer training or was he an unskilled, unwilling conscript? The National Archives (TNA) is the place to start. Most naval records have

the prefix ADM (for Admiralty) followed by a particular code (see opposite). When using the indexes, note whether the service number ends with the letter A or B, or has no letter at all. This will tell you which register you need to order. It's sometimes given at the top of the index page as Series A or Series B.

Naval service before 1853

Until the introduction of continuous service in 1853, men often moved between naval and merchant ships, which makes tracing them

Start your search

1 To search for the naval records of an ancestor, a Jonathan Jones of Lancashire, go to **nationalarchives.gov.uk/documentsonline** and click on **Advanced search**. Fill in his first and last names. The **All categories** box is automatically ticked; untick it, and then tick only the box labelled **Registers of Seamen's Services** and then on **Search**.

First results

2 Jonathan Jones was born in Lancashire, so the correct record is the first one, with the catalogue reference ADM188/1120. You can view the document by either visiting The National Archives in person, or getting a copy of the record. To obtain a copy of the file click on **See details**.

Buy a copy

3 Jonathan Jones's full record will be displayed and you'll see that a copy will cost you £3.50. Click on the **+Add to shopping** button on the page and then click on **Checkout**. Follow the instructions to pay for and download the document.

Ancestors in the RAF

The Royal Air Force was formed in 1918 as an amalgamation of the Army's Royal Flying Corps (RFC) and the Navy's Royal Naval Air Service (RNAS). If your ancestor served in the Royal Air Force before the mid 1920s, you'll be able to search the records on TNA's website. Enter **nationalarchives.gov.uk/documentsonline** and click on **Air Force**. You can then choose from **Officers (AIR76)**, **Women's Royal Air Force (AIR80)** and other categories. Each of these sections is divided by date and whether people were in the RFC or RNAS. Some information is available online, but full details can only be accessed by visiting TNA. Each category not only enables you to search for an individual's records but also contains a number of extremely useful research guides, for example, *Air Records As Sources For Biography And Family History, Information Leaflet 13*.

The RAF records of airmen who served after the mid 1920s are held by the Ministry of Defence (MOD). The MOD will release information to the next of kin for a fee.

The records held by the MOD include details of everyone who served in the RAF, such as these men (right), seen re-arming a Spitfire in 1940.

difficult. Most ships had muster rolls, listing the men on board. To find an ancestor, start with the muster roll and pay books of individual ships (you need to know the name of at least one ship he served on, and a rough date). The muster roll shows where he was before and after his service on that ship.

From 1764 onwards, a muster often provides a man's age and place of birth. From about 1800, description books (which give age, height, complexion, scars and tattoos) may be included with musters. Where a muster is missing, you can use the ships' pay books to confirm that a man served on a particular ship. To trace a muster roll, go to **nationalarchives.gov.uk/records**, click on **Looking for a person?** and then scroll down to **Royal Navy ratings before 1853**. Here you'll find the series numbers you need.

If you think your ancestor may have fought in the Battle of Trafalgar on October 21, 1805, go to **nationalarchives.gov.uk/trafalgarancestors**. This fascinating database can be searched by surname, and also by first name, age on October 21, 1805, birthplace, ship's name, rating and rank.

Naval service 1853-72

From 1853 onwards, seamen joining the navy were given a Continuous Service Engagement, or CS, number. The Continuous Service Engagement Books are held in ADM139; the books list the CS numbers and their holders' date and place of birth, physical features on entry and a service summary.

Naval service 1873-1923

TNA holds records for those who joined the Royal Navy as regular servicemen between 1873 and 1923 in the Registers of Seamen's Services (ADM188). Service details are recorded up to 1928. Here, you should be able to find your ancestor's year and place of birth, period of service, and on which ship or ships he served. Records of those serving from 1892 onwards also contain details on occupation, physical appearance, wounds received, and notes on character and abilities. Records for those who joined after 1923 are not yet open to the public. If your ancestor was in the navy between 1928 and 1938, see the Directory (under Ministry of Defence) for a contact address for further information.

Other sources of information

Sailors who applied for a navy pension gave details of which ships they served on and for how long. Certificates of Service were then compiled and sent to the Admiralty. They are now held in ADM29. To find an ancestor, go to **the Catalogue** on the TNA homepage. Type in the name and put ADM29 in the last box.

Certificates recording the admission of seamen's children into the school known as the Royal Naval Asylum at Greenwich are in ADM73 and are another valuable resource.

Looking for world war heroes

Most families had to make sacrifices in the two World Wars, and many paid the ultimate price of losing a loved one. The 1.7 million British and Commonwealth men and women who served and died are recorded on the Debt of Honour Register – search it online to reveal the fate of lost relatives.

In your family there may be an uncle, cousin or brother who was alive at the time of the First or Second World Wars but whose fate is a mystery. Or maybe you find a medal or other reminder of conflict bearing a name long forgotten. The poignant and sobering Debt of Honour Register, administered by the Commonwealth War Graves Commission (CWGC) **cwgc.org**, allows you to search for those who died in the two wars and also leads you to the names of the fallen who are buried in more than 23,000 war cemeteries around the world. As well as the military casualties, there are listings for more than 67,000 Commonwealth civilians who died as a result of enemy action during the Second World War. If you're armed with some basic information about a relative, the free CWGC website makes it easy to search for that person, investigate the circumstances of the death, and even find a specific location for a grave.

Using medals to trace relatives

Many servicemen and servicewomen were awarded medals, either for a specific campaign, or to acknowledge their acts of gallantry. Mrs Redmond (right) wears her late husband's impressive array of medals with pride.

● Finding a medal can narrow down your search for an ancestor. Along the edge of the medal is usually inscribed a regimental or service number, which can be used as a cross-reference to the CWGC entries.

● A medal can identify the conflicts in which a relative may have served. For example, the 1914 Star, 1914-15 Star, Victory and British War medals belong to the First World War. The medal card index can be searched online at The National Archives (see page 196 for how to do this). Alternatively, visit **www.london-gazette.co.uk/**, where you can examine the archive of the *London Gazette*, which has the official announcements of all gallantry medals.

Take your search further

Once you've found a relative, you can extend your research. You might want to check at The National Archives for a First World War service record, or investigate the circumstances surrounding the death of a relative by examining the final unit war diary entry. The relevant regimental or service museum may be able to supply additional details. You could also pay your respects in person by using the Debt of Honour Register to find the grave or memorial reference for your relative, and the name of the war cemetery where he lies. The Royal British Legion organises trips to war cemeteries – see **remembrancetravel.com**.

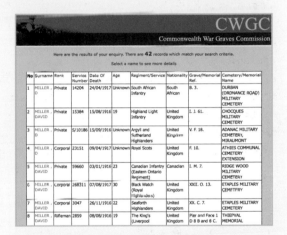

Enter a name

1 To search for the details of a Denis Basil Miller in the CWGC site, go to **cwgc.org** and on the homepage click on **Search our Records**. In the **Search for** box select **Casualty** from the drop-down menu. If you're unsure of the spelling of the surname, type '*' after the name in the **Surname** box. Enter the first initial in the next box to maximise the chances of finding the right person. For example, Denis Basil Miller may be listed only as D. Miller on the database.

Refine the detail

2 In the **War** field, select **First World War** or **Second World War** from the list. If you're unsure, choose **Unknown**. Select dates from the drop-down lists under **Year of death**, if you can, to narrow down the search. Otherwise, select **Unknown**. If you know the branch of the Armed Forces in which your relative served, choose it under **Force**. Select the nationality of the force in which the person served. Click **Submit**.

Read the results

3 Your results appear as a grid, with all the names that match the criteria you entered on the search page. The information is displayed according to the name of the deceased; his rank and service number; his date of death and recorded age, if known; the regiment or service in which he served; his nationality; and the grave or memorial reference followed by the cemetery in which he's buried.

Crime and punishment

If one of your distant ancestors was a criminal you're in luck – there are far more detailed records for convicted felons than for most other people. Though tracking them down can be challenging, it's well worth the effort.

The National Archives (TNA) has a range of research guides that deal with crime and punishment. If your ancestor appeared in court, was charged with a crime, went to prison or was transported to the colonies, you should be able to find out more. On the other hand, you'll also be able to find out more about any ancestors involved in the criminal justice system, as the documents also refer to judges and jurors, witnesses and policemen – along with the innocent victims.

Maker of the law *The First Earl of Rosslyn is shown here in his role as Lord Chancellor, head of the legal system. He is portrayed in all his finery by Sir Joshua Reynolds in 1785.*

Different types of court

Understanding the varying courts your ancestor may have attended will make your research much easier.

QUARTER SESSIONS From the middle of the 16th century until 1972, quarter sessions were held every three months (quarter year) in every county in England and Wales. They tried the less serious crimes, such as arson, assault, burglary and petty theft. They didn't have the power to hear the most serious crimes – treason, murder or manslaughter, for example – though offenders might be brought there for preliminary hearings. Quarter session records are held in local county archives, which can be searched by going to the Access to Archives pages at TNA **nationalarchives.gov.uk/a2a** (see page 170).

ASSIZES The assizes were periodic criminal courts held by judges travelling in 'circuits' around England and Wales. Assizes were generally held twice a year, from the 16th century until 1972. A judge and 12 jurors would try serious crimes, including murder,

infanticide, theft, highway robbery, rape, assault, coining, forgery and witchcraft. A serious offence brought to a quarter session would be referred to the assizes and the accused would then be held in custody until a circuit judge arrived.

CROWN COURTS These replaced the assizes and quarter sessions in 1972. Crown Court records are held at TNA, but generally speaking, case files remain closed for at least 30 years. In certain circumstances, permission to access a closed file is granted under the Freedom of Information Act.

Shortfalls in the system

Unfortunately, the system isn't always helpful when you're trying to trace an ancestor. One of the problems is that not many assizes records survive, and before 1732 most of them were written in Latin, which makes deciphering them difficult for most people. In addition, very few counties have surviving witness statements from before the 19th century, and few Midlands circuit records survive before 1818.

As a rule, neither the age of the accused nor details of their family were included in the court reports. Not surprisingly, aliases were widely used, and you can't always rely on the accused's stated occupation or home town either.

Tracking down a case

Assize records aren't indexed by surname, but are arranged by county, grouped into a number of circuits within the county. In this instance, a circuit refers to a group of places within a county. Kent, for example, would fall in the South Eastern circuit. To find a case, you need to know the name of the accused, the county or circuit where they were tried, and the rough date of the trial.

If you're unsure of this, and are searching for a 19th-century case, check the Criminal Registers for England and Wales. These are at TNA in record series HO27 and cover dates 1805 to 1892. After 1868 you can check the calendars of prisoners tried at assizes and quarter sessions in HO104.

Once you know where and when the trial took place, you can begin your search. Bear in mind that many of the Welsh assize records aren't held at TNA but have been relocated to The National Library of Wales (see page 166).

Youth justice *A young boy stands in the dock as his case is heard in 1891. By then, more enlightened attitudes meant children were no longer treated as severely as adult criminals.*

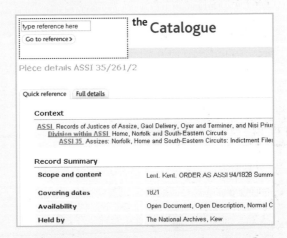

Searching for assize records

1 To search for assize records for a particular county, such as Kent, go to TNA's online catalogue at **nationalarchives.gov.uk/catalogue**. Click on the button labelled **Search the Catalogue**. Enter 'Kent' as a keyword. You can also add a date range to narrow down the search. Then enter 'ASSI' in the **Department or Series code** box (ASSI refers to the department code that's unique to these records at TNA). Click on **Search**.

View the results

2 You'll be taken to a screen that lists the results for the county you're searching, arranged in chronological order. Once you've found the relevant document, make a note of the number on the left-hand side of the screen – ASSI35/261/2, for example. This is a unique TNA document reference. You can't see these original documents online, but if you go to TNA in person, or order copies online, you'll need to quote this reference number.

Check the details

3 Clicking on the link to your particular record will give you a brief catalogue description of what it contains, usually the date and county. You can now confirm that you've found the right document before you decide to take a trip to TNA or order it.

The Old Bailey – a world-famous criminal court

Our ancestors lived in brutal times. Punishments for crimes included burning at the stake and deportation; even children were hanged. The corpses weren't wasted, though – from 1752 to 1809, the bodies of those executed for murder were taken to Surgeon's Hall in the Old Bailey where they were publicly dissected. Relatives could later buy them back for burial.

The first Old Bailey courthouse was built in 1539 but its history goes back to medieval times, when the site was occupied by the notorious Newgate gaol. 'Hanging breakfasts' took place at the alehouse opposite the gates of the gaol, where diners watched the hangings while they ate.

The court takes its name from the street, Old Bailey, which followed the line of the original fortified wall, or 'bailey', of the City of London. The courthouse has been rebuilt several times – the first time was after its destruction in the Great Fire of 1666.

The present-day court was built in 1907, incorporating stone blocks reclaimed after Newgate prison was demolished to make way for the Old Bailey in 1902. It's still used for major criminal trials – including those of serial killers Harold Shipman and Fred West.

Reading the Proceedings

From 1674, transcriptions of Old Bailey trials were published as *The Proceedings*, (right) eight times a year, after each session at the court. During the 1670s, the paper was printed for a popular audience and ran to just a few pages. It was a cheap and popular periodical, publishing descriptions of only the most lurid trials, such as this, from 1679: '…*brought to Tryal, was an unhappy Wench, whom the Devil had seduced to endeavour, to cover the filthy sin of Fornication, with the Scarlet Mantle of*

Murder, having made away her own new-born Bastard-Child, and in a very barbarous manner cut the Throat of it…'. The unfortunate girl was sentenced to death.

No hiding place

A century later, *The Proceedings* ran to hundreds of pages, recording most of the evidence presented – apart from the more salacious details of sex crimes. At this time the courtroom layout emphasised the conflict between the defendant and the court. The accused stood at the bar facing the witness box. He was spotlit by a mirrored reflector, which hung above the bar and reflected light from the windows on to his face – so that the court could better examine his facial expressions as he gave his testimony. His voice was amplified, too, by a sounding board positioned over his head.

Symbol of the court *Poised on the dome of the Old Bailey in London, the gilded statue* Justice *represents the rule of law and impartial justice. Major cases from all over England are tried here, including more than a third of all murders.*

Blood-chilling crimes *Among the notorious criminals tried at the Old Bailey were Dr Crippen in 1910 (below), William Joyce ('Lord Haw-Haw') in 1945, the Kray twins in 1969 and Peter Sutcliffe ('the Yorkshire Ripper') in 1981.*

Death by hanging

The unluckiest of the accused were sentenced to execution. More than 200 crimes were punishable by death in 1800 – including impersonating a Chelsea pensioner and damaging London Bridge – although, in practice, people were only executed for 17 of them, with murder, attempted murder, arson, rape, sodomy and sheep stealing among the crimes on the list.

When the grim moment came, the blindfolded convicts stood in a horse-drawn cart, had the noose placed around their necks and the cart pulled away. Death was slow and painful, and convicts' friends often put them out of their misery by pulling on their legs to hasten the moment. The introduction of a 'sharp drop' system in 1783 made death a quicker business.

Until 1783 most of the condemned were hanged at Tyburn – today's Marble Arch. Then, because of the rowdiness that accompanied these grisly events, the site moved to Newgate or nearby, where, by 1902, a total of 1169 people (1120 men and 49 women) had been hanged. Public hangings were only stopped in 1868.

Morbid curiosity *A Hogarth engraving of 1747 captures perfectly the raucous spectacle of a public execution at Tyburn. Its triangular gallows could hang up to 21 people at a time.*

The Old Bailey online

If you're lucky – or unlucky – enough to have a criminal ancestor in your family, take a look at **oldbaileyonline.org** (right). Details of nearly 200,000 Old Bailey criminal trials from 1674 to 1913 have been transcribed and can be searched online, free of charge. You can use names (of victims and witnesses as well as defendants), dates, places and subject keywords, and you can also view digital images of the 60,000 original pages of *The Proceedings*. The intimacy of the reports can be astounding, including verbatim transcripts of dialogue in the courtroom. This is a fabulous resource that not only helps you learn about any miscreant ancestors you may have had, but gives a vivid picture of the times.

Transportation

During the 17th century, overcrowding in prisons began to be dealt with by transportation. At first, miscreants were sent to the North American colonies, but after American independence in 1776 that was no longer an option.

With the wide open spaces of America no longer available to them, prison authorities turned to newly acquired lands in Australia. On May 13, 1787, what became known as the 'First Fleet' set sail for Australia with six transport ships, two warships and three store-ships, carrying more than 700 convicts, of whom 48 died en route. They arrived at Port Jackson in January, 1788. Many of them would have been convicted and transported on the flimsiest of evidence – but others had cheated death and welcomed the chance of a new life. For more information look at **convictcentral.com**.

All at sea *Jails became so crowded that prison hulks were moored in The Thames estuary and off the south coast. TNA series HO8 and HO9 cover prisoners held in hulks from 1802 to 1876.*

The 'First Fleeters'

There is no single, authoritative list of convicts, but if you think that one of your distant ancestors may have been on that First Fleet, there are some Australian-based sites that may be useful in your search. The First Fleeters Society has a searchable database at **firstfleet.uow.edu.au/search.html**. Another site you might find useful is **members.pcug. org.au/~pdownes/dps/1stflt.htm**. The First Fleet Fellowship offers more information at **home.vicnet.net.au/~firstff/info.htm**.

Transportation was formally abolished in 1868, but it had effectively stopped by 1857. During those 80 years 158,702 convicts

THE "DEFENCE" HULK AND THE "UNITE" CONVICT HOSPITAL SHIP, OFF WOOLWICH.

Read more about it
The National Archives has copies of books that you may find useful. The names of the convicts transported are listed in *The First Fleeters*, edited by P.G. Fidlon and R.J. Ryan (Sydney, 1981).

A list of convicts transported on the second fleet of ships, which left in 1789, during which 278 died, is contained in *The Second Fleet Convicts*, edited by R.J. Ryan (Sydney, 1982).

arrived in Australia from England and Ireland, and 1321 from other parts of the Empire, making a total of 160,023 men and women transported. Sometimes even teenagers were sent, often for crimes that would be considered petty today. The theft of a loaf of bread could be enough to send a starving Briton to the colonies.

Searching for a transportee
The National Archives (TNA) holds various sources relating to transportation, but there's no single index of the names of those who were transported. Very few of these records are searchable online and you'll need to visit TNA if you want to consult them – so it helps to know where to start.

ESTABLISHING A DATE AND SHIP To discover more about a convicted ancestor, you need to know when they were tried and/or the date and ship in which they sailed to Australia. To find this, use one of the published Australian censuses or musters (official rolls) of the penal colonies, which often indicate the place of conviction and the date and ship of arrival in Australia. Censuses were taken periodically between 1788 and 1859, and are in the record series HO10. The census of 1828 (HO10/21 to HO10/27) is the most thorough and contains the names of more than 35,000 people with details of their age, religion, family, place of residence, occupation and any stock or land held. In addition, the census shows whether each settler came free or as a convict (or was born in the colony), and the name of the ship and the year of arrival are also given.

ARRIVALS IN NEW SOUTH WALES The microfiche index to the New South Wales Convict Indents and Ships records the names and aliases of the convicts who arrived in New South Wales and Van Dieman's Land (now Tasmania) between 1788 and 1842. It also indexes ships recorded on the same documents. A copy of this is available at the National Archives library, on a CD.

Taking a risk *If they were caught, even young pickpockets such as these would have been transported overseas to Australia.*

Convict registers held at The National Archives

These registers have information about convicts, their trials and where they were sent.

● **HO11** contains transportation registers listed by ship and date of departure 1787-1871. They tell you where and when the convict was tried, and may lead you to records of the trial.

● **HO26** contains registers of Middlesex prisoners 1791-1849.

● **HO27** contains registers of those Middlesex prisoners who were not tried at the Old Bailey 1809-11, all Middlesex prisoners 1850-92, as well as provincial prisoners 1805-92.

● **HO17** 1819-39 and **HO18** 1839-54 contain petitions for clemency. You'll need to use the registers in **HO19** to find the right one.

● **HO48, HO49, HO54** and **HO56** contain petitions that haven't been indexed.

● **HO47** contains judges' reports 1784-1829 and **HO6** contains circuit letters 1816-40.

Finding the date and place of trial

Prison registers indicate where the prisoner was held before trial, and any movements from prison to prison. Many include an index of prisoners. You'll need to consult the following series:

● **HO23** for registers of county prisons 1847-66.

● **HO24** for prison registers and returns 1838-75.

● **HO9** for miscellaneous registers relating to convict prison hulks 1802-49.

● **HO8** for quarterly returns of convicts in prisons and hulks 1824-76.

● **T38** for material on convict hulks 1802-31, with lists of crews and convicts.

● **HO77** for lists of prisoners tried at Newgate 1782-1853.

Further information

Some wives applied to be transported with their convicted husbands. If their petitions were made between 1819 and 1844, they'll be in **PC1/67** to **PC1/92**. Those from 1849 are in **HO12**, and can also be found in the registers in **HO14** under 'miscellaneous'.

● **CO360** and **CO369** contain other names that are held in New South Wales Registers, from 1849.

● **CO202** contains names from the Australian Entry Books from 1786.

● **HO11** contains convict transportation registers 1787-1867. The registers provide the name of the ship on which the convict sailed as well as the date and place of conviction and the term of the sentence. Contracts with agents to transport prisoners, with full lists of ships and convicts, are in **TS18/460** to **TS18/515** and **TS18/1308** to **TS18/1361** with a few stray lists 1840-3, in **PC1/2715** to **PC1/2719**.

● **CO201** has further lists of convicts, together with emigrant settlers 1801-21, in New South Wales Original Correspondence.

● **CO207** has Entry Books relating to convicts 1788-1825. Both of these are available only in microfilm.

Some of the lists from these records have been printed in L.L. Robson's, *The Convict Settlers of Australia* (Melbourne, 1981).

Sources in Australia

The Australian National Archives doesn't hold records on convicts or colonial migration, but suggests you should contact the 'First Fleeters' at the web address given opposite, if you want to trace individual convicts.

Hard labour and houses of correction

From the early 18th century, any ancestors convicted of serious crimes would have been sentenced to swift and brutal punishment. After 1853 you're more likely to find them serving a long-term prison sentence instead.

Until 1853, people convicted of a serious offence were dealt with quite simply – by execution, or by transportation to North America or Australia. Lesser criminals, such as vagrants or debtors, were kept off the streets and put to work in houses of correction, while people awaiting trial or sentence, or anyone convicted of a minor offence, were kept in county gaols, sometimes with short, sharp spells of hard labour. Then in 1823, houses of correction and county gaols were amalgamated and renamed 'prisons'.

Prisoner or convict?
People held in prison were known as prisoners, but those sentenced to transportation or hard labour were convicts. John Little (above), aged 17, was sentenced to six weeks hard labour in Lambeth prison in 1873 for stealing two sixpences.

Prisons take the strain
The Penal Servitude Act (1853) substituted the transportation of convicts to the colonies with a term of imprisonment in Britain – though in practice, convicts were still being transported until as late as 1867. Prison sentences ranged from three years to life and usually included hard labour. This was meant to show offenders the errors of their ways and teach them to be industrious; it was also extremely unpleasant, with a view to deterring others from a criminal path.

Forms of hard labour
The most soul-destroying aspect of most forms of hard labour was their uselessness. Prisoners were sometimes put to working a water pump for hours on end; others were set far more unpleasant tasks.

THE CRANK MACHINE A prisoner had to turn a handle that forced paddles through sand inside a drum several thousand times a day, while a counter registered the number of turns. The guard could make the work harder by tightening a screw – which explains the slang term 'screw' for a prison warder.

Harsh lessons *Prisoners, overseen by a warder, are forced to pump cold water inside Coldbath Fields Prison, London, in the early 1800s.*

THE TREADMILL A vast elongated drum, resembling the wheel of a paddle steamer, had steps instead of paddles. The prisoners had to stand in individual booths over these steps hanging onto a bar or strap. As the wheel turned under their weight, the prisoners had to keep climbing or fall off.

SHOT DRILL In this exercise a row of prisoners had to pick up heavy cannon balls in time with each other, without bending their knees, and bring them up slowly to chest level. They then took three steps to the right, put the ball down on the ground, took three paces to the left and started again.

Tracing a prisoner

To find an ancestor whom you believe was imprisoned, it helps to know the name of the prison and the date of their imprisonment or release. Don't assume that an individual would have been incarcerated near their home, because prisoners were often moved between prisons, depending on where there was room for them.

Surviving prison records are held at individual county and city record offices and at The National Archives (TNA).

Records at The National Archives

The criminal registers held at TNA list just about everyone accused of a criminal offence – regardless of the verdict – in the 19th and 20th centuries. They're arranged by county and include the following information:
- the result of the trial
- the sentence, in the case of conviction
- the date of the execution of a prisoner who was sentenced to death
- personal details about the prisoner, though these are only occasionally given.

You can see these records at TNA, where the microfiche indexes are arranged alphabetically and by county. Those with the reference code HO27 cover England and Wales from 1805 to 1892. Records in HO26 cover Middlesex from 1791 to 1849 (records from 1850 onwards for Middlesex are in HO27).

Information about finding records for the convicts who were transported to Australia is given on page 206.

PRISONER REGISTERS There are specific reference codes at TNA for prisoner records:
- PCOM2 covers 1770 to 1951
- HO23 records inmates held in rented cells in county prisons from 1846 to 1866
- HO24 records prisoners held in Millbank, Parkhurst and Pentonville prisons in London from 1838 to 1874.

- PRIS1 to PRIS11 include records for King's Bench, Marshalsea and Fleet (London debtors' prisons) during much of the 18th and 19th centuries.

JUDGES' REPORTS These are in HO47 and cover 1784-1829. To search these records, go to **the Catalogue** on the TNA website. In the box on the top left of the screen, type 'HO47' and click on **Go to reference**. Then click on the **Browse from here** button. HO47 is the second entry on this page.

Finding crime records

1 The National Archives provides a detailed online guide to discovering crime and punishment records. Go to the TNA homepage at nationalarchives.gov.uk and choose **Records** from the menu bar. From the menu options that open out select **Looking for a subject?**. From the resulting screen go to the **Political history** section and select **Crime and punishment**.

Did your relative have a photo album?

2 The National Archives also has more than 600 Victorian prisoners' photograph albums online. Go to nationalarchives.gov.uk/ documentsonline and from the **Quick links** on the left of the screen choose **Other records**. Scroll down to **Victorian Prisoners Photograph Albums (PCOM 2)**. You can download the original records: each one costs £3.50.

The poor and the destitute

You may find you have ancestors who fell upon hard times and had to ask for what was called 'poor relief'. Sometimes local parishes helped, but often the shame and hardship of life in the workhouse was all that lay ahead.

Until Henry VIII dissolved all the monasteries in the 1530s, the poor were usually cared for by the monks and nuns of religious houses.

Hard times *The extremes of poverty that affected many people are captured in illustrations from Henry Mayhew's 1862 book* London Labour and the London Poor.

With these havens burnt or ransacked, the poor were meant to be cared for by individual parishes, but the system was haphazard and ineffective. Parishes were expected to raise money from their parishioners to provide for the poor and for orphaned children.

Dealing with the poor

The rules for the care of the poor in England and Wales were formalised by the Poor Law Act of 1601, and lasted for more than 200 years. Records cover the system of outdoor relief for the so-called 'deserving poor' (where money or food and clothing were given, but people remained at home) and the houses of correction (see page 208) for those who were considered the 'undeserving poor'.

For records of the Elizabethan Poor Law, outdoor relief or houses of correction you'll need to go to county record offices. A useful reference book is *An Introduction to Poor Law Documents before 1834*, by A. Cole.

The dreaded workhouse

Between 1832 and 1834 the Poor Law was reformed and rationalised, with parishes organised into Poor Law Unions, each with its own workhouse. The official view now was that the poor were largely responsible for their own plight, so the workhouse was designed to be a harsh place, discouraging the poor from seeking relief there. Controversy over workhouse conditions led to a New Poor Law in 1847, which imposed a rigorously implemented, centrally enforced, standard system for all, which centred on the workhouse. The records generated all relate to admission to these dreaded institutions.

The officers of poverty

The website **nationalarchives.gov.uk** holds information about the records of the governing bodies – the Poor Law Board and the Poor Law Commission – under the code MH (Ministry of Health). If you have an ancestor who was a workhouse official, you'll find records of the staff between 1837 and 1921, with details of dates of appointment and salary, in MH9. In MH12 you'll find the names of thousands of individuals listed by poor law union, with notes of the dates of correspondence, but with no indication as to the subject.

The 'lucky' poor in Scotland

Scotland was way ahead of England and Wales when it came to caring for their poor. The Poor Law (Scotland) Act came into force in 1579. Although records are sparse, it seems that the poor were cared for by wealthy landlords of the parish, who were known as 'heritors'. Payments were noted in the minutes, accounts and heritors' records of the parish Kirk Sessions. Names of the poor receiving relief appear on the Poor Rolls, which are held by the National Archives of Scotland (see Directory). The Poor Rolls show the amounts paid and the recipients' disabilities – which can add poignancy to your research.

Ireland and its poor
Before 1838, when Poor Law Unions were formed in Ireland, private and religious charities took care of the poor. Some towns had almshouses where records may have been kept, but generally, few records were kept of recipients. When the Poor Law Unions were introduced in Ireland, there was only 'indoor relief', which meant that paupers were taken into grim workhouses.

Each Poor Law Union kept records of the people it helped. In many cases, inmates were encouraged to emigrate to North America, Canada, Australia and South Africa, to get them off the list. Details of who went, their ages, names and where they came from, as well as who went with them and where they

Map of distress *Poor Law Union boundaries are shown on this faded 1890 Ordnance Survey map of Ireland. It was once hand-coloured to show the degrees of anticipated distress – acute, severe or light – even 40 years after the Irish Famine.*

were going, can be found among individual Poor Law Union records. Many are held at the Public Record Office of Ireland. You can find out more about the Irish Poor Law Unions at **ancestry.co.uk**, **rootsweb.co.uk** and in the civil registration lists at **genuki.org.uk**.

Life in a workhouse

If your ancestors were unfortunate enough to suffer from incapacitating ill health, or were unemployed for long periods of time, they may have ended up within the grim walls of a Victorian workhouse.

Based on the unforgiving sentiment that the poor were feckless and had brought their fate upon themselves, workhouses were forbidding and uncomfortable places. They were nationally established by the Poor Law Amendment Act of 1834 (see page 210), although many individual workhouses existed before this. Under the Act, local parishes were grouped into Poor Law Unions and each union had to provide a workhouse.

The workhouse system was eventually abolished on April 1, 1930, but the records hold fascinating information and can add heartbreaking details to a search for an ancestor whose life took a turn for the worse.

Inmates were free to come and go as they liked, but life within the workhouse was deliberately made as austere and mortifying as possible so that layabouts and vagabonds would not be tempted to use them as a free hotel. Only those who were truly desperate would apply to live there.

Searching for a workhouse

1 To find an ancestor, for example a James Brown who worked in a workhouse in Kent – possibly Sevenoaks – go to the homepage **workhouses.org.uk**. If you're not sure whether there was a workhouse in the town, click on **Workhouse Locations**, then on **Poor Law Union Maps**.

Choose a location

2 This will open another menu, which has organised the nation into regions. You know James Brown was in Kent, and think it was Sevenoaks. Choose **S.E. England**. Click on the region for **Sevenoaks**, shown on the map.

Find the workhouse

3 The page reveals a brief history of the workhouse in Sevenoaks, with maps and photographs of the building, both past and present. There's also a link near the top of the page under 'Records' to relevant county records – here the Centre for Kentish Studies. From the links at the top of the page, click on **Staff** to be taken to the section of the site that deals with workhouse staff and inmates.

When people went into a workhouse, they were given a thorough medical examination, and if they weren't found to be infirm or chronically ill, they were put to work breaking stones or picking hemp, crushing bones, digging ditches or cutting firewood. Women were given lighter tasks, such as mending and laundry. Elderly men were put to work in kitchen gardens.

Families were split up and the sexes were segregated, making the experience particularly traumatic for children. The only good thing that can be said for the institution was that vulnerable people were given basic shelter and food, and rudimentary medical care – which was better than being out on the streets.

Researching online

To find out more about workhouses, go to **workhouses.org.uk**. It has lots of detail about the Poor Laws, the English, Welsh and Irish Poor Law Unions, as well as maps, locations and photographs of all known workhouses.

There are examples of workhouse rules and links to relevant archives. It's an extremely easy-to-use website with a wealth of interesting information, even if you're not searching for a particular person.

Young, poor and infirm *The grim comforts of the workhouse are evident in this 1897 photo of inmates of the Ormskirk Workhouse in Lancashire. Workhouse registers, such as that from Whitechapel (right), provide invaluable detail on the circumstances leading to admission.*

See the staff and inmates

4 This gives you the option to view the staff or inmates, as shown in the 1881 census. Clicking on **1881 census**, under **Staff**, will reveal a list of staff in order of position. Here we find James Brown, Master of the Workhouse, and further details about him, his marital status, age, relation to others in the workhouse and occupation or position. Directly below this are records of the inmates in alphabetical order.

1881 Census: Residents of Sevenoaks Union Workhouse, Kent

Name	Mar	Age	Sex	Relation	Occupation
Staff					
James BROWN	W	59	M	Master	Master Of The Workhouse
Phillis ROBERTSON	U	38	F	Matron	Matron Of The Workhouse
William Arthur BRAILEY		6	M	Visitor	
Frederick HICKS	M	33	M	Porter	Porter Of Workhouse
Rosalie HICKS	M	32	F	Nurse (Wife)	Hospital Nurse
Selina CONWAY	W	35	F	House Nurse	House Nurse
CARD	U	20	M	Schoolmaster	Schoolmaster
Inmates					
Ann ALLEN	W	71	F	Inmate	No Occupation
John ANNETT	W	66	M	Inmate	Agricultural Labourer
Charles BAKER		8	M	Inmate	
Charles BAKER		11	M	Inmate	
Elizabeth BAKER		4	F	Inmate	
Ann BALL	W	83	F	Inmate	No Occupation
Joseph Bartholomew	U	61	M	Inmate	Housekeeper
William BARTHOLOMEW	U	61	M	Inmate	Pot Boy
William BELL	W	54	M	Inmate	Rope Maker
Hannah BERRY	W	63	F	Inmate	Hawker
Frederick BOAKS		13	M	Inmate	
Jane BOAKS	W	40	F	Inmate	Domestic Servant
Louisa BOAKS	O	13	F	Inmate	
Alice BOND	O	12	F	Inmate	

Taxpayers and their records

Nothing can be certain except death and taxes, so the saying goes. What's also certain is that both yield excellent information for the family historian.

Taxation goes back a long way and so do its records, offering a wealth of detail about people and their social status. The records of particular interest to family historians include the intriguingly named Fifteenths and Tenths, as well as returns from Poll Tax, Hearth Tax and Tithes. Many tax records can be searched online at The National Archives (see opposite).

Taxes of the Middle Ages

Records of medieval taxes are plentiful, but most are written in Latin and relate almost entirely to England. Wales was only included in the taxation system by the Act of Union in 1536. At this time, the king could tax people only to subsidise unusual expenditure, such as a war. He could also impose taxes directly, in the form of feudal levies or forced loans.

The Fifteenths and Tenths

In 1332, Edward III imposed a tax known as the Fifteenths and Tenths. It was levied at the rate of a fifteenth of income in the country and a tenth in the city. Two years later, he levied it again, at the same rate, and the amounts that he collected in 1334 became the basis of all taxes for the next three centuries. A system of fixed quotas on individual townships was introduced, and the same amount was due every time Parliament granted the king's request for a tax to be imposed.

The much-hated poll tax

Poll taxes were levied on individuals, rather than property. Everyone over a certain age had to pay a given amount, so documents including them may have information about your ancestors. The widely loathed poll taxes, introduced in 1377, 1379 and 1380, led to the Peasants' Revolt in 1381. These records aren't online, but *The Poll Taxes of 1377, 1379 and 1381* by Caroline Fenwick (British Academy Records of Social and Economic History, new series, 1998-2004), contains surviving receipts from these taxes.

The Tudors tax movable goods

The early Tudors changed taxation, assessing the value of a person's movable goods or income from land (whichever was the greater) and taxing it at a given rate. Under Henry VIII, these taxes became the norm. From 1523, the names and contributions of individual taxpayers were recorded.

After 1563, the threshold was fixed at a higher rate and so only wealthier people were required to contribute – which means records beyond this period are less extensive.

Counting the hearths

Between 1662 and 1689, a levy on hearths was introduced. Each householder had to pay a shilling for each hearth in their property, every year. Many of the records also include

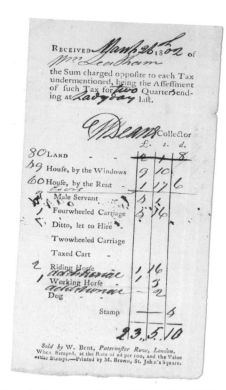

Proof of payment *Dated March 25, 1802, a tax receipt for the two quarters ending on Lady Day includes £9 10s for the number of windows in the house and £4 16s for a four-wheeled carriage.*

lists of those who were exempt – so you'll find records of hearth taxes a good source of names. You can search the records in series E179 at TNA (see opposite, far right) – just select **Hearth tax** from the drop-down menu when you search by tax type.

Tithes – a tenth of income

Tithes were payments to the church of one-tenth of a person's crops or livestock; they reveal how wealthy people were. In 1836, payment in kind was dropped in favour of money payments – a process known as 'commutation'. The resulting Tithe Files include letters to the Tithe Commissioners and records of the commutation in some areas. The records are usually only available on microfilm at TNA, in series IR29. Tithe maps are held in IR30 and you can look at the original maps, in person; fragile maps can be seen as microfilm copies only. Some County Record Offices have tithe projects, so check your local office.

A tax on the land

If your ancestors were landowners, they should appear in the Land Tax records, but remember that owners weren't necessarily resident on their land. The Land Tax was introduced in 1692 and abolished in 1963; its records list the landowners (and occupiers) in each parish and give some indication of their social status. Survival of land tax records varies from county to county and the most complete records cover 1780 to 1832.

Land Tax records are kept in the relevant County Record Office, but can be searched at **nationalarchives.gov.uk/a2a/**. On the **Search** page enter **Land tax** as a keyword. Use the drop-down menu to find the relevant archive.

How to search tax records at TNA

The most informative tax-related documents at TNA are in series E (for Exchequer) 179, which contains the majority of records relating to tax assessment and collection in England and Wales from the 13th to the 17th centuries. These records show how taxes were administered and also reveal much about the people who paid them.

You can search E179 by place, date, tax and document type, or a combination of these. Although names of individual taxpayers aren't included in the database E179, it can be used to identify documents containing the names and you can then consult this document in person at TNA. The database is also linked to both the online TNA catalogue and, for visitors to Kew, to the document ordering service (see page 163).

Search for a Fifteenth tax record

1 To search for Fifteenths relating to Devon, from 1550 to 1559, go to **nationalarchives. gov.uk/e179**. Then click on **Search E179**. Enter 'Devon' in the **Place** box and confirm it by clicking **Lookup** then **Select** on the page that appears. Under **Tax**, click on **Search by years and/or tax type**. Click on the **Specify** button, then use the drop-down box under **Tax** to select **Fifteenth** and enter '1550' and '1559' into the **Year range** boxes. Click on **Search the database**.

Choose a document

2 You'll see a list of documents. To find out more about the document you're interested in, click on the link on the left-hand side. You'll be shown a document that you can see by visiting The National Archives (TNA). Make a note of the details.

Insurance records

Fire was a great hazard when most houses were thatched. With open fires and candles in every house, the chances of a fire breaking out were high. Enterprising characters established fire insurance offices in London in the late 17th century and in the wider country a few years later. The registers contain details of thousands of businesses and homes. Local record offices hold the records for local companies, and the Guildhall Library (see Directory) holds those for more than 80 London-based insurance companies. You'll need to know the policy number to find the right entry in the register. The a2a pages, **nationalarchives.gov.uk /a2a/**, can help you to find insurance records. Enter **Insurance records** and a county as keywords. Follow the links that are offered.

Read all about them

Newspapers are a rich source of information for the family historian, not only for notices of births, marriages and deaths, but also for news items about events that might have affected our ancestors.

It's likely that your ancestors will have made the odd appearance in the newspapers of their day, and it's fascinating to try to trace them through national and local papers.

The earliest papers were no more than news sheets and, in the 17th century, were largely political, taking sides in the Civil War. But in the 18th century, they became of more interest to the upper classes, professional people and merchants who looked to them for political and business news. By 1785, there were eight morning papers in London alone; one of them, *The Daily Universal Register*, was renamed *The Times* in 1788.

Spreading the words

Most 18th and early 19th-century papers published outside London were called 'provincials'. One of them, the *Norwich Post*, first published in 1701, ran both national and local news. By 1750, most counties had their own papers. They played an important role, keeping people up to date with new laws and taxes that might affect them, as well as with the latest news, both local and from London.

The rapid expansion of the railway network in the mid 19th century made it easier to get newspapers, hot from the press, to all parts of Britain, and meant that local papers could incorporate national and international news. And when the stamp duty

on papers was repealed in 1855, the lower production costs meant newspapers became affordable for the masses. This got *The Daily Telegraph* off to a flying start in 1855.

Reduced costs had a marked effect on local papers: the number of titles proliferated and most areas had at least two, taking opposing political stances and vying with each other to carry the most interesting stories. Local news now included news of sudden deaths, inquest reports, funeral notices and obituaries of both well-known and even more ordinary people.

News of the ancestors

Towards the end of the 19th century, local papers carried news of flower shows, sporting events, the arrival and departure of doctors and clergy, and reports on societies – all rich hunting grounds for news of your ancestors.

The obvious place to search is in the births, marriages and deaths section of the paper, but remember that most local people wouldn't have appeared, as they had to pay to have a notice published. So your ancestors may be found if they were wealthy and important, or had reached a grand old age, worked for the gentry for many years, had died suddenly or in suspicious circumstances – or had left a number of orphans for the parish to care for. By the 1880s, far more middle-class families were prepared to pay for announcements.

Dramatic moment *Suffragette Emily Davison flings herself in front of the king's horse at the Epsom Derby on June 4, 1913. Although not online, some original papers can be viewed at local archives and libraries.*

Limitations of online searches

Most local papers aren't online, so to access this rich source of information, you may have to visit newspapers' archives, or your local library, and leaf through collections of old papers. They're usually stored in date order, so you'll need a rough idea of the date of the event you're researching.

If you're not sure which newspaper archive you want, or where it is, go to the Access to Archives website, **a2a.org.uk**, which allows you to search local newspaper archives by location, keyword and date. Another impressively comprehensive source of information is the the British Library's Newspaper Library at Colindale, in London.

The British Library catalogue

The British Library lists its huge collection of newspapers in its catalogue, which has entries for more than 52,000 newspaper and periodical titles. The collection includes all UK national, daily and Sunday newspapers from 1801 to the present; most UK and Irish provincial newspapers, some dating from the early 18th century; selected newspapers from around the world in European languages, some dating from the 17th century; and a range of periodicals from the UK and Ireland covering fashion, music, hobbies and trades.

Go to **bl.uk/catalogues/newspapers** to see what papers are held, but to view the actual journals you'll have to travel to the British Library's reading room in Colindale, north London (see Directory).

Searching the catalogue online

Each entry in the British Library's newspaper catalogue shows the title, place of publication and the dates held. The catalogue may be searched by entering a keyword – such as a title or place name – or by a combination of keywords. The search results you receive may

be sorted and displayed alphabetically, by title or place of publication, or by year of publication. You can limit your search to a specific period of time by combining a keyword search with a date search. Simply select the **Date search** facility and enter the appropriate keyword(s) and year(s). The results will list the relevant newspapers in the collection, and tell you whether they're kept on microfilm, microfiche or hard copy.

Visiting the British Library

On your first trip to Colindale, you'll have to apply for membership of the library for a minimum period of three months. You'll need ID and a plan of what you intend to research. Some newspapers are kept on open shelves, and you'll be given a shelf-mark to help you to find them. Most will need to be ordered from the stacks. The items you select can only be read in certain reading rooms.

If you are unable to visit, the British Library offers a newspaper search service. For £50, a researcher will search up to four newspapers and report on articles found. You can then order copies if you want to.

> **Newspapers in Scotland and Wales**
> For national and local newspapers of Scotland and Wales, check the collections held by the National Library of Wales at **llgc.org.uk** and the National Library of Scotland **nls.uk**.

The word on the street *A group of newsboys in 1910 wait for fresh supplies of the latest papers to sell to a public hungry for news and sensation.*

National newspapers online

Some national newspapers have digitised their early editions and scanned their images. This has created a wonderful resource for you to search for news of your ancestors or find about the lives they led.

The newspapers described on these pages have the best online collection of early newspapers. Most national papers have their own website with online archives available to search by keyword, but they rarely go further back than the date that they first began publishing current issues on the website, usually from the late 1990s. The National Archives, at **nationalarchives.gov.uk** doesn't hold collections of newspapers, although it does have a few papers that might have been sent to government departments because they were considered politically sensitive.

The Times online

Of all the online collections of digital records, *The Times* has the most comprehensive. It has been split into periods, each with its own search engine.

☛ *The Times* and *The Sunday Times* have an online archive that can be searched back to 1985, at **newsint-archive.co.uk**. It's free to search by keyword, date range, headline, writer and section, but if you find pages you'd like to view, you'll need to subscribe. This costs a minimum of £10 for 10 downloads, but each download is cheaper if you invest in a more expensive subscription.

☛ The Times Digital Archive is a digital edition of *The Times* from 1785 to 1985 that you can search by keyword to find facsimile

images of either a specific article or complete page. It contains a wealth of birth, marriage, death and funeral announcements, obituaries, court summaries and criminal reports, as well as details about change of name and address, and advertisements that may have been posted by one of your ancestors' businesses.

This archive can only be accessed via the InfoTrac database, which is a subscription-only facility designed for institutions. To use it, you can visit the British Library or The National Archives (see Directory) and use their subscriptions, free of charge, on computers in the reading rooms.

In addition, many local libraries hold subscriptions, which you may be able to access online from home, using your library card number and a pin number the library will supply you with. For some libraries, your library card number is all that is needed to access this superb resource. Contact your local library to find out how to access their InfoTrac system from home.

The Scotsman digital archive

If you have Scottish forbears, you'll find **archive.scotsman.com**, *The Scotsman*'s digital archive, really helpful. The paper was first published in Edinburgh on January 25, 1817, as a liberal weekly, pledged to 'impartiality, firmness and independence'. It's now a well-established daily national

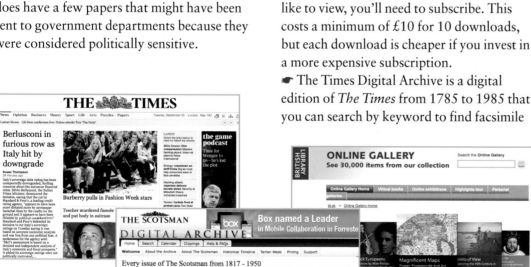

The past, online *These three news websites are treasure troves of valuable and fascinating family history – not just for details of births, deaths and marriages, but also for the exciting times that framed the major events in your ancestors' lives.*

newspaper, and every edition of *The Scotsman* from 1817 until 1950 can be searched online.

You can search the **Calendar** to find issues from specific dates, or use the **Search** facility to look for a keyword, within a date range, from advertisements, articles and pictures. It also contains birth, marriage and death announcements.

The newspaper is free to search, but to view full articles you'll need to take out a subscription. An Archive Pass can be bought online for about £8, which gives 24 hours' unlimited access, or longer periods can be purchased at discounted rates. Students who've been provided with an ATHENS Login password by their educational institution can access the digital archive free of charge.

Penny Illustrated Paper

The British Library's British Newspapers 1800-1900 website, **newspapers.bl.uk/blcs**, includes a complete digitised and indexed run of the *Penny Illustrated Paper*. This paper, published in London between 1863 and 1913, reported news from across Britain and the Empire to many eager readers and is an enthralling source of information.

To access the 52,000 pages and 500,000 images, go to the **British Newspapers 1800-1900** homepage and type 'Penny Illustrated Paper' in the **FIND** box. That takes you to a page offering a range of editions, as well as the option to search the collection. You can download the results free of charge. Clicking on the **Publications List** tab informs you about all of the newspapers that are available in the collection.

Official news in the Gazettes

From the late 17th century onwards, all legal notices in the UK were published in *The London Gazette*, *The Belfast Gazette* and *The Edinburgh Gazette*. These publications may sound rather dry, but they're essential if you're searching for important events in your ancestors' lives.

Not only do the Gazettes contain information relating to State, Parliament and ecclesiastical issues, including official appointments, but you'll also find insolvency and bankruptcy notices, deed polls, name changes, and military medal and honours awards – any of which could apply to one of your ancestors.

The historic archive covering the 20th century – and even earlier for *The London Gazette* – has been uploaded by The Stationery Office (TSO) to provide free access for everyone. Go to **gazettes-online.co.uk**, where you can choose to visit the homepage of *The London Gazette*, *The Belfast Gazette* or *The Edinburgh Gazette*.

Searching the Gazettes

Click on the Gazette you wish to search. This takes you to the newspaper's own homepage. To make a simple search of all the notices, enter a keyword, such as a name you're looking for, in the **Search archive** box, and then click on the **Search** button. For a more refined operation, first click on the **Advanced Search** button: here you can enter more detailed keywords, a range of dates, or select from a list of historic events from the Great Fire of London to the Normandy landings.

To see your search results, scroll to the bottom of the window where they are listed as a series of pages. Each entry lists the date, the issue number, the page number and a percentage match between your search criteria and entries in the Gazette. The highest-rated matches appear at the top of the list.

You can read online or download pages by clicking on the **See PDF** button. Or you can click on **Buy Gazette** to find how you can purchase your own copy.

If you chose to view the PDF, your keyword will not be highlighted on the document you are shown. You can use the **Find** facility on the program that allows you to view pdfs to look for the word or words you are interested in.

The news from Ireland

The Dublin Gazette, known as *Iris Oifigiuil* since 1922, has a website at **irisoifigiuil.ie**, but its online archive goes back only to 2002.

Where they lived

Finding out where in the British Isles your ancestors lived is crucial to your search. It can be a puzzle working through the administrative and geographical changes over the years, but there are plenty of websites to help you.

How the British Isles divides

Over the centuries the boundaries of counties, boroughs and other administrative areas have varied. When researching, you need to understand the changing divisions – this can affect where old documents are kept, how they are arranged and what survives.

The British Isles are divided into the major administrative regions of England, Wales, Scotland, Northern Ireland, the Republic of Ireland, the Channel Islands and the Isle of Man, but the administrative geography of individual regions has changed several times. Once you understand the changes, you'll be able to target your search better. It will also help to explain why there's so much material available on the internet for some parts of the country and not for others.

The Republic of Ireland

In 1922, when Ireland was divided, 26 of the 32 counties became the Republic of Ireland, and the remaining six counties stayed under UK administration. This means that records for Ireland are split according to time and place: material for all Ireland until 1922 and the Republic since then is located in The National Archives of Ireland in Dublin; material for Northern Ireland after 1922 is in the Public Record Office of Northern Ireland, in Belfast (see page 100).

Pancake day *Local customs and traditions exist throughout the British Isles, and your ancestors will certainly have watched or taken part in some. Here, women in Olney, Buckinghamshire, celebrate Shrove Tuesday in 1951 with their annual pancake race. The tradition began in 1445 to celebrate the final day before Lent.*

Isle of Man and Channel Islands

All these islands are self-governing. Of the Channel Islands – Jersey, Guernsey, Alderney and Sark – only Sark doesn't have its own administrative centre (see Directory).

Mainland counties

In England and Wales, the administrative districts are the counties (also referred to as shires), and most documents relating to local areas will be found in the relevant County Record Office. Counties are made up of smaller administrative districts whose boundaries have often changed. Knowing about changes in the past will help you to find records at the relevant County Record Office.

THE 'HUNDREDS' Ancient counties in England and Wales had sub-divisions known as 'hundreds' that were used in census-taking until 1834 when many gave way to Poor Law Unions (see page 210). In 1889 Municipal Boroughs and Urban and Rural Districts, governed by County Councils, were introduced. This new system brought the number of counties to 62.

COUNTIES AND GREATER LONDON By 1965, the total number of counties had decreased to 58, and the boundaries of Greater London were established. Some towns that are now in Greater London, such as Harrow and Barking, were officially in Essex, Kent, Hertfordshire, Surrey or Middlesex before 1965. The administrative county boundaries were abolished in 1974 and replaced by six Metropolitan counties and 39 counties that were non-Metropolitan.

Scotland

In the 17th century, Scotland was divided into counties and burghs, which were ancient urban settlements given trading privileges by the Crown. Burghs of Barony were granted to some landowners, Royal Burghs were mainly sea ports, and Police Burghs had a town council to take care of policing, paving, lighting and cleaning. The numbers of burghs increased with time and boundaries moved. County Landwards and Parish Landwards were areas of land within a county or parish that did not fall within a burgh.

Knowing what type of burgh or county your ancestor lived in is helpful, because separate valuation and electoral rolls were compiled for Royal Burghs and Police Burghs until 1975. After that, burghs were replaced by district councils, and then by local authorities in 1996. Burghs also produced court books, guild records, registers of deeds, financial accounts and records of Burgh institutions such as schools and libraries.

A land captured in the Domesday Book

More than 900 years ago the new Norman masters of England created one of Britain's oldest public records, full of names and details of places, many of which still exist. The priceless original is housed in Kew at The National Archives – but you can read the entries online.

When William the Conqueror urgently needed to raise funds to prepare to combat a threatened Scandinavian invasion in 1085, he commissioned the Domesday Book. Commissioners were sent all over England, and asked such detailed questions that landowners likened the process to the Last Judgment – or 'Doomsday' – described in the Bible. The data recorded was deemed 'final proof' of legal entitlement to land – and in some cases still is. As recently as the 1960s, information in the Domesday Book was used to settle a dispute over land and property rights.

The first draft, completed in August 1086, held records for 13,418 settlements in the English counties south of the rivers Ribble and Tees; many northern counties were exempt from royal taxation, or were not yet fully under Norman administration. The Domesday Book is, in fact, two volumes (see right): Little Domesday – a detailed survey of Norfolk, Suffolk and Essex – and Great Domesday, comprising the rest of England. London and Winchester (the capital of England in 1086) were surveyed, and spaces left for them in Great Domesday, but for reasons that are unknown today were never entered. Bristol and Tamworth were also omitted.

Domesday online

The National Archives (TNA) has transcribed each entry from the Domesday Book into a database that's searchable by place or person, at **nationalarchives.gov.uk/domesday**. This means that local and family historians can learn about the medieval history of a settlement and its population, as well as something about what life was like in the 11th century. If, for example, you enter Halnaker in West Sussex, you get a transcription of the original entry listing the names of people mentioned, such as 'Guntrum' and 'Thorkil, free man', and the village's Domesday name – Helnache; you can also download an image of the original for a small fee.

Answer the following questions...

Domesday was not a population census. Instead it itemised land and landowners at various points in time – at the death of Edward the Confessor (1066); when the new owner received the land; and at the time of the survey (1085-6). Each landowner,

Not so small
Little Domesday (right) may not be as big as Great Domesday (above) but its entries contain more information.

Twenty years on *Every schoolchild knows that William the Conqueror won the Battle of Hastings in 1066 (illustrated above in the Bayeux tapestry); fewer could date the Domesday Book – 1086 – which William commissioned to establish the value of his latest conquest.*

In your best hand *Little Domesday took around six scribes up to 12 weeks to write using quill pens. Great Domesday was mostly the work of one scribe, with help from five others, who would often have to go back and make corrections.*

or a designated representative, had to visit the local court and, after being sworn in, would be asked a series of questions by commissioners-under-oath in front of a jury of barons and villagers. The questions included:

What was the name of the manor?
Who held it in the time of King Edward?
Who holds it now?
How many hides [land measurement]?
How many ploughs?
How many men, either free, tenant or slave?
How much wood, meadow and pasture?
How many mills and fishponds?

The information was recorded in Latin in black and red ink on sheepskin parchment by one or more scribes, and then double-checked by another. According to the contemporary *Anglo-Saxon Chronicle*, 'there was no single hide nor a yard of land, nor indeed one ox nor one cow nor one pig which was left out'.

Reading the power of a great abbey

A number of local history societies have used the Domesday Book to reconstruct a picture of local life in the 11th century. Details of the entry for Peterborough Abbey can be seen at **cottinghamhistory.co.uk/domesdaybook.htm**. The transcript reads: 'Land of Peterborough Abbey. The Church itself holds in STOKE Hundred COTTINGHAM. 7 hides. Land for 14 ploughs, in lordship 2; 4 slaves; 29 villagers and 10 smallholders with 10 ploughs. A mill at 40d; meadow, 12 acres; woodland 1 league long and ½ league wide. The value was 10s; now 60s'. The website explains what each entry means and gives a map of the area.

Old money *From Domesday until the Dissolution of the Monasteries in the mid 16th century, Peterborough Abbey was rich and powerful, and owned large areas of fertile – and taxable – farmland.*

Local history – and how to find it

Once you know where your ancestors lived, it's really rewarding to explore websites about their locality. These sites provide useful information and fascinating details about the lives they led.

When you start trying to find out about a particular area in the British Isles, you'll need to consult some of the websites that can help you to identify local administrative boundaries, research local history and locate records. Here are a few of the more comprehensive.

genuki.org.uk

Genuki has an excellent breakdown of information about the whole of the British Isles on its county, town and parish pages, with links to family history websites, history societies and archives. For more about the site, see page 44. From the UK and Ireland page you can choose to search the administrative regions of England, Wales, Scotland, Northern Ireland, the Republic of Ireland, the Channel Islands and the Isle of Man.

curiousfox.com

Curious Fox is a website aimed at helping family and local history researchers with interests in the same villages or towns to connect with each other and share their knowledge. You're free to search the database of posted entries, which you do by location, but to make the most of the site, it's best to become a paid-up member for £5 a year. This allows you to send messages to other members who may have information useful to your research, and it allows you to search the posted entries by surname. The website covers England, Wales, Scotland and Ireland.

victoriacountyhistory.ac.uk

Known as VCH, Victoria County History was founded in 1899 in honour of Queen Victoria, and is an encyclopedic record of England, arranged by county, from the earliest times to the present day. Information on the VCH website is based on original

documents and work done by historians across England and tells what life was like in each area of England, gives detailed accounts of cities, towns and villages, and explains the social and economic history of each county.

The VCH index is arranged by county. It lists the publications that are available for each county, with a description of the topics discussed. It has links, via British History Online (a digital history library), which enable you to read many of the publications free of charge. If the volume you're interested in is still in print, you can order it online, but you'll find most libraries have copies of the volumes that cover their local area.

Although the VCH website concentrates on England, you'll find Scottish records and documents are also accessible through the site's link to British History Online.

Local gems *Information about every section of the British Isles is there on the Genuki website (left). It will be a great help to your quest for ancestors and information about how they lived.*

Curiosity satisfied *Searches on Curious Fox (right), by county, town, village or surname, should yield details of that elusive ancestor and his home, lifestyle and times.*

Blair Castle *The archives held in this Scottish castle include letters from Charles Stuart, the Young Pretender, and Queen Victoria's childhood notebooks. Many other documents are there, too – such as the letters Sir Harold Goodeve Ruggles-Brice wrote to his wife while fighting in the Boer War. You can access these documents through ARCHON on The National Archives website (see below).*

nationalarchives.gov.uk/archon

The ARCHON directory, which is accessed via The National Archives (TNA), holds contact information for archives around the British Isles, as well as details of institutions from all over the world that hold manuscripts and documents that are useful for local history research.

Use the interactive map to get an alphabetical list of repositories for each county, or use the search engine to find archives in a specific town or county. For example, select Scotland from the map, and scroll through the alphabetical list of record

offices and archives to Blair Castle. Click on the name for full details of what is held in the repository and you'll be swept up into another world (above). It includes address and contact details, a street map and a list of what National Register of Archives indexes are held in the castle. The wealth of information is encouraging if you want a picture of what your Scottish ancestors' lives were like, and the events that affected them.

visionofbritain.org.uk

The Vision of Britain Through Time website was created by the Great Britain Historical Geographical Information System Project, and is a wonderfully detailed site designed for people interested in local history. Its resources describe Britain and its localities, showing how they've changed over the centuries.

The site has used statistics from census returns between 1801 and 1961, information from 19th-century gazetteers and travellers' tales dating back to the 12th century to create a wealth of local histories that can be searched by a village or town name.

Local knowledge *From Scotland to the Home Counties, the breadth and depth of information offered by websites like these is fascinating to family historians.*

Getting down to the grass roots

When you start to reveal those missing ancestors, it's enthralling to find out how they lived day-to-day in their communities. Local history websites can bring those worlds to life.

How did the village where your relatives lived look all those years ago? What were their workplaces like, or their houses, and can you still visit them? What kind of clothes did they wear? Seeing pictures of other people who lived in the same area in the same period, or reading contemporary personal accounts, can give you a vivid impression of the daily life your ancestors might have led.

More and more local authorities and history societies are building websites with photographs, moving images, personal documents and oral history that provide deep insights into a local area. Check the local history society, record office, library or county council websites in the area of interest to you, to see if they have projects as packed with information as these examples.

Handsworth – village to suburb

The Digital Handsworth Project at **www.digitalhandsworth.org.uk** holds an online collection of historical material about the ancient parish of Handsworth near Birmingham. The project charts the area's change from a rural village with medieval roots to its urbanisation from the 1850s to the 1940s, and its later development into a multicultural suburb. There are valuable contributions from local libraries, archives, museums and community groups who've uploaded photographs, prints, personal documents, newspaper extracts, old maps, and video and audio clips.

You can search these resources by keyword or theme – **People**, **Place**, **Subject** and **Time**. There's also a quick-search facility which is useful for finding out about a particular event, such as the Blitz. A map explorer helps to find information about a specific location in or around Handsworth.

Handsworth's history *Browsing the Digital Handsworth site for historical events on Handsworth's past yields a wealth of information, backed by first-person accounts, pictures of people and places and enthralling journeys into bygone days. If your ancestors lived here, this will be a gold mine for you.*

The website has an interactive timeline with key events that have occurred in the local area from the Roman period to the present day.

Digital Handsworth is one of seven projects forming the Digital Midlands initiative. The other projects are: Exploring the Potteries, Literary Heritage – West Midlands, Revolutionary Players, Secret Shropshire, Staffordshire Past Track and Windows on Warwickshire. See the website **www.digitalmidlands.org.uk** for details.

Spotlight on south London

The history of six London boroughs and their people are the focus of the Ideal Homes website, **www.ideal-homes.org.uk**. On the site, Bexley, Bromley, Greenwich, Lambeth, Lewisham and Southwark are explored through old maps, photos and historic documents. Ideal Homes explains the history behind suburbia and what it would have been like to live in these residential developments, using places such as Streatham and Norwood to show how suburbs were created and why. There are also personal memories, such as tales of Coronation street parties in 1953.

It's through these personal documents that life in south London suburbs springs vividly to life – and even if your ancestors aren't mentioned by name, you'll understand more about how they lived and the sorts of things they cared about. Links to each of the six

IDEAL HOMES :
A HISTORY OF SOUTH-EAST LONDON SUBURBS

Exploring the origins and
significance of suburbia as
revealed through the history of
South East London

Life in the suburbs *London's borough of
Lambeth was once a country village and may
have taken its name from 'lamb' and 'hythe',
suggesting a landing place for sheep on the river
bank. Pearly kings and queens (below) add to the
colourful traditions of the area. The Ideal Homes
website brims with colourful facts.*

boroughs take you to a summary of the
history of each area, with further links to
other places within the borough where you
can find more specific historical accounts
and photos.

You can contribute your own photos,
documents and memories of south London
to the website and search other people's
contributions.

Great ports of England

A breath of sea air seems to sweep through
www.portcities.org.uk as it takes you on a
journey through the history of five of our
great maritime centres – Bristol, London,
Hartlepool, Liverpool and Southampton.
As an island nation with ancient seafaring

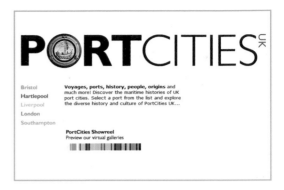

Sailing into the past *From the Romans to the
20th century, PortCities explores Britain's
maritime past and its impact on people's lives.*

traditions, Britain has been hugely influenced
by its ports. PortCities explains the impact
of the maritime world on British culture by
telling the stories of people who lived and
worked in port communities, looking at the
key events that affected their lives and the
industries and leisure activities that grew up
around these commercial hubs.

The PortCities website is supported by
museums, libraries and archives from across
the UK. You can search all five ports at once,
or just explore one in detail.

The site's contents can be browsed by
time and by topic, and its collections can
be searched by keyword. PortCities holds
photos, images, stories, videos and expert
information about all aspects of maritime
life. If your ancestor was a mariner, you
can look for images of the ships he may
have worked on.

Even if your family didn't live in one of
these centres, the website is a wonderful place
to get a feel for what life would have been
like living in big ports around Britain.

Going local in Scotland, Ireland and Wales

Local authorities and history societies in these countries are doing a great job of digitising material about their areas. Online photographs, documents and personal experiences give a real flavour of how your ancestors lived.

Local history sites are easy to use and are often interactive, with links to forums, offline and online, where you can contribute your own memories. The following websites are good examples of the wealth of online material about places and people.

Life in the Highlands

The Gaelic Village, or Am Baile, website, **ambaile.org.uk,** created by the Highland Council, is a digital archive of the history and culture of the Scottish Highlands and Islands. Its material is gathered from archives, libraries, museums and private collections.

An alphabetical subject index allows you to browse tales of Scotland's history, such as the story of the Scottish clans, complete with a Highland clan map. If you have even a scrap of information about the clan your ancestors belonged to, you'll be able to use a keyword search to find images, maps, audio, film footage or narratives about people, objects, themes or places. There's also a page where you can read other people's memories.

Highland highlights *The Gaelic Village site is a must for those with Scottish ancestors. It's an entertaining way to find out all about the heritage and culture of the Highlands and Islands of Scotland.*

Gateway to Ireland

The Island Ireland site, **islandireland.com,** is full of valuable information for researching your Irish local history, with links to many aspects of Irish life, including architecture, archaeology, folk culture, language and music. There's a link on the home page to **Irish Counties & Towns**, which leads to some links with fascinating details. For example, the link to the Limerick's Life website gives information about Limerick's colourful history, as well as old and new images of the city, extracts from historic quarter sessions records and some old newspaper excerpts.

Island Ireland also has links to genealogy sites, in and beyond Ireland, along with details of Irish local history societies that you can join.

	AROUND IRELAND Tourism, travel and community information for Ireland and the Irish abroad... Irish Counties & Towns	IRISH INFORMATION RESOURCES General information on Ireland, archives & libraries, Irish phone directory, government sites, Irish directories & search engines... Irish Museums
	IRISH HISTORY The Celts, the Famine, 1916 Rebellion, Northern Ireland, transportation, politics... Irish Genealogy & Local History	IRISH ENVIRONMENT Irish plants and wildlife, environmental concerns, gardens, landscape... Outdoor Activities
	IRISH ARTS & MUSIC Current events, Irish music and song, traditional instruments, Irish dance...	IRISH FOLK CULTURE Traditional life, clothing, recipes, folklore, customs,

Island Ireland is an Internet directory to Irish art, culture and environment with hand-picked links to Irish history,

Emerald enlightenment *An enthralling cross-section of all things Irish is stored on this site. You can browse the index list for directories.*

Wales revealed in all its glory

Welsh Wales offers an enthralling history of Wales and its people on its colourful website, **welshwales.co.uk**. It contains links to specific parts of Wales, with particular emphasis on Swansea. As much of the information is written by local people with a passion for their roots, this is a valuable resource for your family research.

Click on the link to **History,** for example, and you'll find a comprehensive history of Swansea describing its many industries from ship-building to mineral exploitation. The site contains fascinating images of the town as it was, and compares old buildings with their present-day appearance. The **Golden Yesterdays** section is an illustrated history of the area, showing how the town was structurally affected by events from the Norman conquest in the 11th century to the 'three-night Blitz' of 1941. There's also a fascinating study on the Mumbles railway, described as the world's first railway, that explains why it was built and describes how it was abruptly dismantled in 1960.

Forgotten faces *You may be able to recognise an ancestor in a group photograph. This procession in Wales in 1911 is to celebrate the coronation of George V.*

Wales time-travelling *A vivid tour through Welshwales (left) will help to recreate the lives of your Welsh ancestors. Maybe they were among the world's first train passengers on the Mumbles railway (below).*

Historic Swansea

From a pre-historic settlement and hideout for Viking invaders, to home of the world's first railway service, Swansea has an absorbing history - the gold sand and rugged green hills have so many colourful tales to tell.

In Swansea's own lifestory, a history of ship building in the 14th Century turned to considerably more delicate porcelain manufacture and followed by exhaustive oyster harvesting; mineral exploitation and copper exporting came in the burgeoning 19th Century. At one time the most powerful seaport in the world, Swansea's historical heritage is as captivating as it is surprising and contrasting.

The Mumbles Train
- World's first railway service

On 25 March 1807, a railroad carriage converted to carry people was conveyed by horse along the perimeter of Swansea Bay, travelling between "the dunes" at Swansea, and destined for Mumbles, an oyster harvesting and fishing village on the west of the bay. The people who undertook this journey were unknowing pioneers - they were the first railway passengers in world history.

The story of the "Mumbles Train", as it came to be known, is as heart breaking as it is fascinating. Considering its myriad achievements and world records, it's incongruous that the railway isn't more famous. It is disgraceful also that the railway was abruptly dismantled in 1960 (at that time electric tram powered) - 153 years after those historic first steps in 1807. To the commuter age and the world of

Trade, postal and street directories

Family historians love finding the right local directories, because these old records can often provide an exact location of a business or home address of a relative. Most are in local libraries and record offices, but some are online.

A few trade directories exist from the late 18th century, but most were produced from the early 19th century up to the 1970s. They began as an aid for commercial travellers, and as the 19th century wore on, the information in them became more comprehensive. From the 1860s directories included private residences as well as tradesmen.

Early trade directories
The first trade directories tended to focus only on a specific town or region. But greater co-operation between directories and the Post Office made compiling the directories more efficient, which led to the emergence of large-scale directories covering substantial areas of the UK. The best known of these were Pigot & Co.'s Directories that date from 1820 and Kelly's Post Office Directories, organised by county and published from 1845 until the mid 20th century.

Annual directories are the most useful. They're a wonderful resource for tracing people's movements, and for filling in missing information for the ten years between each of the censuses. They also play an important

role in tracing relatives after 1901, because census records since then are closed – 1911 records won't be fully available until 2012.

Useful for Scotland and Ireland
You'll find directories especially helpful for tracing your ancestors in Scotland and Ireland, particularly in those areas where fewer genealogical sources are available. There's good coverage for both countries from the 1890s, with one directory for Dublin and one for Glasgow dated 1846. There are also the odd directories available for earlier dates, such as Pigot & Co.'s 1824 Directory of Ireland.

Detective work with directories
Local directories can contribute to your research in two ways. First, they can be used to find the address of a person when you only know a name. But more importantly, they can help you to find the person's name when you only have an address or company name to go on. Once you have that name, you'll be able to locate your ancestor in other sources, such as electoral registers and in the census.

Types of directory
Directories were organised in a variety of ways – usually in alphabetical order, by town, by street name and house number, by occupation or by surname. Some directories included more than one type of index, which makes your hunt easier.

Invaluable resources Ranging from the late 18th century to the mid 20th century, trade and street directories such as these can be searched for fascinating details about your ancestors.

The Post Office and its workers

Ever since Charles I established the 'royal mail' in 1635, there's been a need to have a record of people's names and addresses.

With the growth in literacy, followed by the dispersal of people during the Industrial Revolution, the Post Office was kept busier and busier delivering letters. By the late 19th century, it employed around 170,000 people. Their records, showing appointments, pensions and dates of retirement, may also reveal birth date, wages received and reason for retirement. You can find out more about them at **postalheritage.org.uk**.

Mass communication *Postmen in 1930 sort through millions of parcels during the annual Christmas rush. Accurate use of addresses was never more important.*

TRADE DIRECTORIES These were most often arranged by town and then alphabetically by trade, sometimes with a second index of surnames. They give the name of the business, its address and the owner's name. They sometimes have a residential section as well, supplying the names of people not listed in the commercial section. This combination is particularly helpful to family historians.

POSTAL DIRECTORIES Arranged by county and then alphabetically by town, these directories usually give a short description and introduction to each place, with the names of local gentry and prominent people and institutions, a list of local traders grouped by occupation and, sometimes, even a residential list.

STREET DIRECTORIES All types of premises were covered, arranged by town, and then alphabetically by street name and numerically by house number. This kind of directory can be particularly useful if you're looking into the history of your own home (see page 234), because you can go straight to the address in the directory, without needing to know the name of the person who lived there.

Points to bear in mind

When using directories to help you to find an ancestor, there are some limitations to the information they can provide. For example, trade directories give only the head of the household or owner of the business, not the names of everyone living or working at the address. Consider these facts, too:

- House numbers and street names have changed over time, which can make it difficult to pinpoint a modern address. For example, most streets named after Nelson Mandela will have had an earlier name. Using directories in conjunction with old maps (see page 242), electoral lists (see page 294) and rate assessments helps to identify how and when the name changed.
- People renting rather than owning a property weren't usually listed.
- Private residents could choose not to be listed, which can confuse your search.
- It's easier to trace men than women through directories, as women were less likely to be listed as the head of a household or the owner of a business, or to own property of any kind.

Finding old directories

Your search will be speeded up if you know just where to look for trade, postal and street directories. Help is available, online or offline.

Most local archives and libraries hold the directories relevant to their area. You may be able to find them on the shelves, or ask to see copies that have been kept on microfilm. They are usually arranged chronologically.

If you can't track down the directory with information you want, there are some useful reference books on the subject. Try looking in *British Directories: A Bibliography and Guide to Directories Published in England*

and Wales (1850-1950) and Scotland (1773-1950) by Gareth Shaw and Allison Tipper (2nd edition, 1997) or in *Guide to the National and Provincial Directories of England and Wales, Excluding London, Published before 1856* by J. Norton. Your local reference library should have copies.

Sweet treats *Customers line up to buy in a Victorian grocer's. This and all other shops would have appeared in a local trade directory.*

Websites that help in the search for a directory

These sites will help you to find the old postal, trade and street directories that may be able to take you further in your search for relatives. You could also try the Society of Genealogists' Library at **sog.org.uk** (see page 173).

The Digital Library of Historical Directories

The University of Leicester is compiling an online database of English and Welsh trade, postal and street directories from 1750 to 1919, available at **historicaldirectories.org**. There's no charge for searching the scanned directories by location, date or keyword.

The keyword search is particularly useful if you're not sure of where your ancestor lived, because it lets you search for a surname even if the directory is indexed by occupation or address. You can find out which directories are available for each county by selecting the **Find by location** search option.

Genuki

Genuki has transcriptions and surname indexes to some trade directories at **genuki.org.uk**. Navigate to the relevant county page and then look under the **Directories** section to see if there are any indexes or transcriptions for that county. For example, the Kent County page has transcriptions of part of Pigot's 1840 and Kelly's 1936 directories, as well as surname and place name indexes for Pigot's 1823 and 1839 Kent directories.

Fáilte Romhat

This privately run site, at **failteromhat.com/pigot.htm**, has scanned copies of Pigot & Co's *Provincial Directory of Ireland, 1824*. You can search the site by province and town, and can choose from Connaught, Leinster, Munster and Ulster. Click on the one you want and an alphabetical list of towns and counties will appear, with links to scans of the pages for that town or county.

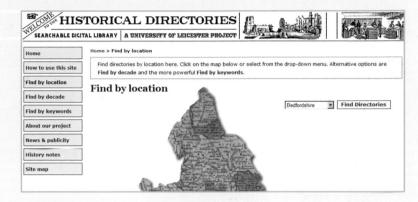

Directories

Pigot and Co.'s Royal National and Commercial Directory

The flysheet of the 1839 edition continues ...

" ... comprising classified lists of all persons in trade, and of the nobility, gentry and clergy, resident in the towns and principal villages in the above counties. An account of every mode of convenance by railway, road and water; Post-Office regulations, &c."

Alec Whitfield has compiled indexes to surnames and place names for the Kent volume of the 1823 and 1839 editions which have been republished are fairly readily available to researchers.

1823 (available on CD from S&N Genealogy Supplies)
Pigot 1823 (Kent) surname index
Pigot 1823 (Kent) place name index

1839 (available on CD from Archive CD Books)
(facsimile edition published 1993 by Michael Winton - ISBN 0-9504069-5-3, now hard to find)
Pigot 1839 (Kent) surname index
Pigot 1839 (Kent) place name index

1840 Janet and Richard Mason have transcribed parts of the Pigot 1840 Directory.

Pigot & Co's Provincial Directory of Ireland 1824
Connaught

Scanned images of Pigot & Co's Provincial directory of Ireland 1824. These are in PDF format so that they can be more easily viewed. Please note these files are large. The average size is 250k. Pigot & Co's directory goes through the towns of Ireland alphabetically. It lists a detailed description of the town or city, post office information and shows the names of nobility and gentry living in or close to the town. The traders of each town are arranged according to their trade. Pigot & Co's Directory was first published in 1820.

Province of Connaught	Castlerea	Gort	Sligo
Ballina	Castlerea	Jamestown	Strokestown
Ballinamore	Colooney	Killala	Swineford
Ballinasloe	Drumsna	Loughrea	Swineford
Ballisodare	Elphin	Manor-Hamilton	Tuam
Ballymote	Eyrecourt	Manor-Hamilton	Ballinrobe
Boyle	Galway	Roscommon	Ballinrobe
Carrick-on-Shannon	Galway	Sligo	Westport
Castlebar	Galway	Sligo	

Who's been living in your house?

Tracking down your ancestors' homes and learning more about them helps you to build up a more personal picture of your relatives. It can also reveal what their social status was and what sort of lifestyle they enjoyed.

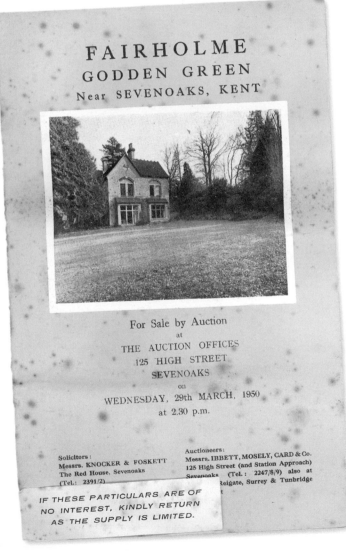

FAIRHOLME
GODDEN GREEN
Near SEVENOAKS, KENT

For Sale by Auction
at
THE AUCTION OFFICES
125 HIGH STREET
SEVENOAKS
on
WEDNESDAY, 29th MARCH, 1950
at 2.30 p.m.

Solicitors:
Messrs. KNOCKER & FOSKETT
The Red House, Sevenoaks
(Tel.: 2391/2)

Auctioneers:
Messrs. IBBETT, MOSELY, CARD & Co.
125 High Street (and Station Approach)
Sevenoaks (Tel.: 2247/8/9) also at
Reigate, Surrey & Tunbridge

IF THESE PARTICULARS ARE OF
NO INTEREST, KINDLY RETURN
AS THE SUPPLY IS LIMITED.

Did they live in a grand detached house with acres of garden, or was it life above a shop? Was their home situated in suburbia or did it jostle its neighbours in a former slum? There's a variety of resources available online to help you to make a start with researching the history of the homes your ancestors lived in – or, perhaps, finding out more about who lived in the house that you're living in now.

Where do you start?

The census and civil registration certificates you'll have already found are the best starting point. You can trace the addresses given on these documents on old maps (page 242), in electoral registers (page 294), in rate books, in street directories (230-3) and land tax documents

Desirable property *It's wonderful when you come across the sale particulars of your ancestors' home. Often they'll give you details of the interior, as well as the size of the grounds and the benefits of living in the area. This house was built by the Blackall family in 1864, and it wasn't put on the open market until 1950.*

(page 214) to learn more about the building, how long your family lived there and what it would have looked like. If you're really lucky, you may even find the deeds, original plans and old photos of the property. Then, using modern maps, you can establish whether the house you're looking for is still standing and if the street has the same name. The highlight of the search will be visiting that street and seeing the house for yourself. If the present owners are friendly, you might even get a chance to look inside.

Searching online

By using the aids available online, you can start to build a good foundation for your research. The websites shown on the right help to map a home today and yesterday, and fill in colourful social detail of many areas.

Need help?

If you get stuck with your house history research and need some expert help, go to the Hidden House History site at **hiddenhousehistory.co.uk** where there's an **EXPERT'S ARCHIVE** link. It takes you to a page where you there's a long list of answers to previously asked questions. Alternatively, you could visit the **Online house detectives** at **house-detectives.co.uk** to find out about the seminars and workshops they run or to commission them to further your findings.

Mapping the history of a home – online

Map websites are a great start. Once you've found the place you're looking for, you can zoom in or out to find your house, and you can cross-refer old and modern maps, to see how areas change over time. Note any outstanding landmarks, like railway lines or large institutional buildings. Not only will this help you to find the house, but these are the features that alter with time. Always make a note of the date of a map, especially if you're printing it.

Bing Maps

Begin with a modern map site. Bing Maps (formerly Multimap), at **bing.com/maps**, allows you to search by postcode, and will provide you with the location of your property, as well as a larger view of the surrounding area. This will be useful when matching up a house with older maps.

Old Maps

Once you've found your property on a modern map, try to match it up with an earlier map. Old Maps, at **old-maps.co.uk**, has a vast number of historical maps. It's searchable by place name, or map co-ordinates. Enter a search term and this should give you a picture of a historic map. For example, enter Broadstairs and you are shown a selection of old maps to choose from. Click on the one you want to see.

The Francis Frith Collection

It's a good idea to look at the Francis Frith collection at **francisfrith.com**. It has historic photographs of more than 7000 towns as well as maps and shared memories of specific places. This site is easy to search: just type in the place you're looking for, such as **Ipswich**, and it will direct you to the relevant page. If you're lucky, there'll be old photographs, maps that you can buy online and information about the town and how it has changed.

Vision of Britain

Information about the parish where the house stood is invaluable. Vision of Britain, at **visionofbritain.org.uk**, lets you search by place name or postcode. Here, a search under the Broadstairs postcode 'CT10 2EE' takes you to a page from where you can explore historical writings, statistics and the like. Click on **Historical units & statistics** and you arrive at a list of units that covered Broadstairs. Click on **Thanet District** to see some fascinating topics to explore.

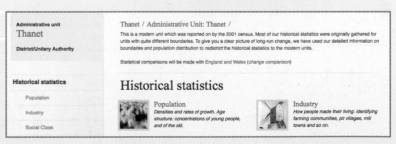

Maps – portraits of a landscape

You can discover much about the lives of your ancestors through maps of the local world they inhabited. These documents give you a sense of the landscape, the size of villages and towns and the rivers, roads and railways that gave access to the area – snapshots in time of how places looked.

Whether researching a local area, or the history of an ancestor's home, you can use past and present maps to find out where people lived, how an area has changed, whether the streets still have the same names – even whether or not the streets still exist and the houses still stand. Great swathes of residential housing were demolished in the late 19th century to make way for railways, stations and goods yards. Other areas were obliterated by bombing during the Second World War. Then, in the 1960s, row after row of Victorian 'slum' terraces were bulldozed and their inhabitants rehoused in shiny new tower blocks.

Maps to augment documents

When a census return or trade directory doesn't give a house number, but you want to find out exactly which building your ancestor lived or worked in, you can use a contemporary map to provide that vital clue. Look on the map for a labelled building, such as a pub or post office, that's near your ancestors' home. Then find that building in the census return or trade directory. You

Surveying the scene *This dapper surveyor and his fine theodolite, of around 1900, were essential to the detailed and extensive work carried out by the Ordnance Survey map-makers.*

can work your way along the street on the map, following the households listed in the census return or trade directory, and find out exactly which building your ancestor lived in. For more information about using census returns and trade directories, see pages 104-129 and 230-233, respectively.

Using old maps with new maps

If you compare a modern map with old maps of the same area, you'll soon notice that historical landscape features are echoed by modern ones. Former field boundaries and ancient footpaths dictate the routes of modern roads and the boundaries of housing estates, keeping the old shapes but in new guises. You can use these repeating patterns to help you to pinpoint a specific landmark from map to map, regardless of how extensively an area has been built up. Look out also for permanent landmarks such as rivers and lakes – they're unlikely to change, however much the areas around them do.

Maps online

The internet has made finding and using modern maps easy – all you need to do is key in a postcode, street or place name into a map-finding search engine (see page 238) to see an instant image of the area. A number of websites offer this free service.

Using Ordnance Survey maps

A marvellous aid to tracking your ancestor's whereabouts are the detailed, accurate and to-scale surveys of Great Britain's countryside and towns, dating from the early 19th century, especially the Ordnance Survey (OS) maps that now cover every inch of Britain.

Taking the high road *An Ordnance Survey map of 1929 shows an evocative Cairngorms view. The OS one-inch-to-the-mile map series was trusted by motorists and walkers alike.*

Back in 1791, in response to fears of invasion by France during the French Revolution, the Board of Ordnance (the government body responsible for military stores and weapons) was ordered to create an accurate map of the south coast of England. The first OS map, covering Kent, was published in 1801. Between 1867 and 1870, the OS undertook mapping for the whole of Great Britain in what became known as the 'First Edition Ordnance Survey Map'. Since then, regular surveys have recorded changes to Britain's

countryside and towns. On a large scale map, you can even work out the dimensions of individual buildings and houses. By comparing maps of the same area from different years, you can track alterations or extensions to any house or other building.

You'll find historical OS maps in most major archives, local libraries and record offices. Free online access to its modern digital maps is available on the OS website at **ordnancesurvey.co.uk**. These can be searched by place name, postcode or grid reference.

Finding an OS map

1 Enter **ordnancesurvey.co.uk**. Click on the tab labelled **Leisure**, and from the drop-down menu choose **OS getamap**. Enter the place name or postcode you want in the search box on the left at the top – in this case, 'W1U 7PA'. Click on the **Locate** button.

View your chosen map

2 A map of the area in question appears and you can use the tools at the top left of the map to move around the map and zoom in or out. Tools at the top right include ones that allow you to save or print a map, although you do have to register. If you want information about buying a more detailed map, click on the **shop** tab in the menu bar for your options.

The digital miracle of modern maps

Thanks to the internet you can have unprecedented access to modern maps of all kinds, from simple street maps to stunning satellite images which allow you to see the very buildings in which your ancestors lived, worked or worshipped.

A number of websites allow you to view modern maps online, free of charge. Most can be searched by postcode or place name and let you zoom in and see an area close up in great detail, or zoom out to see a building or street in its wider context and in relation to other places. This makes searching for your ancestors' homes far easier than if you were limited to printed maps and atlases. Before you start searching one of the digital map websites for an address that you're not too sure of, it's a good idea to have a 'dry run', and look for your own home, your old school or your workplace. Once you're confident, you can start your search in earnest.

Using Streetmap to search for a map

On **streetmap.co.uk** you can search UK maps by a range of categories including place name, street name, postcode and phone code. Enter a postcode, for example, and click on **Go**. This will take you to a map of the area, from which you zoom in and out, using the control functions below the map. If you want to enlarge the map area, click on the large map icon under **Map Size**. To see further in any direction, press the relevant arrow at the edge of the image.

Search Bing for your street

1 You can use **bing.com/maps** to search the UK by postcode or place name. Key in the postcode you require – here W1U 7PA and click **Find**. A straightforward street map appears.

Get an even better view

2 The image you see is a London street map view of the area. The second tab from the left on the menu bar toggles between **Aerial** and **Bird's Eye** options. If you click on **Aerial** you will see a hybrid view of the map – an aerial photograph overlaid with road names. The pin highlights the exact location of your search. If you click on the pin a pop-up panel appears, showing details of nearby stations and other information.

How to download Google Earth

If your PC is equipped with Windows XP, Vista or 7, or you have an Intel Mac, you should be able to download Google Earth to see wonderful aerial shots of places anywhere in the world, such as Hampton Court, Surrey (left).

This application is free of charge. Go to **earth.google.com**, click on the **Download Google Earth** button and follow the instructions to install the software.

Using Google maps

With **maps.google.co.uk** you can search by street name, place name or postcode, worldwide. Enter the address into the **Search** box and click on the search icon. A red pin points to your location and a bubble gives the full address, with links to enable you to get directions. You can zoom in and out and move around. If you click on the **Satellite** button an aerial photo of the area will appear.

Google Earth for the big picture

1 The Google Earth program features a breathtaking map of the world, created using satellite images and aerial photographs. It lets you zoom from a country overview to a photographic image of a well-known landmark – or even your own home – close up. Having installed it on your PC (see box above), double-click on the **Launch Google Earth** icon on the desktop. A satellite photo of the Earth appears with a **Fly to** box, into which you key the address you want.

Explore with Google Earth

2 When you click on the magnifying glass, the screen zooms in to your chosen location, which may take a couple of seconds to appear. You can zoom in more closely and look at individual buildings using the control features at the top right-hand corner of the image, and the map can be 'grabbed' and moved around using your mouse.

Watching Britain evolve

By comparing maps through the ages, you can see just how and when the green and pleasant acres that your ancestors knew were smothered by buildings and restructured by industry, transport and all the facilities of modern life.

The earliest-known English county maps were drawn by Christopher Saxton in the late 1500s. They're fascinating and beautiful but not very useful to the family historian, as few are to scale and none show any roads.

In the early 17th century, a cartographer called John Speed changed all that. He was born in Cheshire in 1552 and worked as a tailor in the family business. After a while he moved to London and began mixing in academic circles, which stimulated a passion for history and map making. Speed joined the Society of Antiquaries, where he found fellow enthusiasts more than willing to advise him, and soon he was able to give up tailoring and become a full-time cartographer. His maps of 1605 to 1610 are more comprehensive and detailed than Saxton's, and include the first town plans of England and Scotland.

Enclosure maps, 1750 to 1830

The earliest detailed surveys of most parishes are enclosure maps – large-scale maps of rural Britain drawn up between 1750 and 1830. The enclosure scheme was introduced by the government to make farming more efficient, in order to cope with the population explosion in the 18th and 19th centuries.

Before enclosure, most English peasants owned a few strips of land on which they grew their food. These strips were redistributed every year – so if you got poor land one year, you'd get a fertile strip or two the next. And every villager had commoners' rights, which meant that even the poorest could graze their animals and cut turf and wood for fuel. Enclosure took away these rights, consolidated all the strips of land and redistributed them as permanent plots. If you got an infertile plot, you were stuck with it. It also obliged the new landowners to fence their plots, which many couldn't afford to do, so they sold their land. Many people lost what little independence they'd had and ended up labouring for the new landowners, or migrating to the growing cities to staff the burgeoning factories. Enclosure maps were drawn up to show how the land had

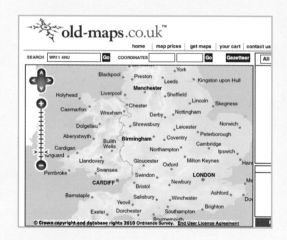

Search for old maps

1 The best place for viewing national historic maps online is at **old-maps.co.uk**. The site holds the digital Historical Map Archive for Great Britain and has collections of historical maps from the OS County Series at scales of 1:2500 and 1:10 560, dating from 1840 to 1948. Click on the **get maps** tab in the menu bar positioned at the top of the page.

Four ways to search the site

2 You can enter an address – town name, modern postcode or street name and number; or use British National Grid co-ordinates, remembering to enter first Easting and then Northing; or use the gazetteer to search by county and then town name (click on the **Gazetteer** button).

been divided into 'awards' – 5,341 in England and 229 in Wales. They outline fields, farms and settlements, land ownership and parish and township boundaries.

The National Archives (TNA) holds some enclosure maps and tithe maps (see box, right), but the best information as to their location is on **hds.essex.ac.uk/em/**, a free online database, complementing the book *The Enclosure Maps of England and Wales, 1595-1918* by R.J.P. Kain, J Chapman and R.R. Oliver (Cambridge University Press, 2004).

Official taxation maps

After the Finance Act of 1910, the Valuation Office used Ordnance Survey maps (see page 237) to devise a new tax based on property values. It surveyed houses, farms and workshops. Each property was identified and numbered. Details about the property, including its owner, occupier, how many rooms it had and its value were entered into a 'Field Book'. Valuation Office maps for England and Wales are at TNA (series IR121 to IR135); Field Books are in series IR58.

Using tithe maps to track the land

Tithes were originally payments in kind (see page 214). The Tithe Act of 1836 brought in cash payments, and maps were drawn to show the areas on which a tithe was payable. Every map shows the boundaries of woods and fields, roads and waterways and the location of buildings. With the maps were tithe apportionment books, whose numbers correspond to plots on the maps. From these you can find out addresses, names of occupiers, landowners and types of property.

Using a modern postcode

3 To match a postcode of today with an old map, enter, for example, the postcode 'WR11 4NU' into the **SEARCH** box. Press the **Go** button. This brings up a results page – in this case with 39 matches – from which you can choose an address match, say 21 Lanesfield Park; click on the address.

Pinpoint the house

4 The location of 21 Lanesfield Park is now shown on a modern map. To see an old map of the area (above) choose a map from the scrolling menu selection on the right. The image of the map will then be downloaded. You can zoom in or out and move in different directions around the map. If you picked an early map, Lanesfield Park does not show up, but you can get an idea of what was there before it. (the first map that Lanesfield Park can be seen on dates to 1985).

Choose alternative maps

5 You can look at other historic maps whose dates are shown along with the map image, compare the old map with a modern map or buy a printed map. The collections are free if you're using only the earliest 1:10 560 scale map. If you want more detailed or later maps you'll have to pay for them. Click on **Add to cart** if you want to do this, and then follow the payment procedure.

Finding old maps online

You can use old maps to help you to work out exactly where your ancestors lived. From a location on a census return you can use current or historic Ordnance Survey maps, and tithe or enclosure maps to take you back in time.

Some family history societies are putting local historical maps online and the process is a continuing one. So if you don't find what you're looking for at first, it's worth checking regularly for new material. The following websites provide access to local historical maps or information about where to find them. For more information on tithe and enclosure maps, look back at pages 214 and 240.

Nonsuch Park In 1538, Henry VIII built a great palace and park here. This map was drawn up after his death to settle a property dispute.

Tracking down your ancestors' homes

The following websites will make it easier for you to find the elusive map that will give depth to the detail you've already collected.

Genuki

You can check what's available online in a specific locality at **genuki.org.uk**. For example, if you want to find a map of an area of Cumberland, go to the United Kingdom and Ireland homepage; select **England**, then **Cumberland**, and choose **Maps** from the alphabetical topics list. This takes you to a page of map links – from the old to state-of-the art 2007 satellite images from Flash Earth.

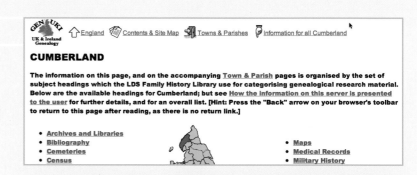

Your Old Books & Maps Online

There's a great range of old maps and etchings, as well as digital facsimiles of old historical and military books, available both on CD and online at **youroldbooksandmaps.co.uk**.

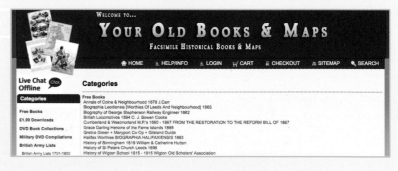

MAPCO

The MAPCO website, **mapco.net**, holds images of 18th and 19th-century maps of London, the British Isles and Australia that you can view for free; shown here is Bett's map of Scotland, 1847. Either key a place of interest into the Google search box towards the bottom of the page, or click the links on the page to access your area of interest. Once you've chosen a map, you can see close-ups of different areas by clicking on the relevant square in the interactive grid.

MOTCO

If you're interested in London, go to MOTCO, at **motco.com**, where several maps can be viewed online for free – four of them are linked with contemporary surveys of the city. Click on the link from the homepage to **MAPS – REFERENCE DATABASE**, where you can scroll through the descriptions and choose the map you'd like to see; shown here is part of a map of Westminster and Southwark in 1746. Use the link to the left of the page to access the index of places on your map.

British Library

The main map collection is now stored as part of the British Library's Online Gallery. Some maps are available online, others are held at the British Library itself (see Directory). To see which maps can be viewed online, go to **bl.uk/onlinegallery**, and click on the tab labelled **Online exhibitions**. In the page that follows, click on **View all** and scroll down the list until you reach the section **Maps and views**.

The National Archives

Although The National Archives (TNA) holds maps from the 16th to the 20th centuries, you can't view them online, but you can find out what's in the collection via the catalogue at **nationalarchives.gov.uk/catalogue**. Click on the **Search the Catalogue** link. In the **Word or phrase** box type 'map AND [place name]' or 'plan AND [place name]'. You'll then see a page of results and codes. Click on the code to see a description of the document(s). If you want to see any items at TNA, write down their reference numbers.

Photographic collections online

Historic photos are a great way of adding colour to your family story. You might not find photos of your relatives in an online collection, but you can supplement your own pictures with images of places that they knew, to give depth to your discoveries.

Two views of Bournemouth *The photo below was taken in 1904, and the smaller inset in 1925. Although taken from a similar viewpoint you can see how the area has changed in the intervening years.*

Picture libraries often hold photographs of workplaces, railway stations, football grounds, streets and buildings with which your ancestors may have been associated. Try looking for something specific to your family, such as a place of worship, a sports club or a factory.

Public photo albums

Pictures of ordinary people from a particular era can give you a good idea of how your ancestors lived and dressed. The Francis Frith or Mary Evans (see right) libraries have pictures dating from the beginnings of photography, 150 years ago.

You'll find the Francis Frith Collection at **francisfrith.com**. It's the result of one man's ambition to photograph every town and village in the UK. Frances Frith was a Quaker born in Chesterfield, Derbyshire, in 1822. Originally a grocer, then a printer, in 1855 he sold all his businesses to devote himself to his photographic ambitions. At first he took the photos himself but, as the business grew, he hired assistants. He liked to include people in his views, both to give a sense of scale and to say something about contemporary fashions, transport and pastimes. Today, the library is an invaluable record of the changes in Britain's towns, villages and countryside from 1860 to 1970. You can search the website by place name, postcode or through the online gazetteer.

When you've found a location, there will probably be some personal memories relating to the place below the area where the pictures are displayed. These are a priceless resource and add an extra dimension to this site.

Local photographic collections

Across the UK there are picture collections that will enhance your view of the past. Some are accessible online; others you need to visit.

☞ **Glasgow Museums Photo Library, glasgow.gov.uk/en/Visitors/Museums Galleries/photolibrary.html**, holds more than 20,000 art and photography images. Use a keyword to search its online images, then sort the results using the subject titles Art & Design, Transport & Technology, Natural History and Human History.

☞ **PhotoLondon, photolondon.org.uk,** lists addresses and searching information on how to locate images from archives such as the Guildhall Library, Museum of London, London Metropolitan Archives and Westminster Archives. There's also a section to help you to trace individual photographers working in London between 1841 and 1908.

☞ **Manchester Local Image Collection,** at **images.manchester.gov.uk**, contains more than 80,000 historical photos from the past 100 years that you can search online.

Visit the Mary Evans Picture Library

1 There are more than 200,000 images available online at **maryevans.com**, with around 500 new ones added every week. There's a broad spectrum of topics and subject areas, which often extend far beyond the traditional notion of a historical picture.

Search the online collection

2 To make a free search of the online collection, key a word, such as 'milliner', into the **Quick Search** box and press **Go**. A selection of thumbnail pictures appears, each of which can be clicked on to enlarge the image and display the date of the image and a detailed description.

In search of a better life

For hundreds of years people have been coming to the British Isles, often to escape religious or political persecution – and many Britons left to find work and greater opportunities elsewhere. So there's a good chance of finding a migrant somewhere in your family tree.

A story of new peoples

From Saxons, Vikings, Normans and 16th-century Huguenots to Jews escaping persecution in the 19th and 20th centuries, and post-war West Indians and Asians, Britain's story is closely linked to immigration. The documents generated include many potential ancestors.

The records made when people first arrive in Britain are key sources of information – they include passenger lists, certificates of arrival and naturalisation records. There was no official registration of foreigners, or 'aliens', until the 19th century, but some documents do exist from as far back as 600 years ago.

Where to start looking

A good place to begin your search for immigrant ancestors is The National Archives (TNA). It has some of the oldest records for immigrants, which are filed under a wide range of series codes (see below).

NATURALISATION CERTIFICATES An important TNA resource is the series of naturalisation certificates issued by the Home Office from 1844 to 1948. They were issued to people once they had satisfied certain criteria, such as length of stay, other family members living in the UK or having performed some sort of service to the nation. The records are a great help if you're trying to trace the records of an ancestor who arrived in Britain in the late 19th or early 20th century. But records after

New lives *Thousands of Jews left Eastern Europe in the late 19th century. Many settled in cities such as London, Leeds and Manchester, establishing new communities and businesses.*

1922 are officially closed for 100 years – although in some instances the Home Office will review an individual file's status if there's a sufficiently good reason.

Most of these files would have been the concern of the Home Office, so they have the prefix HO preceding the file number. The certificates fall into four groups, depending on the date on which they were granted.
- HO1 – from 1844 to 1871
- HO45 – from 1872 to 1878
- HO144 – from 1879 to 1934
- HO405 – from 1935 to 1948 (Some of this series is still retained by the Home Office; you should contact them if you require access. The address is in the Directory.)

Multi-cultural London *People from all over the world flocked to London, bringing with them their cultural and religious identities. The London Muslim Centre (left), opened in 2004, was the realisation of an idea born in 1910. Russian steam baths (below) in London's Brick Lane, maintained the propriety of 'Ladies only' days.*

SEARCHING ONLINE FOR A CERTIFICATE You can search the appropriate series to find your ancestor's records using TNA's online catalogue at **nationalarchives.gov.uk**. It's possible to do a search by surname, but unless you're looking for a rare name, it's a good idea to narrow the field before starting your search by adding details such as a person's forenames, date of birth and place of birth. This will save time by making your search much more effective.

Immigrant communities

Arrival records of individuals date from the Napoleonic wars, when legislation was introduced to monitor people entering the country. The mass of paperwork that immigration generates is a rich hunting ground.

There has always been a steady flow of people into the British Isles, but in modern times it has increased. For example, between the years of 1948 to 1962 any citizen of the British Commonwealth was automatically entitled to British nationality upon arrival. After 1962, there was a tightening of the immigration rules, though large numbers of people continued to arrive throughout the 1960s and 1970s. There are several websites that can help you to trace the 'new Britons' who arrived at this time.

A website that tells it as it was

Funded by the Heritage Lottery and supported by The National Archives, the Moving Here website, **movinghere.org.uk**, looks at the history of 19th and 20th-century

migration to England. To help minority ethnic groups to document their own history of migration it provides free access to an online catalogue of material related to migration history. The material is divided into four broad themes – stories, a gallery, migration histories and help with tracing your roots.

STORIES In this collection of immigrants' oral histories, you can listen to people telling their own tales or simply read transcripts of the recordings. There are hundreds of stories, ranging from a Pakistani's memories of moving to Huddersfield to a Caribbean migrant's experiences after arriving on the SS *Empire Windrush* in 1948.

If you have a story to tell, you can do it – the website tells you how. In the **Stories** section you'll also find themed collections of memories on a wide range of subjects. These have been compiled by museums and family history organisations working with the Moving Here project.

THE GALLERY You'll find this wonderful collection contains the most diverse images, arranged by theme and reflecting different aspects of migration. Subjects include food and drink, faith, faces, war,

> **'No blacks. No Irish. No children.'**
> England was not as welcoming to the new Britons as some might have hoped. One Jamaican man, Owen, recalls his brother's hunt for lodgings: '…he went to this house and he knocked and the lady said, "No, there is no vacancy". Soon as he walked out on the pavement, she came over with a bucket of water and throw (*sic*) water on stairs outside and start scrubbing it. He was really shocked'. His experience wasn't unique.

politics and identity. You can download the images free of charge, and even send them as e-postcards.

MIGRATION HISTORIES The experiences of four immigrant communities – Caribbean, Irish, Jewish and South Asian – are looked at in fascinating detail. Each immigrant history provides information on the reasons people migrated from their home country, finds out what their journeys were like, asks about people's experiences of arriving and settling in England, and asks how people make contact with their family's original home country.

A timeline for each community gives the story a historical perspective, so that you'll get the whole picture. You can download some of the sources – such as newspapers and photos – that were used to compile the histories.

TRACING YOUR ROOTS Perhaps the most important section, if you're tracing your family, is the section on tracing your roots. After an excellent introduction, there are sections devoted to Caribbean, Irish, Jewish and South Asian groups.

Each of these sections gives a thorough guide to researching your roots within that community. For example, if you click on **Tracing Caribbean roots**, you're offered links to life events, occupations, land and property information, a section on slavery and another on migration. Within each of these there are more options and the depth of information is remarkable. For example, the land and property page gives you information that includes deeds and patent registers, maps and plans, probate records and plantation records.

Pictures, subject overviews and first-person accounts add to the comprehensive amount of detail.

Brightening up Britain *The austerity of 1950s Britain was enlivened by newcomers from the Caribbean with their different cultural traditions.*

Not all 'criminals' committed crimes

If you're researching your West Indian ancestors, don't overlook criminal records: many islanders were labelled criminals for violating the smallest law – such as a black woman wearing a silk slip (only white women were allowed to wear silk). Slaves or servants could also be arrested just for whistling in public. Your ancestor just might be listed as a 'criminal' for doing something very minor. The only positive legacy of this harsh system is that it makes people easier to trace.

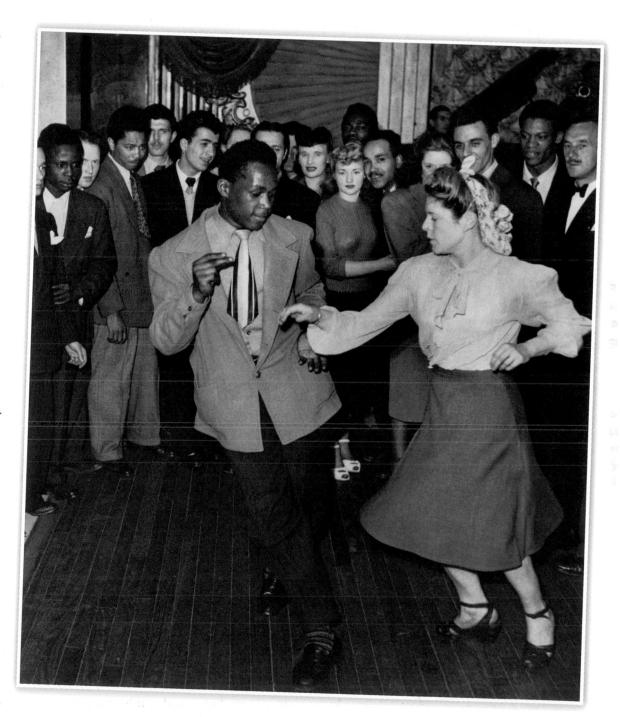

Jewish resources online

Over the centuries, many Jewish people have settled in Britain and there's a wealth of information about them available on the internet. Much of it has been collected by charitable organisations and is free to access.

The first Jewish communities in England can be traced back to the 11th century. At that time the Jewish population was largely made up of Norman-French Jews who were followers of William the Conqueror and had travelled to England in 1066, acting as the king's financiers. But in 1290 Edward I's Edict of Expulsion meant Jews were expelled, forcibly converted or killed. It wasn't until the mid 17th century that Jewish immigrants were permitted to settle here again.

Large numbers of Jewish refugees came to Britain during the last two decades of the 19th century, fleeing from the persecution inflicted on them in parts of Eastern Europe under the Russian Tsars, Alexander III and Nicholas II. Then in the 1930s, the Nazi persecution of Jews brought a further wave of refugee immigrants.

Seeking the Jews of Britain

This migration of Jewish people into Britain over the centuries has generated a great deal of information, and there are a number of websites that can help those researching their Jewish ancestors. You can start your search in conventional civil registration and census documents. But it's important to remember that many Jews changed their names, especially during the two world wars, to anglicise them. The unusual sounding names were often misspelled on official documents, so you may need to do a little lateral thinking. Also bear in mind that some Jewish marriages would have gone unrecorded as Jews were not subject to the Marriage Act of 1753, which stated that weddings must take place in an Anglican place of worship.

Jewish records at TNA

The National Archives (TNA) has various sources relating to Anglo-Jewish history in its collection, found within many different records. The earliest records occur in the Home Office (HO) collections, while the Colonial Office (CO) and the Foreign Office (FO) records contain information for Jewish communities abroad, both in British colonies and foreign lands. TNA's records for immigration and naturalisation could also be relevant, particularly for the large influx of Jewish refugees in the late 19th century.

To search TNA's indexes, go to **nationalarchives.gov.uk** and select **The Catalogue**. Click on **Research guides** and then use the alphabetical list to find the section on **Jewish history**. The list that comes up describes the different sources available and where to access them.

Child refugee *Tired and alone, 8-year-old Josepha Salmon, the first of 5,000 Jewish and non-Aryan refugees, arrives at Harwich on December 2, 1938 in an exercise known as the* Kindertransport. *She'd come from Germany, and was destined for Dovercourt Bay camp.*

Websites that help you to trace your Jewish ancestors

In addition to Cyndi's List (at **cyndislist.com/jewish.htm**), which will give you many links to Jewish resources all over the world, you may like to try these websites.

Genealogy Resources on the Internet

American genealogist, the late John Fuller, developed an extensive database of genealogy resources on the internet. The site he founded continues to provide mailing lists for Jewish genealogy from many parts of the world, including Britain, America, Israel, Germany and Russia. Enter **rootsweb.ancestry.com/~jfuller/gen_mail.html** into your web browser, then click on any links that interest you.

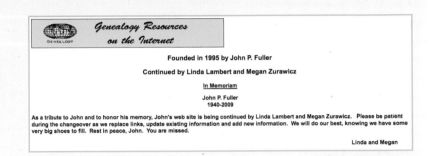

JewishGen

The website **jewishgen.org** is dedicated to Jewish genealogy throughout the world. JewishGen is a non-profit-making organisation that aims to share as much information as possible. The site has a number of online databases, such as a Worldwide Burial Registry, Holocaust Database and Communities Database, as well as discussion forums and various ongoing projects. The website is free to search, but you'll need to register.

London Metropolitan Archives

London has long been an important home for the Jewish community and the website **cityoflondon.gov.uk** has links to various resources. For a time, from the 1650s to the 1730s, most Jews in England were London based, so the archives have sources important to Jewish genealogy for this period, including some synagogue records. From the City of London homepage, type 'Information Leaflets' into the **Quick search** box then click the search icon. On the page that appears click on **Information leaflets** then scroll down to **24 Jewish genealogy.**

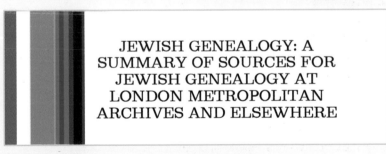

The Jewish Genealogical Society of Great Britain

This volunteer-run, non-profit-making organisation has its own website at **jgsgb.org.uk**. The website is free to use, although there's also a members-only area which has databases that can be viewed online. The website has details of a number of family trees that it holds in its library, but they can't be viewed online.

Finding new homes

If your family came from the Caribbean, West Africa or Asia, or ancestors emigrated to Commonwealth countries or worked in colonial India, these websites may help you to understand more about them and their new lives.

The family historian who's interested in the records of Britain's colonial past and the slave trade can get hold of a vast amount of material online. But this is only the tip of the iceberg. There's so much more – hundreds of thousands of pages – stored on microfilm and microfiche, or in the form of letters and other papers, books and photographs. Much of this material can be viewed only where it is stored – at libraries such as the Commonwealth Institute in London, at family history societies all over the UK and at a variety of other museums and archives. The good news is that what is available online is increasing, as dedicated volunteers locate, transcribe and upload the data.

The Commonwealth Institute website (see below) and the four websites shown opposite are primarily concerned with immigrant and emigrant communities. While they may not help you to draw your family tree, they will provide valuable and often moving insights into the background of your community, and help you to establish lines of inquiry.

The Commonwealth of countries

The Institute of Commonwealth Studies in London (see Directory) has a website at **commonwealth.sas.ac.uk**. It has no simple 'find your roots' links, or lists of names for you to search, but the library (catalogued online) holds more than 160,000 items of Caribbean, Southern African and Australian information. For those with West Indian ancestors there's an online exhibition at **commonwealth.sas.ac.uk/libraries/caribbean/default.htm**, called Routes to Roots, which covers Caribbean history, explaining what archives are available and providing links to other relevant websites.

New citizens *People from the Caribbean began to arrive in Britain as early as the 17th century. Many Jamaicans, like those seen here arriving at Plymouth in 1955, were eager to enjoy a new way of life in England. If your family came from the West Indies, you'll find their records through one or more of the websites here.*

Searching farther afield

World Gen Web

One of the most important resources for all family historians is WorldGenWeb, at **worldgenweb.org**. It's a project run by volunteers, and is designed to provide genealogical and historical records and resources to the public, via the internet. Eventually it hopes to have every country in the world represented online, hosted by researchers who are familiar with the records in their own country. It's divided up into countries, then each area within that country, and is free and simple to use.

The National Archives

An online exhibition, **nationalarchives.gov.uk/pathways/blackhistory**, focusing on black history in Britain from 1500 to 1850, has been created by The National Archives (TNA) in partnership with the Black and Asian Studies Association. You'll find six separate 'galleries' to visit and superb interactive 'learning journeys', such as a virtual tour of the Black and Asian influence on three English cities – London, Bristol and Liverpool. Follow the links to maps of each of the cities, with further links to the Black and Asian presence in particular areas.

The British Library India Office Records

The British Library is the home of the records and archives of British families in South Asia from the early 17th to the mid 20th centuries. Start your search at **indiafamily.bl.uk/UI** for links to numerous family history sources such as records for British families who settled in India during the colonial period. And there's an informative section on the Asians in Britain before the large-scale immigration that began in the 1950s and 1960s.

London Metropolitan Archives

The London Metropolitan Archives has researched groups of immigrants, including French, Irish, Black and Asian, living in London over the past 500 years. Go to **cityoflondon.gov.uk** and click on the tab labelled **online services.** From the drop-down menu select **online databases**. On the page that opens, scroll down and select **London generations**. Here you will find a number of resources and external links.

Emigration and the colonies

As Britain expanded its empire, so the opportunities for Britons to live or work overseas increased. Some people chose to go, others were forced – but whatever the reason for their departure, a wealth of documentation exists to help you to track down emigrating ancestors.

Large-scale voluntary emigration from Britain began with the establishment of the colonies from the 17th century onwards. Before then, only small numbers of people had left to settle in Europe, including those from England and Scotland who were encouraged to colonise Ireland in the 1600s. Records about the settlement of Ireland during this period can be found at The National Archives (TNA). They include Irish state papers, muster rolls and poll tax records – all of which give snapshots of how many immigrants there were in different Irish counties at any one time.

People on the move

Both voluntary and forced emigration increased in the 17th and 18th centuries. Penal colonies were set up in the New World and many convicts were transported there. After the American War of Independence in the 1770s, new destinations were needed and Canada, the West Indies and newly colonised Australia became home for large numbers of transported convicts (see page 206). Transportation was discontinued in 1868, but by then about 160,000 convicts had been sent to Australia and Van Diemen's Land (Tasmania) alone.

If you have ancestors who went to the New World voluntarily in the early years, their records may exist in the archives of the countries where they settled. But these are

Pioneer homes *This 19th-century immigrants' house in Sydney, Australia, accommodated 72 people, all of them voluntary settlers.*

largely incomplete as there was no systematic record keeping. Detailed passenger lists for voyages out of Britain weren't kept until very late in the 19th century, so their departure may have gone unrecorded.

You'll find Cyndi's List and WorldGenWeb are helpful for this type of search. See page 260 for examples of how to use these sites.

A new life in the sun

The numbers who chose to leave the British Isles peaked in the 19th century, with as many as 10 million people leaving for the USA, Canada and Australia during this period to seek their fortunes in farming and gold-mining. Others spread across the British Empire, mostly employed in running the colonies, or to join civil engineering projects, such as the building of bridges and railways in India. Soldiers and sailors were granted land at the end of their period of service, if they agreed to settle in the new colonies.

The government's introduction, after 1832, of specially reduced passages from the UK to the colonies enticed still more people to emigrate.

More controversially, from the late 1800s, orphanages sent children abroad to help to populate Australia, Canada and New Zealand (see page 300) with 'good British stock'.

Convict records

Because of the nature of officialdom, you've a much better chance of tracking down your emigrant ancestors if they were deported as convicts than if they left of their own volition. In contrast to the records for voluntary emigration, far more detail was amassed for

---

Websites to help you to trace ancestors in Australia

Both New South Wales and Queensland have websites to help you to find ancestors. So if they settled there, you should be able to find them.

New South Wales Try **bdm.nsw.gov.au**. It's the registry for births, marriages and deaths. Then there's **records.nsw.gov.au** for census returns.

Queensland For births, marriages and deaths, go to **justice.qld.gov.au**. For information about assisted passages to Australia between 1814 and 1912, visit **archives.qld.gov.au**.

If you don't know the state in which your relatives lived, one of the following family history sites may help. They are gateway sites that will link you to

archives in various states and territories. Start with **coraweb.com.au**, which has a section dedicated to immigration. Or try the Australian Family History Compendium at **afhc.cohsoft.com.au/**. It will link you to other sites that are geared towards family history research.

In addition, the National Archives of Australia (NAA) holds a quantity of information on its website, **naa.gov.au**. The site has a free online catalogue with descriptions of about 6 million documents, posters, photos, maps, films and sound recordings that you can search by keyword, name and date. Go to the homepage, choose the **Search the Collection** link on the left and then **Search as a guest**.

---

those forcibly removed from Britain. Many of their records are held by Australia's state archives. (See also page 206.)

Emigration records at TNA

The National Archives holds a variety of emigration records dating from the 1600s. Records from the 19th century are the most comprehensive, including not only passenger lists for voluntary emigrants but also detailed criminal records of the convicts and their transportation papers.

It's a good idea to read TNA's guide at **nationalarchives.gov.uk/records/research-guides/emigration.htm** before you begin looking for emigrant records. You'll discover a wealth of information and you can choose to look more closely at the most appropriate section for your search. For example, passenger lists can be very helpful.

Everyone boarding a specific ship was registered on its passenger list.

The lists often give extra family history information, such as age and usual place of residence. If you think you have ancestors who set sail for a new life abroad between 1890 and 1919, you should be able to find their records in the online passenger lists, but not every record has survived and they're not all kept and catalogued together.

Series BT27 holds passenger lists compiled by the Board of Trade (hence BT) for outward passengers from 1890 to 1960, and series BT26 lists all the incoming passengers. The whole list – more than 30 million names – is now available on the subscription website **findmypast.co.uk**. This provides a body of information of enormous value to you if you're tracing an emigrant ancestor.

Tracing family members in India

Britons went out to India in droves, as traders, planters, soldiers or government officials. Although there was no mass emigration at any one time, your ancestors could have been among the 4 million who were born, married or died there.

Britain's influence in India and neighbouring regions goes back a long way. If some of your ancestors lived there for a time, you should be able to trace them.

Birth, marriage and death records, similar to those found in UK parish registers, were kept by both the East India Company and the British Government's India Office. Chaplains of the Company began compiling records from the late 17th century as Christian churches became established in India. You'll need to know where your ancestors lived, as the records are split according to region – the three main areas being Bengal, Madras and Bombay – and cover mainly European and Anglo-Indian Christians. The British Library (see right) holds sets of the registers, but they're not yet available to search online.

East India Company records

Up to 1858 British interests in India were controlled by the East India Company, which recorded a vast amount of information about its activities and its staff – merchants, traders,

mariners and soldiers. Annual army lists were compiled, detailing both native regiments and those commanded and staffed by Europeans.

If your ancestor was a soldier, it helps to know his rank, as one set of records covers commissioned officers and another encompasses 'other ranks' – including non-commissioned officers. The entry papers for officer cadets – the rank held by military cadets during their training to become

commissioned officers – provide valuable genealogical information, such as the names of cadets' parents and details of their births or baptisms.

Starting to piece together the service records for 'other ranks' is rather less straightforward. But you can gather together information by using embarkation lists, depot registers, muster rolls and registers of the East India Company's soldiers.

British life abroad *So determined were Britons in India to 'maintain standards' that they even took their foxhounds along on board. You can search for details of their military and business careers in India on* **bl.uk** *and* **fibis.org**.

Britons in India A typical British household at the time of the Raj would have included numerous Indian staff. Records of the British and Anglo-Indians – including marriages, deaths and the births of their children – can be traced through the websites below.

Two phases of British rule in India

British involvement in India can be divided into two distinct periods. Records for both periods are now held at the British Library (see below).

● 1600-1858 Britain conquered and controlled India through the East India Company.

● 1858-1947 India was governed directly by British government through the India Office. This period was known as 'The Raj' – from a Hindi term for 'rule'. In its prime, the Raj included not just present-day India, but Pakistan, Bangladesh, Sri Lanka, Nepal, Bhutan and Burma. Britons lived and worked in all these countries, so your ancestors may show up in the records.

Searching online for your ancestors in India

The National Archives, at **nationalarchives.gov.uk**, is a natural starting point. Its research guides will help you to understand why people emigrated, and it will give you links to related websites. In addition to the TNA site, you may find that the three websites described here can be helpful in your search for family relatives in India and the surrounding regions. They can be searched online and should help you to track down or piece together the lives of your ancestors.

British Library

A wealth of British Government records exists, from the private papers of the Viceroys of India to key documents about the partition of India. The records have been given alphabetical classifications. Class N, for example, covers baptisms, marriages and burials 'relating mainly to European and Eurasian Christians in India, Burma and other areas administrated by the East India Company and the Government of India' from1698 to 1969.

The British Library is both a great source of information and offers family history researchers a great deal of help. Go to the homepage, **bl.uk**, and click on **Catalogues** in the black menu bar. From the list of options that appears, select **India Family History** under **Other catalogues.** Here you'll find a Quick search option along with information on what is available. You can focus your enquiries by clicking on **Advanced Search** below the **Quick search** box

Families in British India Society

The website of Families in British India Society (FIBIS), at **fibis.org**, gives free online access to the records you'll need if you decide to research ancestors who lived or served in the Indian sub-continent from 1600 to 1947. Its database of transcriptions is still somewhat limited, but this is an on-going project so the scope will broaden.

On the homepage, click on **fibis database** then on the page that appears enter a surname in the **QUICK SEARCH** box then click on **Go**. If there

is a match for the name, you are shown the source or sources in which that name appears. You can also browse the records, selecting from the list on the left of the page. The website has transcriptions of military and maritime records, will, photos, personal papers and directories.

If you're a beginner, the website offers links to research guides that help you to find resources that may not yet be available on the FIBIS website. To find detailed research guides on civil, military and other occupational records that are being updated all the time, click on the **Fibiwiki** link along the top panel of the homepage.

Moving Here

You'll find great tips for tracing your Indian ancestors on the website **movinghere.org.uk**. It gives online access to case studies and records that you can search for free. There's a specific section on Indian ancestors that you can visit by keying in **movinghere.org.uk/galleries/roots/ asian/asian.htm**.

Ellis Island – a new start in America

For thousands of immigrants nearing New York by sea, the Statue of Liberty, torch lifted high in her hand, was guiding them to a better life in America. At her feet lay Ellis Island, their first port of call.

From January 1, 1892, to November 12, 1954, this small patch of land, just off the southern end of Manhattan Island, opened its arms to more than 12 million people fleeing poverty, oppression and disease. The island is named after Samuel Ellis, a local farmer and merchant, who owned it in the 1770s. In its early years it was used for many purposes, including a hanging site for pirates and a coastal fort to stop fleets sailing directly into New York harbour as the British had done in 1776 during the War of Independence.

The US government bought the island from New York State in 1808 and used it as a military base until 1890, when $75,000 was allocated to build the first immigration centre. Landfill was used to double the size of the island, and while it was under construction, the Barge Office at the Battery, on the southern tip of Manhattan, processed nearly 406,000 immigrants.

Symbol of freedom *Dominating Ellis Island, the Statue of Liberty was a gift from the people of France in recognition of American support during the French Revolution. Inscribed on it is a verse by Emma Lazarus that begins 'Give me your tired, your poor, your huddled masses yearning to breathe free...'. True to that promise, a poor Italian family arrive at Ellis Island (right).*

The rough and the smooth of immigration

Not everyone who came to America was a refugee in dire straits. Turmoil in parts of late 19th-century Europe could also affect well-off families, who took advantage of increasingly sophisticated and comfortable ships to travel together to America in search of a safer life. For them, the immigration process was relatively easy. An upper-class family paying first or second-class fares wouldn't have had to visit Ellis Island at all. Instead, the wealthy underwent brief questioning and medical examination on board their ship, and then disembarked at the Hudson or East River Piers on Manhattan Island. The US government calculated that if you had the means to purchase an expensive ticket, then you would not be a financial problem.

Life was different, though, for those in third class or steerage. Once the first and second-class passengers had disembarked, they'd be transferred to a ferry, taken to Ellis Island and put through a medical and legal inspection. Even if you were in good health, with all your paperwork in order, the whole process could take up to 5 hours. And yet, even in the peak year of 1897 with 1.25 million immigrants pouring in, a positive effort was made to treat all who arrived with courtesy, and hospital wards were built for those who were ill.

For some, though, the arduous journey across the Atlantic

Welcome to America *Some descendants of immigrants to the USA trace their families' names on Ellis Island's Wall of Honor.*

was a wasted experience. About 2 per cent of people never made it through the immigration process and were returned to their country of origin, usually because they were judged to be of bad character and a potential burden to the state. Others with chronic contagious diseases were also rejected as a danger to public health. To these people and their families, Ellis Island became known as 'The Island of Tears'.

First and famous arrivals

When the Ellis Island immigration centre opened in January 1892, the first person to be processed was Annie Moore, from Cork, in Ireland. She was just 15 years old and described by officials as 'A rosy cheeked Irish girl'. She was just one of 700 people who arrived in New York on that day.

Among the millions, some notable names are on the Ellis Island passenger database, which is searchable online (see right). Walt Disney was one of them. He arrived on September 23, 1919, aged 19, from France, where he'd served as a Red Cross ambulance driver during the First World War. He then headed for Kansas City to concentrate on his career as a cartoonist. Another was

Sigmund Freud, who sailed from Bremen, Germany, in 1909, to deliver a series of lectures. This was his first and only time in America, declaring later that 'America is a mistake, a giant mistake'. More appreciative of this new land were Harry Houdini, Albert Einstein and English entertainers Charlie Chaplin, Leslie Hape (Bob Hope) and Arthur Jefferson (Stan Laurel), who were all to find fame in Hollywood.

Perhaps luckiest of all the arrivals at Ellis Island was the less-famous Barbara West. She arrived, aged just 10 months, on the RMS *Carpathia*, which had rescued her from a freezing sea on the night of April 14-15, 1912. The ship that she'd been aboard was the *Titanic*.

Star immigrant *A 16-year-old stilt-walker called Archibald Leach arrived at Ellis Island from England on July 28, 1920. By 1931 he had arrived in Hollywood and changed his name to Cary Grant.*

Ellis Island ancestors online

The website **ellisisland.org** is a great resource if you have immigrant ancestors who arrived at Ellis Island. It has a free searchable database, and all you have to do is register your email address to search the records. By using a simple name search, you can trawl the passenger lists or ships' manifests – the shipping companies' records of all passengers. You can also download and print a certificate for your family history records.

The website (right) also links you to the site of the American Immigrant Wall of Honor at Ellis Island (above), a permanent memorial of individual or family names. There are 700,000 names on the wall and more are being added all the time. Your ancestor or family may be eligible for addition to the wall if they arrived at Ellis Island in the past.

Did your ancestors go adventuring?

The thrill of striking out into the unknown was irresistible to many men during the 19th century. They dreamed of bringing the benefits of 'civilisation' to great swathes of the world that made up the British Empire. Sometimes their families went along for the ride, too.

Although most British emigrants settled in the colonies of North America and Australia, some people went to places with far smaller British communities. Those who went as missionaries often ventured into previously uncharted regions.

As the Empire expanded during the 18th and 19th centuries, many people were bound to explore new territories abroad through their service in the armed forces, as civil servants or as traders in places as far flung as Kenya and Malaya. Others were motivated to go overseas to heal the sick or teach.

Searching for ancestors abroad

When you start on the trail of these daring relatives, remember that only a few records were kept, so searching can be quite difficult. As always, the more information you have – such as a date of departure, arrival, a ship name or a destination – the more chance of success you'll have.

Many primary resources that would be useful to you are located overseas. If you can't find what you're searching for online, you may want to consider hiring a researcher abroad, or even visiting the land of your forefathers yourself. If the adventurous blood that coursed through your ancestor's veins still runs in yours, you'll find the challenge exciting and, with luck, rewarding.

The websites shown here may be helpful if you're trying to track down ancestors in other parts of the world. In most cases, they will have travelled to far-off countries by ship, so it makes sense to start by looking at passenger lists of people leaving the UK. If you know which ship your ancestors sailed on, you may be able to track their passage at **ancestorsonboard.com** (which is part of FindMyPast) or **ancestry.co.uk**.

The Baltic States ~ Estonia, Latvia & Lithuania

Category Index
- FEEFHS ~ Federation of East European Family History Societies
- General Resource Sites
- History & Culture
- How To
- Language, Handwriting, & Script
- Libraries, Archives & Museums
- Locality Specific
- Mailing Lists, Newsgroups & Chat
- Maps, Gazetteers & Geographical Information
- Newspapers
- Professional Researchers, Volunteers & Other Research Services
- Publications, Software & Supplies
- Queries, Message Boards & Surname Lists
- Records: Census, Cemeteries, Land, Obituaries, Personal, Taxes and Vital
- Religion & Churches
- Societies & Groups

Related Categories
- Eastern Europe
- Finland
- Germany / Deutschland
- Jewish
- Poland / Polska
- Scandinavia & the Nordic Countries
- Western Europe

Migration Routes, Roads & Trails

Category Index
- General Resource Sites
- The California Trail
- Locality Specific
- Mailing Lists, Newsgroups & Chat
- Maps, Gazetteers & Geographical Information
- Mormon Trail
- The National Road
- Oregon Trail
- People & Families
- Publications, Software & Supplies
- Santa Fe Trail
- Societies & Groups
- Wagon Trains
- Wilderness Road
- Zane's Trace

Related Categories
- Canals, Rivers & Waterways
- Immigration & Naturalization
- Orphans
- Passports
- Railroads
- Ships & Passenger Lists
- U.S. - History

Consult Cyndi's List website

1 A good place to begin researching records for other parts of the world is at **cyndislist.com**. It's comprehensive, free to use and has pages for many geographical regions. Find lists for a region or country by selecting one from the page revealed by clicking on **Categories**. Country or region lists, such as this one for the Baltic States, can provide links to libraries and archives, mailing lists and information about published sources and local family history centres and societies.

Follow your ancestor's trail

2 The main categories list covers topics as well as regions. For example, click on **Cowboys, Ranchers & the Wild West**. This will bring up the list that offers, among much else, **Migration Routes, Roads & Trails**. Click on it and you're offered links to a list that includes **Wagon Trains**, **Orphans**, **Passports**, **People & Families**, **Ships & Passenger Lists** and the **Mormon Trail**.

Was your ancestor a missionary?

Fortunately for family historians, 'mission headquarters' expected to be kept updated on their missionaries' progress through regular letters and reports – many of which survive. Missionary work was not a male prerogative: young women were involved, too. If your female ancestor was a missionary, you may be able to discover a lot more about her from missionary records than you would from a census return.

The School of Oriental and African Studies (SOAS) in London has a large archive of documents, photographs and published materials related to missionary work. Find out more at **helpers.shl.lon.ac.uk**. On the homepage click on the link to **Helpers descriptions** and a list appears. Scroll down until you find an entry for the Methodist Missionary Society. Click on that for information about missionary societies.

Using the WorldGenWeb Project

The website **worldgenweb.org** differs from Cyndi's List in that it often contains primary information, not just links. It's free of charge, and from links on the homepage you're taken to individual countries' genealogical pages. Each country's page is hosted by a volunteer co-ordinator, so the level of detail varies from one country to another – many of the counties have no host and contain only basic information.

Searching Africa

You can access a country's website from the relevant continent or region's homepage. So if you're interested in Zimbabwe, for example, go to the Africa homepage **africagenweb.org** and select **Zimbabwe**. Only some of the African countries have hosted websites, but all of them provide general information. Some, such as Zimbabwe, offer more detail than others, for example, Somalia.

Did they go East?

If you're looking for ancestors in Japan, you'll be taken via the AsiaGenWeb page to the Japan page, **rootsweb.ancestry.com/~jpnwgw**, where you can select a language (Japanese, Spanish or English). Choose **English** and you'll see a Welcome page. Scroll down and you'll find numerous links to relevant websites including family history connections and people who have transcribed lists from immigrant ships.

Making contact

One of the many rewards of tracing your ancestry is the opportunity to join in the wider family history community. By making contact with other researchers you can enhance your own experiences, share frustrations and make new friends. Thanks to the web your family can join in your discoveries – you may even find long-lost relatives along the way.

Looking for help online

Tracing your family history is a very personal journey but it doesn't have to be undertaken alone. Your research can be greatly advanced by contact with other researchers who may be able to offer help and advice.

To make faster headway with your search for family members, you can combine the use of traditional research, using birth, marriage and death certificates and census returns with help from the millions of people who make up the online community.

Many of the websites mentioned in this book offer mailing lists, discussion groups and web forums where researchers can meet and discuss areas of common interest and help each other with search problems. For example, **ancestry.co.uk** has Community web pages where family trees can be shared and message boards used. The American site **genforum.genealogy.com** may be able to assist you in finding relations overseas or help with foreign records. Genes Reunited, at **genesreunited.co.uk**, encourages you to upload your tree to its site and conduct searches of other members' trees.

Joining a networking community

To become part of a mailing list that you think will suit your interests, you'll have to send an email asking to subscribe to that list. Your computer must have the capacity to receive daily emails concerning the subject of your group. See page 280 for more about mailing lists and how they work.

The people you meet online who are researching the same or similar topics to those that interest you will often be able to help you to extend your family tree. They may have information you need, and even be distantly related to you.

Web forums are also helpful, and all you need to do is regularly check the site for updated discussions. If you want to ask or answer a query on a website message board, you'll be prompted to create an online profile so that people can contact you about the message you have left.

Speed up your search

Use sites like **friendsreunited.co.uk** and **facebook.com** and you can quickly see if the people you've identified in your research are listed there. As more people sign up to sites

Finding your family Genes Reunited (above) is a spin-off of the popular Friends Reunited website and helps long-lost family members to find each other. On the American-based site **genealogy.com** *(left) you can find* **genforum.genealogy.com**, *which is useful if you suspect your ancestors are spread around the world.*

like this, there's a good chance you'll find someone you know. For example, if you sign up to Genes Reunited and upload your family tree for others to view, you'll get email updates when someone shows an interest in your ancestors. This way, you'll link in to other people's family trees, and maybe find a whole new branch of family members.

The online directory **192.com** (see pages 293 and 295) offers searches of phone directories, electoral rolls, company reports and more. If you find the correct person, the site will give you an address, postcode and sometimes a phone number. It's free to search but there's a fee to view full entries. If you're looking for people abroad, **cyndislist.com** has a link to worldwide directories.

Despite all the information you can find by searching for people on these various online sources, not everyone is listed, so success isn't always guaranteed. A way round this is to put an appeal for information into online message boards or discussion groups. Post a message with the name of the person you're looking for, prominently displayed, and see if anyone replies. If you've an idea of the general area in which the person lives, you can find the local family history society through **ffhs.org.uk** and make an appeal.

Getting help with your search

If you still can't find the person you're looking for, consider trying one of the agencies that specialise in tracing people.

Lookupuk.com

Not only does lookupuk.com offer advice, but it also gives access to a huge range of indexes, phone directories, email addresses and newsgroups, as well as offering links to other family research sites such as Ancestry. In addition, you can search the thousands of messages posted on the site – and leave your own messages – making this a really comprehensive site that will help you to contact missing ancestors.

Salvation Army Family Tracing

At salvationarmy.org.uk/familytracing you'll find the Salvation Army's Family Tracing Service, which aims to reunite family members. The service is closely linked to colleagues in 100 countries, allowing far-flung families to be reunited more easily. A full-time staff can help you to find relatives, for which a small fee is charged – donations are also accepted. A search can take as little as 5 minutes or a few years, and the success rate is 85 per cent.

People Trace Online

This agency specialises in tracing people through its website at peopletraceonline.co.uk. It carries out searches on people and property, using electoral rolls and civil registration indexes. You can trace property ownership details, which is helpful when you're trying to trace the movements of your ancestors and their descendants. You have to pay for the service you choose, but prices aren't high – sometimes as little as 30 pence.

Why make contact?

The internet's a marvellous tool for sharing information. You can put your family history online so that relatives can see what you've achieved, and you may even discover information about your family that's already out there.

Contacting other researchers allows you to correspond with – or even meet – people with common interests, and can help you to discover more about your own family tree in the process. Best of all, a member of the online community may have the answer to one of your problems, or at least be able to point you in the right direction.

How to contact other people

There are a number of ways of contacting people to find answers to your questions. Here are a few of the most popular.

• Mailing lists are an email exchange forum made up of people interested in the same research topic. By subscribing to the list you will receive all the email messages that are posted to that list, in either 'mail mode' or 'digest mode'. Mail mode means that you receive each message as it's posted; digest mode combines a week's worth of messages in one email. When you post a message, it's automatically circulated to all the subscribers on that mailing list.

• Newsgroups work by posting messages on an online message board. You don't need to be a subscriber to use the service.

• Web-based forums are websites that act as message boards. Like newsgroups, they are a place where researchers can post messages for others to read. Both newsgroups and

web-based forums have the advantage of not inundating you with emails; their only disadvantage is that you may miss crucial postings if you don't check the message boards regularly for updates.

Family history databases

Another way to join an online community is to sign up with **genesreunited.co.uk** or **ancestry.co.uk**. Once you've uploaded your tree, the database will alert you when it detects a match in another member's tree. You can contact that member via the website to see if their match really is part of your tree, or mere coincidence. This can help you to broaden your familytree – as well as open up the possibility of meeting living relatives.

  GENUKI UK & Ireland Genealogy — GENUKI Contents

Genealogy Mailing Lists and Usenet Newsgroups

The newsgroups soc.genealogy.britain and soc.genealogy.ireland which the GENUKI Web server has been created to support, are just two of a number of newsgroups devoted to various topics and regions, worldwide. John Fuller provides descriptive listings of the much larger set of genealogy mailing lists that now exist. (GENUKI's listing of UK&I-related mailing lists is maintained in conjunction with John Fuller's much more general list.)

Genealogy Resources on the Internet

GENEALOGY

Founded in 1995 by John P. Fuller

Continued by Linda Lambert and Megan Zurawicz

In Memoriam

John P. Fuller
1940-2009

As a tribute to John and to honor his memory, John's web site is being continued by Linda Lambert and Megan Zurawicz. Please be patient during the changeover as we replace links, update existing information and add new information. We will do our best, knowing we have some very big shoes to fill. Rest in peace, John. You are missed.

Linda and Megan

Using Genuki for your search

1 Genuki has links to information sites for every region of the British Isles, as well as information on Irish and UK genealogy (see page 44). Go to **genuki.org.uk/wg**.

Search the world

2 Genuki supports a number of newsgroups and mailing lists from around the world, as well as the UK. If you click on **Mailing lists** you will now be linked to the John P. Fuller genealogy resource, which has worldwide mailing lists that may be relevant to your research.

Establish your boundaries

If you decide to join an online community, you'll find a vast range of topics from which to choose – from surname research sites to those that focus on locations, religions, occupations and countless other subjects. It's important to know what you are trying to achieve so that you can adopt a methodical approach and stick to lists relevant to your search, rather than searching randomly. Here's how to search on two of the most popular websites, Cyndi's List and Genuki.

Present every Sunday
Names of the parishioners from churches all over the world can be viewed on Cyndi's List. You may be able to track down one of your ancestors on this site by searching the appropriate country, year and denomination.

Genealogy Categories

A   B   C   D   E   F   G   H   I   J   K   L   M
N   O   P   Q   R   S   T   U   V   W   X   Y   Z

▸ Acadian, Cajun & Creole (127)
Updated September 14, 2011

▸ Adoption (188)
Updated September 24, 2011

▸ Africa (86)
Updated June 2, 2011

▸ African-American (677)
Updated September 24, 2011

▸ Ancestry.com: The Basics (173)
Updated September 22, 2011

▸ Antarctica (41)
Updated December 5, 2010

▸ Asia & The Pacific (292)
Updated September 7, 2011

▸ Newspapers (729)
Updated September 22, 2011

▸ Norway / Norge (330)
Updated September 11, 2011

▸ Novelties & Gifts (70)
Updated September 1, 2011

▸ Numbering Systems (37)
Updated August 29, 2011

▸ Obituaries (458)
Updated September 26, 2011

▸ Occupations (385)
Updated September 25, 2011

▸ Odds & Ends (55)
Updated July 5, 2011

Mailing Lists

Category Index

▸ Briefly Defined
▸ Complete Resource for Genealogy Mailing Lists
▸ General Mailing Lists
▸ General Resources
▸ How To
▸ Internet Resources
▸ Mailing List Archives
▸ Military
▸ Miscellaneous
▸ Queries & Surnames
▸ Vendors: Buy, Sell or Trade

Related Categories

▸ Ancestry.com: The Basics
▸ Blogs for Genealogy
▸ Chat & IRC
▸ FamilySearch
▸ Handy Online Starting Points
▸ Internet Genealogy
▸ Newsgroups
▸ Podcasts for Genealogy
▸ Queries & Message Boards
▸ RootsWeb & ROOTS-L
▸ Search Engines
▸ Volunteer Projects
▸ Wikis for Genealogy

→ **AMREV-HESSIANS Mailing List**
For anyone with a genealogical interest in the Hessian soldiers (German auxiliary troops employed by King George III of England) who remained in America after the American Revolution. Archives: browse or search.

→ **BLACKWARHEROS Mailing List**
For anyone with a genealogical or historical interest in Black Americans who were heros during any war. Archives: browse or search.

→ **FOB-LIST - Friends of the Boers - E-mail List**
The primary topic of this mailing list is the centenary commemoration of the 2nd Anglo Boer War (1899-1902).

→ **FRENCH-INDIAN Mailing List**
Archives: browse or search.

→ **Genealogy Resources on the Internet - Wars / Military Mailing Lists**
Most of the mailing list links here point to this site, wonderfully maintained for years by John Fuller. This site indexes links for all known genealogy mailing lists, including RootsWeb and others.

→ **RootsWeb: Genealogy Mailing Lists: New Zealand**
The majority of genealogy mailing lists are hosted by RootsWeb.com. Messages on RootsWeb lists are archived. The links to RootsWeb here also point you to the archives (browse or search).

→ **SEMINOLE-WARS Mailing List**
Archives: browse or search.

→ **The Anglo Boer War Discussion Page**
This mailing list is for the discussion of the Anglo Boer War and other military related topics pre-1900.

Using Cyndi's List

1 If you are keen to contact the mailing list for an online community, there's a range of subjects to choose from on the Cyndi's list website (see page 46). Go to **cyndislist.com** and from the homepage, click on the **Categories** tab in the menu bar, and then on the letter **'M'**. Now click on **Mailing Lists** on the page that appears.

Choose your topic

2 You can see from the list that there are many options from which to chose. For example, the **Military** link will take you to message boards from across the globe dedicated to that subject.

Join a mailing list

3 To join the mailing list of your choice you simply click on the link and follow the instructions as to how to join.

Shared interests

It's encouraging to know you may be only a phone call or web search away from finding someone who is trying to track down the same piece of family history as you – or who may already have found it!

Using family trees online

Finding a family tree that matches and overlaps with yours is exciting, and may open up whole new areas of research. But before you incorporate new family members into your tree, check them against original sources first.

The data uploaded by other researchers into online family trees is what's known as secondary material, and isn't always accurate. It's compiled data, unlike online indexes, and may contain errors of judgment as well as mistakes in reading and typing. Using primary sources – originals – is the only way to ensure the greatest accuracy.

Sorting out your sources
The tendency is to believe what you see on a site, assuming that if it's there, it must be true. Unfortunately this isn't always the case, so it's important to be able to tell a primary source from a secondary one.

PRIMARY SOURCES These are the actual records made by people present at the occasion in question – whether it's in official documents or personal papers. They include parish registers, civil registration certificates, census returns, letters, diaries, newspaper articles and photographs. Usually, the only primary sources that you'll be able to access are photographic images of the original documents, which you can view online.

All in it together *Memories and experiences seem richer and more intense when shared by people with something in common, like these workers on a jaunt in Rhyl, north Wales, in the 1920s.*

Original documents *If the new information you receive can be confirmed by birth certificates, census records or letters, enter it into your tree.*

You can also request photocopies of original documents from archives and record offices, which they'll send you for a small charge.

SECONDARY SOURCES These are records made about a past event, by people who weren't present. Online genealogy, by its very nature, relies heavily on secondary material. The original, which may be damaged, faded or written in an old-fashioned and often illegible script, has been read by someone and copied out – often several times – before it

appears in an online index. The chances for errors to creep in are high, which is why you need to verify any second-hand data.

Confirming the 'facts'
Sometimes the information in other people's online family history can't be backed up, such as when it stems from family stories or memories passed down through the generations. On other occasions, all you need to do is check that the researcher obtained the relevant certificates. It's also worth double-checking spellings, as old handwriting is notoriously hard to read. Here are some useful guidelines to consider before putting other people's research into your own work.
• Ask the original researcher where they found the information and what documents they have.
• Find out if they were unable to find certain primary records.
• Use their names, dates and locations only as a starting point for ordering your own certificates, or for finding parish records, census returns and other primary sources to verify the research and confirm that it ties into your family tree.

Copyright and privacy issues
Online resources are publications and subject to copyright and privacy considerations. When people put material online, they're essentially publishing it. Don't simply copy and paste large amounts of text that don't belong to you. And don't publish online any data you've received without first checking where it comes from and if the person who provided it is happy for you to do so.

Online family trees genesreunited.co.uk

With about 11 million members, Genes Reunited offers you a great chance of making contact with unknown relatives, once you start searching.

The website lets you search its database of family trees for your ancestors and possible relatives. You need to register before you can make full use of the site, then you can upload your own family tree onto the site for free. It works best when users include as much detail as possible, so try to get your whole family involved – the more information on the site, the greater the chances of finding relatives and discovering shared ancestors. The search engine looks for matches in other people's uploaded trees, and alerts you if it finds any. If you want to contact that someone and view their family tree, you have to take out a subscription. This takes only a few moments and prices start at £15 for six months' standard membership. If you choose to share information with other Genes Reunited members, your privacy is protected, as all messages are exchanged via the website.

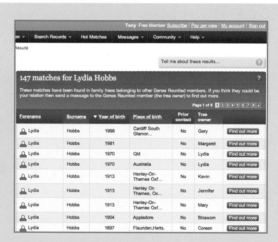

Sign up as a member

1 To become a member of Genes Reunited, go to the homepage, **genesreunited.co.uk**, click on **Register FREE** and fill in your name, date of birth, place of birth and contact details and so on. You can then begin uploading your family tree (see page 312) and carry out searches of other people's trees.

Do a quick name search

2 A quick search can be made by entering a first and last name in the **Quick search** bar. In this case we'll look for an ancestor named Lydia Hobbs.

Check the matches

3 This screen shows the results for a quick search for a Lydia Hobbs. There are 147 matches dating back from 1998. Look through the dates and places of birth to see if any of these matches the ancestor you're interested in. If so, you can contact the tree owner by clicking on **Find out more**. If you've not yet paid for full membership, you'll be asked to upgrade.

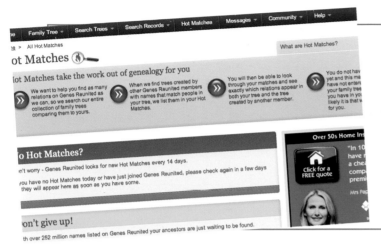

Shared information

Members of Genes Reunited can double-check secondary sources (see page 269) by accessing the census returns from 1841 to 1901, as well as the birth, marriage and death indexes. When you find what you want, you need to buy credits to view the images and details. Fifty credits cost £5 and are valid for 30 days.

Writing a 'Trying to find' message

When you put a 'Trying to find' message online, start with the name of the person you're searching for, written in capital letters. This makes it much easier to spot for anyone who may be scanning a long list. Then include as much information as you can to maximise the chances of identifying a match. Wherever possible, give a full name, date and place of birth, and details about the person's parents, along with any other helpful clues you can think of.

Try 'Hot matches'

4 You can also click on the **Hot matches** tab from the menu bar. The search engine will scan other family trees in its database and list other members who have the same names as yours in their family trees. It shows how many names overlap – the more there are, the likelier you are to be related.

Using 'Search Trees'

5 A third option is to click the **Search Trees** tab on the menu bar, then use Search All Trees. This searches family trees in the database to see how many have the same surnames as your family tree. This is more useful for unusual surnames. Common names will throw up so many matches, you'll be overwhelmed. But 100 or so matches to an unusual name may well be worth investigating. Again, you can contact the owner of the tree by clicking on the **Find out more** button.

Read and post messages

6 As well as looking for matches in family trees, you can also read and post messages if you click on the **Messages** menu bar. You may also participate in message boards – these can be found by clicking on the **Community** tab in the menu bar.

How to develop your family tree online

If you've joined Genes Reunited and found other researchers who might be connected with your family, you'll want to upload your family tree so that you can share information with them. Here's how.

Follow the step-by-step instructions below to upload your family tree to the Genes Reunited website. This can be time-consuming, but it's quite straightforward, so don't be daunted. It doesn't matter if you add only one or two names at a time to your tree, and it's easy to go back in to edit and adapt your entries as you discover new information. One way to navigate your way about is to use the buttons at the top of the Genes

Reunited homepage. You'll see eight tab-like buttons: those with downward pointing arrows by them offer a choice when you click on them. Under **Family tree** you'll find links to **My tree** and **Import GEDCOM** (see opposite). Select **My tree** and you are taken straight to your family tree (see below). This is where you get to see your tree and can add to it and edit it. You can choose to see just your immediate

Starting your online family tree

1 On the **genesreunited.co.uk** homepage, click **Family Tree** in the top panel and select **My tree** and you'll see the details you entered at registration – name, year of birth, gender and place of birth – below a panel showing your tree. This is, in effect, your tree's starting point. You can personalise the form by adding other details – such as your nicknames or your job, and you can also add photographs. When you are happy with your page click **Save changes**.

Add your parents

2 Now you can add other members of your family tree. Click the **Add Mother** link and fill in her details in the form provided. Save the changes and then do the same for your father. Your female relatives appear in pink boxes, and males in blue. Every time you complete a form, click on **Save changes**.

Add more family members

3 To add more names to your tree, such as your paternal grandparents, click on the blue box for your father, then click **Add Father** to add his father or **Add Mother** to add his mother. The same applies for adding partners, siblings or children. If you click on any individual box you may find that it expands to give 'Tree matches' and 'Record matches'. This means someone else's tree includes an ancestor with the same name and year of birth.

family or the full tree, as well as looking for ancestors or descendants of any relations on the tree. There is also a button marked Map where you can plot birth locations.

If you click on the **Search Trees** button, one option is to **View people in your tree,** which lists all the entries in your family tree. Click **Search trees** to discover if any other Genes Reunited members share that relation with you. **Search records** looks through the historical records on Genes Reunited to see if there are any matches.

Another option under **Search Trees** is **Search all trees**. On the page you are taken to, you can search all of the nearly quarter of a million names in all the family trees on the site. The only compulsory field is 'Surname', but if you know the 'Forename', 'Year of birth' and 'Birth place' of the relation this will help narrow things down.

Faster on your computer *Once you've collected a fair amount of information about your family, it's helpful to upload it onto a family tree on the Genes Reunited website.*

Making connections

4 In this example, we set up an entry for the tree owner's maternal grandfather, John Carpenter. Move the mouse over his name and you will see a notice indicating that there are 33 'Tree matches'. Click on the link to open a new window listing details of all 33 matches, along with their place and year of birth.

Sending messages

5 Click the **Find out more** button next to the tree owner's name and type your message in the text box. Explain which member of their tree you are interested in and ask for permission to view their tree. This facility keeps your details safe, as your own email address is never given to anyone else.

Save duplicating work with Gedcom

Gedcom is the term used for the standard file format used by most family historians. For more information about it, see page 278.

If you already have a gedcom file containing your family tree, you don't need to re-enter your family tree details on the Genes Reunited site. You can simply upload the gedcom file. Click on the **Family Tree** and select **Import GEDCOM** on the page that appears, make sure you read the text under 'Important – Before you begin' before clicking on the **Import GEDCOM** button.

You can also export your family tree as a gedcom file. From the same page click **Export GEDCOM** under **Your Tree** at the left of the page. Your gedcom file will then be emailed to the address you gave when you first registered with Genes Reunited.

Sharing online family trees

Seeing other people's trees online may inspire you to take yours further or give you useful pointers on presentation. You may even be lucky enough to discover one, already compiled, that features some of your own ancestors.

Tracing your family's history is so popular now that it's quite likely that someone, somewhere, is researching a family history that has links with your own. It can be tremendously exciting to link up with distant relatives who share one or more ancestors – and physical quirks – with you. You might find that dad's red hair, granny's lovely voice or George's photographic memory might be replicated elsewhere in your extended family.

When sharing information and finding links between your family tree and someone else's, always be aware that data can be put onto the internet by anyone, and you don't know how just thorough they may have been in their checks.

Double-check everything you find, and use the information only as a starting point for your searches. Mistakes can be made unintentionally, but you don't want to perpetuate them by incorporating them into your own family tree.

Searching the Ancestral File

1 To search other people's family trees for a Thomas Proctor, who married a Susanna Arabella Garraway early in the 1800s, go to **familysearch.org** and click on the **Trees** icon in the menu bar beneath the title.

Enter details

2 On the page that opens enter all the details you have – names, locations, dates – and click on the **Search** button.

Read the first results

3 You get one search result for Thomas Proctor and it shows that he married in 1810. Click on the name **Thomas Proctor**.

Familysearch

On **familysearch.org** (see page 138) there's an area devoted to online family trees, known as the **Ancestral File**, which holds thousands of pedigrees put together from submissions by members of the Church of Jesus Christ of Latter-day Saints (the Mormons) and others, since 1978. The search process for this site is similar to that for searching on the International Genealogical Index (IGI), shown on page 138. Below is an example of how to do a search using the Ancestral File.

Rootsweb

This website, **wc.rootsweb.ancestry.com**, has a vast database of family trees. There are around 500 million names online and the collection continues to expand. It offers mailing lists and message boards, to help you to keep in touch with other family researchers. You can submit your family tree to RootsWeb free of charge, after registering; if you've already registered on Ancestry's website, you can use the same login. On the right, you'll see how to use the website and manage your family tree.

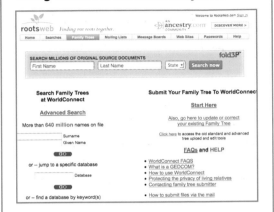

Using wc.rootsweb.ancestry.com

To upload your family tree, go to the WorldConnect site. Under the **Submit Your Family Tree To WorldConnect** heading, click **Start Here**. You'll find instructions on how to convert your family tree to Gedcom (see below) format – don't worry – this won't change your original file. Once reformatted, choose a name for your family tree and follow the steps for uploading it.

You can also change or remove any previously uploaded information by clicking **Update or correct your existing family tree**. This takes you to the **Manage tree** page, which lists all your trees. The editorial options are on the right-hand side of the page, under **Tree settings**. Click on the appropriate option – for example, **Delete tree** to delete the tree from the website.

What is Gedcom?

You'll find the term Gedcom will crop up frequently as you get more involved with online family trees. It comes from Genealogical Data Communications and is the standard file format used by most family history software. Look at page 278 to find out more about it and learn how to use it, if you're not already familiar with it.

Ancestral File

« Back to search results

```
      name:  Thomas PROCTOR
    gender:  Male
      birth: 1773
      death: 31 May 1836
             Birmingham, Warwickshire, England, Uk
        afn: V851-R2
```

Parents

```
    father: William PROCTER (AFN: V851-PP )
    mother: Mary MORTIBOYS (AFN: V851-QV )
```

Marriages (1)

```
    spouse:   Susanna Arabella GARRAWAY (AFN: V854-J8 )
  marriage:   25 Sep 1810
              Chester, , Eng
              Show children (7)
```

Submitters (2)

```
      name:  mrproctor1815489
      name:  gedmunds2353979
```

Ancestral File

« Back to search results

```
      name:  Robert Lord Of INNSBRUCK
    gender:  Male
      birth: Abt 946
             Of, , , Germany
        afn: 18JR-Q2L
```

Marriages (1)

```
    spouse:   Mrs-Robert (AFN: 18JR-Q3S )
  marriage:   Abt 971
              , , , Germany
              Show children (2)
```

Submitters (1)

```
      name:  bpsurname2413231
```

Source Citation

"Ancestral File v4.19," database, *FamilySearch* (https://familysearch.org/pal:/MM9.2.1/M72Z-8DJ : accessed 1 October 2011), entry for Robert Lord Of INNSBRUCK.

Source Information

Look at the details

4 Up come Thomas Proctor's birth and death dates, the names of his parents and date of his marriage to Susanna Arabella Garraway. The data has been submitted by individuals and not checked, so you should verify the information using original parish records – perhaps by visiting the relevant county archive in person – before putting the data into your own family tree.

Going further

5 If you click on a spouse's name or on parents' names, you may find information that has been submitted about these ancestors. Here, one branch of Susanna Arabella Garraway's tree goes back numerous generations to a Robert Lord of Innsbruck in 10th-century Germany, though the information given is rather vague.

Sharing online family trees
Who can see your tree?

There are many sites that allow you to upload your family tree and share data with fellow users. If you've already created a family tree on your home computer using one of the popular brands of software, you can convert it into what's known as a Gedcom file (see page 278) and upload it onto several sites.

This will maximise your chances of finding another family member who's working on a branch of your tree.

In all the excitement of getting your tree online and being able to offer it to others to share, it's important to take a little time to decide just who should be able to access it.

Public or Private?

When you save your tree for the first time (see step 2, below), there is a tick box on a window that pops up, which if left ticked 'Allows others to view this tree'. For more information about what this means click on **how will this help me** by the tick box.

You can change your tree from public to private or vice versa at any time. On the home page, select **Family Trees** then from the options that appear, choose the name of the tree whose settings you wish to change. On

Put your tree on ancestry.co.uk

1 Here, you can build your family tree from scratch or, if you've already created a tree using a program such as Family Tree Maker or Family Historian, you can upload this as a Gedcom file (see page 278). On the homepage, click on the **Family Trees** tab and select **Start a new tree** from the drop-down menu.

Begin your online family tree

2 The page opens up with a blank family tree. To add yourself has the head of the tree, click on **Add Yourself**. Enter your name, gender, and date and place of birth in the box that comes up. Click on **Continue**. Then click on **Add Father** and a similar box will appear – this one also gives you the option of adding his date and place of death. Click on the **Save** button.

How your tree will look

3 This is what an Ancestry online tree looks like – and it's simple to add new family members. By clicking on + **Add Mother**, for example, you can quickly and easily develop your tree. To the left of the window you can see navigation tools that allow you to manoeuvre through large, detailed family trees.

the page showing the tree click on **Tree pages** and select **Tree Settings** from the options. On the page that appears click on the **Privacy Settings** tab and choose either **Public Tree** or **Private Tree**. When you've done this click on **Save Changes**.

You can search other Ancestry member's trees to see if you've relatives in common. Go to the home page and click on **Search** then choose **Public Member Trees**. On the page that appears enter the name and other details of the ancestor you're interested in.

Filling in the detail

4 Clicking on any individual on your tree will open up a window dedicated to that person. If you click on the **Edit this person** button you will be able to add more detailed information, or even photographs, audio and video clips. If a green leaf icon appears next to any names on your family tree, it means that the Ancestry database contains a record that may match that person. Click on the icon and you will be taken to a list of those records.

Using a 'global tree' website

The free-to-use website **gencircles.com** is a 'global tree' site, which means that people from all over the world upload their trees to it, giving you a potential worldwide audience for your findings. You can also post messages on their **Clubs** section. The site is easy to use and you can do basic searches without registering. If you want to upload your family tree and allow others to search it, you'll need to register. Click on the **Register** link on the homepage (see below, right) and follow the prompts. Once you've registered, you can use the Smart Matching facility, which looks for matches by comparing all the people on your tree with all those on other trees already uploaded on the website.

If you want to upload your tree, you'll need to have it in Gedcom format, which your family tree software should be able to do for you (see page 278). From the homepage, you can then navigate to upload your Gedcom file and follow the prompts.

The great thing about this site is that, unlike some other family tree sharing sites, you still 'own' your data, and GenCircles won't pass your details on to any other third party. This also is the case with your email address – which you use to register – so you won't receive any spam email.

If you decide that you don't want your tree on GenCircles any more, you can simply delete it so that it can no longer be seen or searched by any visitors to the site.

Worldwide families *GenCircle's homepage lists the latest family trees to be uploaded. Note how most titles are clear about their content (right).*

Controlling the use of your tree

You can also upload your family tree findings on **genealogy.com**. The site will detect that you're a UK user, and will offer to direct you to **ancestry.co.uk**, its sister site. You have the option, though, to remain on the main site, where you can create your own family tree homepage, upload photos, add links to other sites and edit your page as you would like it.

It's important to bear in mind that the hosts of **genealogy.com** own the rights to your information once you've uploaded it. This means that they can use your information for publicity stories, in articles and on the website if they wish to. If you don't want your family information used by any third party, always check the details of any website to see just who owns the rights to it, and how it will be used once it's posted online.

Using Gedcom files

Each family history software program has its own file format, so you can't just distribute copies of your family tree file and assume every one else will have software that can make sense of it. Fortunately, Gedcom solves this problem.

Gedcom, which stands for **G**enealogical **D**ata **Com**munication, is a file format designed to make it easier to exchange data between one program and another. All family history databases, whatever their own file format, can import Gedcom files and convert their own data to the Gedcom format.

Sharing a Gedcom file

To create a Gedcom file of information that you want to share with someone else, you'll need to use your family history database's Export option.

If the person you're sharing with doesn't already have family history software on their computer, there are several free options that will let them view your family tree. One is LegacyFamily Tree, available through **legacyfamilytree.com**. Another is Personal Ancestral File on **familysearch.org/eng/paf**.

Family Historian software

Unlike other family history databases, Family Historian (see page 38) doesn't need to convert Gedcom files, because it uses Gedcom as its own internal file format – that's why Family Historian files end in **.ged**. If you have Family Historian installed on your computer, then double-clicking on a Gedcom file will automatically start up the Family Historian software with that file loaded.

These programs can be downloaded and installed free of charge. As another option, there are free Gedcom viewers which can be used to view a family tree, although you won't be able to add to it or edit it. You can find Gedcom viewers listed on the Gedcom page on Cyndi's List at **cyndislist.com/gedcom.htm**.

Receiving a Gedcom file

What do you do if someone sends you a Gedcom file of their family tree? If you have the software called Family Historian installed on your computer (see page 38), you can simply double-click on the file and the program will display it.

With other software, you'll need to use the **Import** option to convert the Gedcom file to your program's own format. Before you do this, it's essential to create a new, blank family tree in your database to take the new data – never import a newly received Gedcom file directly into your existing family tree, as this could overwrite or duplicate information already in your tree with new material that you haven't had a chance to check.

Merging a file

Once you've had a look at a Gedcom file you've received from someone else, you need to combine it with your existing database.

You'll have to take into account that each family history database carries out this procedure in its own way. The option is normally called **Merge** or **Match**, so you'll need to look for these words in the index of the online help that goes with your software program. Before you merge any of the new data, make sure to make a back-up of the master file of your family tree, so that if anything goes wrong with the merging, you still have an original, undamaged version of your family tree to use in your next attempt.

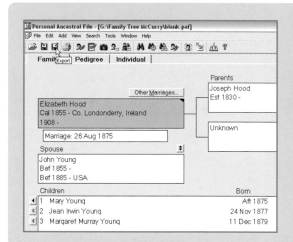

Creating a Gedcom file

1 All family history databases will have an **Export** option, usually on the **File** menu. In Personal Ancestral File (PAF), shown above, there's also an **Export** icon on the toolbar. To create a Gedcom file for exporting, click on the **Export** button.

Protecting privacy

Before you start sharing your Gedcom file with anyone outside your immediate family, you should think carefully about which individuals you include and what information about them is revealed.

Don't forget that once you've given your Gedcom file to someone else, you'll have no control over what they do with it. They could pass it on to other, more distant family members, or they might even submit it to one of the online pedigree databases.

There's no law in the UK against publishing biographical information about individuals without their permission. But even so, many people don't like the idea of their personal details being broadcast, and there's a risk you might fall out with members of your family because you've made public something they feel is private. Certainly, if there's anything in your family that you know is 'not talked about', you should take care to exclude it from a file that may be viewed by complete strangers.

Filtering information

To help you to avoid privacy problems, most family history databases have some kind of 'filtering' facility, which will let you create a Gedcom file containing only individuals who are no longer alive. Some websites will automatically exclude the details of anyone who was born within the past 50 years.

Also, there are separate programs you can use that will do the same thing – such as GEDclean, which can be downloaded free from **raynorshyn.com/gedclean/**.

Choosing parameters

2 In the **Export** dialog box, click on the **Other Gedcom 5.5** button. Choose what to include or exclude from the list on the right. You might deactivate **Full information on living** if you're sending your Gedcom to non-family members. You can also choose to include the whole tree or just selected individuals. Once you click on the **Export** button, PAF will prompt you to type in a file name before creating the Gedcom file. Other family history programs should be broadly similar.

Merging a Gedcom file

1 If you're in Family Historian, make a back-up of your family tree master file, then open your family tree with the program. From the **File** menu click on **Merge/compare file** and select the file you want to match and merge. The software compares all the individuals in the two files and the **Merge file** window shows which are potential matches. It indicates whether they can be merged without difficulty or whether some of the information in the two files conflicts.

Examining any conflicts

2 Where there's a conflict, you can expand the details of the individual to see where the problem lies, by clicking on the name. In this example, the original file has only an approximate birth date for Thomas Joshua Parker, while the new file has more precise information (and many additional details). Obviously this is a good match, and to add these details into your master file, click on **Merge**.

Making the most of mailing lists

There are thousands of family history mailing lists – any one of them could help you to learn more about your ancestors or share information with other researchers. Getting onto a mailing list is easy to do.

Using a mailing list has many advantages. Most importantly, it can help you to find answers to problems – either by connecting with someone who has already found information on the area you're looking into or, more often, by pointing you in the right direction. And as you gain more experience, you may find that you can help other people. Apart from being excellent tools for family research, mailing lists are also a great place for social networking, as you keep on meeting like-minded people who share your interests.

Finding the right mailing list

The all-embracing nature of family history opens up many avenues of research, including surnames, locations, occupations and ethnic groups. Mailing lists therefore have to cover a vast range of topics, so to begin looking for a suitable list, first decide on the subject that you want your mailing list to be about.

Rootsweb offers a large index of mailing lists that you can search to find the one that suits you. Go to **rootsweb.com** and click on **Mailing Lists** in the website's tool bar. You then have two search options. The first is to search the mailing list archives. This can provide information that has already been posted to the mailing list. For example, if you're interested in finding out more about an ancestor whose occupation was a cordwainer (a shoemaker), you can use this search box to see what, if any, messages have already been posted. Enter the occupation and press **Search** and you'll find numerous links to sites that have information about cordwainers.

The second option is to search for a specific mailing list that you wish to join. Here you enter the surname, location or keyword that you want the mailing list to be about, and then click **Search**. Another way to use this search option is to click on **Browse mailing lists**. It allows you to browse for a mailing list by surname, location or topic.

Master of his trade *An early 19th-century baker eases a large pie into his oven. You'll be able to find out more about master bakers, and many other occupations, by joining a mailing list.*

BAKER

If you don't see what you want straight away, scroll down the page to the box labelled **Other** and browse through the options offered. Click on **Occupations,** for example, and you'll be taken to an alphabetical list. Find the occupation you're interested in, such as **Blacksmithing.** By clicking on this you'll be taken to a page where you can subscribe to the blacksmithing mailing list.

Choosing a 'mode'

The way in which you receive messages from your mailing list is called a 'mode'. There are two options and it's best to decide on your preferred mode before you join the list. The first is to join the mailing list in a 'mail' mode. This means that every time a message is posted on the mailing list it will be forwarded to you as an individual email.

The second is called 'digest' mode, and it groups together several messages and sends them out as one large message. So, instead of receiving lots of individual email messages you'll only receive a couple which contain several messages.

Joining a mailing list

To get onto the blacksmithing mailing list, for example, click on the **Subscribe to BLACKSMITHING-L** link for mail mode, or **BLACKSMITHING-D** for digest mode. An email opens up automatically and you send only the word **subscribe.**

Once you've sent your email to subscribe to your chosen list, you'll receive a confirmation email welcoming you to the mailing list. This message includes information about how to use the list, and how to unsubscribe.

Mailing list manners

When using mailing lists, news groups and forums, it's important to remember that they have a set of rules. Some of these are set out in their FAQs (Frequently Asked Questions), but others are largely unwritten. These codes of behaviour ensure that online communication is effective and polite. The complete text of Virginia Shea's book on 'Netiquette' can be found and read online at **albion.com/netiquette/book/**. The main points she raises are:

● Make sure that the messages you send are relevant to the list you've joined – if not, the list owner or other members of that list will ask you to discontinue your line of interest.

● Always be polite and clear in the posting of messages, and if you receive an abusive message known as a 'flame' don't retaliate, but try to ignore it.

● Don't include the whole message that you're replying to – just send your reply or, if necessary, include only a small part of the message that you're responding to.

● Don't post messages that are all in upper case because it INDICATES SHOUTING. Only use upper case letters for surnames, so if you're sending a query, enter your surname in upper cases letters – for example, Emma BELL.

● When you respond to an individual, be careful to check that you're sending the response to the desired recipient only, rather than to the whole group. Always check your **To:** line before you click on **Send**.

● Check that your subject heading is appropriate and explains what your message relates to.

● Be careful about the information you're sending. It's unwise to post large portions of written works, as you may be violating copyright laws; similarly don't post messages containing data from other people or from CDs.

● If you've been sent a message personally, don't send that message on to a mailing list unless you have the permission of the person who sent it to you. They may have meant it to be for you only.

Leaving a mailing list

The time may come when you want to leave a mailing list, either because you have all the information you need, or you find that the list isn't what you want.

Instructions for how to leave the list are shown on the same page as instructions for how to join. To unsubscribe from the list, you send an email just as you did to subscribe, but this time the message contains only the word **unsubscribe.** Within a few moments you'll be sent an email confirming that you have been taken off the mailing list.

Using Genuki for war-related lists

Genuki has a directory of mailing lists which includes war-related lists that will be of interest if you're researching UK and Irish relatives. This site is useful because it contains all the mailing lists that are relevant to British family historians. Go to **genuki.org.uk/indexes/MailingLists.html**. Say you're interested in the area of Birkenhead in Cheshire, scroll down to find that listing and click on it. You'll then be redirected to a mailing list hosted by Rootsweb and you subscribe in the way described, left, in 'Joining a mailing list'.

Tracing your living relatives

Some of your relatives may be complete strangers, yet they share your heritage and genes because you share common ancestors. The exciting thing about looking for your ancestors' descendants is that you'll find and meet new family.

Working forward in time

Most of us know our first cousins and some of us know our second cousins. But very few people can even name their more distant relations, let alone say where they live and what they're doing.

Tracing the living descendants of your direct ancestors' siblings or cousins through several generations can be challenging, but the rewards are great. You might discover, for example, that your recently found distant relatives have family information that's new to you, or they may possess fascinating heirlooms that you knew nothing about.

Journey to find the living

The process of tracing living relatives from distant ancestors is known as 'forward reconstruction'. The best way to do this is to choose one particular relative in your family tree – perhaps your great grandfather's brother – and follow him and his descendants forward through time to the present day. It's best to select someone who was a child in 1901, as they would be of marriageable age after the date that civil registration indexes started to include cross-references. These are likely to lead you to other documents that might provide new information.

If you've chosen someone born some decades before 1901, you'll need to track them through the various census returns,

until you reach the 1901 census and then follow the path, through subsequent birth, marriage and death certificates, to living descendants in your own generation.

You're fortunate if the surname you're looking for is uncommon, as it'll make searching easier. Also, you can narrow your search if you know the area that the family came from, as many people lived and married close to where they were born.

As you work forward through the generations, you'll find the most useful clues come from marriage certificates, though you may need to order more than one in order to check all the details. You'll know you have the correct marriage when you see the name of the bride or groom's father, which will appear on the certificate. He'll be someone you've already identified.

Then search for the children from that marriage using the spouse's surname or maiden name (listed in the birth indexes after 1911) as the unique identifying factor. Frome here on, it's simply a question of repeating the process until you find living relatives. Depending on how far back you started, it can take a little time, but it's worth it when you find a new branch of your family.

Keep in mind that the descendants of your chosen ancestor may not have married or had children, or may have died in childhood.

Family reunion *Through your research you may discover new relatives. Making contact with them could lead to shared memories and valuable information – even big family get-togethers.*

Contacting new relatives

If you're lucky enough to find a branch of your family that's new to you, and have managed to find contact details, here are a few common sense tips about contacting them.

Never turn up at their home unannounced or even phone out of the blue. They may not have any idea of who you are, or even whether you're genuine. It's best to write a letter with your home address and contact details so they can get in touch. Include a family tree diagram, so they can see at a glance where everyone fits in, and some pictures, so they can see that the tree is genuine.

Generation game *From great grandmother to new-born, four female generations pose for a photo in 1905 – a vital family history find.*

From census to phonebook

As your research progresses beyond the 1911 census towards the present day you'll find that phonebooks and other more recent directories become rewarding resources. Much of the information is online.

Once you have identified a living relative you'll probably want to get in touch. One way of doing this is by using phone and street directories, following the research that has probably led you to the area where your relative is likely to be living. Birth and marriage certificates, for example, give exact addresses, so it's worth checking a street directory to see if any members of the family still live there. Alternatively, you might be able to find your relative in a local phone book – assuming the family hasn't moved on.

Using online directories

It's possible to check some directories online, and the amount of information available is growing all the time. Here are some suggested routes that may be helpful.

TRY BRITISH PHONE BOOKS The Ancestry website, **ancestry.co.uk**, is expanding its database of family history sources, and this includes putting phone books (1880 to 1984) online. From the Ancestry homepage, click on **Search**, then choose **Schools, Directories & Church Histories**. On the page that appears click on **British Phone Books, 1880-1984,**

Making connections *Women operators at work in the exchange of the National Telephone Company in 1903. As use of the telephone increased, phone books became essential.*

which should be under **Featured data collections** on the right of the page. This will take you to the search page. Currently the database offers near full coverage of English counties, plus considerable records for Scotland, Ireland and Wales. This is a useful source for tracing people's movements after the 1911 census. Looking at older phone books can also give you an indication of people's social status – only the wealthy had telephones in the late 19th and early 20th centuries, and it wasn't until the 1950s that most families had a phone.

As the entries go right up to 1984, you may even find the phone number of a living relative. Remember that STD codes, now called 'area codes', have changed a number of times in recent years, so check them, too.

EXPLORE 192.COM The homepage at **192.com** offers a range of search services when you're looking for people, businesses or places. You can search direct from the homepage or focus your search. Under **People**, you can access electoral rolls, details of births, marriages and deaths, as well as Directory Enquiries (see also page 295). Under **Businesses**, there is access to a directory, company credit reports and company reports. **Places** links you to maps and aerial photos and you can also browse by postcode.

SEARCH THE YELLOW PAGES If you discover that your relative is involved in a specific business, you can find the business contact details through **yell.com**, the website version of the *Yellow Pages*. The difference between this and the local printed directories is that

yell.com allows you to see entries for the whole of the UK. It's essentially a business listing, free to use and you don't need to register to access it.

If you have a specific name for a business you can search for the address and phone number of that business by entering the name in the **I'm looking for** box. If you don't know the company name, enter the type of business in the box, then click on Search. You can limit the search by entering a geographical area, town or city, or postcode in the **in** box

Using early directories

Phone directories have been compiled since 1880, and some street directories date back to the early 18th century. Various publishers were responsible for producing directories, the most well known being Kelly's, Pigot's and the Post Office. Depending on the period, directories were issued annually or every two or three years. Most can be consulted at local libraries and record offices. For more about different types of directory, especially old ones, see page 232.

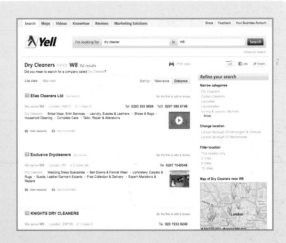

Fill in the details of a business search

1 Say you want to search for a newly discovered relative's dry-cleaning establishment in Kensington, in west London. Go to the **yell.com** homepage. You know that Kensington has the postcode W8. Enter 'dry cleaner' in the **I'm looking for** box, and 'London w8' in the **in** box. Then click **Search**.

Examine the results

2 All the relevant matches will appear with links to individual websites of these companies, where they have them. Click on the link to the one you want for further information.

Modern directories and the electoral roll

The phone book is an obvious place to look for living relatives, but some may have chosen not to be in it or traded in their landlines for mobile phones. If this happens, you can turn to the electoral roll.

Electoral rolls have been compiled every year since 1832, when the Great Reform Act was passed, changing the British electoral system. Until then, booming new cities like Manchester had no MPs to represent them, while other tiny, old constituencies – known as rotten boroughs – could return up to two MPs to Parliament. The Act got rid of rotten boroughs and redistributed the seats to the new towns. But as only householders who owned property worth at least £10 could vote, you won't find any of your working class ancestors on these early electoral rolls.

All electoral rolls are available to the public, right up to the present day, and you can use them to locate a living relative. They include everyone of voting age who's registered to vote in a particular area.

Unfortunately, just as a phone subscriber can go ex-directory, so a voter can opt out of the public access version of the electoral roll – but even so, it offers more comprehensive coverage than phone listings.

Examine historic electoral rolls

As well as being able to access modern registers, you can look at past lists – such as the electoral rolls for the neighbourhood where the relative you're tracking was last known to have lived. You can also use historic records to plot your family's movements. If, for example, you want to

Votes in secret – and for women *Voting by secret ballot (above) was introduced in Britain in 1872. All women got the vote in 1928, after a violent struggle by the WSPU – the Women's Social and Political Union (right), known as the Suffragettes.*

find out how long your ancestors lived at the address recorded on a census return or a civil registration certificate, you could plot this using successive electoral rolls.

Poll Books keep no secrets

If you're looking for information from before 1832, you'll need to look at land tax returns (see page 214) or browse through Poll Books in local record offices. The books list the names of electors, each voter's parish of register and how he voted (secret balloting was not introduced until 1872).

Votes for women

From 1918, the electoral rolls became much larger, because the right to vote was extended to include soldiers in barracks, policemen, domestic servants – and, most significantly, women over 30 (the vote was not extended to all women until 1928). The data was now organised into 'electoral wards'.

Electoral enquiries online

Electoral records from 1700 onwards can be consulted at local archives and record offices. The British Library also holds a detailed nationwide collection. In addition, there are websites, such as **192.com**, which are now putting electoral roll information online. This website evolved from the old British Telecom Directory Enquiries service and it offers the electoral rolls from 2002 to 2011. Its links include search facilities for the 1861 census and the General Register Office's birth, marriage and death indexes.

It doesn't charge for online directory or local business enquiries, or for general searches of its website, but if you want detailed electoral roll data, you have to pay for it. The site operates a credit scheme; the minimum charge is £9.95 for 6 credits, and it costs 1 credit to view an entry.

Another site is **theukelectoralroll.co.uk**. It offers searches of the electoral roll that will give dates of birth and phone numbers, and also gives UK property ownership details, as well as deaths and marriages.

You can search by forename, surname or full name, as well as by address and post-code. Once you've found the type of search you want, you choose the payment package that suits you and are prompted to make your payment. The search results are emailed to you immediately, or simply shown onscreen.

The modern electoral roll

The UK Electoral Roll includes adults over the age of 18. Despite the fact that it's a legal obligation for every adult to enter their details, a percentage of the population continues to avoid giving their information to the compilers.

People not on the electoral roll include young people under 18, homeless people, travellers and gypsies, active members of the serving forces, certain government personnel, people in prison and non-British citizens.

Search the electoral roll

1 If you want to search for a David McMahon, say, who was last known to have been living in Windsor, go to the homepage of the **192.com** website. Enter his name, preferably his full name, in the **Name** box under **Search People**. Enter 'Windsor' in the **Location** box. Click on **Search**.

Read the results

2 A list of all possible entries will be displayed. In this case, a number of matches appear for David McMahon, all of them in various electoral rolls. If you want to see any of the records, click **View**; this will cost you 1 credit.

Making connections through the internet

The internet has made it easy to track down old friends and relatives through contact sites. If you're trying to find someone who served in the armed forces, they too have dedicated sites for making contact.

Perhaps the most well-known website for providing listings of former school friends is **friendsreunited.co.uk**. Since its launch in 2000 the website has enjoyed huge popularity. It began as a simple site where users could contact old school and work colleagues within the UK, but now has expanded to include other parts of the world, with separate pages for genealogy, job seeking and dating. As well as tracking down

old friends, the site can be used to find relatives from all over the world who may be registered on it.

When you register on the site you can post your own information online and look at what other people have posted. If you want to go further you can initiate contacts with other users of the site. There is no charge for using the website.

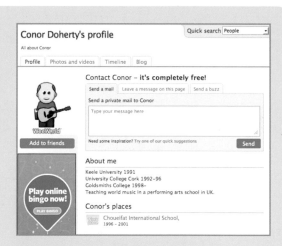

Register with Friends Reunited

1 Go to **friendsreunited.co.uk** and register. This gives you access to the main site so that you can start your search for information about your old school friends, workplace colleagues or relatives. Once registered, you'll be sent to your homepage. You can then access different areas of the site, such as Genes Reunited, Dating, Jobs Board and Connections (which is a way to meet people interested in the same things as you).

Enter the name you're looking for

2 Search the site by first clicking on the **Friends** tab in the menu bar, and select **Find Friends** from the drop-down menu. Enter the forename and surname of the person you want to find; if you know their age and where they live you can add that as well. If, for example, you're searching for a lost friend, Conor Doherty, who studied at the University of Keele in Staffordshire when you were there, enter his name and click on **Search** to view all the Conor Dohertys listed.

View the person's profile

3 The search produces five possible listings, including the correct entry at the top of the page. Click on the name of the person that fits your match to see his entry. Profiles are uploaded by each individual, so they'll vary in detail – some people put in photographs and give other personal information. You can send a message to the individual. (This feature was formerly exclusive to subscribers, but now, like all other aspects of the website, is free of charge.)

Looking for war veterans

If you know that a relative is or was in the armed forces, it might be worthwhile checking out one of the sites dedicated to military veterans. The Ministry of Defence has a website dedicated to veteran issues at veterans-uk.info, run by the Service Personnel and Veterans Agency. It aims to centralise and improve services for current and former employees of the British Armed Forces, but it also includes such groups as the Bevin Boys who worked in the coal mines during the Second World War. Other useful sites include the Royal British Legion, and for locating American friends or relatives in the services, there's the Veterans History Project.

Veterans UK

On the homepage at veterans-uk.info you'll see a number of topics, including **Service Records, Medals & Badges**. If you click on that and then on **Service Records**, you are taken to a page which provides guidance about how to obtain service record information on servicemen and women.

Royal British Legion

The Royal British Legion is dedicated to supporting members and ex-members of the British Armed Forces and was founded in 1921 as a means of giving ex-servicemen a voice, after the horrors of the First World War. Through its website, at www.britishlegion.org.uk, you can contact a network of clubs and branches of the Legion that can put you in touch with lost colleagues or relatives who fought in past wars.

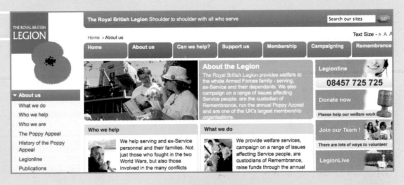

Veterans History Project

Go to loc.gov/vets and you'll find a site run by the Library of Congress in the USA. It aims to share the stories of veterans from the First and Second World Wars, the Korean War, the Vietnam War, the Persian Gulf War and ongoing conflicts in Iraq and Afghanistan. Click on **Search the Veterans Collections** and you'll be taken to a screen where you can enter a person's name, and search the records by conflict(s) or branch of service.

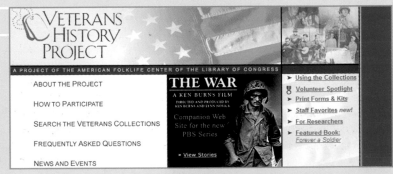

Was your ancestor adopted?

Adoption, with its consequent name changes and shroud of confidentiality, can obscure the trail when you're tracking down some ancestors. Keep persisting, though, and investigations can bear fruit.

Until the 20th century, there was no formal process of adoption, so few paper trails were created when children were given new homes outside the immediate family. Where children were adopted within the extended family, by grandparents, aunts or uncles – perhaps to mask cases of illegitimacy – any surviving information may lie only in letters or documents passed down through the family.

Name-change problems

Searching for a relative who was adopted can be difficult where the name has altered. For example, if you were looking for all six siblings of the novelist Jane Austen, you might miss one. One brother, Edward, was given up for adoption when he was a boy, to his childless uncle and aunt, Mr and Mrs Thomas Knight of Godmersham, in Kent. They made him their heir, and he changed his name to Edward Austen Knight. He would have appeared in subsequent censuses under his adopted name, not under his birth name.

Adoption becomes official

The informal adoption arrangements came to an end in 1926, with the passing of the Adoption of Children Act. From January 1, 1927, a certificate of adoption was issued for each adopted child in England or Wales, with the process formally recorded in the Adopted

A writer's uprooted sibling Edward Austen, *brother of Jane Austen, took his uncle's name when he was adopted and, as Edward Austen Knight, was later recorded as a landowner.*

Help on the internet

Although these websites don't list adopted children, they can help you in starting the difficult task of searching for biological family members.

adoptionsearchreunion.org.uk

The British Association of Adoption's website provides information about the adoption process, and various ways of contacting relatives. England and Wales are thoroughly covered and information is being expanded to cover Scotland and Northern Ireland. The site also has different sections explaining the adoption system, including one on locating adoption records with a database to help you to do this.

search-line.co.uk

The Searchline website attempts to find long lost relatives – adopted people, in particular. It was started by Gwen Richardson after she tried to find her sister, who was given up for adoption when they were very young. The organisation has a large number of databases that it uses to help to trace missing relatives. There's also a contact register where people can leave their own stories.

Children Register compiled by the General Register Office (GRO). The register is open to the public, indexed by the surname of the adoptive parents, not the birth parents. The certificates include the child's date of birth, the name and address of the adoptive parents, the date of adoption and which court issued it. The child's birth parents aren't recorded.

Scotland has had a separate register since 1930 and it's held at the National Archives of Scotland. Similarly, Northern Ireland has held its own register from 1931 at the General Register Office (Northern Ireland). See pages 96-101 and the Directory for contact details.

Seeing original birth certificates

If you were adopted, and want to see your original birth certificate and details of your biological parents, you can apply to the Adoptions Section of the relevant register office. In England and Wales it's the GRO; in Scotland it's the General Register Office for Scotland (GROS); and in Ireland it's the General Register Office (Northern Ireland). You have to be over 18 in England and Wales, and over 16 in Scotland before you can request this information, and all the countries recommend counselling before you go ahead, particularly if you were adopted before November 11, 1975.

Contacting your birth family

There are rules about contacting your biological family. In England and Wales the GRO's voluntary Adoption Contact Register regulates the process. The Register has two lists: one giving the biological parents (and other close blood relatives) and the other

A home for the unwanted

Not all abandoned children in the 18th century were lucky enough to be adopted. Many of London's unwanted children lived wild and rough on the streets. Retired shipbuilder and sailor Thomas Coram became so disturbed by the plight of the destitute and dying children he saw on London's streets that he conceived the idea of a home for them. With the considerable help and influence of his friends – the artist William Hogarth and the musician George Frederick Handel – and a royal charter from King George II, he opened the Foundling Hospital in 1739. It became a refuge for abandoned children where they could be cared for and educated, and it was the first children's charity in England. The charity was renamed the Thomas Coram Foundation for Children, and is known today simply as Coram Family. You can search the site at **coram.org.uk**.

Foundlings
Smiling outside the London Foundling Hospital in the early 20th century, these children were given a second chance at life. Many mothers left tokens of remembrance, as above, for their children.

the adopted children. There are also contact details for a mediator between the two parties. Contact is made only if all parties agree to it. The Adoption of Children Registration Act, 2002, though, gave birth parents more rights: since December 30, 2005, birth parents have been able to inform their adopted adult 'child' of their desire for contact. There are details in the Directory for adoption organisations such as Adoption Search, Birthlink (Scotland) and the Irish Adoption Contact Register.

Children dispersed around the world

It may seem amazing today, but child labourers were once sent to the farthest reaches of Britain's empire. Others went as a result of the authorities' desire to give them 'a better life' – a misguided promise for many.

From as early as the 17th century, small numbers of children were sent to the new American colonies to provide labour for the settlers. The practice continued until the American War of Independence (1775-81), after which America was no longer an option.

A new life far away

After 1850, when the new Poor Law Unions began to take responsibility for the poor or orphan children in their area, the rate of child migration speeded up. Moving children to new locations was seen as a philanthropic solution to child poverty, although often the parents' consent was not given, particularly if they were in prison or a mental institution. If the children were orphans, they were sent without any real understanding of where they were going and for how long.

There was an underlying political motive to the movement, too, for most of the children were sent to Canada, South Africa, Rhodesia, Australia and New Zealand to provide good 'white stock' for these young or developing countries. The policy continued until 1967 by which time approximately 150,000 children had been affected.

The policy of child migration had a huge emotional impact on the children who were forced to migrate. Many went believing their parents were dead or did not want them; some, as young as three, soon forgot their parents and weren't even sure when or where they had been born. This can make tracing them in their new countries quite difficult, but it's worth persevering.

Evacuation from the danger zones

Migration on a lesser scale took place during the Blitz of the Second World War, when children were evacuated from London and other large cities and towns and placed in safer rural areas.

In some cases entire school classes were sent to the same place, to minimise the disruption in the children's lives. For some, evacuation, with name labels, tightly clutched suitcases and gas masks, was an exciting adventure (right). They found themselves in wonderful rural environments and knew a sense of freedom and closeness to nature they could never have had in the city. For many of them, these temporary refuges became their second homes. But for others it was a traumatic experience, often marked by meanness and cruelty from the people who took them in. There is no national list of child evacuees, but the BBC has a section on the memoirs of evacuees at **bbc.co.uk/ww2peopleswar/categories/c1162/**.

How to trace child migrants

Tracing children who were sent away is an exciting challenge, and there are websites that can help. Here are four of them.

Child Migrants Trust

In 1986 Margaret Humphreys, a social worker, heard from a woman in Australia who'd been sent there at the age of four and now wanted to trace any family she might still have in Britain. Margaret was so appalled that she set up the Child Migrants Trust, **childmigrantstrust.com**, to reunite former child migrants with their long-lost families. The Trust is based in Nottingham, with two offices in Australia.

Barnardo's

The children's charity was founded by Thomas Barnardo in the East End of London in the late 1860s. Barnardo was an enthusiastic proponent of child migration, believing the children would benefit. The Australian branch of Barnado's recognises the role it played in child migration and retains records of the children that passed through its hands. If an ancestor was affected by the scheme, you'll be able to get more information by contacting **barnados.org.au**.

Library and Archives Canada

Canada was one of the main destinations for British child migration. Children sent there were known as 'Home children'. The system began in 1839 and continued into the 1930s, by which time approximately 100,000 children had arrived. The Library and Archives Canada holds a variety of documents relating to this migration on its website, **collectionscanada.ca**. Or you can try **bifhsgo.ca**, which is based in Ottawa and holds digitised lists of children.

National Archives of Australia

Australia was a hugely important destination for child migration and the National Archives of Australia houses a comprehensive collection of records relating to it. Go to **naa.gov.au** and click on **The collection** and select **Publications and podcasts**. On the page that appears click on **Research Guides**. Scroll down to and click on the book *Good British Stock* by Barry Coldrey, which outlines the history of child migration, and provides a timeline of the main events. You can either buy the book, or click on **Read online**.

Tracing divorce records

A broken marriage can also disperse family members. Before 1858, divorce was almost impossible, then, particularly from the 20th century onwards, it became much easier. This can cause hiccups in your family research.

If you're trying to trace more recent members of your extended family, you may find that someone suddenly disappears from family photos and correspondence. If you're sure that person didn't die or emigrate, it's possible that a marriage broke down and there was a divorce or a legal separation.

The details of a divorce could name a place of residence and living children, as well as the people who were divorcing. From this, you can trace further marriages, offspring of the named children and then their addresses through trade or phone directories.

Family complications *Divorce or separation can create difficulties in finding ancestors. But divorces are recorded so should be traceable, particularly if they took place in the 20th century.*

The early story of divorce

Divorce was almost unheard of in the 17th, 18th and early 19th centuries, largely because it was too expensive for all but the richest aristocrat. As marriage was conducted in church, only church courts had the power to approve a legal separation; Henry VIII went so far as to change the law so he could divorce Katherine of Aragon and marry Anne Boleyn, in the hope of having a male heir.

If a couple wanted to remarry, their first marriage had to be declared null and void on the grounds of lack of ability to marry – for example, if they were underage and therefore incapable of giving consent – or there was a legal bar to the first marriage, such as consanguinity (too close a blood relationship).

Divorce after 1858

The Matrimonial Causes Act 1857 allowed husbands in England and Wales to divorce through the civil courts on the grounds of a wife's adultery. A wife couldn't do the same, unless she could prove cruelty as well, and this remained the case until 1925.

From January 1858, the Court for Divorce and Matrimonial Causes heard all divorce cases, and all in London. Lawyers had to be appointed, and the couple had to appear in court, which required time and money – so only the wealthy and very determined could divorce. From 1875, the Probate, Divorce and Admiralty Division of the Supreme Court heard all divorce proceedings.

From 1878, poor women could apply to the local magistrate for a separation and maintenance order if the husband had been convicted of aggravated assault against her. This changed again in 1886, when a wife could apply on the grounds that her husband had deserted her and any children. The husband would then be ordered to pay £2 a week as maintenance.

By 1895, the system had changed to protect all women and children with violent or neglectful husbands. But discrimination was rife. Women who were considered immoral weren't covered and, if the woman had already committed adultery, the husband wasn't obliged to maintain her. Within five years more than 10,000 orders had been applied for. These orders are kept in local record offices, but their survival rate is patchy and few records can be found online.

From 1914, poor people could seek financial aid for divorce under the Poor

Person's rules. This was extended in 1923, when women were allowed to petition for divorce on the sole grounds of their husband's adultery.

The Second World War saw many marriages end, with an increase in rates of divorce as it became easier to obtain. But it wasn't until the Divorce Reform Act of 1969 that irretrievable breakdown of marriage could be used as sole grounds for divorce.

Where the post-1858 records are

If you're looking for legal proof of a divorce from 1858 onwards, the union indexes for the whole of England and Wales are kept at the Principal Registry of the Family Division, London (see Directory). For each divorce case, a file was created and given a unique number. They're arranged in chronological order, and contain the petition, copies of any relevant certificates, detail of the status of the plaintiff, affidavits and the decrees *nisi* and *absolute*. Some are at TNA.

Public humiliation *A witness is cross-examined at a London divorce trial in 1900. Until the law changed in 1969, one or other party in a marriage always had to be proved 'guilty'.*

- 1858-1937: the case files are at TNA in class J77 with an index in J78, and have a fairly good survival rate. Surviving decrees are at the Principal Registry.
- 1938 onwards: no case files survive, but surviving decrees are at the Principal Registry.

If there's no surviving case file, check local newspapers of the time, as many divorces were announced in print, especially before 1920. Local records offices may have microfilmed copies of newspapers, with the main repository being at The British Library newspaper archive in London (see Directory).

Records of property disputes

From 1583 onwards, when couples achieved a form of legal separation, disputes often arose about the legal status of any property

Divorces in Scotland and Ireland

Ordinary people could file for divorce from 1560 in Scotland, making it easier than in England and Wales. The Commissary Court of Edinburgh heard cases up to 1850, and thereafter the Court of Session took over. All these records are held at The National Archives of Scotland (see Directory).

From 1855 to 1984, records of divorce were recorded on Scottish marriage registers – with the words 'Divorce RCE' (Register of Corrected Entries). The General Register Office of Scotland holds an index of divorces from 1984 onwards.

In Ireland, various Acts of Parliament forbade divorce until 1995. But on rare occasions, before 1870, Church Courts granted separations, and after 1870, some divorces were agreed by Act of Parliament. After 1995, couples who'd lived apart for five years could divorce, and the records are held in the court where the divorce took place.

shared or promised as part of the marriage settlement. Most property disputes were recorded in the Courts of Chancery, and are likely to be held at TNA in series C78. The Privy Council also ensured that separation settlements were honoured: some entries are in the Privy Council Registers in series PC2.

Between 1532 and 1832, appeals from Church Courts were heard by the High Court of Delegates, and from 1832 to 1858, they were heard by the Judicial Committee of the Privy Council. Copies of the proceedings are kept at TNA. If they occurred between 1609 and 1834 they're in series DEL1 (with an index in DEL11/7) and from 1834 to 1858 they're in PCAP1. None of these records is available online; they have to be searched in person at TNA.

Putting your family history online

Creating your own website allows you to share your family tree and other discoveries with family and friends. As you add more to it, and your relatives start to join in, you'll have created a valuable family and social document.

Setting up a website

Your personal website can be as simple as a single page. Or you may want to be more ambitious by adding images, family biographies and links to other sites. It's up to you how much you make of it and what you choose to include.

Creating your own website gives you the freedom to decide how your family history will be told, where images will be displayed, the layout and design of your pages, and what links to other websites are included. A family history website can be built easily and cheaply using the most basic software. Once you've gained a little confidence, you may want to invest in more complex packages, but this section of the book will look at the most straightforward means of going about building your first website and where to get advice in the process (see pages 306-11).

It might be possible to use your ISP to host your site for you as your subscription package probably includes enough free web space for an online family tree, which you can illustrate with photos and family stories. However, some ISPs that previously made it simple to set up a site have now removed instructions from their websites as to how this is done. If you find that your ISP can be of use, your ISP will allocate you a web address that contains the ISP's name. You may be able to change the address, if you want to, as long as the new one is available.

An alternative is to have a site with its own domain name. You can go to one of the many UK domain-hosting sites, such as **easily.co.uk** and **ukreg.com** (see right), who supply domain names for a small annual fee.

Choosing a name

Each domain name must be unique, so you may find that your first, second or even third choice of name has already been registered by someone else. When you get round to choosing a name, it's a good idea to select one that tells people what your site's about – 'higginsfamilyhistory.co.uk', for example. Calling your website something obscure like 'briansbigadventure.co.uk' or quirky like 'frankfromthepark.co.uk' might amuse you, but will probably only confuse your friends and family.

The cost of using a domain-hosting site is not excessive – it ranges from about £3 to £30 a year. Domain names cost about £4. Shop around to find one that seems good value.

Domain name-hosting

There are many different websites in the UK that offer this service. It's a good idea to shop around the basic search engines, such as Google, Ask or Yahoo!, as the prices can vary. Remember that popular names may cost more – for example, domain names that end with **.co.uk** or **.com** may cost a bit more to register than those that end with **.biz** or **.net**.

Planning the contents of your website

Creating your own family history website is a chance to be as creative as possible with your family tree. But before you launch yourself on a flight of fancy, you need to have a clear idea of what you want the end result to look like and the impression you wish to make on visitors to the site.

It's important to decide on the contents before you get to the really creative part of your website – the layout and look of it. Work out exactly what you want your site to show and the message that you're trying to get across. Ask yourself these questions:
● Which area of your research do you want to focus on? You may want to show the entire family tree, or just focus in on one particular branch of interest, such as a surname, its roots and meaning.
● How much information do you want to include about each ancestor? Do you want to include information on families connected through marriage, or stick to blood relatives?
● How far do you want to go back in time and how much of your family's recent past do you want to cover? Bear in mind that some of your living relatives may not want their information posted on the internet, so be sure to check with them first.

Create a plan
Once you've decided on the content, and how you want to display it, you then need to decide what it will look like. You may want to create what's known as a storyboard (see right). You can display your information in many ways – perhaps as one page of narrative, concentrating on an overview of your research or perhaps a timeline, with

links to other ancestors and information, which will make it clear and easy to see.

Having made up your mind about all this, you're ready to decide on the features that you want to display, as this will affect how the website is going to look. Consider the format of the various pages – what colour palette to use, what style of font, how many pages you want, how they'll link together and whether you're going to include any special design features. By keeping the design and formatting relatively simple, you'll create a user-friendly website that others can enjoy.

WRITING THE TEXT Try to make the text interesting, so that you engage your audience. You could perhaps write in a biographical style about some of the fascinating characters in your family tree, or tell some of the stories that were passed down to you by previous generations.

CHOOSING THE PICTURES Images are crucial for bringing your family's story to life and making it as engaging as possible for all those who visit your page. It's quite easy to attach images or stream a video clip onto your website using the software described on pages 36-39. If you have a scanner or digital camera, you can upload images of your documents, such as wills, baptism certificates

and personal letters onto your computer, and then transfer them to your website. See page 310 for more advice on using images.

DISPLAYING THE INFORMATION The next step is to work out the detail of how you want to use all your information. For example, you might want to have a photo of each of the people on your tree next to their name, or just have one big gallery with the photos and documents organised in chronological order. Remember that if you're using web space provided by your internet service provider (ISP) or by a web hosting service, it will usually be limited and the more images and videos you include, the quicker you'll find yourself using up the space.

Be aware of copyright rules
Your website is a publication accessible to the entire online world. This means you can't legally include copyright material which belongs to other people, unless you get their permission first.

So, for example, you can't scan a photo of your ancestor's village from a local history book or postcard and put it on your site. Neither can you include chunks of material you've copied from a CD or from another website, or any of the census images you may have paid for on one of the data services.

Creating a storyboard for your website

Start by drawing up a visual plan, sometimes called a 'storyboard', for each page of your website, so that you can see exactly what information goes where, how it will be presented, and how it will link to each page and ancestor. Putting your thoughts down on paper, deciding how you want your information presented on each page and working out how a user can access it from the homepage will save you time and confusion once you go online and actually start to build your website.

The more familiar you become with your computer and software package (see page 308), the more adventurous you'll be when designing and editing your website.

Plan your website on paper *This storyboard for The Brooker Family Website shows a homepage with links to four other pages – the family tree, family biographies, a family album and a contact page. Drawing it up first helps to make sure your website is packed with information and looks great.*

Easy ways to create a website

You've planned your website – now you can put it all into action, and it needn't cost you a penny. It's not difficult to create a website, and there's plenty of software available to help you.

You don't have to go out and buy new software to create your website. Your computer may already contain some suitable software, and if not, there are some good free website editors you can download. Since most web pages use a standard file format, it's easy to switch between different editing programs and try them out – you're not locked into the program on which you initially created a page.

Try your existing software
By using most modern word-processing software installed on your PC, you can create and edit pages and then save them in a web-ready format, so that you'll be able to upload them onto your website.

If you don't have word-processing software loaded on your computer, you can download a free software package for Windows at **openoffice.org**. This software contains all the basic office functions, including word processing, spreadsheets and presentations. The word-processing component, Writer, can be used as a simple web editor.

Other types of software can also save information as a web page – if you've got your family data stored in a spreadsheet, this type of file should convert directly into a web-ready format. If you require specific guidance on how to perform these actions, consult your software's help menu, which should give you step-by-step instructions.

Free website programs
There are a number of free programs available online, which are simple to use and can be easily downloaded on to your computer. The following are two good ones to try:

NVU is a free web editor (see right and page 310), which can be downloaded from **nvu.com**. Click on **Enter Nvu site**, then click on **FREE Download** at the top of the screen. Scroll down the page to **Microsoft Windows,** and click on **Download** then follow any instructions for downloading and installation of the software.

SERIF WEBPLUS is a commercial website creation package, but Serif also has a site which offers website design software for free. Go to **freeserifsoftware.com**, click on the **WebPlus** link under the heading **Websites** and follow the instructions downloading and installation of the software.

Website templates
A quick way to create a website is to use a company like Homestead, **homestead.com**, or Moonfruit, **moonfruit.com**, which offer templates that you simply fill in with your own text and images. You pay a subscription for this service and for your site to be 'hosted' on the web. This does mean the company can make wide use of your material, so you should check any terms and conditions first before committing to such a service.

Creating a homepage in Nvu

1 Nvu starts up with a blank page. First of all, save your page by selecting the **Save as** option from the **File** menu located at the top left of the screen. You'll be prompted to enter a title for the page you're starting with. Type **Homepage** into the box on screen and click **OK**. Next, in the **Save as** menu, type in a name for your file. Select **Html files**, in the **Save as type** options, then select the folder you've created for your web page files, and click on **Save**.

Getting help

The best place to start is by looking at your program's online help facility – usually accessed by clicking on the **Help** menu at the top of the screen. There are also a number of sites designed to help family historians to create a website including Web Publishing for Genealogy at **spub.co.uk/wpg/**. There are books, too, including *Planting Your Tree Online*, by Cyndi Howells, creator of Cyndi's List.

What makes website text work

Behind the scenes, the computer file that makes up a web page consists of the text on the page along with tags, which tell the browser how to display it. The tags and what they do are defined by the HyperText Markup Language (Html) – you'll often see the initials Html mentioned in connection with website creation.

The files for your pages will end in **.htm** or **.html** – which is how the browser knows that the file is a web page. You can see this if you use your browser's **View page source** option (on the **View** menu). For example, near the top of the page, you might see two tags <h1> and </h1> to mark the start and end of the main heading, with the wording of the heading between them.

The page source for a professionally designed website will look complicated, but the good news is you needn't worry about this. Most web creation software allows you to simply key in the text you want and the program does the rest.

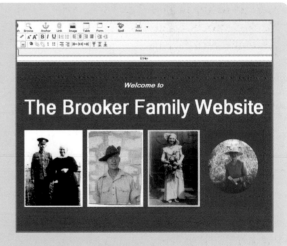

Adding text and colours

2 Choose a title for your homepage and type it into Nvu. Highlight your text and select **Heading 1** from the pre-set sizes in the style box on the toolbar. You could choose **Heading 2** for subheadings and **Body text** for the rest of your text. Click on the **Format** menu, then on the **Font**, **Size** and **Text style** options to style your text. Next, click on the **Page colour and background** option and select **Use custom colours** to choose a colour scheme for your homepage.

Adding images

3 Save the images you want to add in your website folder in jpeg, png or gif format. To add an image to your homepage, first click on the **Image** button on the tool bar. In the **Image Properties** dialogue box select **Choose File** and select an image from your folder by double clicking on the file name. Click on the **Alternate text** button and type in a title for your image, which will appear in its place in text-only browsers. Finally, click **OK**.

Formatting images

4 Your image will appear on the page. To alter the size of the image click on it, then drag the corner handles. If you're adding more images to your homepage, and you want them all to be the same size, go to the **Image Properties** dialogue box, click on the **Dimensions** tab and select **Custom size**. You can then alter the size of the image by **Pixels** or **% of window**. Enter the dimensions into the **Width** and **Height** boxes and click **OK**. See page 310 for more on Nvu.

Getting the most from your website

Once you've set up your first web pages, you can enhance them by adding your family tree and other images, such as photos of ancestors and their memorabilia. This will create a visually exciting family document to impress family and friends, and other family historians.

One of the things you'll probably want to put on your website is your family tree. The best way to produce a tree is by using a family history software package. Some of the most popular packages, such as Family Historian and Legacy Family Tree, are covered on page 38, and on pages 312-15 you'll find information on how to use the software to collate all your ancestral detail and create a family tree. You can then upload the tree to your website.

If you want, you can have more than one tree on your site – say, one for your maternal and one for your paternal ancestors, or perhaps descendant trees for your most important surnames. Just put each in its own separate folder.

Editing and adding pictures

Old family photos are an obvious way to make your website more interesting for visitors. For this you need a scanner to turn the photos into digital images – or a digital camera for up-to-date family shots.

You'll probably want to scan old photos in the best resolution possible, but this will result in huge files, which will be too unwieldy for a website. The answer is to use a program called a graphics editor to make the scanned images smaller – 640x480 pixels is as big as you'd want for a website.

If you have a scanner or digital camera, it will almost certainly have come with a graphics editor free, and this may well be good enough for the basic tasks of resizing photos to a lower resolution or cropping out unwanted areas of a shot. If not, there are plenty of free downloads which can carry out these tasks, such as IrfanView from **irfanview.net**.

If you want to retouch photos – to hide tears or blots, say – you'll need something more sophisticated. Among the commercial graphics editors Adobe Photoshop Elements and Xara are recommended and relatively inexpensive; alternatively, you'll often find older versions of commercial graphics programs given away on computer magazine CDs. The most comprehensive free graphics package is GIMP, available for Windows from **gimp.org/downloads**.

Images are not actually physically part of the page they're displayed on: each one is a separate file and you need to create a link to it on any page where it appears. All website editors can create links to images.

Making it public

Once your website is up and running, it's time to start getting people to visit. First you need to tell everyone in your family about your site, but if you want to make contact with other people who are descended from your ancestors, you'll need to get your site listed in search engines like Google and Yahoo. The most effective way to do this is to submit details to Cyndi's List using the online form at **cyndislist.com/submit** – this will put your site

Creating more pages

1 Once you've created your homepage in Nvu, you're ready to add more pages. To create a new blank page click on the **New** button on the tool bar. Your new page will appear in another tab on your screen. Save the page by selecting the **Save as** option from the **File** menu. Give it the title 'Family Tree Page', and remember to select **Html files** in the **Save as type** options. Give it a heading and background colour as you did on your homepage (see page 308).

on the Personal Home Pages section at **cyndislist.com/personal.htm**. Cyndi's List is visited regularly by search engines looking for new links, and within a few weeks any site submitted to it should be displayed by the search engines. Remember to make sure that your contact details are easy to find on your web site.

Some family history societies have a page on their website for links to members' sites, so if you belong to a society it will be worth checking whether yours offers this facility.

Fonts tips for websites

Choosing the right font is important if you want people to view your website as you designed it. The program you use to create your website may allow you to choose any fonts it finds on your PC, but someone viewing your site who doesn't have those fonts will see only a rough match. It's best to select one or more of a core set of website fonts (see below) that most people will have on their PC. Use **bold** to pick out key words and for headings, and use *italic* for picture captions. Use colour to differentiate between different pieces of information but take care not to use too much. Don't use font sizes above 16 point, except for headings, as the text won't display correctly on most PCs when your material is uploaded to the web.

Arial   Comic Sans   Courier   Georgia   Times   Trebuchet   Verdana

Your family tree

2 Open your family tree in your family tree software (see page 312). Save the diagram as an image file (jpeg, png or gif) into your website folder. You can now insert this image onto your web page by using the **Image** button on the tool bar (see page 309). To change the size of your family tree, click on the image and drag the corners in or out with the mouse. Or you can double click on the image to bring up the **Image Properties** window and alter the size there.

Creating a link on your homepage

3 Once you've completed your family tree page, click on **Save** from the **File menu**. Then go back to your homepage by clicking on the **Homepage** tab. Type the text 'Family Tree' in the space where you want your link to go. Highlight the text, click on the **Link** button on the tool bar. Click on **Choose file**, select your family tree page from your website folder and click **Open**, then click **OK**. The link will now be underlined and active. Click on **Save**.

Putting your website online

4 Click on the **Browse** button on the tool bar. This will display your web page in a web browser with active links. Once you're ready to publish your website, you'll need a domain name (see page 305). When your website is ready, click on the **Publish** button. You'll need to enter a name for your website, its http address and the details of your publishing server. For advice on using Nvu visit **thesitewizard.com/ gettingstarted/nvu1.shtml**.

Using software to create your family tree

Software packages let you create different styles of family tree that you can print out, send to others or put on a website. Most packages work in similar ways, and you'll find using one easy once you start.

There are a number of good software packages that will help you to make a family tree (see page 38). Family Historian, used for the example below, allows you to create a simple pedigree or birth brief family tree (see page 70), as well as the fuller drop-line tree that covers wider family history. You can also add pictures, sounds and videos, and record details of your sources, and so keep track easily of where you found your information – a vital aspect of all research. Family Historian software also lets you see all your information at a glance, displaying it in a different way to most other packages: it gives you a **Records** window that lists all the people you've uploaded with their date and place of birth. When you want to examine and edit each person's full details, you simply view their **Properties** window.

Start loading the family

1 Load the software (in this case, Family Historian) onto your PC, then click on the icon to open it. From the menu, click on **File**, then **New**. You'll see a new file into which you can load your data. The first screen is the **Records** screen (as above). Select **Individuals** and enter the name of the person you wish to record, in this case, Pauline Brooker, starting with her surname. Go to the toolbar menu, and select **Insert**, then **Unrelated individual**.

Add the details

2 This will open another box, which allows you to create a new record for Pauline Brooker. Re-enter her name in the box, then add all the other details you have for her. An **Entry assistant** box will open up to help you to fill in the information. Once you've entered all the details for your starting person, you can begin to build the tree, by entering details of parents. Click on the **Parents >>** button, which you'll find next to the name.

Enter parents' details

3 You'll be asked to select from a drop-down menu that offers **Create new record as parent** or **Link existing record as parent**. At this stage you need to create a new record of a parent, so choose this option and add details, in this case of Pauline's father, Leonard Sawle, and her mother, Florence Sharpe. You can now carry on adding information in the same way.

With all software packages, the best way to learn how to use them is to read through the instructions first. But there's no substitute for experience, so don't hesitate to play around with the software and start uploading branches of your family tree. Once you've gone through the basic steps a few times, you'll quickly gain enough confidence to tackle some of the more advanced features, and soon you'll discover for yourself the full potential of the software, and how you can use it to best suit your needs.

Getting organised

Software packages will let you arrange information in various ways. On Family Historian, for example, material is organised in chronological order – but it also lets you order records alphabetically, by surname, or by place and date of birth. For the latter options, open your family tree in the **Records** window and select the appropriate command. If you haven't entered a date of birth but you know the date of death, the software will estimate the date of birth to 50 years earlier.

Tips to remember

● To find out the name of each button on the tool bar, just hover the mouse cursor over a button and a description of its function will appear.

● When entering names into your tree, it's good practice to enter the surname in capital letters. Then it's easy to see at a glance which names are surnames, especially if your family tree contains names such as Jack James, where the surname isn't obvious. Always use maiden names for women, so you can see where their line starts.

Adding information

If you want to add information about a particular person, for example Florence Sharpe's parents, you need to go to the **Records** window and click once on her name in the **Individual records** list to highlight it. Then click on the **Property dialog** button (shown left), which is on the main tool bar. This will bring up the individual record box, and you can carry on adding information as before.

There are tools to use if your tree contains a great many names and numerous records. If you want to show the chart of a particular person, you can click on any name in the tree, and that will display all the details of ancestors related to that particular individual. By clicking on the buttons in the tool bar, you can display the results either as record sheets or as family tree diagrams, as above. It's a good idea to familiarise yourself with the options.

Searching for a record in your tree

You may wish to search for a particular record in order to add information to it. To do this, click on the **Find record** button (shown left) on the tool bar to open a separate search box. Type in the name of the person you're looking for, and this name will then be highlighted in the **Records** window.

Adding images and seeing your trees

Most family tree software allows you to create links between individuals and any number of images – some packages even let you add sound and video clips. You can keep on enhancing your relatives' files and then choose to view all the information in a number of different family tree formats.

Adding a photo to a record

1 In the **Records** window, highlight the name of the person to whose record you want to add a photo. Now click on the **View multimedia** button located along the tool bar symbolised by a camera (left). This takes you to the **Multimedia records** page. Click on **Insert** from the top panel of options and choose **Pictures** from the drop-down list. The **Insert picture** dialogue box will appear for you to locate your chosen photo from where you saved it on your hard drive. Click on **Open** and the photo will appear in the 'Multimedia' screen.

Linking a photo to other information

2 At the bottom-left of the screen, under **Links and notes**, you'll see the name of the person (or people) that photo has been linked to. If a photo was taken of more than one of your relatives, simply click on the **New link/note** button (left). From the **Create link** box that appears, select whether you want to link the image to an individual, a family, a source record or a note. In the case of a wedding photo showing the bride and groom, you can attach the image to both people in the photo by selecting **An individual** from the list. Then a small version of the **Records** window will appear so that you can find the individual's record.

Choose a viewing option

1 You can view the information in your tree in various ways, using the buttons shown here. From left to right, they are **View ancestors**, **View descendants**, **View ancestors and descendants** and **View all relatives**. Select the name of the person you want the tree to be designed around from the **Records** window. Usually, at this point, it will be yourself or the person whose name you started with. In this case, it's Pauline Brooker. Then click on the **View ancestors** icon on the toolbar. The diagram window opens, displaying a diagram of Pauline Brooker's ancestors.

Creating links to people on your family tree can be enhanced by adding old family photos and images of documents. If you have a wedding photo or a family group, add them to your tree to bring it to life and create a fascinating document of facts and images. Some software packages only allow you to upload photos, but Family Historian (see below) also lets you create links between individuals and 'multimedia' (video or audio) files. You can attach as many photos and images as you want to a person's record and, if a photograph includes more than one person on your tree, you can create links between the image and all the individuals. It's a fairly easy process. If you have a digital camera, you can save and upload family pictures to your computer. Documents can be scanned and uploaded in the same way. If you don't have a scanner, taking pictures of documents using a digital camera, then uploading them onto your PC, can work just as well.

Navigating around your tree

2 You can move around the tree using the following six buttons. From left to right, you can: zoom in, and out, to view the details of a particular ancestor; use the magnifying glass to select areas you want to see close-up; click on the globe to view your complete tree; centre the diagram on the page using the focus symbol; and move the image around using the hand.

You can also change the appearance of the diagram using the following four buttons: the first displays hidden links between relatives; the second adds and removes the text frames, which sometimes makes it easier to read; and the last two buttons display and change the page boundaries.

Adding to your tree

3 As you gather more information, you can add to your tree quickly and easily. When you open your file, you'll see that the information you've already added is displayed in the **Records** window. By clicking on the name you wish to view, and by using the options detailed in the previous steps, you can select different views for different ancestors, as well as for the entire tree if you wish.

Bringing your tree to life

4 If you choose to view **All close relatives – nicknames, dates, pictures** (see step 1), you'll have a far more animated tree to look at. Any pictures, images or documents that you chose to add will be displayed. This has the advantage of bringing your tree to life, as well as creating a clear, accurate family tree document to share with your friends and family. Save as you go along to make sure you don't lose any data if your PC should crash unexpectedly. Click on the **Save** icon on your toolbar, and you'll be prompted to save your file to your hard drive.

Sharing it all on a blog

One of the biggest bonuses of the internet is the ease and speed with which you can exchange information, and one of the most popular ways of doing this is by 'blogging' – great for family historians who want to share their successes and keep on developing their family trees.

Creating a web log – or 'blog' for short – is a good place to start exchanging information online. A blog is an online journal or newsletter that's frequently updated and intended for public viewing. It's a perfect arena to recount your thoughts and experiences and narrate personal journeys.

It also allows anyone who reads it to leave their own comments, stories and perhaps new material that may cast more light on your family's history.

There are two main ways to create blogs: you can use an existing server or website, such as one of those shown on the right, or you can put a blog on your own website (see pages 304-11). This might involve using web space offered by your internet service provider (ISP), buying space from a specialist hosting company or buying your own domain name (the web address for your site) – or even learning a little about HTML (HyperText Markup Language), the language of websites.

Using space on blogger sites

You'll find it far easier to use an existing site to host your blog than to set up your own website. Blogging is an increasingly popular hobby and the number of hosting sites reflects this. Enter the words 'blog hosts' into a search engine and you'll be offered a choice of sites, some that you pay for, others that are free of charge.

Using free blog sites

Free-to-use blog sites are financed by advertising, so a small advertisement banner will be placed on your blog to help to pay for the cost of hosting it. You won't be asked to pay for anything yourself, but neither will you have any choice as to what is advertised on your blog.

Most blogs allow you to store photos but there are limits to the size of the 'photo album' they will allow you, although they're usually perfectly adequate for normal usage.

Made for a blog *Samuel Pepys, seen here at the height of his powers in a late 17th-century portrait by Sir Godfrey Kneller, would have been an enthusiastic blogger. His detailed diaries give a vivid picture of his attitudes and ideas – just as a well-written blog should.*

Choosing a host for your blog

The first three websites shown below will help you to set up your own blog, and the fourth will prove useful as a source of inspiration: you'll be able to see just how – and how not – to set up and run a blog.

Blogger

Owned by Google, **blogger.com** lets you create your own blog, free of charge, in three easy steps: first, create an account by registering your personal details; then name your blog – which can be anything from your name or interest to something more creative; and finally, choose a design template to personalise your blog. Once you've done this, you can start entering information and images. You'll be prompted along the way.

TypePad

You'll be charged for space on **typepad.com**, which provides a choice of templates and technical support. The site offers a free 30-day trial period, and then you can choose from a range of services and prices, depending on what you want to use it for. The website is targeted mainly at professionals and small businesses.

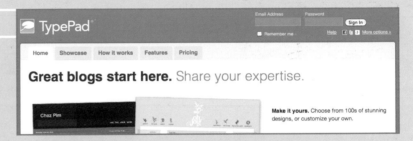

Xanga

Like Blogger, **xanga.com** is a free service that gives you instructions to follow for creating your own blog. All Xanga members receive a 'Xanga Site' consisting of a weblog, a photoblog, a videoblog, an audioblog, a 'Pulse' (mini-blog), and a social networking profile.

Finding family history blogs

If you want to have a look at other people's blogs before designing your own, **cyndislist.com/blogs** has a comprehensive list of the genealogical blogs in circulation. There is also a guide on how to search for and use other people's blogs to help you in your research.

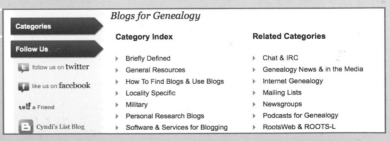

Sharing pictures with your family

Online photo albums and photo-sharing websites are an excellent way in which to store old photographs and record new memories of your family. The first step is to choose the website that's best for you.

When you look for a photo-sharing website, you can be spoilt for choice. It's always wise to go with a well-established site that has already attracted many users. Picasa and the other sites covered here are powerful and versatile, offering all kinds of storage and display features. Remember that websites are constantly changing. And while the appearance of sites and the details of how they work may alter, what they do and the services they provide generally remain much the same. This is also the case for any software. Versions of software may come and go, but the fundamental functionality usually remains, typically being enhanced in later versions. So be prepared for sites to change their style or content and for updated software to seem unfamiliar to begin with or look different.

Take the Picasa tour

1 Go to **picasa.google.co.uk** and, on the homepage, download the software. If you want to have a look at the site before you download, click on the **Learn more about Picasa and Picasa Web Albums** link.

How to use Picasa

2 The page that comes up shows you all the things that you can do with the Picasa software.

Organise your pictures

3 Once you've downloaded the software, all the images currently stored on your computer will be in one handy place. By clicking on the tabs at the top of the screen, you can import photos, create a slideshow or a timeline, or copy them onto a CD.

Picasa

A fast-growing resource for storing photos, **picasa.google.co.uk** is free to use, although you'll need to download the software from the website first. Once you've done this, you can use the site to upload, store and view your pictures. One of the best features of Picasa is that the software automatically searches for every picture you've stored on your computer, and instantly puts them all in one place. This is really useful if you tend to store pictures in a number of different files,

Create an album

4 When you've selected the pictures and images you want to store, you can create an album. This is useful if you want to hold in one handy place a selection of images and documents, that may all relate to one ancestor. Click on **Album**, and you'll be asked to name and describe the contents of the album. You can then share these with friends and family.

because it can find pictures and images that you might have feared you'd lost.

Downloading the software is simple: you just click on the link on the homepage. From there, you click on a series of prompt boxes, and once the software is installed, it will automatically put all the photos on your computer into one file. The whole process should take less than 5 minutes.

Picasa offers the added security of password protection, so only you can see the pictures you've uploaded yourself, if that's what you wish. You can also edit your photos and images, and create slideshows to show to the family. You're allowed up to 1GB of free storage in your online albums, which is about 4,000 standard-size photos.

You can also add captions and comments to any images that you upload, so that you can see at a glance what your image is and what it relates to. If you have friends and family that use Picasa, you'll be able to download their saved images to your own computer.

Picasa constantly works to increase its storage space, so if you're snap-happy, this is a great site for storing all your images. The software supplied is regularly updated, with new features being added.

Flickr

The American website **flickr.com** is one of the largest and most popular photosharing sites. The basic package is free to use, and you can upload 300MB of photos a month by mobile phone, email or from your own computer. Only the most recent 200 can be viewed. Photos can then be seen and shared

by you and your family. You can organise the photos using tags, sets, albums or collections, or sort them by subject. The site also lets you create cards, calendars, prints and DVDs.

Snapfish

Another website where you can upload, share and store photos is **snapfish.co.uk**. Photos can be sent direct to a dedicated email address from a mobile phone or from your own email account. You can customise albums to showcase your pictures and they can all be made into prints or even used to personalise gifts such as mugs and t-shirts.

You can store as many low-resolution photos as you like, provided that the site is used to order prints, enlargements or high-resolution photographs at least once a year, otherwise your photographs will be deleted from the site. (An email reminder is sent after 335 days of inactivity.)

This site is most useful if you regularly order photos or gifts, but not if all you want is free long-term storage.

Photobucket

The creative, free-to-use **photobucket.com** site links millions of uploaded photos, slideshows, graphics and videos daily to more than 300,000 websites, especially the popular social networking ones (see pages 320-1). You can share your photos by email, mobile phone or an instant messenger such as MSN. As well as uploading online you can use the site to create photos, images, videos and music collections, and use different styles of slideshow to play photos back to friends or family members.

Sharing with the family
How to use networking sites

There are many reasons for joining a social networking group. You might want to meet new people who share your interests so that you can exchange stories, photos, videos and other information. Or perhaps you want to stay in touch with other family historians or with family members you've found through your research. You could form a group related to a specific family tree or surname and invite other interested users to join. This group would then have its own homepage, where all the members could write comments, share ideas and developments in their research, and upload photos. In addition, some of the main social networks have extra features that might allow you to create groups sharing common interests or set up forums for discussions on particular subjects.

How a group grows
In recent years, social networking websites and communities have grown massively. Popular sites such as MySpace and Facebook that started with a few thousand users can now claim users in the millions.

Social networking groups grow quickly because each new member can invite non-members to become friends on the website. They receive an email invitation, which they can reply to and use to register their profile on the same site. On most sites, both parties must confirm that they're friends before they're accepted into the group.

Friends you don't know yet
Bear in mind that most users are trying to find new friends and link up with as many other users as possible. So you'll often receive 'friend requests' from people you don't know. This means you need to be careful about the type of information you put on your homepage or personal pages: don't disclose too much, such as your mobile phone number or home address, to other users. These details may be needed to register your profile but they're not in the public domain. A good site will give advice on maximum personal safety and tips on how to stay safe online.

Websites that will help you
Here are some of the most popular social networking sites on the internet. There may be one that can advance your research.

Setting up a Facebook group

1 Anyone with a Facebook page may set up a Facebook group on any subject. This is an ideal way to share genealogy findings. A group page may either be public or restricted to members of your choice – members of your family, for example. Go to **facebook.com** and either sign in or register. On the Facebook homepage, click on **Create group** from the menu on the left. Enter your details into the **Create group** window, and click on **Create**.

What your Facebook group looks like

2 Your new group will now appear under the Group category on the left of the screen. Click on the group name to view the profile. You can edit your profile in a number of ways, including uploading photos and posting salient links. Any postings you or any other members make to the group 'wall' will thereafter be seen by everyone in the group.

- Facebook, at **facebook.com**, is the most popular site in this category. It has more than 800 million active members worldwide, and is used by a wide variety of people, from friends and family who want to talk online, business people interested in networking, bands and groups passing on information to fans, to people looking for a date. Any existing member is able set up a Facebook group devoted to a specific topic. This is an ideal way of sharing your research with your family, or other Facebook users (see opposite).

- YouTube's website, **youtube.com**, is great if you want to share, upload and view items. This enormous site contains film and TV clips and music videos, as well as amateur content such as video-blogging and short original videos. The range of content is extraordinary and seemingly all encompassing.

Unregistered users can watch most videos on the site, but if you're a registered user (see below), you can upload an unlimited number of videos, creating a storeroom for all your family films, and making them accessible to other people, so that distant relatives can view them from anywhere in the world.

- Bebo, at **bebo.com** (see below) started in 2005 to enable users to upload family photos and videos, post comments and send emails in their search for relatives, as well as offering quizzes, picture slideshows and blogs.

- Other networking sites – from the vast selection out there – that you might like to visit in your search for relatives are: **myspace.com**, **orkut.com**, **flickr.com**, **photobucket.com** and **twitter.com**.

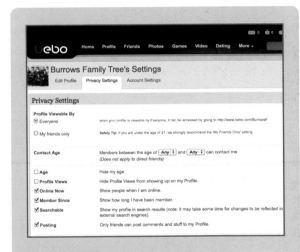

How to join YouTube

1 To create an account on YouTube, go to **youtube.com**. As YouTube is part of Google, if you have a Google account you can use that to sign up. On your homepage you can create your own Youtube Channel in which you can post videos, photographs and comments. Contact other YouTube users – or members of your family – who you think might be interested in subscribing to your channel.

Uploading a video

2 YouTube is at its most effective as a video-sharing site. To post your own videos, on the homepage click on the **Upload** button. A new page opens that enables you to drag videos from your desktop and upload them to YouTube. You can create videos lasting up to 15 minutes, including in high definition (HD) formats. If you're uncertain about the file format of your video, click on YouTube's **Help** button.

Put your profile on Bebo

Bebo works in the same way as most other social networking sites. To create a profile page, register first at **bebo.com**, following the prompts. You can keep your homepage private, if you want to. Once you've signed in, click on your ID on the far right of the screen and select **Settings** from the drop-down menu. Under **Privacy Settings** click on the button labelled **Profile Viewable By Everyone**.

Directory of sources

The Directory lists sources of information mentioned in the book, as well as other useful websites and addresses. All websites are shown without the prefixes http:// or www. If you have any difficulty opening a website, try adding one of the prefixes to its address.

192
192.com
Online business and people directory.

1901 Census
1901censusonline.com
Official 1901 census website.

5 Star Shareware
5star-shareware.com
Software packages to download.

Aberdeen City Archives
aberdeencity.gov.uk
Select Education and Learning, *then* Archives Home
Town House, Broad Street
Aberdeen AB10 1AQ
01224 522513
archives@aberdeencity.gov.uk

Adoption Search
adoptionsearchreunion.org.uk
Website for people wishing to trace birth relatives or adopted children.

Albion
albion.com/netiquette/book
Tips on using message boards and forums.

Am Baile
ambaile.org.uk
History and culture of the Scottish Highlands and islands.

Ancestry
ancestry.co.uk
Website for accessing online records.

Angels
fancydress.com
Fancy dress and historical costumiers.

Anglesey Archives
anglesey.gov.uk
Select Leisure, *then* Records and archives.
Industrial Estate Road
Bryn Cefni Industrial Estate
Llangefni
Anglesey LL77 7JA
01248 751930
archives@anglesey.gov.uk

Antiquus Morbus
antiquusmorbus.com
Glossary of archaic medical terms for diseases and causes of death.

Archives Wales
archiveswales.org.uk
Online catalogue detailing records available in 21 Welsh archives.

ARCHON Directory
nationalarchives.gov.uk/archon
Online database of contact details for all record offices and archives around the UK. Plus some overseas repositories.

Army Museums Ogilby Trust
armymuseums.org.uk
Resource for researching regimental history.
Brigadier C.S. Sibun
58 The Close
Salisbury SP1 2EX
01722 332188
dir@amot.demon.co.uk

Ask.com
ask.com
Search engine.

Avast
avast.com
Anti-virus software to protect your PC.

AVG Free Advisor
free.grisoft.com
Anti-virus software to protect your PC.

AVG Grisoft
grisoft.com
Anti-virus software to protect your PC.

Ayrshire Archives
ayrshirearchives.org.uk
Watson Peat Building
SAC Auchincruire
Ayr KA6 5HW
01292 521819
archives@south-ayrshire.gov.uk

Baptist Missionary Society Archives
rpc.ox.ac.uk
Select Resource Centres, *then* Angus Library
Collections offering material relating to missionary work in many parts of the world.
The Librarian/Archivist
Angus Library
Regent's Park College
Pusey Street
Oxford OX1 2LB
01865 288120
angus.library@regents.ox.ac.uk

Barnardo's (UK and Australia)
barnardos.org.uk
barnardos.org.au
Child welfare agency with child adoption records.

Barnardo's (UK Head Office)
Tanners Lane
Barkingside
Ilford, Essex IG6 1QG
020 8550 8822

Bath and North East Somerset Archives and Record Office
batharchives.co.uk
bathnes.gov.uk
Guildhall
High Street
Bath BA1 5AW
01225 477421
archives@bathnes.gov.uk

BBC (Family history section)
bbc.co.uk/familyhistory
*Tips and hints, plus record sheets
to download.*

BeBo
bebo.com
Social networking site.

**Bedfordshire and Luton Archives
and Records Service**
centralbedfordshire.gov.uk
In the A-Z menu choose Archives *under
A, then* Local History and Heritage,
then click on the link for Bedfordshire
and Luton Archives and Records Service.
Riverside Building, Borough Hall
Cauldwell Street
Bedford MK42 9AP
01234 228833
archive@bedscc.gov.uk

Behind The Name
behindthename.com
History of first names.

Berkshire Record Office
berkshirerecordoffice.org.uk
9 Coley Avenue
Reading RG1 6AF
0118 937 5132

**Berwick-upon-Tweed
Record Office**
**experiencewoodhorn.com/berwick-
record**
Council Offices
Wallace Green
Berwick-upon-Tweed TD15 1ED
01289 301865
ibankier@woodhorn.org.uk

Bing Maps
bing.com/maps
*Modern street directory – formerly known
as Multimap.*

**Birmingham Archives and
Heritage**
birmingham.gov.uk/archives
Central Library
Chamberlain Square
Birmingham B3 3HQ
0121 303 4549
archives.heritage@birmingham.gov.uk

Birthlink
birthlink.org.uk
*Services for people with a Scottish
connection, separated by adoption.*
21 Castle Street
Edinburgh EH2 3DN
0131 225 6441
mail@birthlink.org.uk

Blog
blog.com
Create your own online blog.

Blogger
blogger.com
Create your own online blog.

BMD Index
bmdindex.co.uk
*Online registers for civil registration
documents.*

Bodleian Library
bodleian.ox.ac.uk/bodley
*Main research library for University
of Oxford, with many online resources
accessible to the public.*
Broad Street
Oxford OX1 3BG
01865 277162
reader.services@bodlean.ox.ac.uk

**Bolton Archives and
Local Studies**
**boltonmuseums.org.uk/
bolton-archives**
Le Mans Crescent
Bolton BL1 1SE
01204 332185
archives.library@bolton.gov.uk

Borthwick Institute
york.ac.uk/library/borthwick
Archives at the University of York.
Borthwick Institute
University of York
Heslington
York YO10 5DD
01904 321166
bihr500@york.ac.uk

Bristol Record Office
bristol.gov.uk/recordoffice
'B' Bond Warehouse
Smeaton Road
Bristol BS1 6XN
0117 922 4224
bro@bristol.gov.uk

British Genealogy
british-genealogy.com
Free site for tracing British genealogy.

British Legion
britishlegion.org.uk
Official website for the British Legion.
199 Borough High Street
London SE1 1AA
020 3207 2100

British Library
bl.uk
*The UK's national library website contains
information on the scope of its collections
and how to use its services.*
The British Library
96 Euston Road
St Pancras, London NW1 2DB
020 7412 7676
customer-services@bl.uk

British Library India Office
indiafamily.bl.uk/UI
For contact details see British Library.

**British Library Newspaper
Library**
bl.uk/catalogues/newspapers
British Library Newspapers
Colindale Avenue
London NW9 5HE
020 7412 7353
newspaper@bl.uk

British Origins
britishorigins.com
English and Welsh records online.

British Postal Museum and Archive
postalheritage.org.uk
Information about 400 years'
of postal history.
Freeling House, Phoenix Place
London WC1X 0DL
020 7239 2570
info@postalheritage.org.uk

British Red Cross
redcross.org.uk
British branch of the International Red
Cross, that helps to reunite families.
44 Moorfields
London EC2Y 9AL
0844 871 1111
information@redcross.org.uk

Build Your Website
build-your-website.co.uk
Online help for building your own
web pages.

Bury Archive Service
bury.gov.uk/archives
Moss Street
Bury BL9 0DR
0161 253 6782
archives@bury.gov.uk

Business Archives Council
gla.ac.uk/services/archives
Business archives services, based in the
Centre for Business History in Scotland at
the University of Glasgow.
Duty Archivist
13 Thurso Street
Glasgow G11 6PE
0141 330 5515
enquiries@archives.gla.ac.uk

Cambridgeshire County Record Office
cambridgeshire.gov.uk/archives
Box RES 1009
Shire Hall
Castle Hill
Cambridge CB3 0AP
01223 699399
county.records.cambridge@cambridges
hire.gov.uk

Canada Libraries and Archives
See Libraries and Archives of Canada
(LAC).

Catholic history
catholic-history.org.uk/cfhs
catholic-history.org.uk/crs
Websites for the Catholic Family History
Society and Catholic Records Society.
catholicfhs@ntlworld.com

Catholic National Library
catholic-library.org.uk
Comprehensive collection of Catholic
family history information and mission
registers.
St Michael's Abbey
Farnborough Road
Farnborough
Hampshire GU14 7NG
01252 543818
library@catholic-library.org.uk

Centre for Kentish Studies/Kent Archives Service
www.kent.gov.uk
Select Leisure and Culture, *then*
Archives and Local History
Sessions House
County Hall
Maidstone ME14 1XQ
01622 694363
archives@kent.gov.uk

Ceredigion Archives
archifdy-ceredigion.org.uk
Records of the county formerly known
as Cardiganshire.
County Offices
Marine Terrace
Aberystwyth SY23 2DE
01970 633697/633698
archives@ceredigion.gov.uk

Cheshire Archives and Local Studies
archives.cheshire.gov.uk
Duke Street
Chester, CH1 1RL
01244 972574

Child Migrants Trust
childmigrantstrust.com
Charity reuniting families of child migrants
shipped to Australia, Canada and other
parts of the Commonwealth.
28A Musters Road
West Bridgford
Nottingham NG2 7PL
0115 982 2811

City of Westminster Archives Centre
westminster.gov.uk/services/
libraries/archives
10 St Ann's Street
London SW1P 2DE
020 7641 5180
archives@westminster.gov.uk

ClamAV
clamav.net
Anti-virus software to protect your PC.

Collect Britain
bl.uk/onlinegallery
Showcase of British Library collections.

College of Arms
college-of-arms.gov.uk
Official repository of coats of arms for
English, Welsh, Northern Irish and
Commonwealth families.
Queen Victoria Street
London EC4V 4BT
020 7248 2762

Commonwealth War Graves Commission
cwgc.org
Database of war memorials
and war cemeteries.
2 Marlow Road
Maidenhead
Berkshire SL6 7DX
01628 634221
Use contact form on website for email.

Consumer Direct
consumerdirect.gov.uk
Practical consumer advice.

Convicts to Australia
members.iinet.net.au/~perthdps/
convicts/index.html
*A guide to researching your
convict ancestors.*

Coram Family
coram.org.uk
*Registered children's charity for the
care of vulnerable children.*

Corel
corel.com
Photo software website.

Cornwall Record Office
cornwall.gov.uk
Select Community and living, *then*
Records, Archives and Cornish
Studies
Old County Hall
Truro TR1 3AY
01872 323127
cro@cornwall.gov.uk

Coventry History Centre
theherbert.org/index.php/home/
history-centre
Jordan Well
Coventry CV1 5QP
024 7683 4060
historycentre@theherbert.org

Crockford's Clerical Directory
crockford.org.uk
Details of Anglican clergy.

Cumbria Archive Service
cumbria.gov.uk/archives
Comprises offices in Barrow, Carlisle,
Kendal and Whitehaven.

Curious Fox
curiousfox.com
Website for genealogical enquiries.

Cyndi's List
cyndislist.com
Worldwide portal to genealogy sources.

Denbighshire Record Office
denbighshire.gov.uk
Select Leisure and libraries, *then*
Archives Service
Ruthin Gaol
46 Clwyd Street
Ruthin
Denbighshire LL15 1HP
01824 708250
archives@denbighshire.gov.uk

Derbyshire Record Office
derbyshire.gov.uk/recordoffice
County Hall
New Street
Matlock DE4 3AG
01629 585347
record.office@derbyshire.gov.uk

Devon Heritage Service
devon.gov.uk/record_office
Great Moor House
Bittern Road
Sowton, Exeter EX2 7NL
01392 384253
devrec@devon.gov.uk

Digital Handsworth
digitalhandsworth.org.uk
A history of the town of Handsworth.

DirectGov
direct.gov.uk
*Wide-ranging official British government
website.*

DNA Ancestry Project
dnaancestryproject.com
DNA testing and information.

Dorset Archives
dorsetforyou.com/archives
Dorset History Centre
Bridport Road
Dorchester DT1 1RP
01305 250550
archives@dorsetcc.gov.uk

Dr William's Library
dwlib.co.uk
*Research library specialising in English
Puritanism and Protestant nonconformity.*
14 Gordon Square
London WC1H 0AR
020 7837 3727
enquiries@dwlib.co.uk

Dublin City Archives
dublincity.ie
Enter 'City archives' in Search *box.
Records of the civic government
of Dublin, from 1171.*
138-144 Pearse Street
Dublin 2
00 353 1 6744999
cityarchives@dublincity.ie

Dublin Gazette
irisoifigiuil.ie
Online editions of the Dublin Gazette.

Durham County Record Office
durham.gov.uk/recordoffice
County Hall
Durham DH1 5UL
0191 383 3253
record.office@durham.gov.uk

Easily
easily.co.uk
*Website for purchasing and registering
domain names.*

**East Riding of Yorkshire
Archives**
eastriding.gov.uk
Select Leisure, *then* Archives, family
and Local history.
The Treasure House
Champney Road
Beverley
Correspondence address:
County Hall
Beverley HU17 9BA
01482 392790
archives.service@eastriding.gov.uk

East Sussex Record Office
eastsussex.gov.uk/useourarchives
The Maltings
Castle Precincts
Lewes
East Sussex BN7 1YT
01273 482349
archives@eastsussex.gov.uk

Easyspace
easyspace.co.uk
Website for purchasing and registering domain names and web space.

Edinburgh City Archives
edinburgh.gov.uk
Enter 'City archives' in Search box.
Level 1
City Chambers
253 High Street
Edinburgh EH1 1YJ
0131 529 4616

English Handwriting 1500-1700
english.cam.ac.uk/ceres/ehoc
University of Cambridge online tutorial for reading old handwriting.

Essex Record Office
essex.gov.uk
Click on A-Z of services, select 'A' and scroll down to 'Archives'.
Wharf Road
Chelmsford
Essex CM2 6YT
01245 244644
ero.enquiry@essex.gov.uk

Explore 192
192.com
Index of businesses, people and properties.

Facebook
facebook.com
The world's most popular social networking website.

Family History Centres
The Mormon (LDS) Church's Family History Centres are branches of its vast library in Utah, USA. Its British headquarters and distribution centre for products are also listed below.

Genealogical Society of Utah
www.gensocietyofutah.org
185 Penns Lane
Sutton Coldfield B76 1JU
0121 384 9921

LDS Distribution Centre
399 Garretts Green Lane
Birmingham B33 0UH
0121 785 2200

Aberdeen Family History Centre
North Anderson Drive
Aberdeen AB15 6DD
01224 692206

Aldershot Family History Centre
LDS Chapel
St Georges Road
Aldershot GU12 4LJ
01252 321460

Alloa Family History Centre
Grange Road
Westend Park
Alloa
01259 211148

Alness Family History Centre
Kilmonivaig, Seafield
Portmahomack IV20 1RE
01862 871631

Ashton under Lyme Family History Centre
Patterdale Road
Ashton under Lyme
0161 330 3453

Ayr Family History Centre
2A Mossgiel Road
Ayr
01292 610632

Barrow Family History Centre
Abbey Road
Barrow-in-Furness LA13 9JY
01229 820050

Belfast Family History Centre
403 Holywood Road
Belfast, County Antrim BT4 2GU
028 9076 8250

Billingham Family History Centre
The Linkway
Billingham TS23 3HH
01642 563162

Boston Family History Centre
1 Woodthorpe Avenue
Fishtoft, Boston
01205 353579

Birkenhead Family History Centre
Reservoir Road
Prenton
Birkenhead
0151 608 7723

Blackpool Family History Centre
Warren Drive
Blackpool
01253 863868

Bristol Family History Centre
721 Wells Road
Whitchurch
Bristol BS14 9HU
01275 838326

Cambridge Family History Centre
670 Cherry Hinton Road
Cambridge CB1 4DR
01223 247010

Canterbury Family History Centre
Forty Acre Road
Canterbury
01227 765431

Cardiff Family History Centre
Heol-Y-Deri
Rhiwibina
Cardiff
South Glamorgan.
02920 625342

Carlisle Family History Centre
Langrigg Road, Morton Park
Carlisle CA2 6DT
01228 526767

Cheltenham Family History Centre
Thirlestaine Road
Cheltenham GL53 7AS
01242 523433

Coleraine Family History Centre
8 Sandelfields
Knocklynn Road
Coleraine
Londonderry BT52 1WQ
028 7032 1214

Cork Family History Centre
Sarsfield Road
Wilton, Cork
County Cork
00 353 21 4897050

Coventry Family History Centre
Riverside Close
Whitley, Coventry CV3 4AT
024 7630 3316

Crawley Family History Centre
Old Horsham Road
Crawley RH11 8PD
01293 516151

Dereham Family History Centre
Yaxham Road
East Dereham
Norfolk NR19 1HB
0136 285 1500

Douglas Family History Centre
Woodside, Woodburn Road
Douglas
Isle of Man
01624 675834

Dublin Family History Centre
www.mission.net/ireland/dublin
Ireland Dublin Mission
The Willows
Finglas Road
Dublin
00 353 1 4625609

Dumfries Family History Centre
36 Edinburgh Road
Albanybank
Dumfries DG1 1JQ
01387 254865

Dundee Family History Centre
Bingham Terrace
Dundee DD4 7HH
01382 451247

Eastbourne Family History Centre
18A Furness Road
Eastbourne
East Sussex BN21 4EY
01323 20137

Edinburgh Family History Centre
30a Colinton Road
Edinburgh EH10 5DQ
0131 337 3049

Elgin Family History Centre
Pansport Road
Elgin, Morayshire IV30 1HE
01343 546429

Exeter Family History Centre
Wonford Road
Exeter, Devon EX2 4UD
01392 250723

Forest of Dean Family History Centre
Wynols Hill
Holcot Road
Queensway
Colesford
Gloucestershire GL16 7JB
01594 832904

Gaerwen Family History Centre
Holyhead Road
Gaerwen, Anglesey
01248 421894

Gillingham Family History Centre
2 Twydall Lane
Gillingham, Kent
01634 388900

Glasgow Family History Centre
35 Julian Avenue
Glasgow G12 0RB
0141 357 1024

Grimsby Family History Centre
Linwood Avenue
Waltham Road
Grimsby DN33 2PA
01472 828876

Harborne Family History Centre
38-42 Lordswood Road
Harborne
Birmingham B17 9QS
0121 427 6858

Harrogate Family History Centre
10 Wetherby Road, Harrogate
North Yorkshire HG2 7SA
01423 886537

Hastings Family History Centre
2 Ledsham Avenue
St Leonards-on-Sea
East Sussex TN37 7LE
01424 754563

Helston Family History Centre
Clodgey Lane, Helston
Cornwall TR13 8PJ
01326 564503

High Wycombe Family History Centre
743 London Road
High Wycombe
Buckinghamshire HP11 1HQ
01494 459979

Huddersfield Family History Centre
12 Halifax Road
Birchencliffe, Huddersfield
West Yorkshire HD3 3BS
01484 454573

Hull Family History Centre
725 Holderness Road
Hull, East Yorkshire HU8 9AR
01482 701439

Inverness Family History Centre
13 Ness Walk
Inverness IV3 5 SQ
01463 231220

Ipswich Family History Centre
42 Sidegate Lane West
Ipswich IP4 3DB
01473 723182

King's Lynn Family History Centre
Reffley Lane
King's Lynn
Norfolk PE30 3EQ
01553 670000

Kirkcaldy Family History Centre
Winifred Crescent
Forth Park, Kirkcaldy
Fifeshire
01592 640041

Leeds Family History Centre
Vesper Road
Leeds
West Yorkshire
0113 258 5297

Leicester Family History Centre
Wakerley Road
Leicester, Leicestershire LE5 4WD
0116 249 0099

Lerwick Family History Centre
South Road
Lerwick, Shetland Islands
01595 695732

Lichfield Family History Centre
Purcell Avenue
Lichfield
Staffordshire
01543 414843

Limerick Family History Centre
Dooradoyle Road
Limerick, County Limerick
00 351 61 309 443

Lincoln Family History Centre
Skellingthorpe Road
Lincoln LN6 0PB
01522 680117

Liverpool Family History Centre
4 Mill Bank
Liverpool L13 0BW
0151 252 0614

London Family History Centre
64-68 Exhibition Road
South Kensington, London SW7 2PA
020 7589 8561

Lowestoft Family History Centre
165 Yarmouth Road
Lowestoft, Suffolk NR32 4AB
01502 573851

Macclesfield Family History Centre
Victoria Road
Macclesfield, Cheshire SK10 3JE
01625 427236

Maidstone Family History Centre
76B London Road
Maidstone ME16 0DT
01622 757811

Manchester Family History Centre
Altrincham Road
Wythenshawe
Manchester M22 4BJ
0161 902 9279

Mansfield Family History Centre
Southridge Drive, Mansfield
Nottingham NG18 4RT
01623 662333

Merthyr Tydfil Family History Centre
Nantygwenith Street
George Town
Merthyr Tydfil CF48 1NR
01685 722455

Newcastle Emlyn Family History Centre
Cardigan Road, Newcastle Emlyn,
Carmarthenshire.
01239 711472

Newcastle-under-Lyme Family History Centre
PO Box 457
The Brampton
Newcastle-Under-Lyme
Staffordshire ST5 0TV
01782 630178

Newport, Isle of Wight Family History Centre
Chestnut Close, Shide Road
Newport
Isle of Wight
01983 532833

Northampton Family History Centre
137 Harlestone Road
Northampton NN5 6AA
01604 587630

Norwich Family History Centre
19 Greenways
Eaton
Norwich NR4 6PA
01603 452440

Nottingham Family History Centre
Stanhome Square
West Bridgford
Nottingham NG2 7GF
0115 923 3856

Orpington Family History Centre
Station Approach
Orpington
Kent BR6 0ST
01689 837342

Paisley Family History Centre
Glenburn Road
Paisley
Renfrewshire PA2 8PN
0141 884 2780

Peterborough Family History Centre
Cottesmore Close
Peterborough
Cambridgeshire PE3 9TP
01733 263374

Plymouth Family History Centre
Hartley Chapel
Mannamead Road
Plymouth, Devon PL3 4SR
01752 668666

Pontefract Family History Centre
Park Villas Drive
Pontefract
West Yorkshire WF8 4QF
01977 600308

Poole Family History Centre
8 Mount Road
Parkstone
Poole, Dorset BH14 0QW
01202 730646

Portsmouth Family History Centre
82 Kingston Crescent
Portsmouth
Hampshire PO2 8AQ
02392 696243

Preston Temple Family History Centre
Temple Way
Hartwood Green
Chorley, Lancashire PR6 7EQ
01257 226145

Reading Family History Centre
280 The Meadway
Tilehurst
Reading, Berkshire RG30 4PE
0118 9410211

Redditch Family History Centre
321 Evesham Road
Crabbs Cross, Redditch
Worcestershire B97 5JA
01527 401543

Rhyl Family History Centre
171 Vale Road, Denbighshire.
01745 331172

Romford Family History Centre
64 Butts Green Road
Hornchurch
Essex RM11 2JR
01708 620727

St Albans Family History Centre
Buckthorne Avenue
Stevenage
Hertfordshire SG1 1TX
01438 351553

St Austell Family History Centre
Kingfisher Drive
St Austell
Cornwall PL25 3AZ
01726 69912

St Helier Family History Centre
Rue de la Vallee
St Mary, Jersey JE3 3DL
01534 482171

Scarborough Family History Centre
Stepney Road
Scarborough
North Yorkshire YO12 5BN
01723 507239

Sheffield Family History Centre
Wheel Lane, Grenoside
Sheffield S35 8RL
0114 245 3124

Staines Family History Centre
41 Kingston Road
Staines
Middlesex TW18 4LH
01784 462627

Sunderland Family History Centre
Queen Alexander Road
Sunderland
Tyne and Wear SR2 9BT
0191 528 5787

Sutton Coldfield Family History Centre
187 Penns Lane
Sutton Coldfield
West Midlands B76 1JU
0121 386 4902

Swansea Family History Centre
Cockett Road
Swansea SA2 0FD
01792 585792

Telford Family History Centre
72 Glebe Street
Wellington, Telford
Shropshire TF1 1JY
01952 257443

Thetford Family History Centre
Station Road
Thetford
Norfolk IP24 1AH
01842 755472

Trowbridge Family History Centre
Brook Road
Trowbridge
Wiltshire BA14 9DL
01225 777097

Watford Family History Centre
Hempstead Road
Watford
Hertfordshire WD17 3HF
01923 251471

Wednesfield Family History Centre
63 Linthouse Lane
Wednesfield, Wolverhampton
West Midlands WV11 3EF
01902 724097

Weymouth Family History Centre
396 Chickerell Road
Weymouth
Dorset DT4 9TP
01305 787240

Worcester Family History Centre
Canada Way, Lower Wick
Worcester
Worcestershire WR2 4ED
01905 420341

Worthing Family History Centre
Goring Street
Goring-by-Sea, Worthing
West Sussex BN12 5AR
01903 241982

Yate Family History Centre
Wellington Road
Yate, Bristol, Avon BS37 5UY
01454 323004

Yeovil Family History Centre
Lysander Road
Forest Hill, Yeovil
Somerset BA20 2PE
01935 426817

York Family History Centre
Acomb Road
York
North Yorkshire YO24 4HA
01904 786784

Family Search
familysearch.org
Worldwide genealogical records collected by The Church of Jesus Christ of Latter-day Saints (LDS). Website lists Family History Centres based in the UK.

Federation of Family History Societies (FFHS)
ffhs.org.uk
An umbrella body for more than 200 family history societies around the UK, whose addresses are on the website.
PO Box 8857
Lutterworth LE17 9BJ
01455 203133
info@ffhs.org.uk

Find My Past
findmypast.com
Access to indexes held in the GRO and many overseas records.

First Fleet
firstfleet.uow.edu.au
A searchable database of 780 First Fleet convicts sent to Australia in 1787.

Flickr
flickr.com
Photo storage and uploading software.

Flintshire Record Office
flintshire.gov.uk/archives
The Old Rectory
Rectory Lane
Hawarden
Flintshire CH5 3NR
01244 532364
Use contact form on website for email

Francis Frith
francisfrith.com
Old photos, maps and memories of UK and Ireland.

Free BMD
freebmd.org.uk
Online registers for civil registration.

Free CEN
freecen.org.uk
Census returns online.

Free REG
freereg.org.uk
Parish registers online.

Free Serif Software
freeserifsoftware.com
Software downloads for your PC.

Friends Reunited
friendsreunited.co.uk
Website for re-uniting old friends.

Gazettes online
gazettes-online.co.uk
Online editions of the London, Belfast and Edinburgh Gazettes, official newspapers.

GenCircles
gencircles.com
For sharing online family trees.

General Register Office for England and Wales (GRO)
directgov.uk
For ordering civil registration certificates online.
PO Box 2, Southport
Merseyside PR8 2JD
0845 603 7788
certificate.services@ips.gsi.gov.uk

General Register Office for Northern Ireland (GRONI)
nidirect.gov.uk/gro
For ordering civil registration certificates online.
Oxford House
49-55 Chichester Street
Belfast BT1 4HL
0289 151 3101

General Register Office for Republic of Ireland (GROI)
groireland.ie
For ordering civil registration certificates online.
Government Offices
Convent Road
Roscommon
00 353 90 6632900

General Register Office for Scotland (GROS)
gro-scotland.gov.uk
For ordering civil registration certificates online.
New Register House
3 West Register Street
Edinburgh EH1 3YT
0131 314 4411
Use contact form on website for email.

Genes Reunited
genesreunited.co.uk
Website with access to online records for finding possible relatives.

Genuki
genuki.org.uk
UK and Ireland genealogical information.

Glamorgan Archives
glamro.gov.uk
Clos Parc Morgannwg
Leckwith
Cardiff CF11 8AW
029 2087 2200
glamro@cardiff.gov.uk

Glasgow City Archives
glasgow.gov.uk
Enter 'Archives' in Search box.
The Mitchell Library, North Street
Glasgow G3 7DN
0141 287 2910
archives@glasgowlife.org.uk

Glasgow Museums
glasgowmuseums.com/photolibrary
Glasgow Museums' online photo library.

**Gloucestershire Archives
and Record Office**
gloucestershire.gov.uk/archives
Clarence Row, Alvin Street
Gloucester GL1 3DW
01452 425295
archives@gloucestershire.gov.uk

Google
google.co.uk
Search engine.

Google Earth
earth.google.com
*Aerial, satellite images and information
from all over the world.*

Google Maps
maps.google.co.uk
Modern street directory.

**Greater Manchester County
Record Office**
**www.manchester.gov.uk/info/448/
archives_and_local_studies**
56 Marshall Street
New Cross
Manchester M4 5FU
0161 832 5284
archiveslocalstudies@manchester.gov.uk

Guernsey Archives Service
user.itl.net/~glen/archgsy.html
29 Victoria Road
St Peter Port GY1 1HU
Channel Islands
01481 724512

Guild of One-Name Studies
one-name.org
Organisation for surname studies.

Guildhall Library
cityoflondon.gov.uk/guildhalllibrary
*Records ranging from ancient
guildsmen to fire insurance.*
Aldermanbury
Manuscripts Section
London EC2P 7HH
020 7332 1868/1870
guildhall.library@cityoflondon.gov.uk

Gwent Archives
gwentarchives.gov.uk
Steelworks Road
Ebbw Vale
Bidenau, Gwent NP23 6DN
01495 353363
enquiries@gwentarchives.gov.uk

Gwynedd Archives Service
gwynedd.gov.uk/archives
Caernarfon Record Office
Swyddfa'r Cyngor
Caernarfon LL55 1SH
01286 679095
archives@caernarfon@.gwynedd.gov.uk

Hampshire Record Office
hants.gov.uk/record-office
Sussex Street
Winchester
Hampshire SO23 8TH
01962 846154
Use contact form on website for email.

Herefordshire Record Office
herefordshire.gov.uk/archives
Herefordshire Archive Service
Harold Street
Hereford HR1 2QX
01432 260750
archives@herefordshire.gov.uk

**Hertfordshire Archives and
Local Studies Centre**
hertsdirect.org/heritage
Register Office Block
County Hall, Pegs Lane
Hertford SG13 8EJ
0300 123 4049
hertsdirect@hertscc.gov.uk

Historical Directories
historicaldirectories.org
*Digital library of local and trade directories
from 1750 to 1919.*

Home Office
homeoffice.gov.uk
Records of naturalisation since June 1969.

Homestead
homestead.com
*Online resource for creating your
own website.*

House Detectives
house-detectives.co.uk
*Specialist research service for tracing
the history of your house.*

**Huguenot Society of Great
Britain and Ireland**
huguenotsociety.org.uk
The Huguenot Library
University College, Gower Street
London WC1E 6BT
020 7679 2046
library@huguenotsociety.org.uk

**Huntingdonshire Archive and
Local Studies**
cambridgeshire.gov.uk/archives
Princes Street
Huntingdon PE29 3PA
01480 372738
Use contact form on website for email

Ideal Homes
ideal-homes.org.uk
History of south-east London.

Imperial War Museum (IWM)
iwm.org.uk
Official website for the IWM.
IWM London, Lambeth Road
London SE1 6HZ
020 7416 5000
mail@iwm.org.uk

IWM Duxford, IWM North, HMS
Belfast and The Cabinet War Rooms
See IWM website for details.

India Office Records
See British Library India Office.

Institute of Commonwealth Studies (ICS)
commonwealth.sas.ac.uk
Website of the ICS, dedicated to the study of the Commonwealth.
2nd Floor
South Block
Senate House
Malet Street
London WC1E 7HU
020 7862 8844
ics@sas.ac.uk

Institute of Heraldic and Genealogical Studies (IHGS)
ihgs.ac.uk
79-82 Northgate
Canterbury
Kent CT1 1BA
01227 768664
Use contact form on website for email.

International Ceramic Directory
ceramic-link.de/Seiten/ICD-Historical2.htm
Website for dating old pottery and ceramics.

International Committee of the Red Cross (ICRC)
icrc.org
International organisation dedicated to helping victims of war and disaster.
19 Avenue de la Paix
CH 1202 Geneva
Switzerland
00 41 (22) 734 60 01

Irish Manuscripts Commission
irishmanuscripts.ie
Promotes public awareness of primary source materials and their importance for Irish history, heritage and culture.
45 Merrion Square
Dublin 2
Republic of Ireland
00 353 1 6761610
support@irishmanuscripts.ie

Irish Origins
irishorigins.com
Irish documents online.

Isle of Man Public Record Office
gov.im/registries/publicrecords
Unit 40a, Spring Valley Industrial Estate
Douglas IM2 2QS
Isle of Man
01624 693569
public.records@gov.im

Isle of Wight Record Office
iwight.com/library/record_office
26 Hillside, Newport
Isle of Wight PO30 2EB
01983 823820/1
record.office@iow.gov.uk

Jersey Archives
jerseyheritage.org
Clarence Road
St Helier JE2 4JY
Jersey
01534 833333
archives@jerseyheritage.org

Jewish Genealogical Society of Great Britain (JGSGB)
jgsgb.org.uk
Official website of the Jewish Genealogical Society. Research enquiries are dealt with by email, not by phone.
33 Seymour Place, London W1H 5AU
020 7724 4232 *(answering machine)*
genealogy@jgsgb.org.uk

Jewish Genealogy
jewishgen.org
Website dedicated to Jewish ancestry.

Kent Archaeological Society
kentarchaeology.org.uk
For gravestones and monuments in and around Kent.

Kent Archives Service
See Centre for Kentish Studies.

Lambeth Palace Library
lambethpalace.org
Principal library and record office for the history of the Church of England. Also a significant resource for local and family history.
Lambeth Palace Road, Lambeth
London SE1 7JU
020 7898 1200
contact@lambethpalace.org.uk

Lancashire Record Office
archives.lancashire.gov.uk
Bow Lane
Preston
Lancashire PR1 2RE
01772 533039
Use contact form on the website for email

Last Names
last-names.net
Site for locating surname origins.

Leicestershire, Leicester and Rutland Record Office
leics.gov.uk/recordoffice
Long Street, Wigston Magna
Leicester LE18 2AH
0116 257 1080
recordoffice@leics.gov.uk

Libraries and Archives of Canada (LAC)
collectionscanada.ca
395 Wellington Street, Ottawa,
Ontario KIA 0N4, Canada
Use contact form on website for email.

Lichfield Record Office
staffordshire.gov.uk/leisure/archives
The Friary
Lichfield WS13 6QG
01543 510720
lichfield.record.office@
staffordshire.gov.uk

Liverpool Record Office and Local History Service
liverpool.gov.uk/libraries-and-archives/archives-local-and-family-history
Unit 33, Wellington Employment Park
Dunes Way
Liverpool L5 9RJ
0151 233 5817
Use contact form on the website for email

London Library
londonlibrary.co.uk
The world's largest independent library.
14 St James's Square
London SW1 4LG
020 7930 7705
reception@londonlibrary.co.uk

London Metropolitan Archives (LMA)
cityoflondon.gov.uk
Select Archives and then Records and archives from A-Z.
40 Northampton Road
Clerkenwell
London EC1R 0HB
020 7332 3820
ask.lma@cityoflondon.gov.uk

Look Up
lookup.com
Website for tracing missing people.

LumaPix
lumapix.com
Photo storage and upload site.

Manchester City Archives
Manchester Room@City Library
City Library, Elliot House
151 Deansgate
Manchester M3 2HN
0161 234 1979
archiveslocalstudies@manchester.gov.uk

Manchester City Council Local Image Collection
images.manchester.gov.uk
Images of Manchester, its suburbs and surroundings through the ages.

Manchester County Record Office (Greater)
See Greater Manchester County Record Office.

Manchester University Library (John Rylands University Library)
library.manchester.ac.uk
The University of Manchester
Oxford Road
Manchester M13 9PP
0161 275 3751

Manx National Heritage
gov.im/mnh/heritage/library/nationallibrary.xml
Promotes history and culture of the Isle of Man.
Manx Museum
Douglas IM1 3LY
Isle of Man
01624 648040
library@mnh.gov.im

MapCo
archivemaps.com/mapco
Scanned copies of antique and historical maps.

Mary Evans Picture Library
maryevans.com
Photos, paintings and prints collections online.

McAfee Store
mcafeestore.com
US-based store for firewall and virus protection for your PC.

Memories Nostalgia
memories-nostalgia.com
Site for purchasing archival storage boxes.

Microsoft
microsoft.com
Main Microsoft website – for updates, software and information.

Military Geneology Records
forces-war-records.co.uk
Website with military records of more than two million British Armed Forces personnel.

Ministry of Defence (MOD)
mod.uk
Website for obtaining service records of Army and Navy personnel whose regular or reserve service ended between 1921 and 1997.
Service Personnel and Veterans Agency
Norcross
Blackpool FY5 3WP
0800 169 2277
veterans.help@spva.gsi.gov.uk

Modern Records Centre
modernrecords.warwick.ac.uk
University Library
University of Warwick
Coventry CV4 7AL
024 7652 4219
archives@warwick.ac.uk

MotCo
motco.com
Database of historical maps and plans of London.

Moving Here
movinghere.org.uk
Sources for tracing families who migrated to England over the last 200 years.

Museum of Childhood
vam.ac.uk/moc
The national childhood collection is held here as part of the Victoria and Albert family of museums.
Cambridge Heath Road
London E2 9PA
020 8983 5200
moc@vam.ac.uk

Museum of English Rural Life, Reading University
merl.org.uk
Dedicated to recording the history of rural life in England.
The University of Reading
22 Redlands Road
Reading RG1 5EX
0118 378 8660
merl@reading.ac.uk

Museum of London
museumoflondon.org.uk
150 London Wall
London EC2Y 5HN
020 7001 9844
info@museumoflondon.org.uk

MyBlog
myblog.com
Blog hosting site.

MyDomain
mydomain.com
Website for purchasing and registering domain names.

MySpace
myspace.com
Social networking site.

Name Seekers
nameseekers.co.uk
Site for locating first name and surname origins, and coats of arms.

National Archives of Australia
naa.gov.au
Official website for the National Archives of Australia. Check the website for local contact details.
0061 2 6212 3600
archives@naa.gov.au

National Archives of England and Wales
See The National Archives.

National Archives of New Zealand
archives.govt.nz
10 Mulgrave Street, Thorndon
Wellington. New Zealand
Correspondence address:
PO Box 12-050
Wellington, New Zealand
reference@archives.govt.nz

National Archives of Scotland (NAS)
nas.gov.uk
H.M. General Register House
2 Princes Street
Edinburgh EH1 3YY
0131 535 1314
enquiries@nas.gov.uk

National Archives of South Africa
national.archives.gov.za
Private Bag X236
Pretoria 0001, South Africa
00 27 12 441 3200
archives@dac.gov.za

National Army Museum
nam.ac.uk
Museum dedicated to the British Army, its regiments and history. Online collection of records and images.
Royal Hospital Road
Chelsea, London SW3 4HT
020 7730 0717
info@nam.ac.uk

National Coal Mining Museum for England
ncm.org.uk
History of mining.
Caphouse Colliery, New Road
Overton, Wakefield WF4 4RH
01924 848806
info@ncm.org.uk

National Federation of Women's Institutes
thewi.org.uk
104 New Kings Road
London SW6 4LY
020 7371 9300
Use contact form on website for email.

National Federation of Women's Institutes Wales
thewi.org.uk
19 Cathedral Road
Cardiff
CF11 9HA
029 2022 1712
(*To contact via email, use the website to find address for specific federation.*)

National Library of Ireland
nli.ie
Comprehensive collection of information about Ireland.
Kildare Street
Dublin 2
Republic of Ireland
00 353 1 603 0213
info@nli.ie

National Library of Scotland
nls.uk
Main library:
George IV Bridge
Edinburgh EH1 1EW
0131 623 3700
Use contact form on website for email.

National Library of Wales (NLW)
llgc.org.uk
Aberystwyth
Ceredigion SY23 3BU
01970 632 800
Use contact form on website for email.

National Maritime Museum
nmm.ac.uk
British maritime history and related topics.
Romney Road
Greenwich
London SE10 9NF
020 8858 4422

National Memorial Arboretum
thenma.org.uk
National memorial archive.
Croxall Road
Alrewas
Staffordshire DE13 7AR
01283 792333
info@thenma.org.uk

National Monuments Record
english-heritage.org.uk/
professional/archives-and-
collections/nmr
Public archive of English Heritage, with archaeological information including photos, plans and reports.
Churchward
Swindon SN2 2GZ
01793 414600
nmrinfo@english-heritage.org.uk

National Screen and Sound Archive of Wales
archif.com
National Library of Wales
Aberystwyth
Ceredigion SY23 3BU
01970 632828
Use contact form on website for email.

NORCAP
norcap.org.uk
*Help for adopted adults on issues
of search and reunion.*
112 Church Road
Wheatley
Oxfordshire OX33 1LU
01865 875000
enquiries@norcap.org

Norfolk Record Office
archives.norfolk.gov.uk
The Archive Centre
Martineau Lane
Norwich NR1 2DQ
01603 222599
norfrec@norfolk.gov.uk

**North Yorkshire County
Record Office**
northyorks.gov.uk/archives
Malpas Road
Northallerton DL7 8TB
01609 777585
archives@northyorks.gov.uk

Northamptonshire Record Office
northamptonshire.gov.uk
Enter 'Record office' in the Search *box.*
Records Office
Wootton Hall Park
Northampton NN4 8BQ
01604 762129
archivist@northamptonshire.gov.uk

**Northumberland Archives
Service**
experiencewoodhorn.com
Woodhorn
Queen Elizabeth II Country Park
Ashington
Northumberland NE63 9YF
01670 528080
collections@woodhorn.org.uk

Nottinghamshire Archives
nottinghamshire.gov.uk/archives
County House
Castle Meadow Road
Nottingham NG2 1AG
0115 958 1634
archives@nottscc.gov.uk

Old Maps
old-maps.co.uk
Online archive of historic maps.

One Great Family
onegreatfamily.com
Online family tree building.

Ordnance Survey
ordnancesurvey.co.uk
*Great Britain's national mapping agency.
Maps to view online.*

Origins
origins.net
Online records for Britain and Ireland.

Orkney Library and Archives
orkneylibrary.org.uk
44 Junction Road
Kirkwall
Orkney KW15 1AG
01856 873166
archives@orkneylibrary.org.uk

Oxfordshire History Centre
oxfordshire.gov.uk/records
St Luke's Church
Temple Road
Cowley
Oxford OX4 2HT
01865 398200
oxhist@oxfordshire.gov.uk

Parish Register
parishregister.com
Parish registers and local information.

Parliamentary Archives
parliament.uk
*Archives and records relating to
Parliament, dating from 1497.
Enter 'Archives' in search box.*
Houses of Parliament,
London SW1A 0PW
020 7219 3074
archives@parliament.uk

PC Pro
pcpro.co.uk
*Online newspaper about computers,
software and technology.*

People's History Museum
phm.org.uk
*Celebrates the working lives
of ordinary people.*
Left Bank
Spinning Fields
Manchester M3 3ER
0161 838 9190
archive@phm.org.uk

Photobucket
photobucket.com
Photo sharing site.

PhotoLondon
photolondon.org.uk
*Information about London's historic
photographic collections, history of
photography and other source materials.*

PhotoSharing
photosharing.org.uk
Photo-sharing site.

Picasa
picasa.google.com
Photo-sharing site.

Poppy Travel
poppytravel.org.uk
*Website for arranging visits to war graves
and battle sites.*
The Royal British Legion Village
Aylesford
Kent ME20 7NX
01622 716729
info@poppytravel.org.uk

PortCities
portcities.org.uk
Maritime history of UK port cities.

Powys County Archives
powys.gov.uk
From homepage select Leisure &
Culture, *then* Archives Office.
County Hall, Llandrindod Wells
Powys LD1 5LG
01597 826088
Use contact form on website for email.

**Principal Registry of the Family
Division**
justice.gov.uk
Enter PRFD in search box.
Wills from 1858 to the present day.
First Avenue House
42-49 High Holborn
London WC1V 6NP
PRFD.Familygeneralenquiries
@hmcts.gsi.gov.uk

Public Profiler
publicprofiler.org
Useful for geographical surname locating.

**Public Record Office of
Northern Ireland (PRONI)**
proni.gov.uk
2 Titanic Boulevard
Belfast BT3 9HQ
028 9053 4800
proni@dcalni.gov.uk

Ramsdale
ramsdale.org/surname.htm
Origins of English surnames.

Red Cross
See British Red Cross *or* International
Committee of the Red Cross.

**Religious Society of Friends
Library**
quaker.org.uk/library
*A major collection of material relating to
Quakers, started in 1673.*
Friends House
173-177 Euston Road
London NW1 2BJ
020 7663 1000
enquiries@quaker.or.uk.

**Romany and Traveller Family
History Society**
rtfhs.org.uk
*Website for finding out more
about gypsy and traveller life.*

RootsWeb
rootsweb.ancestry.com
Sharing genealogical information online.

Royal Air Force Museum
rafmuseum.org.uk
Click on Research *and choose* Archive
collections *from the list.*
*Range of archive collections, including
personal papers and logbooks.*
Department of Research and
Information Services
RAF Museum, London
Grahame Park Way, London NW9 5LL
020 8358 4873
Use contact form on website for email.

Royal British Legion Village
rblvillage.legionbranches.net
*Community that houses disabled veterans
and various Royal British Legion industries.*
Aylesford,
Kent ME20 7NZ
01732 870102 *(answerphone)*
Email address changes according to
current secretary. Check site.

Royal College of Physicians
rcplondon.ac.uk/resources/library/
for-historians-and-researchers
*College archives going back to
the 16th century.*
Heritage Centre
The Royal College of Physicians
11 St Andrews Place
Regent's Park
London NW1 4LE
020 7935 1174
Use contact form on website for email.

**Royal Commission on the
Ancient and Historical
Monuments of Scotland**
rcahms.gov.uk
*Independent body responsible for
recording, interpreting and promoting
Scotland's historic buildings.*
John Sinclair House,
16 Bernard Terrace
Edinburgh EH8 9NX
0131 662 1456
Use contact form on website for email.

Royal Irish Academy Library
ria.ie/Library
Resources for genealogical research.
Academy House
19 Dawson Street,
Dublin 2
Republic of Ireland
00 353 1 676 2570
Use contact form on website for email.

Royal Marines Museum
royalmarinesmuseum.co.uk
*The library collection includes Navy
and Marine Officer lists.*
Eastney Esplanade
Southsea
Hampshire PO4 9PX
023 9281 9385
info@royalmarinesmuseum.co.uk

Royal Naval Museum Library
royalnavalmuseum.org
Naval history resources.
Information Service
Royal Naval Museum
HM Naval Base (PP66)
Portsmouth PO1 3NH
023 9272 3795
library@nmrn.org.uk

**Salvation Army's Family
Tracing Service**
salvationarmy.org.uk/familytracing
For tracing missing relatives.
101 Newington Causeway
London SE1 6BN
0845 634 4747

School of Oriental and African Studies (SOAS) Library
soas.ac.uk/library/archives
Information about missionary societies.
Thornaugh Street, Russell Square
London WC1H 0XG
020 7898 4180
docenquiry@soas.ac.uk

ScotlandsPeople
scotlandspeople.gov.uk
Civil registration and census returns for Scotland online.

Scottish Genealogy Society
scotsgenealogy.com
The Library and Family History Centre holds a wealth of material, including a family history index.
15 Victoria Terrace
Edinburgh EH1 2JL
0131 220 3677
enquiry@scotsgenealogy.com

Scottish Jewish Archives Centre
sjac.org.uk
History of Jewish communities living in Scotland since the 18th century.
129 Hill Street
Glasgow G3 6UB
0141 332 4911
info@sjac.org.uk

Searchline
search-line.co.uk
Website dedicated to reuniting lost friends and relatives, particularly adoptees.

Sheffield Archives
sheffield.gov.uk/archives
52 Shoreham Street
Sheffield S1 4SP
0114 203 9395
archives@sheffield.gov.uk

Shetland Archives
shetland.gov.uk/archives
Hay's Dock
Lerwick
Shetland ZE1 0WP
01595 695057
info@shetlandmuseumandarchives.org.uk

Shropshire Archives
shropshire.gov.uk/archives.nsf
Castle Gates
Shrewsbury SY1 2AQ
01743 255350
archives@shropshire.gov.uk

SilverMine
freespace.virgin.net/a.data
Website for dating silverware.

Snapfish
snapfish.co.uk
Photo-sharing site.

Society of Genealogists
sog.org.uk
Family history library and genealogy centre.
14 Charterhouse Buildings
Goswell Road
London EC1M 7BA
020 7251 8799

Somerset Heritage Centre
somerset.gov.uk/archives
Brunel Way
Langford Mead
Norton Fitzwarren
Taunton TA2 6SF
01823 278805
archives@somerset.gov.uk

Southampton Archives Service
southampton.gov.uk
Enter 'Archives' in search box.
Civic Centre
Civic Centre Road
Southampton SO14 7LY
023 8083 2251
city.archives@southampton.gov.uk

Spinning the Web
spinningtheweb.org.uk
History of the Lancashire cotton industry.

Staffordshire Record Office
staffordshire.gov.uk/leisure/archives
Eastgate Street
Stafford ST16 2LZ
01785 278379
staffordshire.record.office@staffordshire.gov.uk

Sticks Research Agency (SRA)
sra-uk.com
Specialist genealogical and historical research organisation.

Streetmap
streetmap.co.uk
Modern online street atlas.

Stoke on Trent City Archives
Staffordshire.gov.uk/leisure/archives
City Central Library
Bethesda Street, Hanley
Stoke on Trent ST1 3RS
01782 238420
stoke.archives@stoke.gov.uk

Suffolk Record Office
suffolk.gov.uk
Entre 'Suffolk Record Office' in search box. There are three branches:
77 Raingate Street
Bury St Edmunds IP33 2AR
01284 741212
bury.ro@suffolk.gov.uk

Gatacre Road
Ipswich IP1 2LQ
01473 584541
ipswich.ro@suffolk.gov.uk

Clapham Road
Lowestoft NR32 1DR
01502 405357
lowestoft.ro@suffolk.gov.uk

Surname db
surnamedb.com
Site for locating surname origins.

Surrey History Centre
surreycc.gov.uk/surreyhistoryservice
130 Goldsworth Road
Woking GU21 6ND
01483 518737
shs@surreycc.gov.uk

Symantec
symantec.com
Anti-virus software to protect your PC.

TalkingScot
talkingscot.com
Forum and discussion for Scottish genealogy.

The Clergy of the Church of England database
theclergydatabase.org.uk
Records of all clergy careers.

The Genealogist
thegenealogist.co.uk
Online records.

The National Archives
nationalarchives.gov.uk
The main repository for government records for England and Wales.
Kew, Richmond
Surrey TW9 4DU
020 8876 3444
Use contact form on website for email.

***The Scotsman* newspaper**
archive.scotsman.com
Online editions of The Scotsman newspaper from 1817 to 1950.

***The Times* online**
thetimes.co.uk/tto/news
The Times *newspaper online.*

TypePad
typepad.com
Blog site.

UK BMD
ukbmd.org.uk
List of websites showing transcriptions of civil registration documents.

UKReg
ukreg.com
Website for purchasing and registering domain names.

Ulster Historical Foundation
ancestryireland.com
Northern Irish genealogy site with access to historical trade directories.
49 Malone Road
Belfast BT9 6RY
028 9066 1988
enquiry@uhf.org.uk

United States of America National Archives
archives.gov/contact
Archives and Records Administration
8601 Adelphi Road
College Park
MD 20740-6001
USA

V&A Museum of Childhood
See Museum of Childhood.

Veterans History Project
loc.gov/vets
Library of Congress site for US war veterans.
Library of Congress
101 Independence Ave, SE
Washington DC 20540
USA

Veterans-UK
veterans-uk.info
Website for tracing war veterans and for putting lost comrades in touch.

Victoria and Albert Museum (V&A)
vam.ac.uk
Cromwell Road
South Kensington
London SW7 2RL
020 7942 2000
vanda@vam.ac.uk

Victoria County History
victoriacountyhistory.ac.uk
An encyclopaedic record of England's places and people.

Vision of Britain
visionofbritain.org.uk
A list of statistics, maps and information for local history.

Warwickshire County Record Office
warwickshire.gov.uk
Enter 'Record office' in the Search *box.*
Priory Park
Cape Road
Warwick CV34 4JS
01926 738959
recordoffice@warwickshire.gov.uk

Wellcome Library
library.wellcome.ac.uk
Books, manuscripts, archives, films and pictures on the history of medicine.
183 Euston Road
London NW1 2BE
020 7611 8722
library@wellcome.ac.uk

Wesley Historical Society Library
wesleyhistoricalsociety.org.uk
Large collection of Methodist information.

West Sussex Record Office
westsussex.gov.uk
Enter 'Record office' in the Search *box.*
3 Orchard Street, Chichester
West Sussex PO19 1RN
Correspondence address:
County Archivist
West Sussex Record Office
County Hall, Chichester
West Sussex PO19 1RN
01243 753602
records.office@westsussex.gov.uk

West Yorkshire Archive Service
archives.wyjs.org.uk
Offices are in Bradford, Calderdale, Kirklees, Leeds and Wakefield. The Wakefield office also holds the West Riding Registry of Deeds.
Registry of Deeds
Newstead Road
Wakefield WF1 2DE
01924 305980
wakefield@wyjs.org.uk

Wiltshire and Swindon History Centre
wshc.eu
Cocklebury Road
Chippenham
Wiltshire SN15 3QN
01249 705500
heritageadmin@wiltshire.gov.uk

Women's Library

londonmet.ac.uk/thewomenslibrary

Most extensive collection of women's history in the UK.
London Metropolitan University
25 Old Castle Street
London E1 7NT
020 7320 2222
moreinfo@thewomenslibrary.ac.uk

Worcestershire Record Office

worcestershire.gov.uk/records

County Hall
Spetchley Road
Worcester WR5 2NP
01905 766351
RecordOffice@worcestershire.gov.uk

Workhouses

workhouses.org.uk

Site dedicated to the history of workhouses.

Xara

xara.com/products/webstyle

Web graphics website.

Yell

yell.com

Directory of listed businesses.

York City Archives

york.gov.uk/leisure/libraries/archives

Records and documents covering 500 years of life in York.
York Explore Centre
Museum Street
York YO1 7DS
01904 552800
archives@york.gov.uk

Yorkshire Record Offices and Archives

See East Riding of Yorkshire Archives, North Yorkshire County Record Office *or* West Yorkshire Archive Service.

You Tube

youtube.com

Social networking site.

ZoneAlarm

zonealarm.com

Online store for PC security packages.

Index

Page numbers displayed in **bold** type indicate main entries.
Numbers in *italic* refer to illustrations and their captions.

1837online *see* findmypast.co.uk
1901censusonline.com 106, 107, *107*, **116-19**
1911 census 49
192.com 264, 293, 295
3D Family Tree 37

A

abbreviations **8**, 31, 126
Access to Archives *see* a2a.org.uk
addresses
   directories 231
   findmypast.co.uk 121
   1901censusonline.com 116-19
   tracing houses 234
Adobe Photoshop 310
adoption 37, **298-9**
Adoption Contact Register 299
adoptionsearchreunion.org.uk 298
advanced searching 40
aerial photographs 238
Africa, emigration to 261
African immigrants 252
agriculture 17, *125*, **190-1**, 240-1
airmen **199**
Albert, Prince *108*, 109
Alderney 221
Alexander III, Tsar 250
Alien Registration Cards 163
alphabets, handwritten 175
Am Baile 228, *228*
American War of Independence
254, 300
ancestorsonboard.com 260
ancestral home, tracing *45*
ancestry.co.uk 16, *16*, 48, 49, **50-51**, 59, 74, **90-91**
   Catholics 147
   census records 106, *106*, 111, **112-3**
   forums 283
   DNA testing service 51
   military pensions 196
   parish registers 133
   phone directories 292-3
   Poor Law records 211
   sharing family trees 264, 276-7, *276-7*
   wills 161
Angels costumiers 27
Anglican Church *see* Church of England
antivirus software 31, 41
apothecaries 183, 185
apprenticeships 53, 179, 184, **186-7**
Apprentices of Great Britain 186
Archbishop of Canterbury 142, 183
Archdeaconry Court of London Wills Index 160
archives 30, **162-75**
   a2a.org.uk 170-1
   directories 232
   Ireland **166**
   libraries **172-3**
   newspapers 216, 218-9
   Northern Ireland **166**
   online catalogues **168-9**
   reading old handwriting **174-5**
   Scotland **164-5**
   Wales **166-7**
   see also The National Archives
ARCHON directory 159, 171, 225, *225*
Army lists 53
Army Museums Ogilby Trust 193
Army Roll of Honour 53
Asia, emigration to 261
Asian immigrants 248, 252, 253
assizes 202-3
a2a.org.uk 170-1
   criminal records 202
   fire insurance records 215
   newspapers 216
   parish records 136, 137, *137*
audio records, plug-ins 40-41
Austen, Jane *155*, 298
Australia
   child migration 300, 301
   emigration to *254*, 255
   transportation to, 166, 179, **206-7**, 254
Australian Family History Compendium 255
Avast 41
AVG 41

BIRTH CERTIFICATES

birth certificates 21, 22-23, 28, 48, 73
   and adoption 299
   ancestry.co.uk 90-91
   bmdindex.co.uk 86-87
   content *75*
   findmypast.co.uk 52-53, 84-85
   freebmd.org.uk 82-83
   General Register Office indexes **78-79**

B

badges 26
Bank of England Wills Extract Index 160
banns, marriage 51, 142, 144
baptism *79*
   Nonconformists *148*
   parish registers 74, 134, 138, *141*, 144-5
Baptist Church 148, *148*, 149
bargemen *121*
Barnardo's 301
Bath Record Office 153
BBC 15, 300
Bebo 321, *321*
Belfast Gazette, The 219
Berners-Lee, Tim 35, *35*
Bibles 23
bing.com/maps 235, 238, *238*
birth briefs 70, *70*
birth certificates *see panel*
birth registers
   India 256
   Ireland 100-1
   missing data 102-3
   parish records 133, 134
   Scotland 96, 98, 99
illegitimacy 74
ordering **94-95**
planning websites 306
Scotland 56
tracing living relatives 292
ukbmd.org.uk 92-93
what's now online 49

births, newspaper announcements 216

bishops' transcripts 133

black immigrants **252-3**

Blair Castle *225*

blogger.com 317

blogs **316-17**

bmdindex.co.uk 74, **86-87**

Board of Trade 255

bookmarking websites 31

Boots *168-9*

Borthwick Institute 55, 160

boundaries, administrative regions 221

Bournemouth *244*

Boyd's London Burial Index 133, 143

Boyd's Marriage Index 133, 143, 173

Bristol 227

The British 19th Century Surname Atlas 58, 62

British Army 163, 178-9, **192-3**, **196-7**
  see also military records

British Association of Adoption 298

British Genealogy 283

British Isles, administrative regions 221

British Library 172
  Collect Britain website *218*, 219
  electoral rolls 295
  India Office Records 253, 256, 257
  maps 243, *243*
  Newspaper Library 216-7, 303

British Medical Association Library 183

British Telecom Directory Enquiries 295

browsers 40

Buchan, John *123*

bulletin boards 267

Bunyan, John *148*

burghs, Scottish 221

burials *see* graves

Business Archives Council 182

C

calendar, Julian and Gregorian 175

Callington Area Heritage 153

Canada
  censuses 106
  child migration 300, 301
  emigration to 255
  transportation to 254

Caribbean immigrants 248, *249*, 252, *252*

Catholic Church 100, **146-7**

Catholic Family History Society 147, 286

Catholic National Library 172

Catholic Record Society 147

cemeteries *see* graves

CEMSEARCH-uk 153

censuses *see panel*

ceramics 26

certificates *42*
  adoption certificates 298
  naturalisation 247
  see also birth certificates; death certificates; marriage certificates

Channel Islands 112, 221

Chaplin, Charlie 109, *109*, 259

Charles I, King 231

Charles II, King *146*, 148, 192

charts
  birth briefs 70, *70*
  drop-line 70, *70*
  pedigree 13, 68, 70, *70*

chat rooms 13

Chaucer 58

Cheshire, wills 159

Chester, wills 159

CENSUSES

censuses 28, 28, 42, 48, 49, **104-29**
  ancestry.co.uk 112-13
  confidentiality 105
  content 105, 106
  dates 105
  enumerators 108-9, *109*
  errors 126
  ethnic information 123
  familysearch.org 54
  findmypast.co.uk 52-53, **120-1**
  handwriting 122, 126
  history **108-9**

chests, parish registers *134*

Child Migrants Trust 301

children
  adoption **298-9**
  in censuses 106, 126
  evacuation 300, *300*
  foundlings 299
  illegitimacy 298
  migration 255, **300-1**
  in wars 195

Christie, Agatha *81*

Church Courts 155, 158, 303

churches
  Genuki Church Database 45
  memorial inscriptions **150-3**
  tithes 214-15
  see also parish registers

Church of England 146
  clerical records 179, 182-3
  marriage records 51

inaccuracies 103, 105

Ireland 107, 114, **124-5**

missing ancestors **126-7**

1901censusonline.com 116-19

online records **106-7**, 111

origins.net 114-15

parishes 135

Scotland 96, 107, 112, 115, **122-3**

tracing houses 234

tracing living relatives 291

tracking surnames 62

transportation records 206-7

using the census **110-11**

memorial inscriptions 152

parish registers 134-5

Church of Ireland 166

Church of Jesus Christ of Latter-day Saints (LDS, **familysearch.org**) 17, *17*, **54**
  census indexes 110
  Family History Centres 101, 136-7, **138-9**, 172
  Irish records 101
  Nonconformists 148
  online family trees 274-5, 278
  parish registers 48, 59, 133, 136-7, **138-9**

Church of Scotland 164

Churchill, Winston 190

City of London burials 143

civil registration 42, 48, **73-103**
  findmypast.co.uk 52-53
  General Register Office indexes **78-81**

information provided **74-77**
Ireland **100-1**
local indexes **92-93**
missing data **102-3**
national indexes **82-91**
ordering certificates **94-95**
Scotland **96-99**
see also birth certificates; death certificates; marriage certificates
civil service 181
ClamAV 41
clans, Scottish 228
clerical records 179, 182-3
clocks 27
clothing 24, 26
coalmining *170*, 188
Coastguard 163
coats of arms 12-13, *12*, *173*
Coldbath Fields Prison, London *208*
Collect Britain website *218*, 219
College of Arms 13
Colonial Office 250
commemorative objects 27
Commissary Court of Edinburgh 303
Commonwealth immigrants 248, 252
Commonwealth Institute, London 252
Commonwealth War Graves Commission (CWGC) 48, 200-1
company archives 168-9
computer viruses 41
Confederation of British Industry (CBI) 189
Congregationalists 148, 149
contacting other people *see* making contact
convicts *see* criminal records
cookies 40

copyright 29, 269, 306
Coram Family 299
Coram, Thomas 299
coraweb.com.au 255
coroners 81
counties 93, 221, 240
countryside
    farming **190-1**
    migration to towns 181
County Councils 221
County Record Offices 210, 215, 221
county records, Genuki 44-45
courts
    Church Courts 155, 158, 303
    Courts of Chancery 303
    criminal records 202
    Old Bailey **204-5**
cousins 8
craftsmen, guilds 184-5
crank machines, hard labour 208
credit cards 41
criminal records **202-9**
    Old Bailey **204-5**
    prisons **208-9**
    Scotland 164
    transportation 166, 179, **206-7**, 254, 255
    West Indians 249
Criminal Registers for England and Wales 203
Crockford's Clerical Directory 182
Cromwell, Oliver 192
Cromwell, Thomas 133, *133*
crown courts 202
curiousfox.com 224, *224*
Cyndi's List 15, **46-47**
    blogs 317

creating websites 309
Jewish resources 251
migrants 255
online communities 267
overseas ancestors 260, 264
publicising your website 310

D

databases
    family history software **36-39**
    merging 278
dates
    dating documents 175
    dating objects 27
    in parish registers 134
Davison, Emily *216*
death certificates *see panel*
death registers
    India 256
    Ireland 100-1
    missing data 102-3
    parish registers 133, 134, *137*
    Scotland 96, 97, 98
deaths
    death penalty 205, *205*

DEATH CERTIFICATES
death certificates 22-23, 48, 73
    ancestry.co.uk 90-91
    bmdindex.co.uk 86-87
    content *74*, *77*
    findmypast.co.uk 52-53, 84-85
    freebmd.org.uk 82-83
    General Register Office indexes 78, **81**

memorial inscriptions **150-3**
newspaper announcements 216
Debt of Honour Register **200-1**
delicious.com **43**
dentists 53, 183
diaries 23
Penguin Dictionary of British Surnames 65
A Dictionary of Surnames 58
Digital Handsworth Project 226, *226*
Digital Library of Historical Directories 233
Digital Midlands project 226
digital scrapbooking 25
diigo.com **43**
Directgov 94-5
direct.gov.uk/gro 15
direct.gov.uk/en 78, 83
directories
    occupational records **182-3**
    of surnames 65
    tracing living relatives 292-3
    trade, postal and street 178, **230-3**
discussion groups 264, 265, **284-5**
Disney, Walt 259
Dispensary Districts, Ireland 100
district councils 221

inaccuracies 103
ordering **94-95**
planning websites 306-7
Scotland 56
suspicious deaths 81
ukbmd.org.uk 92-93
what's now online 49

divorce 84, **302-3**
DNA **128-9**
　online databases 129
　testing (Ancestry) 51, 129
dnaancestryproject.com 61
doctors 53, 182, 183
documents, transcribing *30*
dolls 27
domain names 305, *305*
Domesday Book **222-3**
drop-line charts 70, *70*
Dublin City Archives 187
Dublin City 1851 census 114
Dublin City Rotunda Ward 1901 census 114
Dublin, directories 230
Dublin Gazette, The 219
Dun & Bradstreet 293
Dunant, Henry 130

E

East India Company 256, 257
Edinburgh Gazette, The 219
Edward I, King 250
Edward III, King 214
electoral rolls 234, 293, **294-5**
Elizabeth I, Queen 133, 146
Ellis Island **258-9**
Elphin 1749 census 114-15
emails
　email exchange forums 266-7
　mailing lists 264, **280-1**, 282
emigration *see* migration
employment *see* occupational records
enclosure maps 240-1
enumerators, censuses 108-9, *109*

ephemera 23
Episcopalian church 144
estate records 17, *110*, 178
ethnic information, censuses 123
etiquette, mailing lists 281
Exchequer Court of York 160-1
executions 205, *205*

F

Facebook 264, 320, *320*
factories *180*, 181, 188
Fáilte Romhat 233
'false' relatives 8
Families in British India Society (FIBIS) 257
Family Historian 38, *38*, 278, 312-13, *312-13*, 315, *315*
family history **12-13**
　Bibles 23
　coats of arms 12-13
　collecting family memories **20-21**

FAMILY TREES
　developing **272-3**
　filtering facility 279
　format options **70-71**
　Gedcom files 276, **278-9**
　genesreunited.co.uk **270-3**
　'global tree' websites 277
　online family trees **269-74**
　privacy **276-7**, 279
　setting out **68-69**
　sharing **274-7**
　software **312-15**
　on your website 310-11

creating your own website **304-11**
'false' relatives 8
　photographs **24-25**
　relationships 8
　societies 13, 45, 110, **286-9**
　software **36-39**
　terminology **8-9**
　tracing living relatives **290-303**
Family History Centres 101, 136-7, **138-9**, 172
familyrelatives.com 74, **88-89**
familysearch.org *see* Church of Jesus Christ of Latter-day Saints
Family Tree Maker 39, *39*
family trees *see panel*
farming 17, *125*, **190-1**, 240-1
The Federation Ezine 289
Federation of Family History Societies (FFHS) 13, 110, 150, 286, **288-9**
Fifteenths and Tenths taxes 214, 215
Fildes, Sir Samuel Luke *72*
files
　backing-up 31
　Gedcom files 273, 275, 276, **278-9**
　merging databases 278
filtering facility, online family trees 279
findmypast.co.uk 16, *16*, 48, **52-53**
　apprentices 186
　census records 107, *107*, **120-1**
　emigration records 255
　memorial inscriptions 150-1
　national indexes 74, **84-85**
　occupational records 182, 183
　parish records 133
　ships' passenger lists 179
　wills 160
fire insurance 215
firewalls 31, 41

First Fleet, transportation 206
First World War 23, *24*, *52*
　Debt of Honour Register 200-1
　Imperial War Museum 194-5
　'land girls' 191, *191*
　military records 48, 49, 196-7
　National Archives 163
　Red Cross 130
Fleet Prison 149
Flickr 319
Foreign Office 250
fonts 311
forenames
　alternative names 83, 126
　shortened forms 102, 126
　variant spellings 102, 126
format
　family trees **70-71**
　planning websites 306-7
forums 264, 266-7, **282-3**
Foundling Hospital, London 299
Four Courts building, Dublin *101*
Fox, George 149
Francis Frith Collection 235, 245
fraud, online 41
freebmd.org.uk 74, **82-83**, 90, 93
Freedom of Information Act 202
French immigrants 253
Freud, Sigmund 259
Friends Reunited 264, 296, *296*
Frith, Francis 245
Fuller, John 251

G

Gaelic Village 228, *228*
gaols 208

Gazettes 219

gazettes-online.co.uk 200

gbnames.publicprofiler.org/ 62-3

Gedclean 279

Gedcom files 37, 273, 275, 276, **278-9**

gencircles.com 277, *277*

genealogy.com 277

Genealogy in the UK and Ireland
   see genuki.org.uk

Genealogy Resources on the Internet
   251

General Medical Council 183

General Register Office (GRO) 15, 42-3,
   74, 295

   Adopted Children Register 298-9

   ancestry.co.uk 90-91

   birth indexes **79**

   bmdindex.co.uk 86-87

   death indexes **81**

   errors 92

   findmypast.co.uk 52, **84-85**

   Ireland 100-1, 299

   marriage indexes **80**

   Nonconformist registers 148

   ordering certificates 78, **94-95**

   ukbmd.org.uk 93

   using the indexes **78-79**

General Register Office for Scotland
   (GROS) 42, 56-57, 164, 165

   adoption records 299

   divorce records 303

   scotlandspeople.gov.uk 144

   Statutory Registers 96-97

genesreunited.co.uk 17, *17*, 107,
   264, 266, **270-3**

genetic genealogy 128

Genfair 150-151, 289

genforum.genealogy.com 264, 283

GenoPro 37

genuki.org.uk 15, **44-45**

   family history societies 287

   Ireland 125

   local history 224, *224*

   mailing lists 281

   maps 242, *242*

   occupational records 181

   online communities 266

   parish registers 134, 136

   Poor Law records 211

   trade directories 233

German names, anglicisation 61

GIMP 310

Glasgow, directories 230

Glasgow Museums Photo Library 245

'global tree' websites 277

Google

   blogger 317

   finding parish registers 136

   Google Earth 239, *239*

   maps 239, *239*

   publicising your website 311

   using effectively 40

government employees 181

Grant, Cary *259*

graphics editors 310

graves

   inscriptions **150-3**

   parish registers 134, *137*, 143

   war cemeteries 48, 200, 201, *201*

Great Britain Historical Geographical
   Information System Project 225

Greater London 221

Great Famine, Ireland 114

Gregorian calendar 175

Griffith's Valuation 1847-64 114, **124-5**

Grocers' Company 183

Guernsey 221

Guildhall, London 183, **184-5**, 245

Guild of One-Name Studies 61

guilds 184

gypsy weddings *102*

H

hackers 41

Hampshire, wills 159

Ham's Yearbooks 182

Handsworth 226, *226*

handwriting 122, 126, **174-5**

hangings, public 205, *205*

hard labour **208-9**

Hartlepool 227

hearth tax 214

Hemingway, Ernest 130

Henry VIII, King 12, *37*, 133, 146, 210,
   214, *242*, 302

heraldry 12-13

Heritage Centres, Ireland 101

Heritage Lottery Fund 248

Hertfordshire Family History Society
   153

Hidden House History 234

Highland Council 228

historicaldirectories.org 178

*Historic Parishes of England and
   Wales* 135

HM Customs and Excise 179, 182

homeless people *103*

Home Office 247, 250

houses **234-5**

   ancestral home *45*

   fire insurance 215

   maps 236

   ownership 178

   renting 178

   taxes 214, 241

Howells, Cyndi 46, 309

HTML code 309

Huguenots *46-47*

'hundreds' 221

I

ideal-homes.org.uk 226-7

identity cards *20*

illegitimacy 37, 74, 298

Illustrated London News 105

immigration *see* migration

Imperial War Museum (IWM) 27,
   194-5, 289

India, emigration to 53, 255, **256-7**

India Office 256

Indian immigrants 252, 253

industrial trades and skills **188-9**

inherited objects **26-27**

Inland Revenue 186

INTERNET

   beginning your search **14-17**

   errors 29

   firewalls 41

   getting the best from the
      web **40-41**

   making the internet work for
      you **35**

   search engines **40**

   security precautions 41

   starting your search **42-43**

   terminology **9**

   what's now online 49

   see also websites

IRELAND
administrative regions 221
apprenticeships 187
archives **166**
Catholics 147
censuses 107, 114, **124-5**
civil registration **100-1**
directories 230, 233
divorces 303
emigration to *125*, 254
Great Famine 114

inscriptions, memorial **150-3**
Institute of Commonwealth Studies 252
Institute of Heraldic and Genealogical Studies (IHGS) 73, 147
insurance records 215
International Ceramic Directory 27
International Genealogical Index (IGI) 54, 133, 138, 139, 148, 173, 275
internet *see panel, left*
Internet Explorer 40
Internet Surname Database 61, 62
interviewing family members **20-21**
intestacy 155
Ireland *see panel*
Ireland-Australia Transportation database 166
irishorigins.com 114, **124-5**
Irish Poor Law Act (1838) 100
Irish Wills Index (1484-1858) 114
Iris Oifigiuil 219
iscrapbook.com 43
Island Ireland 228, *228*
Isle of Man 112, 221
ISPs, creating your own website 305

immigrants 114, *114*, *125*, 248, 253
local history 228, *228*
medical profession 183
origins.net 55
parish registers 142
Poor Law records 211, *211*
property records 114, 124-5
wills 114, 155, 161
see also Northern Ireland

J
James, Charles 141
Japan, emigration to 261
Jarrow March (1936) *178*
Jersey 221
jewellery 26
Jewish Genealogical Society of Great Britain 251
Jews
anglicised names 61
immigrants *246*, 248, **250-1**
Second World War 130
John Ryland's Library 189
judges' reports 209
Julian calendar 175

K
keepsakes **26-27**
Kelly's Post Office Directories 53, 230, 293
Kent Archaeological Society 153
King's Bench Prison 149

Kirk Sessions 210
Kitchener, Lord *196*
knights, symbols 12

L
Lambeth 226, *227*
Lambeth Palace Library 179
'land girls' 191, *191*
landowners 17, 215
Land Tax 215, 234, 295
last-names.net 61
Latin language 135, 146, 157, 202
Law List 182
layout, websites **306-7**
Legacy Family Tree 39, *39*, 278
legal profession 182
libraries 30, **172-3**
access to newspaper archives 218
directories 232
picture libraries 245

LONDON
administrative regions 221
Boyd's London Burial Index 133, 143
evacuation of children 300
foundling children 299
Guildhall 183, **184-5**, 245
Imperial War Museum **194-5**
local history websites 226-7
newspapers 216
Old Bailey **204-5**
photographs 245
tenements *116*
wills 160

Library and Archives Canada 301
Library of Congress 297
licences, marriage 142-3
Linton, Sir James Dromgole *142*
Liverpool 227
livery companies 185, 186
living relatives, tracing **290-303**
local authority websites 226
local history **44-45**, **224-45**
houses **234-5**
Ireland 228, *228*
maps **236-43**
photographs **244-5**
Scotland 228
trade, postal and street directories **230-3**
Wales 228-9, *229*
local indexes, civil registration **92-93**
local record offices
occupational records 182
Scotland 164
wills 158-9
London *see panel*
London Apprenticeship Abstracts 186
London Gazette, The 200, 219
London Metropolitan Archives (LMA) 245, 251, 253
London Muslim Centre *247*
London Underground 181, *181*
Lookupuk.com 265, *265*
Luttrell Psalter *60*

M
McAfee VirusScan 41
McColl, John *182*

McIver, Dr Norman *12*
Magna Carta 32-33
mailing lists 264, 266-7, **280-1**, 282
making contact **263-7**, **296-7**
  biological families 299
  blogs **316-17**
  discussion groups **284-5**
  family history societies **286-9**
  forums **282-3**
  Gedcom files **278-9**
  mailing lists 264, **280-1**, 282
  networking sites 264-5, **320-1**
  online family trees **269-74**
  photosharing websites **318-19**
  privacy **276-7**, 279
  tracing living relatives **290-303**
Manchester Local Image Collection 245
manorial court records 178

MARRIAGE CERTIFICATES
marriage certificates 22-23, 48, 73,
  73, 137
  ancestry.co.uk 90-91
  bmdindex.co.uk 86-87
  findmypast.co.uk 52-53, 84-85
  freebmd.org.uk 82-83
  General Register Office indexes
  78, **80**
  illegitimacy 74
  inaccuracies 103
  ordering **94-95**
  planning websites 307
  Scotland 56
  tracing living relatives 291, 292
  ukbmd.org.uk 92-93
  what's now online 49

Manx National Heritage Library 172
MAPCO 243, *243*
maps **236-43**
  tithe maps 215
  tracing houses *45*, 234, 235
marriage
  banns 51, 142, 144
  divorce **302-3**
  Jewish 250
  licence allegations 142-3
  newspaper announcements 216
  Quakers *149*
marriage certificates *see panel*
marriage registers
  India 256
  Ireland 100-1
  missing data 102-3
  parish registers 51, 133, 134,
  139, 142-3
  Scotland 96, 97, *97*, 98, 99
Mary I, Queen 146
Mary Evans Picture Library 245, *245*
matronymic names 60
May Fair Chapel 149
Mayhew, Henry *210*
medals 26, 194, 196, 197, 200, 219
Medical Card Index 48
medical profession 53, 182, 183
medieval taxes 214
memorial inscriptions **150-3**
memorymixer.com 43
Merchant Navy 163, 179
merging databases 278
message boards 13, 264, 265, 266-7,
  282-3
Methodists 148, 149, 261
Metropolitan Police 163, 179
Middleton, Norfolk *135*

midwives 183
migration 53, 179, **246-61**
  black immigrants **252-3**
  child migration **300-1**
  Ellis Island **258-9**
  emigration **254-5**
  Irish migrants 114, *114, 125*,
  248-9, 253
  Jewish immigrants *246*, 248, **250-1**
  missionaries 260, 261
  paupers 211
  to India **256-7**
  to towns 181
  transtlantic 114
military keepsakes 26
military records 23, 48, 49, 178-9,
  192-201
  censuses 126
  Debt of Honour Register **200-1**
  familyrelatives.com 88
  findmypast.co.uk 53, 84
  India 256
  mailing lists 281
  overseas records 103
  sailors and airmen **198-9**
  war veterans **297**
  what's now online 49
miniature portraits 29
mining *170*, 188
Ministry of Defence (MOD) 193, 197,
  199, 297
Mint 149
Mintlyn, Norfolk *135*
missing data **102-3**
missionaries 260, 261, *261*
Montagu, Lord *173*
Mormons *see* Church of Jesus Christ
  of Latter-day Saints

MOTCO 243, *243*
movinghere.org.uk 125, 147,
  248-9, 257
Mozilla Firefox 40
Municipal Boroughs 221
Museum of Childhood 27
Museum of English Rural Life 190, *190*
Museum of London 245
muster rolls, ships 199
MySpace 321

N

names
  domain names 305, *305*
  nicknames 21
  saints' names *65*
  variant spellings 31
  see also forenames; surnames
NameX 65
Napoleonic Wars 105, 108
National Archives of Australia 255, 301
National Archives of Ireland 124, 155,
  166, 221
National Archives of Scotland (NAS) 43,
  164, 187, 211, 299, 303
National Archives (TNA) see The
  National Archives
National Army Museum, London 192-3
National Coalmining Museum for
  England 188
National Farm Survey 190
national indexes, civil registration **82-91**
National Inventory of War Memorials
  289
National Library of Ireland 55, 172
National Library of Scotland (NLS) 165,
  172, 217

National Library of Wales (NLW) 43, 166-7, 172, 203, 217

National Maritime Museum 27

National Register of Address searches 181

National Register of Archives (NRA) 137, *168-9*, 169

National Roll of the Great War 53

National Screen and Sound Archive of Wales 167

National Service 23

naturalisation certificates 247

navy 163, 178-9, **198-9**

Nazis 250

networking sites **320-1**

New Register House, Edinburgh 96

newsgroups 266-7, 281

newsletters **316-17**

New South Wales 255

New South Wales Convict Indents and Ships 207

newspapers **216-19**, 303

New York 258-9

New Zealand 255, 300

Nicholas II, Tsar 250

nicknames 21

Nightingale, Florence 109, *109, 130*

nobility, coats of arms 12-13

Nonconformists 73, **148-9**

non-paternity events 128

Nonsuch Park 242

Normans 60, **222-3**

Northern Ireland 43, 100, 125
   administrative regions 221
   adoption register 299
   archives **166**
   census records 124
   wills 155

Norton 41

numbers, handwritten 174

Nvu 308-9, *308-9, 310-11*

O

obituaries 216

O'Brien (William Smith) Petition 1848-9 114

occupational records 53, **181-201**
   apprenticeships 179, **186-7**
   census information 111, *111*
   directories **182-3**
   farming **190-1**
   findmypast.co.uk 53
   industrial trades and skills **188-9**
   job titles 181
   mailing lists 280-1
   military records **192-201**
   online directories 293
   surnames 60-61
   tracing ancestors 178-9

Old Bailey, London **204-5**

old-maps.co.uk 134, 235, 240-1, *240-1*

Old Parish Registers (Scotland) 48, 56, *56*, 144, 164

Olney, Buckinghamshire *220*

onegreatfamily.com 61

one-name.org 61, 129

one-name studies 129

online communities **266-7**

online family trees *see* family trees

Online Public Access Catalogue (OPAC) 164, 165

OpenOffice.org 308

oral history websites 226

Ordnance Survey *236, 237, 237,* 241

original records *see* archives

origins.net **55**, **114-15**
   apprenticeships 186
   census records 107, *107*
   parish registers 133, **142-3**
   wills 160

orphans 299, 300

overseas registrations 84, 88

P

Pallot's Marriage index 133

parishes
   enclosure maps 240-1
   Poor Law 210

parish registers 48, 73, **132-9**
   ancestry.co.uk **140-141**
   bishops' transcripts 133
   burials 143
   Catholic Church **146-7**
   dating 134
   familyrelatives.com 88
   familysearch.org 54, 136-7, **138-9**
   Genuki 45
   indexes **138-43**
   legibility 135
   marriages 51, 142-3
   Nonconformists **148-9**
   Old Parish Registers (Scotland) 48, 56
   origins.net **142-3**
   parishregister.com 133
   Scotland 96, 142, **144-5**
   tracking down **136-7**

passenger lists, ships' 48, *49,* 53, *85,* 179, 255, 260

patronymic names 60

Peculiar courts, wills 160

pedigree charts 13, 68, 70, *70*

Penguin Dictionary of British Surnames 65

Penny Illustrated Paper 219

pensions, military 196

People's History Museum 188, 189

Pepys, Samuel *316*

period pieces **26-27**

Peterborough Abbey 223, *223*

Phillimore Atlas and Index of Parish Registers, The 135

phone directories 292-3

photobucket.com 319

photographs *19, 22,* **24-25, 244-5**
   aerial photographs 238
   ancestral home *45*
   on blogs 316
   dating 24, 25
   digital scrapbooking 25
   on family trees *70-71,* 314-5, *314*
   inherited 26
   local history websites 226
   photosharing websites **318-19**
   storing 25
   on your website 306-7, 310

PhotoLondon 245

Picasa 318-19, *318-19*

picture libraries 245

Pigot & Co. 230, 233, 293

place names 60, 169

plug-ins 40-41

Police Burghs 221

Poll Books 295

poll taxes 214

Poor Law 73, 100, **210-13**, 300

PortCities 227, *227*

portraits, miniature *29*

ports, local history websites 227

Post Office 230, 231, *231*, 293

postal directories **230-3**

postalheritage.org.uk 231

Prerogative Court of Canterbury 158, 160

Prerogative Court of York 160

Presbyterians 144, 148, 149, 166

Principal Registry, London 155, 158, 303

prisoners of war 163, 194

prisoner registers 209

prisons **208-9**

privacy, online 269, **276-7**, 279

Privy Council 303

probate, wills 133, 155, 156-7, 158, 160-1

property
    divorce and 303
    Irish records 114, 124-5
    taxes 241
    see also houses

public photo albums 245

publicprofiler 62-3

Public Record Office *see* The National Archives

Public Record Office, Dublin 114, 124, 211

Public Record Office of Northern Ireland (PRONI) 43, 124, 125, 155, 166-7, 221

publicity, personal websites 310-1

Q

QinetiQ 116

Quakers (Society of Friends) 148, 149, *149*

quarter sessions 202, 211

Queensland 255

R

railways 163, 179, 181

ramsdale.org 61

rate books 234

records
    beginning your search 19
    interviews 20
    keeping records *19*, **30-31**, 43

Red Cross **130-1**

refugees, Jewish 250, *250*

regiments 192, 193

registers *see* parish registers

Registrar General 73

relatives *see* family history

religion
    Catholic Church **146-7**
    on censuses 109
    missionaries 260, 261, *261*
    Nonconformism **148-9**
    see also Church of England

reviews, software 38

Rhodesia, child migration 300

rmhh.co.uk 181

Romany weddings *102*

RootsChat 282

Roots Magic 39, *39*

RootsWeb 16, *16*
    Jewish records 251
    mailing lists 280-1
    online family trees 275
    Poor Law records 211
    Quaker records 149

Rosslyn, 1st Earl of *202*

Royal Air Force 163, **199**

Royal British Legion 201, 297, *297*

Royal Burghs 221

Royal College of Physicians of London 183

Royal College of Surgeons 183

Royal Commission on Historical Manuscripts 169

Royal Fusiliers *192*

Royal Navy 163, 178-9, **198-9**

Rural Districts 221

Russia, Jewish migration 250

S

sailors **198-9**

St Martin-in-the-Fields, London *136*

saints *65*, 185

Salvation Army Family Tracing 265, *265*

Sark 221

Saxton, Christopher 240

School of Oriental and African Studies (SOAS) 261

schools 23, *57*

Scotland *see panel*

scotlandspeople.gov.uk 48, 96, 74, **98-99**
    censuses 107, *107*, **122-3**
    name searches 64, *64*
    parish registers **144-5**
    wills 161

Scotsman, The 218-19, *218*

Scottish Archive Network (SCAN) 165

Scottish Association of Family History Societies *289*

Scott, Sir Walter *173*

scrapbooking, digital 25

seamen **198-9**

search engines **40**, 311

search-line.co.uk 298

Second World War 23

SCOTLAND

administrative regions 221

adoption register 299

apprenticeships 187

censuses 96, 107, 112, 115, **122-3**

civil registration 48, **96-99**

consulting original documents **164-5**

directories 230

divorces 303

forums 283

local history 224, 225, 228

newspapers 217

occupational records 181

origins.net 55

parish registers 96, 142, **144-5**

Poor Law records 210-11

reading old handwriting 175

scotlandspeople.gov.uk 56-57

wills 56, 96, 155, 161

Debt of Honour Register 200-1

evacuation 300, *300*

identity cards *20*

Imperial War Museum 194-5

medals 219

National Archives 163

National Farm Survey 190

Red Cross 130

secondary sources 269

security, credit cards 41

Serif Web Plus 308

servants, in censuses 113

Shakespeare, William 65, *65*

sharing information *see* making contact

Shea, Virginia 281

ships
  bargemen *121*
  immigrants 258-9
  muster rolls 199
  passenger lists 48, *49*, 53, *85*, 179, 255, 260
  prison hulks *206*
  tracing Huguenots *46-47*
  transportation records 206
shopkeepers *14*
shot drill, hard labour 208-9
Shrove Tuesday *220*
signs, on family trees 69
Singer Manufacturing Company *180*, 181
slavery 33, *61*
Snapfish 319
societies, family history 13, 45, **286-9**
Society of Friends (Quakers) 149, *149*
Society of Genealogists (SOG) 13, 55, 147, 173
software
  creating a family tree **312-15**
  family history **36-39**
  family history websites 305
  Gedcom files 276, **278-9**
  reviews 38
  word-processing 308
soldiers *see* military records
Soundex 64-65
South Africa, child migration 300
South Asian immigrants 248, 253
Southampton 227
Speed, John 240
spellings, variant 40, 61, **64-65**, 102, 126
Spinning the Web 188
Stationery Office (TSO) 219

Statue of Liberty, New York 258, *258*
Statutory Registers (Scotland) 96, 98, 144
Stopher, Richard 108
storyboards, planning websites 306-7, *307*
street directories 178, **230-3**, 234, 292
streetmap.co.uk 238, *238*
street names, guilds and 185
studio photos 24
suburbs, London 226-7, *227*
Suffragettes *294*
Sunday Times, The 218
surnamedb.com 58, 61, 62
surnames **58-61**
  and adoption 298
  in family trees 13, 313
  geographical distribution **62-63**
  Jewish 250
  offline directories 65
  tracing living relatives 291
  variant spellings 40, 61, **64-65**, 102, 126
Surnames and Genealogy: A New Approach 65
Surnames, DNA and Family History 65
Swansea 228-9, *229*
Swindon, wills 159
symbols
  coats of arms 12-13, *12*, 184-5, *184-5*
  on family trees 69

T

Tags, web pages 309
TalkingScot 283
Tasmania 207, 254
tax records 147, 186, **214-15**, 241

teachers 53
telephone directories 292-3
tenants
  censuses *110*
  farmers 17, *125*
  houses 178
tenements, London *116*
terminology **8-9**
Territorial Army 197
testaments, Scotland 48, 56
textile industry 188, *188*
text, planning websites 306
theclergydatabase.org.uk 182-3
The National Archives *see panel*
theukelectoralroll.co.uk 295
The Times 218, *218*

THE NATIONAL ARCHIVES

The National Archives (TNA) 16, *16*, **32-33**, 43, 74, 162
  apprenticeships 186
  Archon directory 159, 171, 225, *225*
  black history 253
  Catholic records 147
  census records 106, *106*, 116
  consulting original documents 163
  criminal records 202, 203, 209
  divorce records 303
  Domesday Book 222
  emigration records 254, 255, 257
  government employees 181
  GRO indexes 78
  Jewish records 250

Thomsons' Directory 293
Titanic 48, *48-49*
tithes 214-15, 241
towns, migration to 181
toys 26-27
People Trace Online 265, *265*
tracing living relatives **290-303**
trade directories 178, **230-3**
tradesmen, guilds 184-5
Trade Union Congress (TUC) 189
Trafalgar, Battle of (1805) 199
transportation, criminals 166, 179, **206-7**, 254, 255
treadmills, hard labour 208
trials, criminal records 202-3
TypePad 317

  local history 225
  maps 241, 243, *243*
  military records 48, 179, 196-7, 201
  naturalisation certificates 247
  naval records 198-9
  newspapers 218
  Nonconformists 148-9
  occupational records 179
  Poor Law records 210
  RAF records 199
  Scottish documents 165
  street and trade directories 178
  tax records 214, 215
  transportation records 206, 207
  wills 48, 157, 158

U

ukbmd.org.uk 74, **92-93**
United States of America
  censuses 106
  child migration 300
  Ellis Island **258-9**
  emigration to 255
  New York **258-9**
University of Leicester 233
University Library of Warwick 189
Urban Districts 221

V

Valuation Office 241
Veterans History Project 297, *297*
Veterans UK 297, *297*
Vicar General Index
  (1694-1850) 142
Victoria and Albert Museum 27
victoriacountyhistory.ac.uk
  224, *225*
Victoria, Queen *108*,
  109, 224, *225*
video, plug-ins 40-41
viruses, antivirus software 31, 41
visionofbritain.org.uk 134, *225*,
  225, 235

W

Wales *see panel*
wars
  Imperial War Museum **194-5**
  mailing lists 281
  Red Cross **130-1**
  veterans **297**
  war graves 48, 200, 201, *201*
  war memorials 289, *289*
watches 27
web addresses 305
web browsers 40
web editors 308
web logs **316-17**
web pages 308-9
websites 35
  beginning your search **14-17**
  bookmarking 31
  cookies 40
  creating your own **304-11**
  filtering facility 279
  'global tree' websites 277
  networking sites **320-1**
  photosharing websites **318-19**
  publicity 310-11
  record keeping 30
  registering with 41
  searching for variant spellings **64-65**

WALES
  administrative regions 221
  archives **166-7**
  censuses 115
  criminal records 203
  local history 228-9, *229*
  newspapers 217
  occupational records 181
  tax records 214

  security 41
  storing information from 31, *31*
  web authoring software **308-9**
  see also internet *and individual websites*
weddings 51, *53, 72, 102*
Wellcome Library 179, 182, 183
Welsh Wales 228-9, *229*
West African immigrants 252
West Indian immigrants 252, *252*
West Indies, transportation to 254
Westminster Archives 245
Westminster Library 147
Whittington, Dick 184
wildcard searches 64, 126, 127
Wilkie, Sir David *158*
William the Conqueror 222, *223*, 250
wills 23, 48, **154-61**
  Ireland 114, 155, 161

  looking for **158-61**
  Scotland 56, 96, 155, 161
Wiltshire, wills 159
women
  on electoral rolls 295
  in First World War 195
  Land Army 191, *191*
  wills 155
Women's Institute 285
word-processing software 308
work see occupational records
workhouses 210, 211, **212-13**
WorldGenWeb 253, 255, 261
World Wide Web 35
writing 122, 126, **174-5**

X Y Z

Xanga.com 317
Xara 310

Yahoo! 284-5
Yellow Pages 293
York Medieval Probate Index 160
York Peculiars Probate Index 160
York University 55
youroldbooksandmaps.co.uk 242
YouTube 321, *321*

ZoneAlarm 41

Acknowledgments

l = left, **r** = right, **t** = top, **c** = centre, **b** = bottom
Front Cover All frames Shutterstock, Inc; TL iStockphoto.com/PJ Jones, TR iStockphoto.com/ Duncan Walker, BL iStockphoto.com/Joey Nelson, BC iStockphoto.com, BR Punchstock; **10** © Reader's Digest **14** Manchester Jewish Museum **16** The National Archives **18-19** Museum of English Rural Life, University of Reading **20** Betty Loving **21** © Reader's Digest **22** Sarah Snape; Anne Snape/UK Passport Service © Crown copyright material is reproduced with the permission of the Controller of HMSO and Queen's Printer for Scotland; David Halford (medal) **23** Imperial War Museum **24** Anne Snape **25** (l) Museum of English Rural Life, University of Reading (r) Sarah Snape **28** (t) Sarah Snape/Office for National Statistics © Crown copyright material is reproduced with the permission of the Controller of HMSO and Queen's Printer for Scotland (b) The National Archives **29** Anne Snape **30** (t) Felicity Cheetham (b) © Reader's Digest **32** © Reader's Digest **32** (inset) The National Archives **33** (tl) The National Archives (cl) Getty Images (br) The National Archives **34** Getty Images; Digital Vision **35** Jaakko Avikainen/Rex Features **36** (t) Calico Pie (b) ancestry.co.uk **37** Sudeley Castle, Winchcombe, Gloucestershire/Bridgeman Art Library **41** © Reader's Digest **42** (l) © Reader's Digest (r) The National Archives **45** (l) Anne Snape (r) Mary Evans Picture Library **48-49** The National Archives **49** (l) The National Archives (r) Getty Images **51** The National Archives **52** Art Archive **53** Art Archive/ Bradford City Art Gallery/Eileen Tweedy **55** Museum of London **56** Reproduced with the kind permission of the Registrar General for Scotland **57** The National Archives **58** Mary Evans Picture Library **59** ©Science & Society/SuperStock **60** AKG Images/British Library **61** Royal Geographical Society **62** Courtesy of Cardiff Council Libraries and Information Services **64-65** Art Archive/Collegio del Cambio, Perugia/Dagli Orti **65** (b) The National Archives **65** (inset) AKG Images **66** Museum of English Rural Life, University of Reading **69** Pauline Brooker **72** Private Collection © Christopher Wood Gallery, London/Bridgeman Art Library **73** Michael McLellan/Office for National Statistics © Crown copyright material is reproduced with the permission of the Controller of HMSO and Queen's Printer for Scotland **74** Mary Evans Picture Library **75-77** Felicity Cheetham/Office for National Statistics © Crown copyright material is reproduced with the permission of the Controller of HMSO and Queen's Printer for Scotland **78** © Reader's Digest **79** Getty Images **80** Anne Snape **81** Getty Images **82** The National Archives **83** (l) The Times (r) Anne Snape/Office for National Statistics © Crown copyright material is reproduced with the permission of the Controller of HMSO and Queen's Printer for Scotland **85** National Maritime Museum **87** Mary Evans Picture Library **88** Jill Steed **91** Museum of London **93** Anne Snape **95** ©Reader's Digest **96** Popperfoto **97-9** Reproduced with the kind permission of the Registrar General for Scotland **100** www.flyleaf.ie **101** Courtesy of the National Library of Ireland **102** Museum of English Rural Life, University of Reading **103** (r) Art Archive/John Meek (t) Mary Evans Picture Library **104** Museum of English Rural Life, University of Reading **105** The National Archives **108** (c) AKG Images/Archie Miles (b) The National Archives **108-9** Mary Evans Picture Library **110** Museum of English Rural Life, University of Reading **111** The National Archives **113** Museum of English Rural Life, University of Reading **115** Mary Evans Picture Library **116** Museum of London **119** Helen Holmes **121** (t) The National Archives (b) Guildhall Library, City of London **123** Mary Evans Picture Library **125** Courtesy of The National Library of Ireland **127** (t) Betty Loving (bl) Felicity Cheetham/Office for National Statistics © Crown copyright material is reproduced with the permission of the Controller of HMSO and Queen's Printer for Scotland (bc & br) The National Archives **128** ©Science Faction/SuperStock **130-1** Getty Images **130** British Red Cross Museum and Archives **132** © Croydon Art Collection, Museum of Croydon/Bridgeman Art Library **133** (t) David

Halford/by kind permission of the Vicar and Churchwardens of St John the Baptist (Croydon Parish Church) and the Surrey History Centre (b) © Collection of the Earl of Pembroke, Wilton House, Wiltshire/Bridgeman Art Library **134** Christie's Images **135** The National Archives **136** Private Collection, The Stapleton Collection/Bridgeman Art Library **137** David Halford/by kind permission of the Vicar and Churchwardens of the United Benefice of St Martin's Church, Dorking with St Barnabas, Ranmore, and the Surrey History Centre **139** Mary Evans Picture Library **141** © Manchester Art Gallery/ Bridgeman Art Library **142** © Bonhams, London/Bridgeman Art Library **144** Getty Images **145** Roy Miles Fine Paintings/Bridgeman Art Library **146** NTPL/Andreas von Einsiedel **147-9** Mary Evans Picture Library **152** ©imagebroker.net/SuperStock **155** Inventory and Valuation for Probate, 1947 (oil on canvas), Elwell, Frederick William (1870-1958)/© Russell-Cotes Art Gallery and Museum, Bournemouth /The Bridgeman Art Library **156** Private Collection/Bridgeman Art Library **158** Private Collection, Photo © Christies Images/Bridgeman Art Library **162** The National Archives **164** Scottish Viewpoint **166** Istock **169** (t) Ms 313, Manuscripts and Special Collections, The University of Nottingham (inset) Boots "The BOOTS™ word and BOOTS script oval are trade marks of The Boots Company plc" **170** Beamish Photographic Archive, County Durham **172** ©Imagesource/SuperStock **173** Lord Montagu of Beaulieu **176** The National Archives **178** Popperfoto **179** The National Archives **180** Mary Evans Picture Library **181** Yale Center for British Art, Paul Mellon Collection, USA/Bridgeman Art Library **182** Anne Snape **184** By courtesy of The Worshipful Company of Gardeners **184** London Stills **185** © 2007 Gerald Sharp Photography **187** Mary Evans Picture Library **188** Popperfoto **191** Museum of English Rural Life, University of Reading **192** © Malcolm Innes Gallery, London/ Bridgeman Art Library **194** Imperial War Museum **194-5** Corbis **196** Mary Evans Picture Library **199** Popperfoto **200** (l) © Reader's Digest Association (r) Imperial War Museum **201** Rex/Paul Webb **202** Lincoln's Inn, London/Bridgeman Art Library **203** Mary Evans Picture Library **204** www.oldbaileyonline.org/Courtesy of Special Collections Department, Harvard Law School Library **204-5** Steve Cotton/artofthestate.co.uk **205** (l) Mary Evans Picture Library (r) Getty Images **206-7** Mary Evans Picture Library **208** (l) The National Archives (r) Mary Evans Picture Library **210** Mary Evans Picture Library **211** The National Archives **213** (t) London Metropolitan Archives (b) Manchester Library and Information Services **214-6** Mary Evans Picture Library **217** Popperfoto **219** Mary Evans Picture Library **220** Popperfoto **222** (t) The National Archives **222-3** AKG Images/Eric Lessing **223** (l) Art Archive/British Library (r) Last Refuge/Adrian Warren **225** Paul Booth Photography **227-32** Mary Evans Picture Library **234** Anne Snape **236-7** Mary Evans Picture Library **242** The National Archives **244-6** Mary Evans Picture Library **247** (t) David Gibson/Photofusion (b) Jewish Museum, London **249** Corbis **250** Getty Images **252** Popperfoto **254** Art Archive/Mitchell Library, Sydney **254-7** Mary Evans Picture Library **258** (l) Angelo Hornak Photo Library (inset) Corbis **259** (l) The Statue of Liberty-Ellis Island Foundation, Inc. and www.ellisisland.org and www.wallofhonor.org (r) Getty Images **261** Mary Evans Picture Library **262** Digital Vision **267-8** Mary Evans Picture Library **269** (t) Michael McLellan/Office for National Statistics © Crown copyright material is reproduced with the permission of the Controller of HMSO and Queen's Printer for Scotland (c) Anne Snape (b) Anne Snape/The National Archives **273** © Reader's Digest **280** Mary Evans Picture Library **285** WI Archives **287** Mary Evans Picture Library **290** Corbis **291-4** Mary Evans Picture Library **298** Bridgeman Art Library/Jane Austen House, Chawton, Hampshire **299** (t) The Foundling Museum, London/Bridgeman Art Library (b) © Coram Family in the care of the Foundling Museum **300** Popperfoto **302** iStock **303** Mary Evans Picture Library **304** Shutterstock **311** Mary Evans Picture Library **316** Royal Society of Arts, London/Bridgeman Art Library

How to trace your family history on the internet
This edition published in 2012 in the United Kingdom
by Vivat Direct Limited (t/a Reader's Digest),
157 Edgware Road, London W2 2HR

How to trace your family history on the internet
is owned and under licence from the Reader's Digest
Association, Inc.

We are committed both to the quality of our
products and the service we provide to our
customers. We value your comments, so please do
contact us on **0871 351 1000** or via our website at
www.readersdigest.co.uk

If you have any comments or suggestions about
the content of our books, email us at
gbeditorial@readersdigest.co.uk

Concept Code UK2142/IC
Book Code 400-571 UP0000-1
ISBN 978 1 78020 051 4

How to trace your family history on the internet
Created for Reader's Digest
by Amazon Publishing Limited
7 Old Lodge Place, Twickenham TW1 1RQ.

Chief consultant
Nick Barratt
Dr Nick Barratt is one of Britain's best-known experts on
family history – a regular face and voice on TV and radio,
and a weekly columnist for The *Daily Telegraph*. His
broadcasting credits as researcher, adviser and presenter
include the Radio 4 series *Tracing Your Roots* and the TV
programmes *House Detectives*, *Hidden House History*,
So You Think You're Royal? and the triple BAFTA-
nominated *Who Do You Think You Are?*. Among Nick's
publications are *Tracing the History of Your House* and
The Family Detective.

Contributors
Sarah Newbery, Sara Khan, Laura Berry, James Higgins,
Freya Beales, David Hey

For Amazon Publishing
Editors
Jill Steed, Helen Spence, Celia Coyne, Jackie Matthews

Technical editors
Tony Rilett, Terry Burrows, Jon Kirkwood

Genealogy consultant
Peter Christian

Picture research
Elizabeth Loving, Nicoletta Flessati

Editorial assistant
Kate Overy

Designers
Colin Goody, Murdo Culver, Stuart Perry

Special photography
David Murphy

Proofreaders
Barry Gage, Sarah Kaikini

Indexer
Hilary Bird

For Vivat Direct
Project editors
John Andrews, Jo Bourne

Art editors
Julie Bennett, Sailesh Patel

Editorial director
Julian Browne

Art director
Anne-Marie Bulat

Managing editor
Nina Hathway

Trade books editor
Penny Craig

Picture resource manager
Sarah Stewart-Richardson

Pre-press account manager
Dean Russell

Production controller
Jan Bucil

Origination FMG
Printed and bound in China

How to
Trace Your
Family History
on the Internet